DATE DUE

12/23/09		

Demco

THE OTTOMAN LADY

THE OTTOMAN LADY

A SOCIAL HISTORY FROM 1718 TO 1918

Fanny Davis

CONTRIBUTIONS IN WOMEN'S STUDIES, NUMBER 70

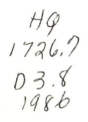

Greenwood Press
NEW YORK • WESTPORT, CONNECTICUT • LONDON

Library of Congress Cataloging-in-Publication Data

Davis, Fanny, 1904–1984.
  The Ottoman lady.

  (Contributions in women's studies, ISSN 0147–104X ; no. 70)
  Bibliography: p.
  Includes index.
  1. Women—Turkey—History. 2. Family—Turkey—History.
3. Turkey—Ottoman Empire, 1288–1918—Social conditions.
4. Elite (Social sciences)—Turkey—History. I. Title.
II. Series.
HQ1726.7.D38 1986   305.4'09561   85-14717
ISBN 0–313–24811–7 (lib. bdg. : alk. paper)

Library of Congress Catalog Card Number: 85–14717
ISBN: 0–313–24811–7
ISSN: 0147–104X

First published in 1986

Greenwood Press, Inc.
88 Post Road West
Westport, Connecticut 06881

Printed in the United States of America

∞™

The paper used in this book complies with the
Permanent Paper Standard issued by the National
Information Standards Organization (Z39.48–1984).

10 9 8 7 6 5 4 3 2 1

Acknowledgment

Illustrations are reproduced from Samuel S. Cox's *Diversions of a Diplomat in Turkey* (New
York: Charles L. Webster & Co., 1887).

To the memory of a great lady
Seniha Sami Moralı

Contents

Illustrations

Preface

Up to this time, the study of the upper-class Ottoman woman has not been systematically pursued. In engaging in it, the author freely acknowledges that she has taken on a large assignment and that her work, far from being definitive, can serve as no more than an introduction to the subject. The subject is a vast one, and the difficulties in locating sources are obvious. The Ottoman did not write about his women. To do so would have been in the worst possible taste on his part. Therefore, it has been necessary to use Western sources, but even there one is limited, for the greater part of the Western observers, being men, were never admitted into an Ottoman harem. Consequently any information they may give about the Ottoman lady is at best second hand. There remain the Western women observers, and this study is greatly indebted to the keen eye and expressive pen of such intrepid lady travelers as Julia Pardoe. Furthermore, two Turkish women—Halide Edip and Emine Foat Tugay—have written memoirs of upper-class life, which have added greatly to whatever value this study may have.

However, there is yet another source on the Ottoman lady—namely, the surviving members of old Ottoman families. Their memories of the last decades of the Ottoman empire and their family archives are treasure troves of information about traditional Turkish family life. During my several stays in Turkey in the 1960s, I had the great pleasure of meeting and interviewing several of these remarkable individuals, most notably Mithat Akçit, Perihan Arıburun, Beraet Bulayır, Leylâ Cebesoy, Nesterin Dirvana, Belkis Erad, Fazilet Keçeci, Nesrin Moralı, Seniha Sami Moralı, Nazli Tektaş, and Emine Foat Tugay. Their personal recollections and the documents they showed me have immensely enriched the fund of knowl-

grateful to Fazilet and Nezih Manyas, Süphiye and Ahmet Gürün, Nesime Moralı, Nuri H. Arlasez, Kemal Kent, Merzuka Nayır and Şehbal Teilmann for sharing their memories, knowledge, and insights with me.

Finally, I am greatly indebted to Professor Tibor Halasi-Kun and Professor Kathleen R. F. Burrill. It is to their inspired teaching and guidance that I owe my interest in the Ottoman Empire and my knowledge of the Ottoman Turkish language.

Fanny Davis

Note: Fanny Davis, the author of *The Ottoman Lady*, died on May 10, 1984. Preparation of her manuscript for publication was made possible by a grant from the Institute of Turkish Studies, Inc.

ERRATUM

The final line on the first page of the Preface was inadvertently left out. It should read: "edge which was available to me through the printed word. I am also very"

Introduction

Over the centuries the road to personal freedom of the women of the Turks has travelled through uplands of opportunity and valleys of seclusion. When we first meet Turks in the eighth century in the Orhon River country of the Altai Mountains of Central Asia, we find their women moving about freely, the wives of their khans commanding respect. In the pre-Islamic Orhon inscriptions of their leader Bilge Kagan, Bilge likens his mother to the goddess Umay and talks of heaven's having granted "them" the state, "them" being both his mother and his father. He calls his mother İlbilgä, *il* meaning "people or state" and *bilgä* meaning "wise."[1]

This free life of the women of the Turkic courts continued for centuries, even after Islamization, as can be seen from Ibn Battuta's reports of his travels in the fourteenth century from Asia Minor to the Kuma River country of the Caucasus Mountains. Coming from the Arab lands where classical Islam ruled and women were secluded, Ibn Battuta was astonished to be honored en route by the daughter of Sultan Muhammad Uzbek Han, and he was amazed at the magnificence of the retinues of that sultan's wives. He says of the Turkic women he met on the journey, "I witnessed in this country a remarkable thing, namely the respect in which the women are held by them [the Turks], indeed they are higher in dignity than men;"[2] and of an emir's wife, "The windows of the tent would be open and her face would be visible, for the women of the Turks do not veil themselves."[3]

This attitude toward women contrasts with the status of the women of the Selçuk Turks, who were centered on Konya in west central Anatolia in the twelfth and thirteenth centuries. Classical Islam was practiced by the Selçuk dynasty, and women were consequently not much in evidence. There is not a great deal to learn about these women except that some of them were patrons of architecture. At that time, it was only the women of the lower ranks who were relatively emancipated. Among them were women who openly followed the religious leader Hacı Bektaş and, in Konya, women disciples who assisted at sheikhs' ceremonies. Moreover, in the Zulkadır region of southeast Anatolia, there are reports of women warriors. The Zulkadırs were, of course, Turkmen and, as such, led a more heterodox life than did the members of the Selçuk court.[4]

Two centuries later in a different milieu we again find freedom being enjoyed by women, particularly by women of importance. In the Akkoyunlu (White Sheep) Turkic confederacy of eastern Anatolia and northwestern Iran, highly placed women played outstanding roles. The most noteworthy of these was Sâra Hatun, the daughter of an Akkoyunlu chief, the wife of another, and the mother of two successive heads of the Akkoyunlu tribal confederacy, Jahangir and Uzun (Tall) Hasan. Since she had a gift for diplomacy, both her reigning sons used her as a mediator, sometimes in their internecine quarrels, sometimes to plead their cause with outsiders.[5] In the rivalry between Uzun Hasan and the Ottoman Mehmet II in the environs of Trabzon, it was Sâra Hatun who made peace between them.[6]

Yet in the same century, the fifteenth, the Ottoman state was changing from a frontier principality to an Islamic empire, and the status of women was changing as well. Before he became sultan, Mehmet II, the Conqueror, married according to his father's wishes and with great pomp Sitt Hatun, the daughter of a Zulkadır chieftain. He had had no hand in choosing her, did not like her, and paid her little attention.[7] Apparently the high rank of her father did not impress him. Nothing much is heard of her. By this time the Ottomans were giving their allegiance to classical Islam, and the *ulema* (members of the religious institution) were gradually succeeding in cloistering women. In the fourteenth-century reign of Orhan, Ibn Battuta was entertained by one of that sultan's wives[8] but by the time of Süleyman the Magnificent in the sixteenth century the public role of women in the Ottoman Empire had come to an end.

However, the change that came over the Ottoman woman's life should not lead one to think that because she was in purdah she was a prisoner. Though her life was limited, led as it was mostly behind closed doors, she was the center of considerable activity. The Ottoman lady was not without influence, albeit it was not openly wielded. Nor was she without social life, though it was confined, outside the family, to contact with other women. Furthermore the first wife, or *büyük hanım* (great lady), of an important man had a large household to run, and in it she was a commanding and even dictatorial figure.

The farther one goes up the social ladder the more opportunity one sees for the Ottoman lady to develop her personality. Although by the time this study starts, at roughly the turn of the eighteenth century, there were no longer such commanding figures as those of the seventeenth-century Women's Sultanate, when the sultans' mothers ruled in fact if not in name, there was still the opportunity for the mother or daughter of a sultan to make her presence felt.

We begin our excursion into the world of the Ottoman lady with a tour of the imperial palace of Topkapı, for it was in that establishment that the strictest rules for the upper-class Ottoman woman's life were laid down.

NOTES

1. Talat Tekin, *A Grammar of Orkhon Turkic*, pp. 265, 267, 268.
2. Sir Hamilton A. R. Gibb, *The Travels of Ibn Baṭṭūṭa, A.D. 1325–1354*, II, pp. 480–481, 482, 484.
3. Ibid.
4. Fuat Köprülü, *Les Origines de l'Empire ottoman*, pp. 112–113.
5. John E. Woods, *The Aqquyunlu, Clan, Confederation, Empire*, pp. 55, 86, 89, 92, 94, 97, 107.
6. Franz Babinger, *Mahomet II, le Conquérant et son temps, 1432–1481*, tr. and ed. H. E. Del Medico (Paris, 1954), p. 233.
7. Ibid., pp. 76–77.
8. Gibb, *Ibn Baṭṭūṭa*, p. 454.

THE OTTOMAN LADY

1

The Palace

THE HAREM HIERARCHY

The imperial harem, the *harem-i hümayun*, was a tightly organized hierarchy. However, in the period under discussion, from about the year 1700 to the end of the Ottoman Empire, certain changes came about in that institution as the influences of Westernization reached the Ottoman court. Here we shall discuss mainly the imperial harem as it was known during the eighteenth century and the early nineteenth century, "before the reforming hand of Sultan Mahmud . . . swept away its medieval splendor."[1]

At the apex of the harem stood the *valide sultan*, or mother of the sultan, whose authority extended officially over the entire harem and unofficially sometimes far beyond. Next in rank came the sultan's daughters, who were also called *sultan*s. After them came the *kadın*s,[2] those women whom the sultan chose as official concubines and set up in their own apartments within the harem, with the social though not the legal status of wife. Most sultans kept to the canonical number of four, although of course a ruler might have more over a lifetime, since from time to time one would die or be retired to the Old Palace.[3] The *kadın*s were designated as first, second, third, and fourth in order of their elevation to that position.[4] The contraction of legal marriage had stopped with Süleyman the Magnificent (ruled 1520–1566),[5] except for the isolated instances of Osman II (ruled 1618–1622) and İbrahim (ruled 1640–1648), and later Abdülmecit (ruled 1839–1861).[6]

There is another title for the sultan's concubines, namely, *haseki* or *haseki sultan*, which was given to any woman who entered the sultan's bed.[7] The word *haseki* comes from the Arabic and means "to attribute something exclusively to."[8] *Haseki* is, therefore, one who belongs exclusively to the sultan. There were also male *haseki*s in the service of the sultan who were housed in the male quarters (*selâmlık*) of the palace. According to Charles White, *haseki* as a title for a woman was in disuse by the time of Abdülmecit in the mid-nineteenth century.[9]

*İkbal*s (favorites), also concubines of the sultan, came below *kadın* in rank. Their number varied, but they too were ranked as head favorite (*baş ikbal*), second, third and so on according to the order in which they had caught the sultan's eye.

In considering the imperial harem, it is important to remember that an elaborate etiquette was observed at all times.[10] The sultan was bound by this etiquette to give the favor of his amorous attentions to each concubine in a given order. Each one had her "night turn" (*nöbet gecesi*).[11] Only when a concubine was indisposed did she lose it.[12]

The woman whose *nöbet* it was ushered into the sultan's bedroom in the harem, unless he chose to visit her in her bedroom. He had notified her by means of the *kızlar ağası*, the chief black eunuch, who had passed the word to the *kâhya kadın* (head housekeeper), who had handed it on to the favored consort's attendants.[13] Sometimes a *kadın* was invited to dine with the sultan, and when this happened in the early years of the Ottoman dynasty she sat at a separate table. Since the time of Mehmet II (ruled 1451–1481) no one but members of the dynasty had been permitted to eat at the padishah's table.[14]

There were other occasions when the sultan came to visit a *kadın* or *ikbal* in her apartment,[15] namely, if she was sick or if she had young children. At these times, in Topkapı Palace days, he wore silver hobnailed shoes to apprise the inmates of the harem of his approach so that they might withdraw, it being considered disrespectful to meet the sultan accidentally. Fortuitously coming upon the padishah was called *hünkâra çatmak*, to encounter the ruler.[16] Moreover, the rule of silence within the House of Felicity (or private domain of the sultan) was strictly observed in the vicinity of the monarch.

Charles White, who took most of his information from the Ottoman historian Ahmet Vefik, relates:

Each kadinn has a small kitchen, and great rivalry is exhibited in seeking to gratify the monarch with dainties, for which he [Abdülmecit] is known to entertain a predilection. The evening is employed in playing with the children, if the kadinn be a mother, in listening to the songs or recitations of the most accomplished slaves, in examining jewellery and dresses—in short, the time is passed much after the manner of all other wealthy Turks, when within the privacy of their harems. On these occasions the Sultan withdraws about the usual hour of repose; for it is a rare occurrence for him to pass the night in any other than his own apartment.[17]

White gives further information about the *kadın*s:

These ladies not being married, the designation commonly given to them, of the "Sultan's wives," is erroneous. Nor are they addressed by the title of Sultana, that being reserved for the Imperial children. Kadinns cannot even sit upon divans or chairs in the sultan's presence, although their daughters enjoy this privilege; their place is upon cushions, spread upon the floor. There is no such person officially as the khasseky (favourite), although former sultans permitted their first favourites to assume this appelation. Preferences naturally exist; but it is difficult for the Sultan to betray them in a marked manner without exciting dangerous jealousies and harassing clamours. The reigning monarch . . . has hitherto only raised five ladies to the rank of kadinn. One of these . . . died in 1842.

The Buyuk Kadinn was a present from Esma Sultana [the sultan's aunt]. . . . The second . . . was purchased by Riza Pasha, and given to Esma Sultana, who educated and then presented her to her nephew. The third was a gift of the Valida. The fourth was educated by Riza Pasha's first wife.[18]

The latter part of this excerpt illustrates the practice of endeavoring to gain influence in the *saray* by presenting to the padishah an extraordinarily beautiful and accomplished slave who stood a good chance of becoming a *kadın*. The Rıza Pasha mentioned was undoubtedly Hasan Rıza Pasha, commander of the Imperial Guard for Abdülmecit. It is highly likely that his wives' personal relations with the two *kadın*s were helpful to him at court.[19] *Kadın*s were not permitted to receive outside visitors or to leave the palace except to accompany the sultan to another of his abodes.[20] An exception was made for women who had formerly been *saray* slaves and had subsequently been allowed to marry. These invariably kept up their palace connections and thus were frequently called upon to act as intermediaries. They were often sought as wives for just those reasons.

One other group of outsiders, the merchant women of the minorities, was allowed to enter the harem, although usually into only one room reserved for the purpose. These tradeswomen supplied the palace women with articles of feminine adornment. Also, it was possible for a foster mother to maintain some contact with a *kadın*. For example, we know that Bezmâra, one of Abdülmecit's *kadın*s, was allowed to visit her foster mother when the latter was sick.[21]

Regarding the rigid seclusion of the *kadın*s, White writes that the reason for it was

to prevent the demands and intrigues of needy relatives,[22] who might put forward claims, as near kin to the different members of the Imperial family—a useful precaution, as Circassia may be said to be one-fourth populated with their connexions, the greater part of whom are serfs or persons of low condition.[23]

Though the *kadın*s were permitted to receive no one not of the imperial harem, the Valida and married Sultanas may, however, exercise their discretion in this respect, and now and then receive the wives of envoys and distinguished strangers. Even Aghas rarely enter the kadinns' apartments, unless commanded to do so, and never see their fair mistresses unveiled.[24]

The monotony was occasionally relieved by day-long outings to a garden kiosk, always arranged with the express permission of the sultan and with orders to the *bostancı*s (gardeners) to absent themselves. Sometimes the sultan joined the women in the kiosk for a meal. This was undertaken with much ceremony and the meal was often prepared under the eye of the imperial *kethüda* (chamberlain) in kitchens of the grand vizier and transported on platters covered with red cloth. The occasion was called *halvet* (time of privacy).[25] This custom of kiosk outings continued into Abdülhamit II's day.[26]

When the *kadın*s left Topkapı for one of the other palaces, the utmost care was taken to prevent their being seen. They left the palace before sunrise, were driven through the *saray* grounds in curtained carriages and, covered with shawls, embarked from the Yalı Köşkü (Shore Kiosk) in boats where they were seated in enclosures. The whole convoy, as it traversed the Bosphorus to, for example, Beşiktaş, was closely guarded by other boats so that no one could approach.[27]

Upon the death of a sultan any of his *kadın*s and *ikbal*s who had not borne a child, or who had borne a girl, or a boy who had died, was usually freed and married to some statesman.[28] The others retired to the Old Palace.

After the *kadın*s and *ikbal*s the next in *saray* rank were the *gedikli*s, the privileged ones (also called *kalfa*s).[29] They were in the personal service of the sultan, and each had a title that indicated that aspect of the service for which she was responsible.[30]

The woman in charge of the harem and head of the entire harem service, the *kâhya kadın*, was a *gedikli*. She was usually chosen by the sultan from among the oldest, most experienced of his women. She carried a silver-decorated baton as her sign of office, and was one of only three persons—the sultan, the grand vizier, and herself—who carried an imperial seal. The girls obeyed her, even the *kadın*s respected her, and when the *valide* had died, the sultan called her "mother." When the court moved elsewhere, she stayed in Topkapı.[31]

Her second in command was the *haznedar usta* (treasurer), who was also an elderly woman. It was her duty to assist the *kâhya kadın* in taking care of the sultan's jewels and valuable clothing and to look after the general economy of the harem. She accompanied the imperial harem when the court moved to any of the other palaces.[32] This arrangement prevailed throughout the eighteenth century and through the nineteenth, probably until the time Abdülhamit II moved to Yıldız. He left the *kâhya kadın* at Dolmabahçe Palace, which made the *haznedar usta* the senior harem official at Yıldız. She had an assistant and three other ranking *usta*s on her staff, as well as 20 ordinary *haznedar gedikli*s or *kalfa*s.[33]

In addition, there were other heads of services, all elderly: the *camaşır usta*, who saw to the laundering of the sultan's attire and acted as chambermaid; the *çaşnigir usta*, a sort of lady butler who looked after the sultan's table in the harem; the *ibriktar usta*, who poured water for the sultan's ablutions and for him to wash his face and hands after meals; a *külhane usta*, the *hamamcı* who was in charge of his bath; a *kahve usta*, ready to brew coffee at all times; and a *kilerci* (pantry) *usta*, who prepared syrups and delicacies for the monarch.[34] Each of these women was a *baş*, or chief, *usta* and had a second (*ikinci*) as well as a number of other *gedikli*s attached to her service. She also had considerable freedom, in that she was allowed to go about the city shopping. In addition there were a number of *kâtibe*s, women clerks who kept inventory and took care of the necessary correspondence, and a *berber usta* who dressed the women's hair.[35]

The most beautiful and accomplished girls were chosen to assist the *usta*s in their personal services to the sultan, and it was from among these that he often chose his *has odalık*s or *ikbal*s: the girls, besides the *kadın*s, whom he took to bed and who were therefore *gözde* (in the eye), or favorites.[36] As vacancies arose among the *kadın*s, these girls moved up to the *kadınlık* in the order of their seniority in the sultan's favor. Although Uluçay says their number was limited by the eighteenth century to no more than six, one cannot but surmise that Ahmet III, with his 52 children,[37] had more. There was, however, by no means as much license in this regard as in former centuries. Murat III, Süleyman's grandson, is supposed to have had 40 *ikbal*s.[38]

But even when there was a large number of *ikbal*s there was no relaxation in their relations with the sovereign. White describes the decorum which was observed at all times:

Should His Highness bathe within the harem . . . he is served by women allotted to this duty. . . . This process is conducted with rigid attention to etiquette and propriety, under the superintendence of two or more elderly oostas. The Imperial bather is enveloped in crimson silk clothes embroidered in gold, called pestamel, and the attendants are attired in light but ample dresses.
. . . The old oostas perform the required services while the sultan is within the heated room; and it is not until he returns to the vestiary that the younger gedekli approach, in order to offer refreshments, and to divert him with song or stories— and this with most severe and rigid respect for decorum.[39]

There have been tales to the effect that when the sultan went afield in his desires and decided to pick a new girl, he sent word to the woman in charge of the harem, the *kâhya kadın*, who lined the girls up for his inspection. When he had chosen one he dropped a handkerchief over her shoulder, whereupon she bent her knee to him, kissed the handkerchief repeatedly, and thrust it inside her clothing. But this is unlikely.[40] Since the most beautiful and talented girls were already in his personal service, he scarcely needed an inspection in order to choose his lady love. Hafise Kadınefendi, the favorite of Mustafa II whom Lady Mary Wortley Montagu interviewed, emphatically denied the handkerchief story. She said that the sultan sent word of his choice to the Ağa of the House of Felicity (the chief black eunuch), who informed the *kâhya kadın*, who informed the girl.[41] The French scholar Jean Deny also calls the handkerchief story a fable.[42] In any case, the other girls gave the chosen one their congratulations, accompanied her to the bath, washed and perfumed her, dressed her, and decked her with jewels. Finally, they led her to the sultan's bedroom with music and song. Given permission to enter the royal bedchamber, she kissed the feet of the sultan. The next morning she was again ceremoniously taken to the bath, this time in the charge of the *kâhya kadın*. If she pleased the sultan, Uzunçarşılı informs us, she was then assigned an apartment suitable for a new concubine of the ruler. However, this could hardly have been possible in cases where the padishah had a very large number of concubines. In such circumstances, as d'Ohsson points out, the *ikbal*s remained with their companions. Both he and Uzunçarşılı assert that an *ikbal* was raised to *kadın* when she became pregnant, but this cannot always have been the case. Alderson records, for example, that Mahmut II had 36 and Abdülmecit 41 children. It is highly unlikely that the mothers of all of them would have become *kadın*s. Moreover, according to Ayşe Osmanoğlu, her mother Müşfika remained an *ikbal* for many years after Ayşe's birth, although she received an apartment of her own.[43]

Müşfika's background serves as a good illustration of how a girl might enter the *saray* in the late nineteenth century. She was the daughter of a Circassian volunteer in the Ottoman army. A senior Turkish officer sent her, as well as her sister, to his wife in Istanbul to be taken care of, for the officer's wife was a Circassian related to Müşfika's family. The officer's wife entrusted the two sisters to Pertevniyal Valide Sultan, who assuaged some of her grief at Sultan Abdülaziz's death by looking after small children. On Pertevniyal's death the girls were brought to Dolmabahçe Palace where, when Müşfika was 14 she caught the eye of Abdülhamit II. She was one of two of Abdülhamit's women who stayed with him until his death. Her sister, meanwhile, had become one of his *haznedar usta*s until she was freed and married when she was 25.[44]

Below the *gedikli*s in rank came the *usta*s who performed the same personal services for the *valide*, *kadın*s and women *sultan*s that the *gedikli*s performed for the padishah. They were organized in groups of 20 or 30 girls, each group bearing the name of the person served, so that there were the *valide*'s *kahve usta*, the *baş kadın*'s *çamaşır usta*, etc.[45]

The next in rank were the *şagird*s, or apprentices, in training for the personal service of the imperial family. They were promoted as vacancies occurred.

Below the *şagird*s came the *cariye*s, the ordinary women slaves, and, at the foot of the ladder, were the *acemiler*, the inexperienced ones, who had just been admitted into the palace. Often they came as children and grew up in the palace. In any case, immediately upon entering they were given a physical examination to make sure they were without fault or blemish. If found acceptable, they went through a course of training called *saray terbiyesi* that consisted of lessons in the Turkish language and the rudiments of Islam, if these had not been previously learned, and in reading, writing, drawing, music and dancing, dressmaking, fine needlework, and good manners.[46]

Uluçay, who has made a study of the writing abilities of the palace women, writes:

It is firmly established that all the girls in the palaces knew how to read and write. We know this fact from the documents in the archives. However, we should admit that these ladies did not have a good education. Their letters are full of spelling, grammar and construction mistakes. Their writing is often untidy and illegible. That their pronunciation was bad and irregular is clearly seen from the written words in their letters. Apparently they wrote the words as they spoke them. On the other hand, the queens' [*kadın*s'] letters were free from such mistakes. The words were correctly spelt, the sentences were regular in construction, and the expressions were vivid and attractive. This proves that the queens had a better education.[47]

The slaves came from several sources. It was the duty of the Chief of Customs, the *gümrük emini*, to pick out attractive girls for the palace. Also, as we have seen, certain individuals presented the sultan with exceptional girls. In addition, the sultan received gifts of girls from his governors and as a yearly tribute from the Crimean Khan.[48] Finally, there were special circumstances, such as an influx of Circassian refugees during Abdülmecit's time, which induced him to accept several into the imperial harem, where they were fed and clothed. Those who had no other connections were kept in the palace and handed over to the service of the *kadın*s. One such girl was assigned to Abdülhamit II's mother and, when the latter died, was transferred to him. She slept in front of his door until the end of her life.[49] The girls were given new names, usually of Persian origin, on entering the *saray*.[50] This *saray* organization set the pattern for the *konak*s (mansions) of the great.

According to d'Ohsson, toward the end of the eighteenth century there were five or six hundred women in the imperial harem.[51] According to Uluçay, in the same century the number varied between four and eight hundred.[52] In the mid-nineteenth century, White found their number to be somewhat in excess of 350, "of whom about one hundred and fifty are negresses employed in low menial offices."[53] Lane-Poole thought there were 1,200 in Abdülaziz's time (1861–1876).[54] We have no figures for Abdülhamit II (1876–1909), but it is generally supposed that he considerably reduced the size of the harem.

The harem of Topkapı was closed off with two bronze and two iron doors at which black eunuchs stood guard day and night.[55] Dolmabahçe's harem was similarly separated from the rest of the palace by iron doors.[56]

Each of the inmates received an allowance from the state according to her rank. In d'Ohsson's time the first *kadın* was given ten *kese* (purses) or 5,000 *kuruş* (piasters) per month; the other *kadıns*' amounts were allotted according to rank.[57] The *kâhya kadın* received five *kese* a month and the *haznedar usta* three. These monies came from the endowment for Mecca and Madina. Since 1689, by the grace of Süleyman II, the *kâhya kadın* had received an additional fifteen *kese* or 7,500 *kuruş* a year.[58] The allowances of the remainder of the women were assigned against Istanbul customs and were paid quarterly: 250 *kuruş* every three months to each *gedikli* and *ikbal*; 200 to each *usta*; 50 to each *şagird*; and 35 to each of the *cariyes*.[59]

The labors of the women slaves were slight. In addition to waiting on the sultan's family, they sewed, spun, embroidered, did various kinds of needlework, and sometimes even made furniture. Their amusements were as limited—they could bathe, make sweetmeats, dress themselves in the best palace fashions, listen to songs and stories, and occasionally have an outing in the gardens or by *kayık* or *araba*.[60] In the latter years of Abdülhamit II some of them were apparently widely read.[61]

The slaves were frequently enfranchised—sometimes when a *kadın* or an *ikbal* had given birth, sometimes as a result of a sultan's vow, often by a new sultan on his accession, and also on special occasions such as a *bayram* (holiday) or a *kandil gecesi* (one of the four yearly night feasts when the minarets are illuminated). On one of the last-named occasions the slave might write a note saying, "The slave desires a favor of my lord," and put it some place where the sultan would be sure to find it. She would then hide from his presence. The sultan usually granted such a wish, gave the girl a trousseau and some money, and sent her to the house of one of the palace people until a suitable husband could be found. The women who were not freed were moved upon their retirement or, in the case of *kadıns* and *ikbals*, upon the accession of a new sultan, to the Old Palace. After Dolmabahçe became the sultan's residence, they were brought to Topkapı. When the padishah moved to Yıldız, Dolmabahçe also became a place of retirement.[62]

As for the harem staff, at least in the latter half of the nineteenth century, a change in sultans resulted in the retirement only of the *haznedar ustas*; the rest stayed to serve the new ruler. The *kâyha kadın* apparently also kept her position. Ayşe Osmanoğlu knew one who had been made a present to Mahmut II by Mehmet Ali of Egypt, and knew several *kalfa*s from the days of Abdülmecit and Abdülaziz. When they were too old to work they were retired to Topkapı. Upon the death of a prince, woman *sultan*, or *kadın*, that person's personal staff was registered in the *saray ocağı* (palace hearth or home),[63] which indicates that the staff also had a place of retirement.

In the case of the death of a slave in service, her effects passed to her owner, the sultan. Even if she had been freed and married, care was taken to protect *saray* property. In 1695, Ahmet II issued an order to the Istanbul *kadı*s (judges), to the effect that the household possessions of deceased *cariye*s who had belonged to the *saray* should not be given to anyone without permission of the *ağa*s (black eunuchs) of the Old Palace, and that the claim of anyone who did not have proof of inheritance should not be heard.[64]

*Kadın*s, being slaves, were subject to the same law of inheritance as the rest of the harem. However, they were usually buried in places of honor. The tomb of Nakşidil Valide Sultan, Mahmut II's mother, contains the graves of two of his *kadın*s and one of his *ikbal*s. In its courtyard lie a *kadın* of Abdülmecit and one of Mehmet V.[65]

THE VALIDE[66]

Valide sultan is a title supposedly instituted by Murat III (ruled 1574–1595). Until then the sultan's mother had been known in the Ottoman Empire, as in some other Eastern states, as *mehd-i ülya*, "cradle of the great."[67] From time to time other titles were added: *valide-i macide*, "illustrious mother," and *valide-i muhterem*, "honored mother." She was the only woman not of imperial blood permitted to use the title *sultan*.[68]

Although a sultan could have several wives or official concubines, he could have only one mother. Therefore, the position of the queen mother was unique—a fact which explains her lofty status at the court. She was the great exception to the inferior position of women in the Ottoman Empire. She had considerable personal freedom, often immense power, and always the respect of the whole court, including her son. She had her own extensive suite of rooms, both in Topkapı and in Dolmabahçe,[69] and undoubtedly in Yıldız.[70] She had her own staff, among whom was a *kethüda* who looked after her affairs outside the palace and who was usually one of the statesmen of the Empire. Mihrişah, Selim III's mother, had a particularly capable *kethüda*, Yusuf Ağa, who was an intimate of the sultan. He was persecuted and finally killed through the machinations of Kabakcı Mustafa in the uprising against Selim III (1808); his *mukataa* (tax farm) was given to Mustafa IV's *valide*.[71]

In the days when Topkapı was still the imperial palace (before 1853) and the Old Palace was used as a place of retirement for former *kadın*s and *ikbal*s, a new *valide sultan* would generally have been living in the Old Palace (the two exceptions to this were Kösem Mahpeyker, who was mother of both Murat IV and İbrahim, his successor, and Râbia Gülnûş, mother of Mustafa II and his successor, Ahmet III). A few days after his elevation to the throne a sultan would send word to officials to prepare his mother's procession, the *valide alayı*, from the Old Palace to Topkapı Palace, for the following day.[72]

On the appointed day, the lady in question would leave the Old Palace by carriage (in early times by sedan chair) and proceed in state from Beyazıt Square down the Divan Yolu (Council Road) to Topkapı.[73]

Uzunçarşılı gives us a vivid description of a *valide*'s procession, based on an account of that of Selim III's mother:

The Divan heralds with plaited turbans fell in front; then walked, also with plaited turbans, those who were connected with the Holy Cities, either as appointees or as administrators; after them came the *valide*'s *kethüda*, Mahmut Bey, with his [turban], and wide-sleeved sable fur and a scepter in his hand; after him *baltacı*s [halberdiers] on both sides, and then the [Ağa of the House of Felicity] with plaited turban, and after him passed the *valide sultan*, in a six-horse carriage with drawn curtains, and behind her another official scattering bright money on both sides. Behind the *valide*'s carriage were the slaves and *sultan*s being transported to the New Palace.

The *valide*'s procession entered through the Bab-ı Hümayun, and when it came to the imperial bakery Sultan Selim came to meet his mother and gave her the oriental salute [*temenna*] three times and kissed his mother's hand through the window of the carriage, which was open on the right side, and fell in in front of her and took her to the imperial harem.[74]

The procession made several stops en route from one palace to the other. The first was at the Janissary guardhouse at Beyazıt, where it was met by the Janissary *ağa* or, if he was on campaign, by the *sekbanbaşı* (head of a certain regiment of Janissaries). The *ağa* first kissed the ground and then was garbed in a robe of honor. He and his staff were given presents, as carefully set forth in a register (*defter*) prepared for the occasion. This present-giving was repeated at each Janissary guardhouse along the Divan Yolu and at the Armory in the first court of Topkapı Palace. The procession proceeded through the Imperial Gate of that palace and crossed the first court, passing between two lines of imperial bodyguards, and stopping at the door of the imperial bakery. Here the *valide* was met by her son, in accordance with the procedure described above.[75]

Selim III was particularly fond of his mother. In fact, when Selim launched his Nizam-ı Cedit (New Order),[76] both his mother and her *kethüda*, by then Yusuf Ağa,[77] were his strong supporters. To encourage the reforms so dear to her son's heart, Mihrişah built a mosque for the Humbaracıhane (barracks of the bombardiers) at Hasköy on the Asiatic shore, and founded a school of medicine at Üsküdar.[78]

The day after the *valide* was installed in Topkapı Palace, she sent the *sadrazam* (grand vizier) or, in his absence, the *kaymakam* (his representative) a *hükümname* (written order), informing him that he was to come to the Pasha Gate of the palace. With the royal command went a sable fur and a dagger. At the same time presents were sent to his suite. In the latter half of the eighteenth century the *valide* also sent the *şeyhülislâm* (the head of the religious establishment) a present of fur, thereby reminding him too of her ascendancy.[79]

It was natural that the sultan should be devoted to his mother. His earliest, most impressionable years had been spent under her influence. She was the only person with whom he could be on truly intimate terms. The layouts of Topkapı and of the palace at Edirne reflect this, for the *valide*'s suite in both instances was the nearest to his personal rooms. Even the new rooms built for the *valide* in the eighteenth century, which are located on the second floor of the Topkapı harem, are contiguous to one of the sultan's rooms.[80] This traditional devotion of the sultan to his mother made it inevitable that the *valide* should be a person of influence. She usually called him *arslanım*, "my lion," and *kaplanım*, "my tiger."[81]

A strong-minded *valide* made her wishes felt in affairs of state, particularly during the Women's Sultanate (Kadınlar Saltanatı), before the period under discussion, but also, to a large extent, throughout the eighteenth and nineteenth centuries. Selim III's mother has already been mentioned in this regard. When Mustafa II was dethroned in 1703 the populace blamed his mother, Râbia Gülnûş, for his preference for Edirne over Istanbul as a place of residence and for the general confusion of life in the capital. Since she was also the mother of his successor, Ahmet III, she remained *valide* during his rule, but the new monarch thought it prudent to keep her out of sight until the feeling against her had died down. And so, on her return from Edirne, she went to the Old Palace for a time.[82] By the time of her death, the people were ready to remember her for her good works, which included building a kitchen for the poor and mosques at Galata and Üsküdar.[83]

An example of beneficent influence occurred in 1755 when Osman III's mother, Şehsüvar, persuaded him not to execute the grand vizier, Hekimoğlu Ali Pasha, who had been imprisoned in Kız Kulesi.[84] On the other hand, an example of constant, narrow-minded interference in affairs of state is the case of the famous Pertevniyal, Abdülaziz's mother. She was partial to the spendthrift *sadrazam*, Mahmut Nedim Pasha, and had made her son so dependent on her that when he heard the crowd that had gathered in front of Dolmabahçe to bring about his dethronement in 1876, he looked to her for comfort and guidance.[85]

Mustafa IV's mother, Sineperver, who was *valide* during the one year of his reign (1807–1808), retired after his death and devoted herself to her daughter, Esma Sultan. She apparently fell on hard times, for she wrote Mahmut II a letter in which she asked him for a house to live in.[86]

It is said of Murat V's mother, Şevkefza (Servetseza), that she was never reconciled to his deposition.[87] On the night of the Ali Suavi incident in 1877, when Murat's partisans tried to reinstate him on the throne, Şevkefza encouraged him to play his part. But Murat was too nervous and upset to head the conspiracy. Given his lack of leadership, the conspiracy never stood a chance of succeeding.[88]

Abdülhamit II's *valide*, Perestû (actually his foster mother), though a non-political figure, was not averse to using her influence in personal matters. Mediha Sultan, a daughter of Abdülmecit, was in love with Samipaşazade Necip Bey, whom she had happened to see. Abdülhamit, who frowned on Necip's family because they had connections with Ali Suavi (the journalist and educator who had attempted a coup against the ruler in 1877), sent him to Paris. It was only when Mediha Sultan's adoptive mother, Verdi Cenan Kadın, appealed to the *valide* that Necip Bey was recalled. He was made a pasha and the marriage was arranged.[89]

The strongest of the *valide sultan*s gave orders directly to the grand viziers and maintained relations with many statesmen through their *kâhyas*.[90] If, as happened, the *kâhya* was venal, he grew rich and the *valide* unpopular. Abdülaziz's *valide*, Pertevniyal, seems to have been inordinately greedy and was in no small measure responsible for the financial chaos of the Empire at the end of her son's reign.[91]

The *valide* maintained a court of her own. E. D. Clarke, who was escorted through the summer harem of Topkapı about 1806 when the court was elsewhere, describes the *valide*'s audience chamber there as being surrounded with mirrors. Steps of crimson cloth led up to a throne encased in latticework. She could summon men to her presence here, while remaining discreetly concealed.[92]

Although the influence of the *valide sultan* outside the palace varied, depending on her strength of character and that of her son or the grand vizier, her influence was always paramount in the harem. On all formal occasions, such as the annual visit of the imperial family to the holy relics, she took precedence. At any harem gathering hers was the place of honor. To her all the other women made obeisance, kissing her hand at each audience. The women who administered the harem, as well as those who educated the women slaves, were responsible to her. She could not be addressed unbidden. To go outside the palace, a woman had to have her permission. When she herself drove outside the palace walls, she was invariably escorted by her suite and saluted by the guards.[93]

Both the dominant position of the *valide* in the harem and her special position vis-à-vis the sultan are shown by the letters which Besm-i Âlem

Valide wrote to Abdülmecit when he was on a trip in Anatolia in 1850.
She tells how his family watched him leave and says:

My beautiful one, all of us, your brother Aziz Efendi foremost, your sister Âdile
Sultan, and your mother press their faces against the dust under your noble feet
and listen for your passing outside, and when they suddenly see the vessel, how
they suddenly lose their heads! . . . Do not be anxious. Look after your affairs in
comfort, everyone is well. For the rest, I trust in God the Creator, my lion.[94]

At other times she wrote that the *kadın efendis* were all asking for him;
that one had written him; that she herself had taken the children to the
bath; that everyone prayed for him. She wanted news of his health. She
had passed out the cloth he had sent to the *kadın efendis*, and to his sisters
and brother. She wrote of the birth of twin sons to one of his *ikbals*, and
finally letters of joy telling of the preparations for his return.[95]

Charles White saw Besm-i Âlem proceeding down the Bosphorus and
the Golden Horn in a caique and has left this account of the event:

Besma Allem (Ornament of the Universe), mother of the reigning monarch, was
a Georgian slave, purchased and educated by the late Sultan's sister, Esma. She
was celebrated for her accomplishments and beauty; of which latter, as far as it is
possible to judge through the folds of a thin veil, she retains a greater share than
is usual with Eastern ladies who have reached their 38th year. . . .

It is a pleasing and most original spectacle to look upon this great lady, accompanied
by her female suite, when she indulges herself and them in a binish (excursion by
water). This pleasure I enjoyed repeatedly: once, among other occasions, when,
with the galaxy of houris in her train, she landed at the imperial Kioshk of
Therapia. . . .

Upon the approach of the imperial kayiks, Captain Mitchell [of a British corvette]
hoisted the Sultan's standard, dressed out his gallant craft in her holiday colours,
manned yards, and fired a salute. Then the . . . crew complimented the fair Turks
with one of those British hurrahs. . . .

On another occasion I chanced . . . to stand upon the southern arch of the bridge
that connects the two shores of the Golden Horn. The Valida was at that moment
returning down the harbour from performing her devotions at Eyoub. . . .

In the first [*kayık*], a richly ornamented, fourteen-oared, imperial boat, was seated
the Valida upon embroidered cushions, placed on a purple velvet carpet, fringed
with gold. Opposite to her, their backs turned to the boatmen, were her Khet
Khoda (intendant or first lady), and her Khasnadar (treasurer and second lady).
Two young Lalas occupied the after-deck, which was covered with a rich Persian
carpet. A third Lala sat in the bow, and the boat was steered by an imperial
coxswain.

As the kayik glided beneath our feet, we uncovered our heads. The Valida, who is well acquainted with European forms of respect, instantly raised her eyes and returned our intended mark of deference with that fixed and penetrating gaze, which is the customary token of imperial recognition, and is the only acknowledgement ever made by the Sultan in return for the salutations of natives or strangers.

The remaining five boats, painted black outside, with yellow mouldings, were rowed by five pair of oars. In the first sat the Harem Aghassy (superintendent). Opposite him was the Oda Lalassy (inspector of chambers), and the Khasnadar Agha (privy purse), and behind were two youthful Lalas, one of whom held a crimson umbrella over the broad face and mishapen figure of his chief. The contents of the four other boats were alike. Seven ladies, pleiades of youth and beauty, sat in each, upon crimson ihrams, fringed with gold, and attended by two black Aghas, whose duty it was to protect the merry groups from wind or sun with large umbrellas, although some of the ladies saved them this trouble by exhibiting the unusual innovation of parasols.[96]

The *valide sultan* was financially supported by special monies designated for her—originally by the revenues from certain *has*, or crown lands, set aside for her use.[97] For a time these revenues were received by her treasurer in the room directly over the Imperial Gate (Bab-ı Hümayun).[98] With the reforms of the nineteenth century this arrangement was discontinued and the *valide* was thereafter supported by an allowance which came directly from the State Treasury. Charles White reported in 1844 that the revenues of the *valide* came partly as an annuity from the civil list and partly from real property, "the fruit of gifts and accumulations." He estimated her entire yearly income at 110,000 British pounds.[99]

The *valide* was a rich woman throughout the days of the Empire and used much of her wealth to beautify the city and to help the poor.

If the sultan died before the *valide*, she was taken back to the Old Palace, but if she died first her son accompanied her body through the palace grounds. Her funeral cortege was impressive as it wound through the city, with the grand vizier and the *şeyhülislâm* in the places of honor. She was buried in a royal tomb, often one she herself had prepared, and 40 days of mourning were observed in her honor.[100]

THE WOMAN SULTAN

The daughter of a padishah bore the title *sultan*, which was placed after her name.[101] She was brought up in the palace by her mother, or, if her mother died, by a childless *kadın* or an old *gedikli*. Although in earlier times *sultan*s had been given in marriage to Muslim princes of the principalities of Asia Minor, by the eighteenth century their husbands were chosen from among the first rank of state dignitaries.[102]

A woman *sultan*, being of imperial blood, had a good deal more freedom than the other women of the *saray*. She was allowed to go out of the palace to call on viziers' ladies, to shop and to promenade and, once married, to have a palace of her own.[103] Unlike the *kadıns*, she could receive outside visitors, even foreign women at times.[104] Melek Hanım[105] and Julia Pardoe[106] paid visits to Mahmut II's sister, Esma Sultan. Selim III's sister, Hatice Sultan, even visited a foreigner's house, namely the villa and gardens of M. de Huebsch, the Danish chargé d'affaires, at Büyükdere, where she saw the work of the famous Austrian landscape architect, Antoine Ignace Melling. This visit was undoubtedly made with Selim's permission, and perhaps even at his instigation, for he was interested in beautifying Istanbul along European lines. Hatice thereafter employed Melling to work on her palace at Beşiktaş.[107]

The ties among the members of the royal family were strong. Though Selim III found it embarrassing that another sister, Beyhan Sultan, should be as extravagant as she was, he nevertheless came to her aid with an apologetic memorandum to Yusuf Ağa, then director of the mint, saying: "At present our expenses are extremely great and I am ashamed to take money from the mint; yet she is my full [womb] sister and is under my protection now, whatever she may or may not do. Hand over 50,000 *kuruş* to her *kethüda*, Abdullah Berri Efendi, quietly without anyone being aware. Do not write it openly in the monthly register."[108]

Mahmut II was especially fond of and tolerant toward his sister, Esma Sultan, a lady who lived her own life to an extent not possible for other women in the Empire. Adolphus Slade has left a vivid description of her:

The sultan's uterine sister, is a lady possessing charms of mind and person, and celebrated for gallantries in the wood of Belgrade,[109] which obliged more than one European to make a precipitate retreat from the country. She was married when young, to Kutchuk Husseyin, the talented, generous captain pasha . . . and was happy in being one of the few princesses of the house of Othman, who have not been debarred, owing to a barbarous policy, the society of their husbands; the object of marrying them off being only to free them from the restraints of the seraglio, and to give them a separate establishment, which the husband supports from the proceeds of this government, usually rich and distant, where he resides without daring to profit from the Mohammedan privilege of a plurality of wives, since on the good graces of his royal bride depends his existence. So warm in the East is the affection which children by the same mother have for each other, that the lady in question has been enabled to pass her widowhood as she pleased, and her eccentricities, in consequence, make the Osmanleys call her the delhi [*deli*: crazy] sultana, by which name she was universally known. Her chief pastime was riding about in an araba. . . . The delhi sultana particularly liked to frequent the places where the Franks resorted, because their unambiguous mode of expressing admiration pleased her, never, woman-like, allowing herself to think their meaning glances were directed to any of the beautiful damsels who composed her train; and if a Frank attracted her notice, she would not hesitate to speak to him, calling him Hekim ["doctor"], which address varnished the impropriety of her condescending to regard an infidel. One day she honoured me with a salutation, and again, to my surprise, she stopped her araba where I was standing; but her guards thinking twice in one day too much familiarity, bade me walk on.[110]

She was a woman obviously trying to extend the dimensions of her life, and this earned her the sobriquet of *deli*. Layard tells how she struck up an acquaintance with him and another Englishman and surreptitiously invited them to her palace, where she questioned them about the ways of the West. This kind of relationship was fraught with danger for the men involved, and one of them fled the country.[111]

Esma Sultan was married in 1792, at the age of fourteen, to one Küçük Hüseyin Pasha and went to live in a palace of her own on Divan Yolu. In 1803 her husband died and, unlike most widowed *sultan*s, she was not pressured into marrying again. She fared well under both of her brothers, Mustafa IV and Mahmut II, acquiring a number of homes. Although there was considerable gossip about her free ways, Mahmut enjoyed her company and spent much time with her. After his death, she apparently ceased to be so well supported, for when she died in 1848 a portion of her estate was sold for debt.[112]

There was another Esma Sultan a generation before her, this one the sister of Abdülhamit I, who was also curious about the West. She received the wife and the mother-in-law of the Baron de Tott (the Hungarian nobleman who served as military advisor to the Turkish government for many years), and not only discussed with them the liberty of European women, but expressed dissatisfaction with the system that had married her, at thirteen, to an old man who had treated her as a child. That pasha having died, she then married a younger man more to her liking, but the practice of sending the *sultan*s' husbands to distant *paşalık*s (governorships) kept them apart.[113]

It was the custom to allow a *sultan* and her bridegroom six months, or sometimes a year, together and then to dispatch the pasha to a far-off governorship (ostensibly to prevent him from establishing a potentially threatening power base in the capital). In this period the *sultan* was not allowed to follow him, although her married daughter, a *hanım* (lady) *sultan* who was one step lower in rank, might follow her own husband.[114] There is one known exception to this. Hatice Sultan, the daughter of Mustafa III (and, as we have seen, the sister of Selim III), was allowed to accompany her husband when he was exiled to Izmit. But three years later, when he was appointed governor of Egypt, she had to return to Istanbul.[115]

The women *sultan*s were engaged to important men, such as the sword bearer (*silâhtar*), the chief of the Admiralty (*kaptan paşa*), or the grand vizier (*sadrazam*) while still infants, and sometimes to more than one before the *nikâh*, or marriage contract, was drawn up. Since the man was sometimes old enough to be the girl's grandfather, and was a prominent man as well, the vicissitudes of age, war, and political intrigue often carried him off before the girl was old enough for the marriage to be consummated. For like reasons the women *sultans* were frequently widowed. It was, however, unusual for them to be allowed to remain in that state; many acquired several husbands during a lifetime. Such a one was Saliha Sultan, daughter of Ahmet III and sister of Mustafa III. She was married first to Sarı (Blonde) Mustafa Pasha; after his death to Sarhoş (Drunken) Ali Pasha, then to the grand vizier, Ragıp Pasha, and finally to Kaptan Pasha Mehmet.[116]

At no time were there more royal engagements and marriages than during the reign of Ahmet III. This is understandable, since he had 52 children, 30 of them daughters. One of them, Ümmümgülsüm, was engaged in 1709 at the age of two to the elderly Abdurrahman Pasha, a vizier. It was an expensive affair for the pasha. He sent to Topkapı a great number of valuable engagement presents, the *nişan takimları*: to his fiancée a seal ring, an aigrette, six *bohças* of cloth, as well as flowers and fruits on trays; to the padishah a handsome horse, a jeweled belt, and five *bohças* of fabric; to the *baş kadın* a diamond bracelet and five *bohças* of fabric. Presents were also given to the other *kadın*s and *sultan*s, to the princes, and to those who arranged the ceremony. Çağatay Uluçay estimates that the engagement cost Abdurrahman more than 10,000 lira.[117] But the pasha died before the marriage could take place.

Ümmümgülsüm, when 16, was married to Damat Ali Pasha with a wedding celebration (*düğün*) that rivaled her sister Fatma's. Yet her life was a troubled one. She and her husband soon found themselves in financial straits, and she appealed to her father for help. There is a letter from her to "My sublime sultan," pointing out the woeful financial condition of his slave, her husband the pasha. Unfortunately we have no knowledge of Ahmet III's reaction to the letter, but undoubtedly he gave her some help, although the state of the Treasury was so serious by this time that the sum offered may have been limited. The Patrona Halil rebellion against her father ended whatever good days Ümmümgülsüm may have had and, in 1732, at the age of 24, she died.[118]

Another unlucky *sultan* was Mediha, born to an *ikbal* and Abdülmecit only five years before the latter's death in 1861. Her mother also died when she was young, and she was adopted by Abdülmecit's third *kadın*, Verdi Cenan. She married—for love—Samipaşazade Necip Bey, but Necip died at 29, whereupon Mediha was pressured into marrying Ferit Pasha, the grand vizier. It was owing to her influence that he sided with Vahideddin, the last Ottoman sultan, during the War of Independence, with the result that both men eventually fled the country.[119]

Tuberculosis took its victims in the palace as elsewhere in the nineteenth century. Among them was Behice Sultan, a daughter of Abdülmecit. There is extant a touching letter to her from one Feleksu Kalfa, herself sick with malaria. The time of Behice's marriage was approaching, and Feleksu was happy for her that she would soon be going to her own palace, but at the same time she worried about her health. "You will be going to the country," she wrote, "where Pertev Kalfa knows many medicines."[120] Behice was thought to be well enough to be married in 1876 and was given a palace at Kuruçeşme, on the Bosphorus. But she died a mere two weeks after her marriage.[121]

The pasha whom a *sultan* married had to divorce any previous wives he might have had and thenceforth was allowed neither multiple wives nor, when his wife came of age, concubines. He could not divorce his imperial wife, although she might divorce him. Even the women *sultans*' daughters, the *hanım sultans*, could not be divorced without the ruler's permission.[122]

D'Ohsson, who has otherwise left us a reliable account of the women *sultans*, says that their male children were all killed at birth, by failure to tie the umbilical cord, supposedly to avoid dynastic rivalry.[123] Many other writers have repeated this statement. However, Uzunçarşılı has proved that this was not so and shows that the sons of several *sultans* were made *sancakbeyi*s (governors general) and one, Sultanzade Mehmet Pasha, grand vizier. The sons of the *hanım sultans* generally went into palace training and were called *beys*.[124]

Each woman *sultan* had a *kethüda* (woman steward) appointed by the padishah who was in charge of her household and financial affairs. She was provided with an allowance, as were the other royal women—a *has*, which was the revenue from a *mukataa* (tax farm) or part of a *mukataa*, or a *malikane suretiyle mukataa*, which was an assignment of revenue for life. These generally consisted of the tax on certain of the produce of the Islands, such as the mastic of Scios, the sponges of Naxos, the wines of Tenedos, and so on.[125] Later on, the *sultans* received a salary from the Treasury. Sometimes the padishah, in setting up a *vakıf* (pious foundation), assigned part of the income to a *sultan*, as did Mustafa III when he founded a *vakıf* for Lâleli Camii. He assigned 1,500 *kuruş* a month to each of his sons, 1,000 to each of his daughters, and 500 to each of his *kadıns*.[126] The *hanım sultans* received a pension of 300 *kuruş* a month each.[127] The wealth of a *sultan* who died widowed and childless went to the monarch.

The great event in the life of a woman *sultan* was her wedding, the magnificence of which depended partly on the state of the Treasury at the time and partly on how much affection the ruler had for her. Although weddings varied in their degree of magnificence, none could be said to have been paltry. Perhaps the most lavish one of all during the last 200 years of the Ottoman Empire was the wedding of Ahmet III's daughter, Fatma Sultan, to Nevşehirli İbrahim Pasha.

Marrying an imperial princess was always an expensive proposition for the bridegroom, who had not only to provide a large *mehr* (marriage settlement) and give what must have seemed an endless array of presents, but also to provide a palace worthy of his royal bride. However, he invariably received a high appointment: many of the *damat*s, or sons-in-law, of the sultan were made *kaptan paşa* (grand admiral). His lot, nevertheless, was not entirely an enviable one. Since he was a mature-to-elderly man, he almost inevitably had children by previous marriages, of whom his new wife was frequently jealous.[128]

The *damat* was, moreover, his wife's slave from the day when the princess was conducted in procession to the palace he had prepared for her. After evening prayer on that day he was dressed in a sable robe which was the gift of the princess, and was escorted by the *kızlar ağası* (black eunuch in charge of the harem) to the room where she awaited him. Outside the door the *ağa* called out, "Illustrious *sultan*, here is your pasha, your slave," and immediately withdrew. According to d'Ohsson, the *sultan* was seated, hidden by a curtain of rich material. With her was the *yenge kadın* (the elderly woman who attended the bride). The latter introduced the couple and even helped them with the marriage particulars. After praying in a corner, the pasha approached his wife, kissed her robe, and waited for a sign to sit beside her.[129]

Since no pasha or princess has written the story of the wedding night, we have to rely on the accounts of people who were not there, and these vary. The above account is according to d'Ohsson. However, Charles White, basing himself on what he claims is an "authority not to be doubted," relates that the *damat* did not enter his bride's bedroom until he was summoned. He then knelt at the foot of the bed, lifted the coverlet, raising it to his forehead and lips, and finally crept up into the bed. White also tells the story of one royal bride, Selim III's sister Şah Sultan, who kicked and scratched her pasha, Kara Mustafa, when he knelt at the foot of her bed, and finally drove him from the room.[130] It is no wonder that theirs was never a close marriage.

Hammer, describing the marriage of Mustafa III's sister, Saliha Sultan, to Ragıp Pasha, gives more details. At the *koltuk* (armchair) ceremony, when the bride and groom first met upon her arrival at his *konak*, the *sultan*, following custom, disdained even to look at him and soon retired from the room. The eunuchs immediately removed the bridegroom's shoes and left them on the harem threshold—a little ceremony that indicated he was now master of the harem. Eventually the bridegroom knelt before his bride and awaited her word in silence. Finally she said, "Bring me water." Having, on his knees, presented to her a ewer of water, he then asked her permission to raise her veil, which was embroidered and ornamented with pearls. Meanwhile slaves had brought in two food-laden trays, one with roast pigeon and the other with sweets. He offered her food which she imperiously rejected. Then he produced magnificent presents which assuaged her to the extent that he was able to lead her to the table for the ceremony of feeding one another. Later, when the festivities were over, a eunuch—the *kızlar ağası*—led him to her bedroom, where he undressed cautiously, so as not to disturb her, sank to his knees beside her bed, and kissed her feet.[131] If the princess did not try to defend herself, the marriage was then consummated. However, if the princess was too young for the marriage to be consummated, the sultan presented the bridegroom with an *odalık* (concubine) to console him until the princess came of age. After that he had to discard the concubine, and the girl slaves of his household were to devote themselves solely to the care and welfare of the princess.[132]

As the nineteenth century got under way and the *sultan*s grew more independent, they became dissatisfied with the very much older men who were chosen for them. Mahmut II made an attempt to pick handsome young men for his daughters. Thus Sait Pasha, Ahmet Fethi Pasha, and Halil Pasha all became imperial *damat*s at a relatively young age. Indeed, from Mahmut II on, youth-and-age marriages ceased to be the custom. Sometimes the girl herself was allowed to choose. Mihrimah is said to have decided on Sait after seeing a picture of him,[133] and Emine Naciye set her heart on Enver even though at the time she was engaged to a son of Abdülhamit II.[134]

Fanny Blunt, who lived in the Ottoman Empire 20 years as daughter and wife of British consuls, thought the *sultan*s of her day deficient in education—"an elementary knowledge of their native language, of music, and needlework, given at leisure and received at pleasure, is considered quite sufficient"—and rather unsavory in reputation:

Wayward and extravagant in their habits, tyrannical, and often cruel, their treatment of their little-to-be-envied spouses furnished cause for endless gossip to the society of Stamboul. The few princesses who formed exceptions to this rule are still remembered with affection by the numerous dependents of their establishments.[135]

The *sultan*s obviously varied in character. Whatever their temperaments—kind or capricious—they were inevitably important personalities in Istanbul society.

THE KIZLAR AĞASI (MASTER OF THE GIRLS, OR CHIEF BLACK EUNUCH)

The *kızlar ağası* or *dârüssaadet ağası* (Ağa of the House of Felicity) was so closely associated with the women of the palace that no discussion of them can be complete without some consideration of him. The chief black eunuch, at the beginning of the period under discussion, was the head of the eunuchs who guarded the entrance to the imperial harem, a duty which the black eunuchs had taken over from the white eunuchs at the end of the sixteenth century,[136] and which they continued to perform until the end of the Empire. The *kızlar ağası* stood third in the state hierarchy, after the grand vizier and the *şeyhülislâm*, with the rank of vizier with three *tuğs* (horse tails). He had access to the sultan, not only as the person who passed on the monarch's messages to the harem, but also as the only individual empowered to carry the grand vizier's communications to the sultan. He seems always to have had access to the *valide*, although theoretically he was not supposed to enter the harem without the express permission of the sultan. Yet there can be little doubt that there was direct communication between them. In the history of the Empire these two, the *kızlar ağası* and the *valide*, were frequent fellow conspirators.[137]

The *kızlar ağası* was personally appointed to his post by a *hat-ı hümayun* of the sultan, who clad him with a robe of honor (*hil'at*).[138] While in service he could be and often was the recipient of a *has* (fief), and, when he was dismissed, he was sent to Egypt,[139] or occasionally to the Hejaz, with a pension called *azatlık* (document of liberation). To attain this lofty position he had first to rise by seniority from *en aşağı* ("the lowest," a post that involved guard duty) to officer and perhaps even commander of the harem guard. When his training was far enough along, he would be removed from the guard and placed in the service of a member of the imperial family. The *valide* and each *kadın*, woman *sultan*, and *şehzade* (prince) had a head *ağa* (*baş ağa*) and several subordinate eunuchs.[140] There was one group of them, the *müsahip ağaları*, whose duty it was to attend the monarch when he was in the harem. There were also black *imam* eunuchs who led the women in prayer, a eunuch treasurer (*haznedar ağası*), and one, the *müsendereci*, who saw to it that the other eunuchs performed their duties. Any of these positions could serve as a stepping stone toward the position of *kızlar ağası*.

The *kızlar ağası* was in charge of all the eunuchs at the court. Furthermore, he had the privilege of having attendants of his own, including female slaves.[141] The *kızlar ağası* was the harem's connection with the world outside its walls. He passed messages between harem and *selâmlık*. He ordered the harem supplies from the palace stores. He had a place in state processions, and took part in the ceremony honoring the holy relics. He was guardian of the Holy Cities of Mecca and Madina and in charge of the yearly dispatch of the *sürre* (the procession of gifts sent to the Holy Cities by the sultan). He walked at the end, in the place of honor, in the funeral procession of a *valide*, *kadın*, or woman *sultan*. He passed on allowances to the women *sultan*s, and he escorted the bridegroom to the door of the imperial bride for the *koltuk* ceremony.[142]

In addition, he was often a person of great influence because of his closeness to the sources of power. In our period there were two especially important *ağa*s, both named Beşir Ağa, who used their influence for political ends. The elder Beşir Ağa served Ahmet III and Mahmut I; the younger served only Mahmut I. The elder Beşir Ağa interfered in affairs of state to such an extent that the grand vizier, Kabakulak İbrahim Pasha, finally persuaded the sultan to dismiss him and send him to Egypt. Beşir got wind of the plan and threw himself at the mercy of the *valide*, with the result that it was İbrahim Pasha and not Beşir Ağa who was dismissed. This same Beşir Ağa is credited with influencing the sultan to reject Nadir Shah's proposal that Iran and the Ottoman Empire might settle their differences if the Empire accepted a Shia group as the fifth sect of orthodox Islam.[143] The elder Beşir Ağa, though fanatical and obsessed with power, left behind many good works, including a number of fountains in Istanbul.[144]

The younger Beşir Ağa, the elder's successor, was even more power-hungry. He managed to get his own man appointed grand vizier and called him his personal apprentice (*çırak-ı has*). On one occasion, he sought the dismissal of a grand vizier. When at first unsuccessful, he arranged to have a fire break out in the city and to have the grand vizier blamed for the disaster so that he eventually lost his post. This Beşir controlled officials by means of bribes, and he finally aroused in the populace and the Janissaries such discontent that he was killed.[145]

The behind-the-scenes influence of the chief eunuchs was so obnoxious to the grand viziers that when Şehit Ali Pasha[146] was *sadrazam*, in 1715, he sent a *hüküm* (command) to the governor of Egypt ordering him to cease the castration of Negroes and the sending of eunuchs to the Porte from Egypt. But the order was never carried out, perhaps because Şehit Ali Pasa died shortly thereafter, in 1716. In that year the *kızlar ağası* increased his power by getting under his control the *vakıf*s (pious foundations) of the imperial family in addition to the *vakıf*s of the Holy Cities, which he already administered.[147]

The political power of the *kızlar ağası* was trimmed when Mahmut II reorganized the government in the 1830s. In 1834 the administration of the Holy Cities and the imperial *vakıf*s was taken away from the *kızlar ağası* and vested in a government department specially created for the purpose, the Ministry of Vakıfs.[148]

However, although the *kızlar ağası* lost his political role and his important *vakıf* posts, his ceremonial duties lasted until the end of the Empire.[149]

NOTES

1. Stanley Lane-Poole, *Turkey*, p. 292. Every house in Turkey was divided into a harem (women's rooms or private section) and a *selâmlık* (men's rooms or public section).

2. Jean Deny (*Grammaire de la langue turque*, Paris, 1920, pp. 783 and 1164) says that *kadın* is an older form of *hatun* and notes: "This word has kept its honorific acceptance only in the usage of the *saray*."

3. The Old Palace was built by Mehmet II, the Conqueror (of Istanbul), and was located where the University of Istanbul now stands.

4. Ignatius Mouradgea d'Ohsson, *Tableau général de l'Empire othoman*, VII,

p. 65; İsmail Hakkı Uzunçarşılı, *Osmanlı devletinin saray teşkilâtı*, pp. 151–153. M. Çağatay Uluçay ("The Harem in the XVIIIth Century," *Akten des Vierundzwanzigsten Internationalen Orientalisten-Kongresses, München, 28 August Bis 4. September 1957*, pp. 394–398) says that in the eighteenth century the number of *kadın*s of a sultan went up to as many as eight, and the number of *ikbal*s varied between four and six. These figures apparently do not hold for the nineteenth century, for Ayşe Osmanoğlu (*Babam Abdülhamit*, p. 235) lists five *ikbal*s of her father plus two who were elevated to *kadın*s, making seven.

5. There is a difference of opinion as to whether or not Süleyman legally married Hürrem. It being before the period under discussion, we shall not attempt to cover the matter here.

6. Osman II married the daughter of Şeyhülislâm Hacı Mehmet Esadullah (A. D. Alderson, *The Structure of the Ottoman Dynasty*, Table XXXV), and İbrahim married a slave named Telli (*The Structure*, Table XXXVII). Alderson says that upon her marriage her name was changed to Hümaşah; d'Ohsson (*Tableau général*, VII, p. 63) says it was changed to Şah Sultan. Abdülmecit married a woman named Bezmâra, who was the adopted daughter of İsmail Pasha, son of Mehmet Ali of Egypt (M. Çağatay Uluçay, *Haremden mektuplar*, p. 167). Ayşe Osmanoğlu (*Babam*, p. 167) says that he went through a marriage ceremony with Perestû, who was the adopted daughter of his aunt, Esma Sultan. She gives details, complete with wedding procession. However, according to d'Ohsson (*Tableau général*, VII, p. 66), two eighteenth-century sultans, Mustafa III and Abdülhamit I, each made a marriage of conscience because there were grounds for believing that the women in question had been born Muslims and hence could not be enslaved and become concubines (the latter all being slaves). In each case the sultan declared the girl to be free and repeated the marriage vow in her behalf before the *şeyhülislâm*, but did this without pomp. D'Ohsson does not record whether there was a dowry, without which a Muslim marriage is not legal. There is evidence that some sort of marriage ceremony was performed by later sultans. Ayşe Osmanoğlu (*Babam*, p. 100) says that Abdülhamit II went through a marriage ceremony (*nikâh*) with her mother, Müşfika, and names the witnesses. Abdülhamit appointed her head favorite (*baş ikbal*), from which she was not promoted to *kadın* until a vacancy in his *kadınlık* occurred after his abdication (*see Babam*, p. 142 where, on the list of people who accompanied Abdülhamit to Salonika, Müşfika is still referred to as *baş ikbal*).

7. In this we have followed Uzunçarşılı (*Saray teşkilâtı*, p. 151 and n. 1) who in turn follows the sixteenth-century Ottoman historian Mustafa Âli. Others, following d'Ohsson, have taken a different view. The present writer doubts that *sultan* was combined with *haseki* to form a title and agrees with Charles White (*Three Years in Constantinople; or Domestic Manners of the Turks in 1844*, III, p. 9) that only members of the dynasty could be called *sultan* (with the exception of the *valide sultan*).

8. J. G. Hava, *Arabic-English Dictionary* (Beirut, 1951), p. 169.

9. White, *Three Years*, III, p. 9. According to Jean Deny ("Wālida Sulṭān," *EI*[1], IV, pp. 1113–1118), the concubines also had the title *sultan* until the beginning of the eighteenth century. In this work, we reserve *sultan*, after the name, for the princesses, as Fatma Sultan, and for the sultan himself before the name, as Sultan Ahmet, in accordance with Ottoman practice. When the word sultan is used to

describe any princess and is not part of a name, it is printed in italics; when it is used to designate the ruler, it is in roman type.

10. Ayşe Osmanoğlu writes that when Abdülhamit II summoned one of his women, he invariably used her title and that he even spoke to the women slaves (*cariyes*) in the polite second person plural (*Babam*, pp. 24–25).

11. D'Ohsson, *Tableau général*, VII, p. 74. Bezmâra, in a letter to Abdülmecit, lamented that her absence from the palace to visit her sick foster mother had made her miss her *nöbet gecesi* (Uluçay, *Haremden mektuplar*, pp. 169–170).

12. D'Ohsson, *Tableau général*, VII, p. 74.

13. White, *Three Years*, III, p. 12.

14. This custom eventually died out. Ayşe Osmanoğlu (*Babam*, p. 23) writes that her mother dined at the table with her father regularly.

15. The apartments of the first and second *kadıns* in Topkapı Sarayı have been located. The main rooms, which are on the ground floor, are elaborately decorated but of modest size. Both suites look out onto the Court of the Valide (Valide Taşlığı) which is an interior court, and open onto only the Hall with the Hearth (Ocaklı Oda) and the Golden Way (Altın Yolu). (*See* Fanny Davis, *The Palace of Topkapı in Istanbul*, pp. 210–211, for a plan of the harem, and p. 212 for the key.) It will thus be seen that the *kadıns* were very much under the eye of the *valide* and well cut off from the rest of the ground floor of the harem. In Dolmabahçe Palace the *kadıns* had single rooms, but they were large and overlooking the Bosphorus. Yıldız Palace has never been available for study, but it would seem from Ayşe Osmanoğlu's description that some of Abdülhamit II's women were lodged in the harem and some in separate kiosks.

16. D'Ohsson, *Tableau général*, VII, p. 74; Uzunçarşılı, *Saray teşkilâtı*, p. 149.

17. White, *Three Years*, III, p. 14. White is writing of the period before Abdülmecit moved into Dolmabahçe Palace. He was probably then living in one of the palaces which no longer stands.

18. White, *Three Years*, III, pp. 10–11. The custom of *kadıns* sitting on the floor had passed by the time of Abdülhamit II; see Ayşe Osmanoğlu, *Babam*, p. 123.

19. Later, Rıza Pasha held the highest posts in the Empire; *see* İbrahim Alâettin Gövsa, *Türk meşhurları ansiklopedisi*, pp. 328–329.

20. Râbia Gülnûş often accompanied Mehmet IV on the hunt; *see* Alderson, *The Structure*, p. 102, n. 1.

21. Uluçay, *Haremden mektuplar*, p. 169.

22. That *kadıns*' relatives were sometimes given official positions is seen in the case of Çerkes Hasan, a brother of one of Abdülaziz's *kadıns*, who was a protégé of the sultan and a member of Prince Yusuf İzzeddin's personal staff, and in the fact that the brother of one of Abdülhamit II's *kadıns* was among that sultan's *bendegân* (courtiers); *see* Osmanoğlu, *Babam*, p. 143.

23. White, *Three Years*, III, p. 11.

24. Ibid.

25. D'Ohsson, *Tableau général*, VII, p. 81; Uzunçarşılı, *Saray teşkilâtı*, p. 150; J. de Hammer-Purgstall, *Histoire de l'Empire ottoman depuis son origine jusqu'à nos jours*, XIV, p. 72.

26. Osmanoğlu, *Babam*, pp. 103–104.

27. D'Ohsson, *Tableau général*, VII, p. 83.

28. Uzunçarşılı, *Saray teşkilâtı*, p. 152. D'Ohsson says that mothers of royal children were not set free but were shut up in the Old Palace. This is disproved by the fact that Hafise (Hafsa), the widow of Mustafa II, left the imperial cloisters and was married, somewhat against her will, to the *reis-ül-küttap* (the state secretary); *see* Lady Mary Wortley Montagu, *Letters*, p. 155. Hafise had a living daughter.

29. *Gedik* means "gap" or "breach," from which it came to mean "a privilege of control" over something. Sir James W. Redhouse, *A Turkish and English Lexicon* (Constantinople, 1921), p. 1531.

30. D'Ohsson, *Tableau général*, VII, pp. 66–67; Uzunçarşılı, *Saray teşkilâtı*, p. 148.

31. D'Ohsson, *Tableau général*, VII, p. 69; Uzunçarşılı, *Saray teşkilâtı*, p. 150.

32. D'Ohsson, *Tableau général*, VII, pp. 69–70; Uluçay, "The Harem," p. 395.

33. Osmanoğlu, *Babam*, pp. 77–78.

34. White (*Three Years*, III, pp. 23–24), writing in 1844, says there were 12 *gediklis* " 'appointed' to perform the functions of pages and attendants on the Sultan's person. . . . They have their distinct oda, bath and meals, and are waited upon by the third and fourth classes. Their dresses and jewels are costly and expensive; and they constantly receive rich presents in money, trinkets, and materials for dresses. . . . They are occasionally allowed to make excursions in arabas or in kayiks, escorted by aghas, specially appointed to attend them."

35. White (*Three Years*, III, pp. 11–12) and Uluçay ("The Harem," p. 396). Uluçay also mentions a palace supervisor who superintended the work quarters of the harem, and a palace commissioner whose duties he was not able to ascertain. He does not give the Turkish titles of these two. His information is based on Topkapı Palace archives. Osmanoğlu (*Babam*, pp. 77–82) lists the same *usta*s for Yıldız, in addition to which she mentions the *nöbetci kalfa*s whose job it was to watch over the harem throughout the night, and a *hastalı usta* who took care of sick *kalfa*s who were sent to Topkapı, which became the place of retirement after the court moved to Dolmabahçe and then to Yıldız. Another difference at Yıldız was that the *kâtibe*s, instead of being clerks or secretaries, were the persons who kept order in the harem. White (*Three Years*, III, p. 18) bears out Osmanoğlu's information about the *usta*s who stood guard.

36. Abdülhamit II, at the time of his abdication, had six *ikbal*s (Osmanoğlu, *Babam*, pp. 146, 235).

37. Alderson, *The Structure*, Table XLI.

38. D'Ohsson, *Tableau général*, VII, p. 68.

39. White, *Three Years*, III, pp. 13–14.

40. Hammer (*HEO*, XIV, pp. 71–73) says that the belief in Europe that the sultan tossed a handkerchief on the girl he chose actually came from the usage whereby a fiancée, in receiving from a eunuch the basket of nuptial presents from her husband-to-be, sent the latter a handkerchief, called "the handkerchief of *nişan*," as a sign that she had received his presents. This ritual was called *nişan makraması*.

41. Here we have followed Montagu (*Letters*, p. 155) and Hammer. Hafise also denied to Lady Montagu that a girl had to enter the sultan's bed at the foot and crawl up it.

42. "Wālida Sulṭān."

43. D'Ohsson, *Tableau général*, VII, p. 67; Uzunçarşılı, *Saray teşkilâtı*, p. 148; Alderson, *The Structure*, Tables XLVI and XLVII; Osmanoğlu, *Babam*, pp. 100, 102, 142.

44. Osmanoğlu, *Babam*, pp. 101-102.

45. Uluçay, "The Harem," p. 395. Also *see* d'Ohsson, *Tableau général*, VII, p. 68; Uzunçarşılı, *Saray teşkilâtı*, p. 148. There is confusion here, in that certain *gediklis* had the title of *usta*, and also seem to have been called *kalfa*.

46. D'Ohsson, *Tableau général*, VII, pp. 68-69; Uzunçarşılı, *Saray teşkilâtı*, pp. 148-149; Uluçay, "The Harem," p. 394; Mithat Sertoğlu, "Gedikli cariye," *Resimli osmanlı tarihi ansiklopedisi*, p. 114.

47. Uluçay, "The Harem," p. 398.

48. D'Ohsson, *Tableau général*, VII, pp. 63-64; Uzunçarşılı, *Saray teşkilâtı*, p. 147.

49. Osmanoğlu, *Babam*, p. 36.

50. Uluçay, "The Harem," p. 397. He says that "beginning with the latter half of the 15th century, it became a tradition to call the concubines, executives, and all the ladies of the Harem including the wives of the Sultan by Persian names. On the other hand, the princesses were generally given Arabic names up to the 18th century." For example, among the concubines of Murat III (1574-1595) there were Mihriban and Nazperver, both Persian names, and among his daughters Ayşe and Fatma, both derivatives of Arabic names. This tradition, however, was not strictly adhered to. *See* Alderson, *The Structure*, Table XXXII.

51. D'Ohsson, *Tableau général*, VII, p. 69.

52. Uluçay, "The Harem," p. 397.

53. White, *Three Years*, III, p. 23.

54. Lane-Poole, *Turkey*, p. 293.

55. D'Ohsson, *Tableau général*, VII, p. 7.

56. Personal observation. It has not been possible for this writer to check Yıldız. Ayşe Osmanoğlu says that the doors of Yıldız harem were locked at 7:30 P.M. and opened at 7 A.M. by the *harem ağa*s (black eunuchs) (*Babam*, p. 58).

57. According to a *hazine-i hassa defteri* (treasury register) of 1278 (1861-1862), after the death of Mahmut II his four *ikbal*s received a monthly pension of 20,000 *kuruş*, and his five *kadın*s 25,000 *kuruş* each (Uzunçarşılı, *Saray teşkilâtı*, p. 148, n. 1).

58. D'Ohsson, *Tableau général*, VII, pp. 72-73.

59. Ibid., p. 73.

60. White, *Three Years*, III, p. 25.

61. Halide Edip [Adıvar], in *Memoirs of Halide Edip* (p. 79), tells about the *saraylı* (woman trained in the palace) who had been a teacher in the palace and who became a wife of her father.

62. D'Ohsson, *Tableau général*, VII, pp. 85-86; Osmanoğlu, *Babam*, p. 80.

63. Osmanoğlu, *Babam*, pp. 79, 81.

64. Ahmet Refik [Altınay], *Hicrî on ikinci asırda İstanbul hayatı (1100-1200)*, p. 20, n. 30.

65. Halûk Y. Şehsüvaroğlu, *Asırlar boyunca İstanbul*, pp. 138-139. The famous Cevri Kalfa, who saved Mahmut II in the mêlée when Selim III was killed, is also in Nakşidil's *türbe* (tomb).

66. *Valide*, "mother," comes from the Arabic *wālada*, "to give birth"; Hans Wehr, *A Dictionary of Modern Written Arabic*, ed. J. Milton Cowan (Ithaca, 1961), p. 1097.

67. Uzunçarşılı, *Saray teşkilâtı*, p. 154. However, Deny ("Wālida Sulṭān") claims that "the practise of calling the sultan's mother *valide sultan* probably started in the reign following Beyazit II," which would be that of Selim I. In Selçuk times she was called *hatun*. Under the Ottomans she was also from time to time referred to as "woman of modesty," "crown of exalted womanhood," "queen of queens," and "diadem of the veiled mistresses, to whom happiness and nobility are submissive and whose chastity flourishes eternally" (Hammer, *HEO*, XIV, p. 72). Another term used in Ottoman times was "mother-of-pearl of the pearl of the Caliphate"; Moriz Wickerhauser, *Eine Deutsch-Turkische Chrestomathie*, p. 53 (Ottoman section).

68. Deny, "Wālida Sulṭān."

69. Personal observation. For Topkapı Palace, *see* Davis, *Topkapı*, pp. 222–226.

70. Abdülhamit II's *valide*, Perestû, had a house of her own in Maçka (Osmanoğlu, *Babam*, p. 14).

71. İsmail Hakkı Uzunçarşılı, "Nizam-ı Cedit ricalından Valide Sultan Kethüdası meşhur Yusuf Ağa ve Kethüdazade Arif Efendi," *Belleten*, 20 (*Temmuz*, 1965), pp. 485–525. Yusuf Ağa was the son of a poor man of Crete who gave him as *evlâtlık* (adopted child) to a Janissary *ağa* named Süleyman Ağa. Süleyman Ağa educated the boy and, when the former was appointed *mühürdar* (keeper of the seals) and *kaymakam* (in this instance assistant to the grand vizier), he made Yusuf his *haznedar* (treasurer) and later his *kethüda* (chamberlain). From there Yusuf rose to become the *kethüda* for Abdülhamit I's sister, Esma Sultan, and also *darphane emini* (director of the mint), and eventually *kethüda* to the *valide sultan*.

72. Uzunçarşılı, "Nizam-ı-Cedit."

73. Ibid.

74. Uzunçarşılı, *Saray teşkilâtı*, p. 155, taken from a collection passed on to Türk Tarih Kurumu by Türk Tarih Encümeni.

75. Ibid., pp. 155–156.

76. The Nizam-ı Cedit was an attempt by Selim III to Westernize the Ottoman Empire's armed forces and, to some extent, its state apparatus. For a full account, *see* Stanford J. Shaw, *Between Old and New, The Ottoman Empire under Selim III, 1789–1807*.

77. Yusuf Ağa was the second *kethüda* of Valide Mihrişah; the first one, Mahmut Ağa, died during his tenure of office (Uzunçarşılı, "Nizam-ı Cedit"). The *hat* (decree) of Selim's appointment of him reads: "I have appointed him *kethüda* to my virtuous, honored mother, and I have robed him in fur in the royal presence." For the *valide*'s and Yusuf Ağa's political influence, *see* Shaw, *Between Old and New*.

78. Hammer, *HEO*, XVIII, p. 65.

79. Uzunçarşılı, *Saray teşkilâtı*, p. 156. It was customary for both the *sadrazam* and the *şeyhülislâm* to wear furred robes. The *sadrazam* also wore a dagger, thrust in his belt.

80. *See* Davis, *Topkapı*, plan of harem, pp. 210–211, and Rifat Osman, *Edirne Sarayı*, fold opposite p. xiv.

81. Deny, "Wālida Sulṭān;" d'Ohsson, *Tableau général*, VII, p. 88.

82. Aubrey de la Motraye, *Travels through Europe, Asia, and into Part of Africa*, I, p. 246. This was Râbia Gülnûş's second stay in the Old Palace. From the death of Mehmet IV, whose *kadın* she had been, until the accession of Mustafa II (*i.e.*, from 1687 to 1695), she had been shut away there (Hammer, *HEO*, XIII, p. 288).

83. De la Motraye, *Travels*, I, p. 246.

84. Uzunçarşılı, *Saray teşkilâtı*, p. 157. The Kız Kulesi, or Maiden's Tower, is a tiny island at the junction of the Bosphorus and the Sea of Marmara.

85. Enver Ziya Karal and İsmail Hakkı Uzunçarşılı, *Osmanlı tarihi*, VII, pp. 109–110.

86. Uluçay, *Haremden mektuplar*, pp. 118–120.

87. Ali Fuat Türkgeldi, *Görüp işittiklerim*, p. 267.

88. Sir Austin Henry Layard, *Autobiography and Letters*, II, p. 412.

89. Uluçay, *Haremden mektuplar*, pp. 199–202.

90. D'Ohsson, *Tableau général*, VII, p. 87.

91. Roderic H. Davison, *Reform in the Ottoman Empire, 1856–1876*, p. 282.

92. Edward David Clarke, *Travels in Various Countries of Europe, Asia and Africa*, III, p. 27f. The summer harem, a separate building on the shore, was originally called Topkapı because it was near the Topkapı, or Cannon, Gate. It burned in 1862/3, and its name was transferred to the main palace, which had theretofore been called the New Palace to distinguish it from the Old Palace. *See* Barnette Miller, *Beyond the Sublime Porte*, pp. 100–103, and Davis, *Topkapı*, pp. 276–278.

93. Osmanoğlu, *Babam*, pp. 60, 65, 71, 87; Uzunçarşılı, *Saray teşkilâtı*, pp. 156–157; Deny, "Wālida Sulṭān."

94. Uluçay, *Haremden mektuplar*, pp. 153–155.

95. Ibid., pp. 148–164.

96. White, *Three Years*, III, pp. 3–5.

97. Uzunçarşılı, *Saray teşkilâtı*, pp. 157–158; d'Ohsson, *Tableau général*, VII, p. 87.

98. Miller, *Porte*, pp. 141–142.

99. M. Tayyip Gökbilgin, "Başmaklık (Paşmaklık)," *İA*, II, pp. 333–334; Sir James W. Redhouse, *A Turkish and English Lexicon* (Constantinople, 1921), p. 326; White, *Three Years*, III, p. 2.

100. Deny, "Wālida Sulṭān."

101. J. H. Kramers ("Sulṭān", *EI¹*, IV, pp. 543–545) thinks that *sultan* as a title for the imperial princesses comes from its popular usage in erotic poetry. However, it doesn't seem necessary to reach that far for an explanation. It is likely that both usages, in the palace and in erotic poetry, stem, perhaps independently, from the fact that the word originally meant "power" or "the person who wielded power."

102. D'Ohsson, *Tableau général*, VII, pp. 88–89.

103. Abdolonyme Ubicini, *La Turquie actuelle*, p. 145.

104. D'Ohsson, *Tableau général*, VII, pp. 93–94.

105. Melek Hanım [Melek-Hanum], *Thirty Years in the Harem*, pp. 26–27.

106. Julia Pardoe, *The City of the Sultans and Domestic Manners of the Turks in 1836*, I, pp. 302–319.

107. *See* Miller, *Porte*, pp. 127–128; Antoine-Ignace Melling, *Voyage pittoresque*

de Constantinople et des rives du Bosphore d'auprès les dessins de M. Melling, I; Celâl Esat Arseven, *L'Art turc depuis son origine jusqu'à nos jours*, pp. 117, 134, figs. 268, 268A, 268B.

108. Uzunçarşılı, "Nizam-ı Cedit."

109. A forest near Istanbul.

110. Adolphus Slade, *Records of Travels in Turkey, Greece, etc., and of a Cruise in the Black Sea, with the Captain Pasha, in the Years 1829, 1830, and 1831*, I, pp. 121–123.

111. Layard, *Autobiography*, II, pp. 145–150.

112. Uluçay, *Haremden mektuplar*, pp. 120–123.

113. *See* Baron de Tott, *Mémoires sur les Turcs et les Tartares*, I, pp. 80–88; Alderson, *The Structure*, Table XLIV.

114. D'Ohsson, *Tableau général*, VII, p. 92.

115. Uzunçarşılı, *Saray teşkilâtı*, p. 164.

116. Hammer, *HEO*, XIV, p. 193; Karal and Uzunçarşılı, *Osmanlı tarihi*, IV, p. 391; Alderson, *The Structure*, Table XLI.

117. Uluçay, *Haremden mektuplar*, pp. 108–113.

118. Ibid.

119. Ibid., pp. 196–203; Alderson, *The Structure*, Table XLVII.

120. Uluçay, *Haremden mektuplar*, pp. 194–196; Alderson, *The Structure*, Table XLVII.

121. Uluçay, *Haremden mektuplar*, pp. 194–196.

122. Uzunçarşılı, *Saray teşkilâtı*, p. 163.

123. D'Ohsson, *Tableau général*, III, p. 316.

124. Uzunçarşılı, *Saray teşkilâtı*, p. 166.

125. White, *Three Years*, III, p. 2. J. H. Mordtmann ("Dāmād," *Encyclopaedia of Islam*, second edition, III, p. 103) says that Süleyman fixed the dowry of a *sultan* at 100,000 ducats (2,500 *kuruş*), and her appanage (*has*) brought her 1,000 to 1,500 aspers (8.33 to 12.50 *kuruş*) a day.

126. D'Ohsson, *Tableau général*, VII, p. 95; a significant indication of rank in the palace. *See* also Uzunçarşılı, *Saray teşkilâtı*, p. 166.

127. *See* d'Ohsson, *Tableau général*, VII, p. 96.

128. An exception to this seems to have been Fatma Sultan, who is credited with not having interfered between İbrahim Pasha and his children by his former marriage. Since he was 50 and she 13 when they were married, his children were older than she; Uzunçarşılı, *Saray teşkilâtı*, p. 165.

129. D'Ohsson, *Tableau général*, VII, pp. 91–92.

130. White, *Three Years*, III, p. 180. White places the anecdote at the time of Selim III's reign. However, according to Alderson, Table XLIII, all of Şah Sultan's three marriages occurred before Selim III's accession. The event may or may not have happened as related; such palace gossip necessarily passed through many people before it reached the Western observer and may have undergone many alterations in the process. Even if this came straight from Ahmet Vefik, White's informant, it had taken place long enough before Vefik's time for some of the details to have become scrambled.

131. Hammer, *HEO*, XIV, pp. 21–24. De la Motraye (*Travels*, I, pp. 253–254) gives the following account: The *sultan* wears in her girdle as a mark of authority a dagger set with diamonds, emeralds, and rubies. When her bridegroom enters

her room the first time he makes three bows between door and girl, kisses the end of her robe, and claps his hand to his forehead. They then play-act a scene in which he professes love and she pretends anger. She takes out her dagger as if to defend herself, but subsides when the bridegroom presents the sultan's *hat* (decree) pertaining to their marriage. She kisses the *hat*, presses it to her forehead, and says, "The sultan's will be done." The man again kisses her robe and withdraws, walking backwards. Later he goes to the palace that he has fitted out for her and where she now is, undresses and crawls into bed softly, from the foot up.

132. Hammer, *HEO*, XIV, pp. 21–24.

133. Malek Hanım, *Thirty Years*, p. 122.

134. Ziya Şakir, "Enver Paşa ile Emine Naciye nasıl evlendiler?" *Resimli tarih* 10 (*Ekim*, 1950), pp. 376–378. Emine Naciye was the daughter of a son of Abdülmecit. We have no authentic information on the titles of these daughters of the sultans' sons born after the ban on the princes (*şehzade*s) having children was lifted. It would seem logical for them to be called *hanım sultan*. However, Emine Naciye is generally referred to as *sultan*.

135. Fanny Blunt, *The People of Turkey*, I, pp. 268–269.

136. The qualifications for a *harem ağa* given in the *Qābūs Nāma* of the eleventh century make an interesting sidelight: "The mark of the slave suitable for employment in the women's apartments is that he should be dark-skinned and sour-visaged and have withered limbs, scanty hair, a shrill voice, little slender feet, thick lips, a flat nose, stubby fingers, a bowed figure and a thick neck. A slave with these qualities will be suitable for service in the women's quarters. He must not have a white skin nor a fair complexion; and beware of a ruddy-complexioned man, particularly if his hair is limp. His eyes, further, should not be langourous or moist; a man having such qualities is either over-fond of women or prone to act as a go-between" (Kai Kā'ūs ibn Iskandar, *A Mirror for Princes, the Qābūs Nāma*, p. 102).

137. *See* Uzunçarşılı, *Saray teşkilâtı*, p. 172; H. A. R. Gibb and Harold Bowen, *Islamic Society and the West*, I, Part 1, p. 363; d'Ohsson, *Tableau général*, VII, pp. 54–62.

138. The *hat* by which Selim III appointed his *lala* (manservant assigned to the care of a child), Bilal Ağa, *dârüssaadet ağası* reads in part, "Because you have been my supporting slave and faithful and beloved *lala*, and because your faithful and upstanding conduct has come to my royal knowledge, I honor you from all my slaves and appoint you *dârüssaadet ağası* and overseer of the *Haremeyn-i muhteremeyn* [holy cities of Mecca and Madina]. I appoint you officer over all the small and great and old and young of all the *ocak*s [guild homes] of the *ağa*s of the harem and the officials of the Old Palace. All of the *ağa*s of the *harem-i hümayun* [imperial harem] and the halberdiers of the Old Palace and the *koz bekçiyan* [a corps of outer guards of Topkapı Palace] and all their servants of the *Haremeyn-i şerifeyn* [also Mecca and Madina] know you are the master in all matters and affairs, and no one will act except you say so, and they will obey you completely." *See* İsmail Baykal, "Silâhdar-ı Şehriyari ve Dârüssaade ağası tâyinleri hakkında hattı hümayunlar," *Tarih vesikaları*, 2 (*Şubat*, 1943), pp. 338–341.

139. *See* Altınay, *İstanbul hayatı*, pp. 45–46, no. 68, and p. 51, no. 73, for documents on Süleyman Ağa's dismissal to Egypt, his killing, and the orders to sell his effects as well as those of his female slaves for the benefit of the palace.

140. The dignitaries of the Empire were also entitled to the services of two or three *ağa*s each in their houses.

141. Uzunçarşılı, *Saray teşkilâtı*, p. 174; Gibb and Bowen, *Islamic Society*, I, pp. 330–331; d'Ohsson, *Tableau général*, VII, p. 54. For further discussion of the black eunuchs, *see* Davis, *Topkapı*, pp. 185–201.

142. Uzunçarşılı, *Saray teşkilâtı*, pp. 163, 180; Osmanoğlu, *Babam*, p. 82.

143. Uzunçarşılı, *Saray teşkilâtı*, pp. 175–177.

144. İbrahim Hilmi Tanışık, *İstanbul çeşmeleri*, I, pp. 380–381.

145. Hammer, *HEO*, XV, pp. 229–232; Uzunçarşılı, *Saray teşkilâtı*, p. 177.

146. *Şehit* means martyr, one who dies in battle.

147. Uzunçarşılı, *Saray teşkilâtı*, p. 172. Gibb and Bowen (*Islamic Society*, I, Part 1, p. 76 and n. 3) wrongly identify the grand vizier as Damat Çorlulu Ali Pasha.

148. Uzunçarşılı, *Saray teşkilâtı*, p. 180.

149. This account of the *kızlar ağası* in the main follows d'Ohsson and Uzunçarşılı. For a variant account *see* Gibb and Bowen, *Islamic Society*, I, Part 1, passim.

2

Childbirth

Next to her marriage, the most important event in the life of an Ottoman woman was the birth of a child. It was attended by almost as much ceremony, both religious and social, as a wedding. Just as the *yenge* is an important figure at the wedding, the *ebe kadın* or midwife is indispensable now.[1]

It was usual for a family to have a favorite *ebe*, one in whom it had confidence. And indeed some of these women acquired considerable skill by purely empirical methods, and were held in high esteem.[2] Only an extremely dangerous delivery could justify calling in a doctor, for to have a male present at such a time was a disgrace to the whole family.[3]

When the prospective mother was six or seven months pregnant, the midwife was brought in to get in order the swaddling clothes and the *nazar takımı*, the outfit of charms against the evil eye. The midwife wrapped all this equipment in a *bohça* (piece of cloth), meanwhile sprinkling fennel seed over it and saying a *bismillah*.[4] Then she attached a small Koran bag to the *bohça* and hung the whole arrangement on the wall in the direction of Mecca.

The midwife was not needed again until the birth was imminent, when she was called back. As soon as the woman's labor had sufficiently progressed, the *ebe* sat her in the childbirth chair, which had side arms, a high back, and a seat scooped out to facilitate the delivery of the child. Just before the baby's head appeared the *ebe* along with the other women in the room proclaimed the *tekbir*: "God is most great." As soon as the child was born they raised their voices in the *şahadet* (witnessing): "I bear witness that I will worship no god but God and that Muhammad is His slave and His prophet."[5] The midwife immediately washed the infant in warm water and cut its navel cord, saying as she did so, "May his voice be beautiful!" She then gave the baby its *göbek adı*, its "navel" or preliminary name, and sprinkled it three times with fennel seed.

The baby was now ready to be swaddled. It was covered with a linen shirt and its feet and shoulders were swathed in strips of muslin. Around its waist was wrapped the *gayret kuşağı*, the girdle of effort of the Turk. On its head was put a skull cap with a pearl tassel, and to it was attached a gold coin or two and a collection of charms which consisted of a bunch of garlic, a piece of alum, one or two verses from the Koran written on blue cloth, and some blue glass beads—all being part of the *nazar takımı*. The midwife then wrapped the baby in the rest of the *nazar takımı*, which comprised a printed blue kerchief (*yazma yemeni*), an embroidered veil of green gauze, and a red ribbon. Thus arrayed, the baby was carried to its mother's bed.

The mother, meanwhile, had been stretched out on her *loğusa yatağı*,[6] a couch (*sedir* or *yataklık*) of wood ornamented with mother-of-pearl and adorned with quilts of satin, velvet, or moire embroidered with spangles, gold, and silver. *Bürüncük*, a chiffon-like fabric, hung from it to the floor. This couch, as richly ornamented as the family could afford, was called the *gelinlik yatağı* (bed of the newly married woman). At its head was hung a Koran in an embroidered bag, and at or near its foot hung an onion impaled on a skewer, wrapped in red muslin and ornamented with garlic and blue beads. These were to protect the mother from the evil eye, to which a new mother and baby were thought to be particularly susceptible.

On the second day a *müjdeci* (bearer of good news) ran to the houses of relatives and friends bringing the news of the birth and carrying a decanter of sherbet, its stopper tied with red gauze. If the baby was a boy, the gauze came down to the throat of the decanter; if a girl, it was tied only to the stopper. At each house the *müjdeci* was rewarded with a tip.[7]

Back at the house of the new mother, or *loğusa*, the woman was dressed up to receive her husband. The father was handed his child and held it toward Mecca. He chanted the *ezan* (call to prayer) and the *şahadet* into the baby's right ear, the *bismillah* into its left, and pronounced the baby's real name, as differentiated from its *göbek adı*, three times.

If the *loğusa* was well enough, she had a *cemiyet* (reception) for friends and relatives on the third day.[8] The visitors did not admire the baby, as that would have shown envy and invoked the evil eye. They either ignored it, called it an ugly thing, or pretended to spit on it in disgust.[9]

However, it was good form to pay plenty of attention to the mother, though if the baby was a girl the guests might commiserate with her somewhat.[10] They brought her gold jewelry edged with pearls and bearing verses of the Koran. They brought diamond *maşallah*[11] charms for the infant. They also brought silver pieces, handsome fabrics, candies, pastes scented with musk, and aniseed cookies.[12]

When the guests left, the midwife straightaway fumigated the room against any evil eye they might have brought in by throwing into the *mangal* (brazier) a clove for each guest. If one of the cloves exploded, that meant the evil eye was indeed present. To exorcise it she threw into the *mangal* a strand of the mother's hair and a piece of the child's (if it had any) and, if it could be secured, a scrap of the clothing of the person suspected. As these burned, she prayed and recited incantations interspersed with frequent spittings.[13] One such incantation went:

> Incense of rue, the air about you,
> Your medicine for every trouble,
> Pale eye, dark eye,
> Blue eye, green eye,
> Yellow eye, topaz eye,
> Whichever the evil eye may be,
> Destroy its evil look.[14]

This activity continued until the baby yawned, which, with the air heavy with incense, might well have been very soon. The yawn indicated that the evil spirits had fled.[15]

The indefatigable Englishwoman, Julia Pardoe, called on a new mother at Çekirge in Bursa some time before 1837, and describes the scene with her usual meticulous detail. Her hostess was the wife of a *kadı* (judge).

Long before I reached [the *hanım's* apartment], I was deafened with the noise which issued from its door; the voices of the singing women—the rattle of tambourines—the laughter of the guests—the shouts of the attendant slaves—the clatter of the coffee and sherbet cups—I could scarcely believe I was being ushered into a sick chamber. . . .

Directly opposite to the door stood the bed of the Hanoum; the curtains had been withdrawn, and a temporary canopy formed of cachemire shawls arranged in festoons, and linked together with bathing scarfs of gold and silver tissue: and, as the lady was possessed of fifty, which could not all be arranged with proper effect in so limited a space, a silk cord had been stretched along the ceiling to the opposite extremity of the apartment, over which the costly drapery was continued. Fastened to the shawls were head-dresses of coloured gauze, flowered or striped with gold and silver, whence depended oranges, lemons, and candied fruits. Two coverlets of wadded pink satin were folded at the bed's foot; and a sheet of striped crape hung to the floor, where it terminated in a deep fringe of gold.

The infant lay upon a cushion of white satin richly embroidered with coloured silks, and trimmed like the sheet; and was itself a mass of gold brocade and diamonds. But the young mother principally attracted my attention.

Her dark hair was braided in twenty or thirty small plaits, that fell far below her waist. . . . Her throat was encircled by several rows of immense pearls, whence depended a diamond star, resting upon her bosom; her chemisette was delicately edged with a gold beading, and met at the bottom of her bust, where her vest was confined by a costly shawl. Her head-dress, of blue gauze worked with silver, was studded with diamond sprays, and ornamented with a fringe of large gold coins, which fell upon her shoulders, and almost concealed her brilliant ear-rings. Her satin antery was of the most lively colours, and her salva were of pale pink silk, sprinkled with silver spots. A glass of white lilies rested against her pillow, and a fan of peacocks' feathers, and a painted handkerchief, lay beside her. Previously to her confinement, she had plucked out the whole of her eyebrows, and had replaced them by two stripes of black dye, raised about an inch higher on her forehead. . . .

I have alluded elsewhere to the facility with which the working classes of Turkey obtain access into the houses of the wealthy. . . . Mothers were there . . . whose sunburnt arms and naked feet bore testimony to a life of toil . . . half a dozen stately Hanoums were seated on the crimson velvet sofa, leaning against its gorgeous cushions, and some of them engaged with the chibouk [pipe].[16]

Such was the life of the *loğusa* as she lay in state on her couch for seven days, drinking no water but only sherbets.[17] On the seventh day the *gelinlik yatağı* was taken away and the maternal grandmother provided the baby's cradle of carved wood inlaid with mother-of-pearl or silver. Two gold- or silver-embroidered swaddling bands a meter long and about a quarter of a meter wide were wound about the baby, one around its feet and the other around its chest, and each was fastened to the cradle. A *sübek* or urinal was provided, which consisted of a tube that led from between the baby's legs to a receptacle.

This seventh day was celebrated by the reading of the *Mevlüt*[18] for the child and the dancing of a gypsy girl, after which the baby led the normal life of an infant at that time and place. Lullabies—*ninnis*—were sung to it, such as:

> God is great,
> The earth is filled with sustenance,
> It is the path of your life,
> Sleep and grow up, *ninni.*[19]

Or perhaps:

> Sleep, my son, and you will be a pasha
> when you grow up.[20]

Incense was burned morning and evening to keep the evil eye away from mother and child, and if the baby was nevertheless fretful, a *kurşuncu kadın*[21] might be called in to exorcise it by pouring molten lead into cold water above the baby's head. The more complex the design the lead took on in the water, the greater the power of the evil eye over the child.[22] This might mean the performance had to be repeated up to three times. Each time as she poured the molten lead, the woman said: "This is not my hand, it is the hand of our mother, Ayşe Fatma."[23] And since the human body has a healthy tendency to heal itself, she was frequently credited with a cure.

For 40 days the mother was thought to be exposed to the influence of evil spirits and for that reason could not be left alone. If there was no way to avoid leaving her alone, a broom was placed behind the door,[24] a practice similar to that of leaving a scarecrow in a field.

At the end of this period, the *loğusa* had her *kırk hamamı*, the 40th-day bath,[25] in the family's private *hamam* (bath) if there was one; if not, in a public *hamam*. With the *ebe kadın* carrying the baby, the mother, relatives, and friends proceeded to the *hamam* for a party that rivaled that of a wedding. The *loğusa* was wrapped in a large embroidered silk towel, and, clacking her silver and mother-of-pearl clogs across the floor and supported by *hamamcı* (bath attendant) and *usta*, she went into the cool room. There she greeted her guests while gypsies danced for her.

Once the mother was bathed, it was the child's turn, and during its bath certain ceremonies, called *kırklama*,[26] were performed. First the midwife recited the names of the 40 saints of Islam. Then, as soon as the child had been soaped and rinsed, she rubbed it with a fresh duck egg which had been beaten in a cup. The egg was supposed to convey to the child the duck's affinity to water. With the child well smeared and the water flowing into the basin, the *ebe kadın* recited three *tekbir*s and three *fatiha*s.[27] The duck egg was washed off in the water that had accumulated in the basin and the baby's first *hamam* bath was finished.[28]

As for the mother, she was covered with an aromatic honey that was supposed to restore vitality, and the paste was left on for an hour. From time to time, in order to partake of its benefits, a guest would transfer some of the paste onto her own finger and lick it off. At the end of the hour the honey was washed off.[29]

At intervals during these proceedings gypsies danced and sang, and such refreshments as *helva*, *dolma*s, sherbets, pickles, and coffee were served. The celebrations would take up the whole day and were always most elaborate upon the birth of a first child.[30] Once the *kırk hamamı* was over, the mother was *loğusa* no more.

Much the same procedure was followed in the event of a royal birth at the palace, except that the arrangements were more elaborate and included the additional ceremony of the cradle processions. When a *kadın* became pregnant, official announcement was made of the fact, and the anticipated birth was celebrated. In the time of Selim III a false announcement had been made of the pregnancy of the *baş kadın* and later had to be retracted.[31] After a royal birth, the *loğusa* was settled in state on a couch, like any other *loğusa*, but her couch was draped in red satin embroidered in rubies, emeralds, and pearls. Red was the only color considered suitable for the dynasty.[32]

The newborn imperial child was favored with three cradles. The first of these had been made ready by the *hazine-i hümayun kâhyası* (chamberlain of the Imperial Treasury), who had it set with silver hobnails at the mint. This one was presented to the Ağa of the House of Felicity without ado and was at hand at the time of birth. The others, provided by the *valide* and *sadrazam* respectively, arrived later in formal processions. Meanwhile the news of the birth was spread.[33] The first announcement, outside the inner palace, came via a *hat-ı hümayun* sent to Paşakapısı, the residence of the grand vizier. In addition, *ağa*s carried the glad tidings to the chief officials, who rewarded the messengers with robes of honor (*hil'at*s), horses with fine trappings, and other presents. The next day the *sadrazam, şeyh-ülislâm, reis-ül-küttap*,[34] and other officials called at the palace to offer their congratulations, at which time they were given robes of honor by the padishah. The governors of provinces and the local judges were informed of the event by *hüküm*, and the general public by a town crier. Three sacrifices were carried out in each *mahalle* (quarter), and the meat was sent to the palace. In five places in the city of Istanbul seven cannons were set off—five times for a boy; three times for a girl. The city was decked out with the decoration and illumination known as *donanma*.[35]

Meanwhile the wives of statesmen received from the Ağa of the House of Felicity or the *kâhya kadın* an invitation to call on the *loğusa*. These women gathered at the residence of the grand vizier and were then taken by carriage to the palace. The women *sultan*s, who had also been invited, arrived separately. The supposition is that the wives of officials needed the escort of the grand vizier's household, whereas the *sultan*s, being royalty, could enter the palace in their own right. On reaching the *loğusa*'s room the guests greeted her, kissed the coverlet on her bed, and seated themselves on a couch. The *sultan*s occupied a higher position across from the *loğusa*'s bed. The baby, during this time, was at the breast of the *sütana* (wet nurse),[36] who sat on the foot of the bed. The guests brought valuable presents to mother and child and to the *kadın*s[37] who were gathered in the *loğusa*'s room. The women stayed at the palace three days, during which time they were entertained with music played by women slaves, as well as by games and imitations.[38]

While the women were thus occupied, the cradle processions took place. The first of these was for the cradle the *valide* had had prepared for the new child. With it were carried a handsome quilt and an embroidered coverlet (*puşide*). The master of ceremonies (*teşrifatcı*) sent the invitations out one day before the event to the officials who were to participate. The procession started in the neighborhood of the Old Palace and Beyazıt Mosque and passed along Divan Yolu to Ayasofya (Santa Sophia) and around to the Imperial Gate (Bab-ı Hümayun) of Topkapı Palace. There it entered the palace grounds and proceeded to the Middle Gate (Orta Kapı) where all dismounted and arranged themselves in two rows. In these ranks and on foot they passed through the Middle Gate and went on to the Carriage Gate (Araba Kapısı) of the harem, where cradle, quilt, and coverlet were presented to the Ağa of the House of Felicity by the *valide*'s chief *ağa*, who kissed the quilt and coverlet before handing them over. The Ağa of the House of Felicity then presented the men of the procession with robes of honor, and presents were handed out according to protocol.[39]

Later, on the *loğusa*'s sixth day, the cradle which was the gift of the grand vizier made its way to the palace in similar procession. This cradle was accompanied by jewels and, if the child was a boy, by an aigrette. As with the procession of the *valide*'s cradle, the invitations to participate had been sent out the day before, and at the appointed time all assembled at the palace of the grand vizier. From there the men walked in a defined order along Divan Yolu and around to the Imperial Gate. At the end of the procession the *mehterhane* (the grand vizier's band) played. Again, as with the other procession, it was met by the Ağa of the House of Felicity at the harem gate. The cradle was presented to him by the chamberlain, it was observed by the sultan, and then it was carried into the imperial harem by the *kâhya kadın*. The men of the procession received the usual robes of honor and other presents.[40]

The cradle was conveyed to the *loğusa*'s room where, as it entered, all the women rose to their feet. The women had placed themselves according to rank, the royal family at the right of the *loğusa*, the other guests on the left. The *valide* tossed a handful of coins into the cradle and the guests followed her example. The midwife first prayed and then laid the baby in the cradle. She rocked the cradle three times, and took the infant out. The guests next covered the cradle with fine fabrics. All this, plus the money that had been thrown in, became the property of the *ebe*.[41]

The role of the *ebe* in Ottoman society was of such magnitude that the government realized relatively early in the nineteenth century the importance of training her. Some knowledge of midwifery was included in the surgery lessons for medical students when the medical school opened in 1826/7; in 1842 the midwives themselves began to receive instruction. In that year a memorandum was given to the authorities by the *hekimbaşı* (chief doctor) announcing the opening of courses in *ebelik*. At the same time, the patriarch, the chief rabbi, and the judges of Istanbul were charged with overseeing the profession of midwifery within their jurisdictions. *Ebes* came to the medical school for lessons twice a week. It was unthinkable at that time for women to be instructed in such matters by men, so two European women were brought in to teach the local midwives. The lessons consisted of acquainting the midwives with the symptoms of illness in a woman about to give birth and instructing them in the general care of a pregnant woman. At this time all the teaching had to be done by means of descriptions, pictures, and models. It was still not possible for *ebe*s to be taught in a clinic or hospital.[42]

By 1845 ten Muslim and 26 Christian midwives had been trained. There was still reluctance to take the course, especially on the part of those midwives who already had a reputation in their profession. The government tried to discourage the people from seeking the services of the latter by issuing an *irade* (decree) which stated that untrained midwives were unregistered and hence should not be held in esteem, but it is doubtful that the *irade* had much effect in that period.[43]

Later in the century the training of midwives became more widespread. According to a memorandum of 1871, most of the *mahalle*s in the district of Ahırkapı Otluk Ambarı,[44] just outside the walls of Topkapı, had orders to set up midwifery schools. In 1885 a plan to build a hospital of midwifery was drawn up, but the project came to nothing. However, a small childbirth clinic had been set up in Gülhane Park in 1862. The public attitude toward it may be judged from the fact that it was popularly called a *piçhane*, or bastards' home. In 1895 an important step forward occurred when *ebe*s began to be trained in actual contact with patients. In 1905/6 a clinic and school were opened for them in Kadırga. The Young Turk Revolution of 1908 gave further impetus to the training of midwives.[45]

But even in the best of circumstances the dangers of childbirth in Turkey were great. Mihrimah Sultan died in childbirth in 1839, only two years after her marriage.[46] Interestingly enough, Mihrimah may have had the services of a doctor, for foreign doctors had been introduced into the palace by the *valide sultan* earlier in the century.[47] However, until Semmelweis[48] developed antiseptic obstetrics in the mid-nineteenth century, it is doubtful that doctors anywhere made childbirth much safer than did midwives.

Although children were a source of pride to the Ottoman woman, many a woman, once she had all the children she wanted, had no hesitation in resorting to abortion.[49] Islamic law allows birth control—with the consent of the husband, in marriage; at the discretion of the master, in concubinage.[50] In practice this often meant abortion, which was neither religiously nor morally frowned upon. The indignation with which Dr. Madden told of a member of the *ulema* asking him to arrange an abortion for one of his slave girls reflects only the Western view.[51] The women seem to have accepted the hazards of abortion and, at times, succumbed to them, although with what frequency we do not know. Lady Blunt came upon an abortion tragedy in her travels. A young wife, distressed at the idea of being a mother before becoming fatter, "used some violent measures . . . in order to procure abortion, and had been found dead in her bath."[52]

However, because of the prestige attached to it, childbearing, despite the lack of sanitary conditions, was certainly more friend than foe to the Ottoman woman.

NOTES

1. The description of birth customs, unless otherwise noted, is from Musahipzade Celâl, *Eski İstanbul yaşayısı*, pp. 20–23.

2. Lady Fanny Blunt, *The People of Turkey*, II, pp. 1-2.

3. Ignatius Mouradgea d'Ohsson, *Tableau général de l'Empire othoman*, IV, p. 320.

4. The *bismillah*, "in the name of God, the Compassionate, the Merciful," opens each chapter of the Koran.

5. For the *tekbir, see* H. C. Hony, with the advice of Fahir İz, *A Turkish-English Dictionary*, (Oxford, 1957), p. 354; for the *şahadet, see şehadet*, p. 333.

6. *Loğusa* is a word taken from the Greek. Mehmet Ali Ağakay (*Türkçe sözlük*, Ankara, 1966, p. 490) defines it as a woman who has just given birth and whose internal organs have not yet returned to their former state.

7. Blunt, *The People of Turkey*, II, p. 4.

8. Ibid.; and Lucy M. J. Garnett, *Home Life in Turkey*, p. 229.

9. Blunt, *The People of Turkey*, II, p. 4; Garnett, *Home Life*, p. 230.

10. Sir Edwin Pears, *Turkey and Its People*, p. 71.

11. *Maşallah* means "What wonders God hath wrought!"

12. Celâl, *Eski İstanbul*, p. 23.

13. Blunt, *The People of Turkey*, II, pp. 5-6.

14. Mehmet Halit Bayrı, *İstanbul folkloru*, p. 10. All translations from the Turkish or French are the author's.

15. Blunt, *The People of Turkey*, II, pp. 5-6.

16. Julia Pardoe, *The City of the Sultans and Domestic Manners of the Turks in 1836*, II, pp. 96-105.

17. Blunt, *The People of Turkey*, II, p. 4.

18. The *Mevlüt* is a poem on the birth of the Prophet.

19. Celâl, *Eski İstanbul*, p. 23. There are several more verses.

20. For a girl: "You will be a *sultan* . . ." (this information supplied by Şehbal Teilmann).

21. A woman who performed the exorcisms described here.

22. Celâl, *Eski İstanbul*, p. 23.

23. Bayrı, *İstanbul folkloru*, p. 91.

24. Halide Edip, *Memoirs of Halide Edip*, p. 42.

25. Lady Fanny Blunt has the ceremonial bath taking place on the eighth day, which is unlikely. However, on the seventh day the *loğusa*'s ceremonial bed was taken away, and presumably after that she led a more active life; Celâl, *Eski İstanbul*, p. 22. Lucy Garnett and Clara Erskine Clement (the author of *Constantinople, the City of the Sultans*) also put the bath on the eighth day, but their accounts of birth customs follow Lady Blunt's so closely as to suggest they were taken from her book.

26. A 40th-day ceremony, *kırk* meaning 40.

27. The *fatiha* is the first *sura* or chapter of the Koran and reads as follows:

In the Name of Allah, the Merciful, the Compassionate.
Praise be to Allah, Lord of Mankind,

The Merciful, the Compassionate,
Master of the Day of Judgment.
Thee do we worship, and to Thee do we turn for help.
Guide us (in) the straight path,
The path of those to whom Thou has been gracious,
Not (that) of those with whom Thou art angered,
nor of those who go astray.

Arthur Jeffery, ed., *A Reader on Islam*, pp. 20-21; translated from the Arabic by the late Prof. Jeffery.

28. This version of the *kırk hamamı* is from Celâl, *Eski İstanbul*, pp. 22-23. Bayrı says the *kırklama* was an Arab custom adopted by the Turks. He makes no mention of the duck egg (Bayrı, *İstanbul folkloru*, pp. 96-97). According to *Türk Dil Kurumu. Söz derleme dergisi—folklor sözleri* (VI, p. 69), in the *hamam*, on the 40th day after the birth of a child, a gold coin or key is submerged in the water of the last basin 40 times, and the child is washed in this water. This was reported from Istanbul, Konya, and Gaziantep. It is also mentioned by Lady Blunt (*The People of Turkey*).

29. Blunt, *The People of Turkey*, II, p. 8.

30. Ibid., p. 9.

31. Tahsin Öz, "Selim III. ün sırkâtibi tarafından tutulan ruzname," *Tarih vesikaları*, 13, (Ağustos, 1944), pp. 26-43.

32. İsmail Hakkı Uzunçarşılı, *Osmanlı devletinin saray teşkilâtı*, pp. 167-171.

33. Royal births, of girls as well as of boys, were important enough to be included in the official chronicles. Raşit, for example, dutifully notes the births of Ahmet III's daughters. For the birth of Saliha Sultan, *see* Mehmet Raşit Efendi, *Tarih-i Raşit*, IV, p. 43; for Râbia Sultan, p. 176.

34. Chief of the scribes; later, foreign minister.

35. Uzunçarşılı, *Saray teşkilâtı*, pp. 167–171.

36. By the act of nursing a child, the wet nurse became *mahrem* (forbidden in marriage) to the child and her own children *mahrem* to the child she nursed. These foster relationships continued through life. D'Ohsson writes that all women, not excepting the *sultans*, nursed their own children and were chagrined if a wet nurse was needed (*Tableau général*, IV, p. 331).

37. This seems to have been the only occasion when the *kadın*s were permitted to see women from outside the palace.

38. Uzunçarşılı, *Saray teşkilâtı*, p. 170.

39. Ibid., pp. 169-170.

40. Ibid., pp. 170-171.

41. Ibid.

42. Osman Ergin, *Türkiye maarif tarihi*, II, pp. 449-452.

43. Ibid.

44. The name means Hay Storehouse of the Stable Gate.

45. Ergin, *Maarif tarihi*, II, pp. 449-452. *See* also Mary Mills Patrick, *Under Five Sultans*, p. 168. The law forbade a midwife to use obstetrical instruments during a birth (Sir George Young, *Corps du droit ottoman*, III, p. 197), but the difficulty of enforcing this is obvious.

46. Mihrimah was the daughter of Mahmut II and Hüşyar Kadın. Her husband

was Sait Pasha (*see* Melek Hanım, *Thirty Years in the Harem*, p. 122; A. D. Alderson, *The Structure of the Ottoman Dynasty*, Table XLVI).

47. Melek Hanım's first husband was doctor to the *valide sultan*; they were married in the 1820s (*see* Malek Hanım, *Thirty Years*, p. 15). We have no information as to when doctors were first called into the palace in cases of childbirth, although we know that Abdülhamit II had them for his women. See Ayşe Osmanoğlu (*Babam Abdülhamit*, p. 103) for the information that her mother was attended by a doctor pending her birth. Because the *valide sultan* patronized Western doctors, and because progress in medicine was an upper-class interest, it is likely that doctors first replaced or supplemented *ebe*s for childbirth cases in the *saray*. According to d'Ohsson, *ebe*s exclusively were used both in and out of the palace in his day, the end of the eighteenth century (*Tableau général*, IV, p. 320).

48. *Columbia Viking Desk Encyclopaedia* (New York, 1963), p. 1926.

49. Blunt, *The People of Turkey*, II, pp. 18-20.

50. Joseph Schacht, lecture notes (Columbia University).

51. R. Robert Madden, M.D., *Travels in Turkey, Egypt, Nubia and Palestine in 1824, 1825, 1826 and 1827*, I, p. 23. Madden reported that the practitioners of this skill were Jewesses. Princess Christina Trivolzio de Belgiojoso (*Oriental Harems and Scenery*, p. 115f) reported being asked to prescribe for an abortion. The girl in question was the daughter of the head of a dervish order. Her husband was away in the army, and her father had no objection to her baby's being aborted.

52. Blunt, *The People of Turkey*, II, pp. 19-20.

3

Education

There is very little to record about the education of the Ottoman woman before the nineteenth century, because there was so little of it. However, a brief survey of the earlier Turkic and Islamic women may throw some light on the educational situation of the Ottoman woman at the turn of the eighteenth century, when this study begins.

In pre-Islamic days the Turkic woman was taught the practical skills of the nomad wife: to ride, to tend animals, to weave, to pitch a tent. There is no record of any women scribes, which does not necessarily mean there were none, but certainly at the present stage of our knowledge it must be assumed they were rare to nonexistent.

One group of early Turkic women, however, received special training: the shamanesses. Under the tutelage of an older shamaness each learned the requisites of the priesthood: the dances, the incantations, the technique of ecstatic flight.[1] But learning in the sense of literacy and book-learning formed no part of her training.

It might be argued that because of the relatively high position of women among the early Turks, they must have received as good an education as the men; therefore, if a Central Asian Bilge Kagan was literate or a Tonyukuk (his minister) learned, so, to a certain extent, must his wife and daughters have been educated. The education of the ruler's women, if it existed, may have survived in the form of the training that the Ottoman palace women received.[2] Certainly the tradition of the shamaness, of the participation of women in religious rites, survived, as is evidenced by the practices of the Bektaşis (one of the most important mystic orders in Ottoman times). Though we have no information about the education of the women of the early Ottoman rulers, we can perhaps construct a meaningful analogy from the customs of the Asiatic Turks during the Middle Ages. Segregation and sequestration of their royal women never took hold, even after they had been subjected to Persian influence and Islamized.

We know that Safvetüddin Padishah Hatun, a ruler of Kerman in the thirteenth century and daughter of the famous Küçük Turkân, was both educated and talented. She wrote prose and poetry, was a very good calligrapher, and was also a *nakkaş*, an illuminator of manuscripts.[3] In the same century Sultan Raziyye, the daughter of Iltutmish and for a brief period ruler of the Delhi Empire of India, was a woman who "loved the learned" (*bilginleri seven kadın*).[4] Since her father thought her more intelligent than his son and appointed her his successor, it is very probable that she was highly literate. A century later Ibn Battuta, visiting Uzbek Muhammed Han, found his second wife, Kabak, reading the Koran.[5] It is significant that she was the daughter of an emir. In the sixteenth century Gülbadan Begum, the highly intelligent and observant daughter of Babur, wrote a family biography, the *Hümayunname*, that is one of the important sources for the history of the Moghul dynasty.

These women were all Muslims.

What precisely was the Muslim attitude toward the education of women? In early Islamic times it seems to have been a permissive one. Among the wives of the Prophet there was one, Hafsa, who could read and write, an ability that seems to have given her a high status in the harem.[6] Others could only read; some were entirely illiterate.

Ignácz Goldziher has recorded an early *hadith*[7] that enjoins both men and women to seek learning.[8] This must, for a time, have represented a general trend; in any case, enough women became distinguished for their learning so as to arouse fear of competition among learned men, with the result that women were gradually excluded from the *ulema*. Meanwhile there was an occasional girl student in the early *medreses* (theological schools). Indeed, there must have been a fair number, for, according to the Arab scholar al-Bukhārī, there were definite days assigned to the instruction of women. Some became scholars in their own right, with student followings.[9] Such a one was the twelfth-century Shushda bint al-'Ibarī, "the pride of womankind," who was famous both as a writer and as an authority on the *hadith*.[10] In the fourteenth century the Arab literary critic, Ṣafadī, taught his daughters to read.[11]

In the days of the Fatimids of Egypt (tenth-twelfth centuries), whose people were heterodox in their beliefs, certain public lectures for women took place in the court of the palace at Cairo, under the sponsorship of al-Azhar University. The Fatimid institution of higher learning, Dār al-Ḥikmah (House of Wisdom), had rooms set aside for women.[12]

Yet in later times one hears nothing about such classes for women or about women scholars. Instead, the attitude toward women that developed is illustrated by the story of Fatima's handmill, a homily that enjoins a woman to bake, to spin, to care for her children, and to be obedient to her husband and hospitable to him in bed.[13] Nowhere does it suggest that she learn to use her intellect.

Among the Selçuks of Rum who were under the influence of classic orthodox Islam, we have no record attesting to the education of women. There is evidence of the Selçuk princesses' handiwork,[14] and of their penchant for good works, but none concerning their literacy or intellectual attainments.

We also have no solid information about the education of the Muslim women of the Ottoman court in its early days, before it was established in Istanbul. However, when Mehmet II made Istanbul the seat of government and set up the Palace School to train the officers of state, he also made arrangements for the education of palace women. They were instructed in the speaking and reading of Turkish and the requirements of Muslim law, as well as in the feminine arts of sewing, embroidering, harp playing, and singing. Nor was that apparently the extent of their attainments. According to the fifteenth century Italian historian, Giovanni Mario Angiolello, who was in Istanbul at the time of Mehmet's death, the Conqueror's granddaughter delivered a funeral oration for her father and was much praised for her wisdom, "her erudition in Arabic literature and expert knowledge on every subject pertaining to a woman in her condition."[15]

There were also talented and educated women outside the palace, although it is hard to tell how numerous they were. The fact that two such women, Zeynep and Mihri, appeared in Amasya in Anatolia in the fifteenth century[16] suggests an open-minded attitude or perhaps even a tradition in favor of the education of upper-class women there. On the other hand, all the women poets we know very much about, up until Nigâr Hanım, who lived at the end of the nineteenth century, were from *ulema* families. Is this, perhaps, some vestige of the early Islamic tradition? Until we have more information, we cannot be definitive.

All these women were, of course, taught at home, by their fathers or grandfathers. Not only were there no facilities for the public education of women beyond those provided in the mosque schools, but even when such facilities materialized in the nineteenth century, the upper-class Ottoman girls continued to be educated, if at all, in the home. So strong was this tradition that even today, in Istanbul, one finds upper-class women who had all or part of their schooling at home.[17]

In Istanbul, there was always an opportunity for a girl to learn to read the Koran. Instruction was provided in private homes as well as in the mosque schools.[18] This was the child's first taste of discipline, for Turkish children were brought up in a very free manner. They went to sleep when they wished and got up when they pleased. In infancy an upper-class child was provided with a nurse or *dadı* who devoted all her time to the toddler's care. At a young age a girl would probably be sent to the mosque school, called *sıbyan mektebi* or *mahalle mektebi*.[19] Halide Edip called these schools "holes in the wall," since they usually consisted of one small room with a domed roof and matting on the floor on which the pupils sat cross-legged.[20] They learned the Arabic alphabet, the *tevcit* (the art of reading or reciting the Koran in proper rhythm), the *ilm-i hal* (catechism), the correct performance of ritual prayers (*namaz*), the recitation of certain verses of the Koran (*ayet*) and special prayers (*dua*), writing, and arithmetic. Later a little history and geography were added.[21]

Osman Ergin, the historian of Ottoman education, considers the mosque schools as having been merely nursery schools (*ana okulu*).[22] There was one connected with the mosque of each quarter, and they were supported by the Evkaf (Pious Foundations). A child's initial attendance was a great event. Halide Edip has described it: the pretty clothes, the gold-embroidered school bag, the procession to school, the kissing of the teacher's hand, and the gold coins passed out to the students by the parents of the newcomer.[23]

Kissing the hand of an elder was a custom that all Turks learned in childhood and observed throughout life—a salute from the younger to the elder, from the lesser to the more important. Called *temenna*, it consisted of carrying the hand first to the lips and then to the forehead while bowing more or less low according to the degree of respect owed the person saluted. If it was a young girl greeting an old lady, the bow was so low as to almost touch the hem of the lady's skirt.[24]

In the old days children started attending these schools at the age of four, although Halide's grandmother maintained that she had learned to read at three and that by seven she had memorized the Koran.[25] The family had decided that Halide was to begin her schooling at home and, perhaps because her father, a palace secretary, was an admirer of the English educational methods, not before she was seven. By dint of coaxing on her part she was able to start at six. Her *başlanmak* (beginning of school) was marked by a home ceremony that took place after night prayers in the presence of neighbors and guests from the palace.[26]

Halide's teacher of Islam was a man, but in many cases the religious teacher was a woman (*hoca hanım*, "lady teacher") who came to the house.[27] This was the extent of most women's education. It is no wonder that many Western observers and, as time went on, an increasing number of Turks had a negative view of it. D'Ohsson, for example, says that girls were taught catechism and moral precepts by their mothers, close relatives, or slaves, and sometimes reading but rarely writing. His scorn for their lack of formal education was, however, tempered by his feeling that they had a natural sagacity and delicacy that counteracted the shortcomings of their education.[28]

A century later Osman Bey, a foreigner who had assumed a Turkish name, thought the Turkish woman to be so ignorant that she did not even understand the Koran and that she spent all her time eating, drinking, dressing, taking promenades, visiting, and going to weddings.[29] Melek Hanım complained that Ayeşa, the daughter she left behind for a time when Kıbrıslı divorced her, was taught by the pasha's second wife only to read the Koran, to write a little, and to sew. Otherwise her time was taken up in gossip.[30]

De Amicis, writing in the late nineteenth century, had virtually the same opinion. Women, he says, had no instruction, either from books or from conversation, and quotes as the attitude of the Turks their old proverb, "Women have long hair and short intelligence." Yet he notes that they were anxious to learn a foreign language so that they could converse with foreign women.[31]

Halil Halit, a Turk who wrote his autobiography at the turn of the twentieth century, reports that his mother could read but not write. There was, he says, an old superstition to the effect that learning to write turned women into witches.[32] A more frequently encountered excuse was that the ability to write tempted them to write love letters.[33] Halil Halit's mother's ability to read did not take her very far afield. Her education had been entirely religious, provided by teachers her son called ignorant, and her favorite literature appears to have been sacred legends and hymns.[34]

How much schooling a girl had depended largely on the head of the family. If he was against schooling for girls, she had little choice but to remain ignorant. Erzurumlu Hafız Mehmet, who was governor of Kossovo and Tripoli under Abdülhamit II, was so opposed to teaching women anything except religion and the household arts that his daughters and niece grew up illiterate.[35] Other men, though they believed in the need for education, had doubts as to how much of it women should receive. Celâl Nuri, a strong advocate of the emancipation of women during the Young Turk period, nevertheless asked: "How capable are the brain and nerves of a woman? Some rare ones can read very well and possess the talent to remember . . . [but] will a little advanced knowledge make a woman haughty, arrogant, discourteous, and even ignorant? . . . A woman may read everything that comes to hand, but can she digest it?"[36]

Even in the palace, where women had long been literate, there were doubts as to how far their education should go. Abdülaziz's eldest son, Yusuf İzzeddin, whom he unsuccessfully conspired to place on the throne, thought it wrong to educate a woman to the same degree as a man. He believed that excess of cleverness and intelligence only brought her harm; it was her chastity and charm alone that counted.[37] Abdülhamit II, who has often been called a tyrant, was actually more liberal in this matter. He objected not to the education of women per se, but to their education in foreign schools.[38]

But in spite of doubts expressed by many of the most powerful figures of the realm concerning the wisdom of educating women, there was growing pressure (at least in Istanbul and other cosmopolitan centers) for giving women more educational opportunities during the last few decades of the nineteenth century. This was reflected by the literature of the time. The prominent writer and journalist, Namık Kemal (1840-1888), for example, was an ardent champion of the education of women. "We know," he wrote, "that in civilized countries the women, like the men, are educated." He then pointed out that in those countries girls under twenty were so well educated that they became teachers and that the learned chose their wives from among them.[39] In 1880, the encyclopedist and lexicographer Şems-eddin Sami (1850-1904) published a small book entitled *Kadınlar* (*Women*), in which he argued that inasmuch as women constitute half the human race they should be educated. He believed that women should be trained in their girlhood not only to administer a household and bring up children, but also to acquire skills which they could put to use once their children had left the home.[40]

Another influential writer on the subject of women during that period was Kasim Amin (1865-1908), who lived in Egypt but whose works were widely read and discussed in the Ottoman capital. In his *Tahrir al-Mar'a* (*Women's Emancipation*), and *Al-Mar'a al-Jadida* (*The New Woman*), he asserted that only if women were educated could they fulfill their function in modern society.[41]

Recognizing the need to offer girls at least the rudiments of a general education, the Ottoman government, at first timidly but then increasingly boldly, undertook the necessary reforms. In 1858, the girls' first *rüştiye*, or secondary school, was established in Istanbul. This was so great an innovation that in its official publication, *Takvim-i Vekayi* (*Calendar of Events*), the government thought it imperative to point out to men the advantage of having literate wives:

The creation of the facilities for women to read and write, as well as for men, will make it possible to relieve men of household affairs so that they can look after important matters.[42]

A further opportunity for women to broaden their horizons was offered when Suphi Pasha, the Minister of Education, founded what later became the Archaeology Museum in 1867 and decreed that the new institution should be open to women one day a week.[43]

In 1869, the Ottoman government enacted a public education law which had far-reaching consequences and played a major role in the moderni-zation of Ottoman education. One of its provisions mandated the estab-lishment of separate *rüştiye*s for the different *millet*s (nationalities) in the Empire, the children of each to be taught in their own language and to be given instruction in their own creed. For the Muslim *millet*, the law specified that the curriculum should include the Ottoman, Arabic, and Persian languages; history; geography; elementary mathematics; elementary natural science; music; painting; and various practical skills (*enva-ı ameliyat-i hayatiye*).[44]

Each school was to be under the charge of a director at a salary of 1,500 *kuruş* a year. Teachers and *usta*s would receive 750, and servants 150. The system was put into effect a year and a half later, although some subjects had to be postponed for lack of qualified teachers. In 1870 an examination system was instituted for the *kız rüştiyesi*. Minister of Education Saffet Pasha, with the aid of a group of lesser officials, examined 32 girls in grammar (*emsile*), arithmetic (*amal-ı erbaa*), geography (*coğrafya*), spelling (*imlâ'*), calligraphy (*sülüs yazısı*), drawing (*resim*), painting (*nakış*), and dressmaking (*heyat*). Everyone passed.[45] By 1874 there were nine *rüştiye*s in Istanbul and its suburbs, with 38 first-year, 35 second-year, 55 third-year, and 120 fourth-year pupils; 248 in all.[46] These figures show a gradual increase in the numbers of girls entering secondary school, which in turn indicates a growing acceptance of the principle of educating women. By 1901 there were 11 *kız rüştiyesi*s with 1,640 students and 40 teachers.[47]

With the proliferation of the *rüştiye*s for girls, the problem of staffing them became increasingly acute. Because there still was strong opposition to the mixing of the sexes, it became necessary to train a cadre of women teachers. Until this could be done, only elderly men of impeccable character were appointed to the *kız rüştiyesi*s.[48] To remedy this situation, the Dârülmuallimat, or Women's Teachers' Training School, was established in Istanbul in 1872.[49] Although it had only 29 students to start with and for a time did not have permanent quarters, it soon flourished. By 1895 its student body had grown to 350.[50]

The Dârülmuallimat attracted some exceptional women, among them Ayşe Sıdıka Hanım, the first wife of the distinguished Turkish writer Rıza Tevfik [Bölükbaşı]. She was the daughter of an *enderun hoca* (palace teacher) of Topkapı Palace, Mustafa Hoca, a man who quite evidently believed in education for women. He sent his daughter to the Zaption, a Greek school, and, when she was graduated from there, to the Dârülmuallimat. After graduation from the teachers' college she was appointed, in 1891, teacher of *fenn-i terbiye* and *usul-ı tedris*, "the science of education" and "the principles of instruction." Sıdıka was not only a pedagogue, but also a musician and a painter, and she embroidered beautifully. She died when still fairly young, or more would undoubtedly have been heard of her.[51]

In 1875, an American school, which later became the Constantinople Women's College, opened in Üsküdar.[52] Though at first only girls from minority families attended, in the closing years of the nineteenth century three Turkish fathers braved Abdülhamit II's wrath to have their daughters educated there. All came from upper-class families. The first was Gülistan İzmet, whose mother was a *saraylı* (palace woman) and whose father was an army colonel; the second was the famous Halide Edip, daughter of a palace secretary; and the third was Nazli Halit, granddaughter of a former important official. For none of them was it an easy step. The school, being supported by the Protestant Board of Missions, felt it necessary to acquaint the students with the Bible. In her memoirs, Halide Edip tells how the members of her father's household hid the Bibles she brought home in order to memorize verses for school, and how friendless she felt at first among the girls of the minority cultures. Adjustment to an entirely new environment was not the girls' only problem. Harassment by government officials was constant. As a result, Halide's father withdrew her for a time, and Nazli was in and out depending on the pressure the sultan brought to bear on her family. At one point the school authorities hid Gülistan in the library when Abdülhamit's men came to search the school for her. In spite of these problems, all three girls graduated.[53]

In 1877, the first *kız sanayı mektebi*, or girls' arts and crafts school, was established. The Ottoman Empire was indebted to Mithat Pasha for this institution. While governor of the Danube province, he had opened the first such school, for orphan girls, in Rusçuk in 1865. With machinery imported from Europe, he had the girls taught to make clothing for the army. After he returned to Istanbul, he was influential in the establishment of the first *kız sanayı mektebi* there. It trained girls to work in the Yedi Kule (Seven Towers) factory that turned out bandages and underwear for the armed forces.[54]

In 1878 Ahmet Vefik, an Ottoman historian and statesman, opened a school of three grades in Üsküdar. The purpose of his school was to train women to support themselves, and thus spend their time in ways other than dressing up (*giyinmek*) and arraying themselves (*süslenmek*). In 1881 Suphi Pasha, who was now Minister of Education for the second time, converted this school into a second *kız sanayı mektebi*. At first it followed the *rüştiye* program but later it added an atelier, so that its course of study took seven years to complete. In 1912, it was about to be reorganized out of existence. Its energetic director, Fatma Zekiye, protested so vigorously that although its name was changed, its program, a combination of the scholastic and the practical, remained basically unchanged.[55]

In 1879 a third arts and crafts school was added in the vicinity of Topkapı Palace. This one was a boarding school—a further innovation. According to Osman Ergin, it was located in the *konak* of Tursunlu Mehmet Pasha in the Sultanahmet district until 1907. During the first month or so only three girls applied for admission to this school, but five years later, in 1884, it had 75 boarding and 125 day students. Its original aim was the "securing of skill and knowledge by female children."[56] The *kız sanayı mektebi*s, with their curricula which combined the scholastic and the practical, went through numerous changes of name and location, but lasted throughout the remaining days of the Empire.

Several girls from upper-class families studied in this public school system. One of these was Hamiyet Hanım, who was a daughter of Suphi Pasha. Born in 1876, she went to the Leylî Sanayı Mektebi in Istanbul, which her father had founded. She later led a very productive life. During the First Balkan War of 1912, she founded the Esirgeme, a society for the protection of refugees. She also became active in the Hilâl-i Ahmer Cemiyeti (Red Crescent Society). She married, was widowed, and, during the Republic, became a teacher of music at the Erenköy Lisesi. She died in 1930.[57]

Another product of the public school system created during the second half of the nineteenth century was Nimet Günaydın. She was the daughter of Kâmil Bey, who was a secretary to Abdülhamit II and who represented Turkey at the International Congresses of Orientalists in 1894 and 1897. She was probably born in 1885. Her mother was a Circassian who died when Nimet was three. Her father married again and had one or more other daughters, whose education he promoted as actively as he did that of Nimet. They completed the seven-year course at Emirgân Rüştiye Mektebi, which was then, under the efficient headmistress Fıtnat Hanım, the best organized school for girls in Turkey. Nimet was graduated *pek iyi* (very good). After that she had lessons at home, studying Arabic and history. She was especially interested in history.

In 1895 she accompanied her father to London, where he represented Turkey at the International Congress of Geography. They traveled through Belgrade, Budapest, Vienna (where they stayed three days), Paris (where they stayed a fortnight), and finally reached London (where they spent a month). She was only 12 years old when she lost her father.

Nimet Hanım was 19 when she married. The marriage was unhappy, and she and her husband were divorced. She had four children, of whom three survived her. Her elder daughter married Tevfik Bey, son of the İsmet Bey who was a foster brother of Abdülhamit II and Grand Master of the Robes. Tevfik Bey is a first cousin of Ayşe Sultan, daughter of Abdülhamit II.

When Turkey entered World War I and women were employed in order to substitute for the men who had been conscripted, Nimet Hanım was one of the first 15 women to be hired in the Ministry of Finance. These women still wore the *çarşaf* (veil) and were given offices separate from those of the men.

Nimet Hanım traveled a good deal in Europe, North Africa, Syria, and Lebanon. In 1960, she published a book of her impressions of Lebanon, *Gölde bir gece ve Tedmür Melikesi Zennuba (One Night on the Lake and Zenubia the Queen of Tedmur)*.[58]

But women like Hamiyet Hanım and Nimet Günaydın were exceptions to an unwritten rule, namely, that girls from upper-class Ottoman families were to be educated entirely in their homes. Traditionally, if they had any education at all, they learned classical Arabic and Persian, so as to be able

to read the Koran and Persian poetry.[59] However, as the tempo of Westernization accelerated during the second half of the nineteenth century,
girls were given foreign governesses so that they might learn Western
languages as well. At first French was the favorite European language.
Later German and English also became fashionable. These languages made
it possible for them to gain access to the rich tradition of European literature, opening a new and exciting world to them.

An excellent representative of this group of women, Emine Foat Tugay,
who was the granddaughter of Gazi Ahmet Muhtar Pasha, the hero of the
Russo-Turkish War of 1877-1878, and the Khedive Ismail, has given us a
clear picture of the upper-class Ottoman pattern of education in her family
biography, *Three Centuries, Family Chronicle of Turkey and Egypt*. She
says that when she was taught foreign languages great emphasis was put
on proper pronunciation, so the children of the family had as teachers
native speakers of the languages they learned—German, French, and English. They also had lessons in Turkish, Persian, and Arabic grammar, since
such knowledge was considered requisite for a thorough understanding of
Turkish. They were also instructed in Islamic and Turkish history, and
even calligraphy.[60]

This was the situation in the early twentieth century, but a generation
earlier, in the days of Princess Nimetullah, Mrs. Tugay's mother, the system
of governesses already prevailed. This lady had first an English and then
a French governess. The latter also gave her piano lessons, which were
later undertaken by the German-Huguenot conductor of the khedival military band. With the advent of Westernization the ability to play the piano
had become an important part of a girl's education.[61]

Princess Nimetullah, a daughter of the Khedive Ismail, was the first
generation of the khedival family to have Western governesses. Her mother,
who had been a Circassian slave brought up in Istanbul by the wife of a
pasha, had been taught only religion and reading, but not writing.[62] The
khedival family was of course Turkish, and however independent it might
be politically, it followed Ottoman customs socially.

The same pattern of education was followed by Seniha Moralı. Like
Emine Foat Tugay, she had a male teacher—hers was an old man who
wore a turban—several days a week for reading and writing Turkish, Turkish history, and the history of Islam. Later she had a *hoca hanım* for Turkish
literature and grammar (a different kind of person than the *hoca hanım*
who taught religion). In due course there were both English and French
governesses. As in most Ottoman families, these people taught all the
family children of like age, Seniha, her sisters, and her cousins.[63]

Seniha Moralı's paternal grandfather, as we have seen, was Suphi Pasha,
a Minister of Education who did a good deal to advance the public education of women. Yet all his daughters except one had private instruction
and foreign governesses.[64]

Another daughter of a Minister of Education was Lûtfiye Hanım, whose father, Zühtü Pasha, held his post in the late nineteenth century. Although he was concerned with education, he does not seem to have seen any necessity to provide advanced schooling for his daughter. She went only to the primary school which her father had founded in Kızıltoprak,[65] where they lived.[66]

Still another was Seniye Cenani, the daughter of Saffet Pasha, a Tanzimat Minister of Education. She was taught at home in the way then fashionable among Westernized families: a French governess for the French language and literature, an elderly Turk for Turkish and Persian literature and Arabic syntax, and a German for the piano. She also learned to play the lute, to sing, to draw, and to paint. Such a method of education could be afforded by few, but it produced women of broad culture.[67]

At the time there was considerable criticism of the employment of foreign governesses, and it is still not easy to ascertain how much of it was well-founded. Mehmet Emin, writing in the magazine *Hayat* in 1928, thought families picked up foreign governesses in Beyoğlu (the European quarter of Istanbul) because it was fashionable to have their children learn a foreign language, but the women whom they chose often had no qualifications for teaching. He believed the result of this practice was that the children lost their patriotism and "became good-for-nothing," even losing their proper Turkish accent.[68] However, Mehmet Emin was a Turkist and seems to have viewed the *mürebbiye*, or governess, from an ultra-nationalist viewpoint.

Marmaduke Pickthall, the Englishman who became a Muslim, thought Turkish parents did not know how to select a governess and therefore sometimes chose disreputable characters. One English governess, he says, spent her time in bed, drinking.[69] Yet most of them must have been good teachers, for many cultivated Ottoman women came from their hands. Even Pickthall admits that the Ottoman women were "often highly cultivated and familiar with the art and thought of Europe."[70]

These women in turn saw to it that their daughters were educated. Many of them took an active part in the modernization of Turkey. Though there were no doubt governesses who deserved dismissal, much of the opposition to them must have come from the traditionalists who were opposed to all innovation. In any event, governesses were a definite part of upper-class life. There was even a novel written on the subject, Hüseyin Rahmi Gürpınar's *Mürebbiye* (*Governess*), first published in 1895, in which the governess is depicted as a dissolute creature.[71]

Under the Young Turks, educational opportunities for women were further extended. The *idadiye*, a step up from the *rüştiye*, became accessible to girls in 1911, and the University of Istanbul opened its doors to women in 1916.[72] At first women were not eligible for a degree but could merely listen to lectures—in classes separate from the male students. By 1919, however, they were both matriculating and sitting in the same classrooms as the men.[73] According to Hans Kohn, "In February, 1914, special courses for women were started at the University of Stambul, with two hundred and fifty students enrolled. The subjects taught were hygiene, domestic science, and the rights and duties of women."[74] In 1913 a Turkish woman teacher of gymnastics was appointed to the Sultaniye lycée for girls, which represented yet another step forward.[75]

After the departure of the xenophobic Abdülhamit from the scene, many more Muslim girls entered the American College for Girls, and its influence became more widely diffused. Of the 24 Muslim girls graduated through the year 1922, 16 became teachers and thus added their talents to the cause of women's education in Turkey. Two of the 24 became doctors. One became a lawyer. Several wrote. Others were engaged in social service work. All became people of influence.[76]

Halide Edip, who was one of the graduates, was persuaded to teach by Sait Bey, then Minister of Education, who, she says, was "the pioneer advocate of the modernization of women's education in Turkey."[77] "Pioneer advocate" may be the wrong phrase, since certainly other Ministers of Education did their share. Yet Sait Bey took over the ministry at the advent of power of the Young Turks, a time when it was possible to make major reforms. However, Halide Edip is certainly right when she points out that although there were many prominent men in the post of Minister of Education, there was "a lack of clearness of aim and principles." She credits Emrullah Efendi, another Young Turk Minister of Education, with being "the first man to have clear ideas of what he wanted in public education."[78] He organized the *lise* (lycée) program, and in doing so opened preparatory schools to women. Şükrü Bey, his successor, opened the university to them.[79] Under the Young Turks, women were for the first time sent abroad to study.[80]

In 1914 two American women of the American College for Girls in Istanbul published an article outlining Turkish education for women at the time. They said there were then at the American College "eight students supported by the Government, and these girls are pledged to several years of service in the Government schools." Twenty-six Turkish girls were then being educated in schools in Europe at the expense of the government. Some had been sent to Switzerland to study drawing and the technique of education.

The Young Turks' first idea was to send educated girls from Istanbul to teach in the provinces, but this proved difficult because of the Muslim restrictions on women. Instead it was decided to bring the provincial girls to Istanbul and educate them there. This was successful enough so that when Ellis and Palmer were writing their article in 1913 they could count 143 girl students, including some from the minorities, studying at the Dâr-ülmuallimat. However, the girls were still veiled in the presence of the men teachers.[81]

Meanwhile the Society for Excellence in Ottoman Women (Osmanlı Kadınların Cemiyet-i Hayıresi) had been formed for the purpose of organizing girls' schools. One of these, in Nişantaşı, opened in the fall of 1913. A similar organization founded during this period was the Society for the Defense of the Rights of Ottoman Women (Osmanlı Müdafaa-ı Hukuk-ı Nisvan Cemiyeti), which not only promoted the education of women but also strove to increase their personal freedom and to replace the veil with a head scarf, thus leaving the face visible. The organization had some success in its work, as attested to by the fact that a Turkish girl of good family was given a job in the Constantinople telephone system. The society published a magazine, *Kadınlar dünyası*, which we shall discuss later.[82] Women themselves began to look to the education of their sex. In 1908 Halide Edip helped organize an association of women, Teali-i Nisvan Cemiyeti, that arranged courses and conferences for women in Istanbul. According to her, it was the first women's club in Turkey, and it invited men of a variety of professions to lecture to the members. It also brought into being childcare centers.[83]

The Balkan Wars, stirring up as they did the patriotism of women, was a spur to their quest for personal freedom. In 1913 we find both Halide Edip and Princess Nimetullah (the mother of Emine Foat Tugay) speaking at a crowded meeting of women in the hall of the then University of Istanbul and, a few days later, Fatma Aliye in the same hall rousing women to give their jewels for the sake of the fatherland. Of this the newspaper *Tasvir-i efkâr* said, "Certainly these conferences have beautifully proved what great moral assets we have in our women."[84]

By the end of World War I all legal restrictions on the public education of women had been removed. It remained for time and a change of attitude to remove personal restrictions. The catalyst had been provided by the private education of upper-class women and the public education of some of the middle class. From the time of the Young Turks, the desire for a secular, Western-type education for girls was to spread swiftly. As a result, with the advent of the Republic and its emphasis on the equality of the sexes, there was a cadre of educated, articulate women to further its aims.

NOTES

1. Mircea Eliade, *Shamanism: Archaic Techniques of Ecstasy* (New York, 1964), pp. 115–122, 189.

2. Hans Kohn (*A History of Nationalism in the Near East*, p. 241) says: "The Mediterranean religions—Judaism, Christianity, and Islam—have always accorded to women a position of inferiority; the priestly office was confined to men." If this be so, the Altaic region with its Shamanism placed women in a much higher position than did the eastern Mediterranean, despite the latter's being the cradle of many cultures. *See* also Fuat Köprülü, *Influence du chamanisme turco-mongol sur les ordres mystiques musulmans*, p. 8.

3. Bahriye Üçok, *İslâm devletlerinde kadın hükümdarlar*, p. 91.

4. Ibid., p. 26.

5. Sir Hamilton A. R. Gibb, *The Travels of Ibn Baṭṭūṭa, A.D. 1325–1354*, II, p. 487.

6. L. Veccia Vaglieri, "Ḥafṣa," *EI²*, III, pp. 63–64.

7. A *hadith* (*hadis*) is a saying or action attributed to the Prophet Muhammad.

8. Ignácz Goldziher, *Muhammedanische Studien*, II, p. 300.

9. Johannes Pedersen, "Mescid: Talebeler," *İA*, VIII, p. 69.

10. Reuben Levy, *The Social Structure of Islam*, p. 132.

11. Seeger Bonebakker, *Some Early Definitions of the Tawriya and Ṣafadī's Fadd al-Xitām 'an at-Tawriya wa-'l-Istixdām* (The Hague, 1966), p. 67, n. 10–11.

12. Bayard Dodge, *Al-Azhar: A Millennium of Muslim Learning* (Washington, D.C., 1961), p. 17.

13. Arthur Jeffery, *Islam, Muhammad and His Religion*, pp. 217–222.

14. Faruk Sümer, "Eski Türk kadınları," *Türk yurdu*, 3 (*Eylül*, 1954), pp. 191–194. There were, however, two prominent Selçuk women who might be called intellectuals: Müneccime Hatun (Lady Astrologer) and Erguvan Hatun, a literary figure; *see* A. Afetinen, *The Emancipation of the Turkish Woman*, p. 24.

15. Quoted in Barnette Miller, *The Palace School of Muhammad the Conqueror*, pp. 30–31.

16. Elias John Wilkinson Gibb, *History of Ottoman Poetry*, II, pp. 123–125, 135–137.

17. A case in point is Nesterin Dirvana, professor of Romance literature at Istanbul University, who received all her education at home until she matriculated at the university. She comes from a family with a tradition of private instruction; personal interview, July 1966.

18. Vedat Günyol, "Mektep," *İslam ansiklopedisi*, VII, p. 659; information on private instruction from Seniha Moralı.

19. Lady Fanny Blunt, *The People of Turkey*, II, pp. 157–159.

20. Halide Edip, *Memoirs of Halide Edip*, p. 351.

21. Mehmet Zeki Pakalın, "Sıbyan mektebi," *Osmanlı tarih deyimleri ve terimleri sözlüğü*, III, pp. 201–203.

22. Osman Ergin, *Türkiye maarif tarihi*, II, pp. 381–382.

23. Halide Edip, *Memoirs*, pp. 86–87.

24. Personal communication from Nesrin Moralı, 1968.

25. Halide Edip, *Memoirs*, p. 85.

26. Ibid., pp. 87–89.

27. Personal interview with Seniha Moralı, July 1966.

28. Ignatius Mouradgea d'Ohsson, *Tableau général de l'Empire othoman*, IV, p. 338. D'Ohsson goes on to say that he has been astonished by the purity of the language, the facility of the elocution, the fineness of the thoughts, the noble tone of the conversation, and the graces of the women he claims to have met at the homes of ministers, seigneurs, and magistrates. Because he was the Swedish Minister in Turkey and was married to a woman from Istanbul, d'Ohsson was one of the few Europeans to become acquainted, however remotely, with Ottoman ladies.

29. Osman Bey [Frederick Millingen], *Les Femmes de Turquie*, p. 50.

30. Melek Hanım, *Thirty Years in the Harem*, p. 211.

31. Edmondo de Amicis, *Constantinople*, p. 225.

32. Halil Halit [Khalil Khalid], *The Diary of a Turk*, p. 19.

33. Personal interview with Seniha Moralı, July 1966.

34. Halil Halit, *The Diary of a Turk*, p. 19.

35. Personal interview with Süphiye Gürün, a member of Hafız Mehmet's family, December 1967.

36. Celâl Nuri [İleri], *Kadınlarımız*, pp. 121, 123.

37. Necmeddin Erim, "Yusuf İzzeddin'e dair yeni vesikalar", *Tarih dünyası*, 1 (*Haziran* 15, 1950), pp. 211–213. Yusuf İzzeddin's views are reminiscent of the old verse, "Be good, sweet maid, and let who will be clever."

38. Joan Haslip, *The Sultan: The Life of Abdul Hamid*, p. 155; Mary Mills Patrick, *Under Five Sultans*, p. 164.

39. Mustafa Nihat Özön, *Namık Kemal ve İbret gazetesi*, pp. 86–90.

40. Tezer Taşkıran, "Şemseddin Sami ve kadınlar," *Türk yurdu*, 1 (*Haziran*, 1955), pp. 946–950.

41. Thomas Philipp, "Feminism and National Politics in Egypt" in Lois Beck and Nikki Keddie, eds., *Women in the Muslim World* (Cambridge, Mass., 1978), pp. 278–279.

42. Ergin, *Maarif*, II, p. 557.

43. İbrahim Alâettin Gövsa, *Turk meşhurları ansiklopedisi*, p. 358; Seniha Moralı, "Arkeoloji Müzesi, Suriye ve Lübnan ile Kanlıca Körfezine dair," *Hayat tarih ve edebiyat mecmuası*, 4 (*Nisan*, 1978), pp. 56–61, and interviews, August 1966. Suphi Pasha (1818–1886) was the son of the famous vizier Sami Pasha (1795–1878) and the paternal grandfather of Seniha Moralı. Under the Republic, Seniha Moralı became the curator of the Archaeology Museum.

44. Ergin, *Maarif*, II, pp. 557–572.

45. Ibid.

46. Ibid, pp. 381–382.

47. Ergin, *Maarif*, III, pp. 740–742.

48. Ergin, *Maarif*, II, p. 557.

49. Reşat Ekrem Koçu (*İstanbul ansiklopedisi*, I, p. 447) says 1867.

50. Stanford J. Shaw and Ezel Kural Shaw, *History of the Ottoman Empire and Modern Turkey*, II, p. 113.

51. Ergin, *Maarif*, II, pp. 557–572; Munissa Başıkoğlu, Ayşe Sıdıka's daughter, personal interview, August 1966.

52. Now called Kız Koleji, it moved to Arnavutköy, on the European shore of the Bosphorus, in 1914. Today it is part of Boğaziçi University.

53. Halide Edip, *Memoirs*, pp. 148–150; Patrick, *Under Five Sultans*, pp. 56–57, 192–194, 251–252.

54. Ergin, *Maarif*, II, pp. 572–581.

55. Ibid.

56. Ibid.

57. Seniha Moralı, "Çocuk esirgeme kurumu'nun kurucunlarından Hamiyet Hanım," *Hayat tarih mecmuası*, 1 (*Şubat*, 1969), pp. 69–71; also personal interview, 1966.

58. Personal communication from Seniha Moralı.

59. Blunt, *The People of Turkey*, II, p. 161; Lucy M. Garnett, *Turkey of the Ottomans*, p. 241.

60. Emine Foat Tugay, *Three Centuries, Family Chronicle of Turkey and Egypt*, pp. 240–241. Mrs. Tugay was also known as Princess Emine.

61. Tugay, *Three Centuries*, p. 208.

62. Ibid., p. 179.

63. Personal interview with Seniha Moralı, July 1966.

64. Personal interview with Seniha Moralı, July 1966.

65. A suburb of Istanbul.

66. Lûtfiye developed into a woman with much force of character. During World War I she turned her house into a hospital and maintained it at her own expense. Her descendants remember her as a woman of great charm, famous for her hospitality; Nezih Manyas, Lûtfiye's grandson, personal interview, April 1967.

67. Personal interview with Seniha Moralı, July 1966; Kadri Cenani, Seniye Cenani's son, personal interview, August 1966.

68. Mehmet Emin, "Mürebbiye," *Hayat*, 4 (*Ağustos* 6, 1928), pp. 1–2.

69. Marmaduke Pickthall, *With the Turk in Wartime*, pp. 98–99.

70. Ibid., p. 153.

71. Hüseyin Rahmi [Gürpınar], *Mürebbiye*, passim.

72. Bernard Lewis, *The Emergence of Modern Turkey*, p. 225; Patrick, *Under Five Sultans*, p. 304.

73. Patrick, *Under Five Sultans*, p. 304.

74. Kohn, *Nationalism*, p. 243.

75. Ellen Deborah Ellis and Florence Palmer, "The Feminist Movement in Turkey," *The Contemporary Review*, 105 (January-June, 1914), pp. 857–864.

76. Personal communication from the Alumnae Office of the American College for Girls, January 1967; by the kindness of Nesime Moralı.

77. Halide Edip, *Memoirs*, pp. 297-300.

78. Ibid.

79. Ibid.

80. Halide Edip, *Conflict of East and West in Turkey*, p. 263.

81. Ellis and Palmer, "The Feminist Movement," pp. 859–860.

82. Ibid.

83. Tezer Taşkıran, via communication from Seniha Moralı, 1978; Edip, *Conflict of East and West*, p. 262.

84. "The Patriotic Awakening of the Turkish Woman," *The Literary Digest*, 46 (January 1913-June 1913), pp. 563–564.

4

Marriage

The Ottoman girl began her adult life[1] with marriage.[2] This took place at so early an age, from 12 to 14, that she scarcely had time for growing up, which would have to come later under the tutelage of her mother-in-law. In the Ottoman Empire marriage was considered the natural state of women. Widows, for example, were encouraged to marry again quickly. But before her first marriage, this momentous event that would henceforth shape her life, a girl played her part in an age-old drama with a rigid set of conventions. The first scene of this drama was the visit of the *görücü*[3] (viewer) or *kılavuz*[4] (guide).

The *görücü* was a woman dispatched by the family of the prospective groom to scout for a bride.[5] She might be his mother, a close female relative, or a woman hired for the purpose. If a relative, she had probably, like the grandmother in İrfan Orga's *Portrait of a Turkish Family*, been picking and choosing from among the naked girls she saw bathing in the *hamam*: "She had eyes only for the budding . . . maidens of thirteen years old or thereabouts, and she would tell some delighted mother at great length that she would certainly be well advised to marry such a daughter as soon as possible to the strongest young man that could be found."[6] If a professional matchmaker, she was usually an old neighborhood character, perhaps the same person as the *kıra*[7] or tradeswoman who sold articles to the harems of the quarter. Her entrée into the harems enabled her to know in which houses attractive and marriageable girls were to be found. She then set out to call on the most promising girls, sometimes accompanied by the prospective groom's mother.[8]

Occasionally a family friend acted as *görücü*, as did Melek Hanım,[9] the wife of the Ottoman official, Kıbrıslı Mehmet Pasha. In this instance the

would-be groom was one Gözlüklü Reşit, a pasha who was without female
relatives in Istanbul. He specifically required that his bride be tall and
slender like a European woman, but whenever Melek turned up such a
girl he added new requirements. Seated on innumerable sofas in houses
with nubile daughters, Melek looked over girl after girl as each would come
into the room dressed in her best, salute the guest with handkerchief and,
with downcast eyes, hand out dainty coffee cups (*fincans*) set in silver
containers (*zarfs*). Melek would drink the coffee slowly in order to have
time for inspection—for when the coffee was consumed the girl withdrew[10]—
and also to keep from hurting the girl's feelings by a too hasty dismissal.
Then, as soon as the girl left the room, the elders would get down to
business. The girl's mother would ask Melek's opinion, and Melek would
inevitably give a flattering one, true or not. The mother listed the contents
of the girl's trousseau, including jewelry. Melek would listen carefully,
making allowances for the customary exaggerations.[11]

She called on the harems of ministers, generals, *ulemas*, and other high
dignitaries, but Gözlüklü Reşit was still not satisfied. Finally, weary of the
hunt, she chose a tall, healthy girl with red hair, the daughter of a pasha
with a palace on the Bosphorus. She dyed the girl's eyebrows a fashionable
black and, without consulting Gözlüklü Reşit, presented her with the diamond he had provided for such an occasion. Melek triumphantly reports
that the marriage was a success. The pasha lived with his redhead all his
life and—the most convincing proof—never added another wife to his
household.[12]

Halide Edip, in discussing the *görücü* visit, this first step toward marriage,
emphasized the importance of the ceremony of the coffee cups. According
to her, the girl withdrew when the first lady guest put her cup back on the
tray, and: "One often heard it asked with painful excitement after a geuruju
visit whether they had handed back their coffee-cups too soon or not."[13]

Other aspects of the visit were also regulated by ceremony. When the
görücü was met at the door, she would announce, "We have come to see
the little lady." She would be ushered into the best room to be entertained
with small talk while the girl was being arrayed in her most fetching outfit.
As the girl put on *şalvar* (harem trousers) and *entari* (dress) with slit skirt,
the nurse or maid who was helping her would admonish her to keep her
eyes lowered and to say little, lest the *görücü* think her bold. She would
enter the room slowly and diffidently and later left it in the same manner.
She sat with bowed head, raising it only at the *görücü*'s words: "My little
chick, raise your head a little and let us see your beautiful face."[14]

For most girls of the nineteenth century the custom of being looked over
was accepted as a matter of course. Though the girl might be understandably nervous at the approach of the *görücü*, it is unlikely that she would
have resented the visit. Yet the institution of arranged marriages could
leave a tragically wide gulf between a girl's dreams and the reality she

faced, a gulf that grew wider as education gave the girl a wider field for dreaming. This unhappy predicament is reflected in a story written by Hüseyin Cahit Yalçın in 1899.[15]

Its heroine, Seniha, was no longer an old-fashioned Ottoman girl. For one thing, she read novels at a time when reading was not yet a widespread female accomplishment. These and her daydreaming conjured up in her mind the image of a slender young *bey* with light brown hair and blue eyes, a youth at once courteous and educated. Would these daydreams and longings, she wondered, be apparent to the two *görücüs* who suddenly appeared at the door? Fear that they might guess her thoughts made her blush with self-consciousness.[16]

The details she had heard from the older girls in the neighborhood school, details to which she had listened with undivided attention . . . these things she had awaited with unendurable impatience and curiosity, now they were becoming real.

And this made her afraid. She understood from the malice in their eyes that the pair of strangers would search for all sorts of defects and would want to find fault, even though they wouldn't be open about it. She understood that their unfriendly scrutiny, which would assault her from her hair and eyebrows down to her feet, would oblige her to say farewell to the entire life of her childhood. She felt that this *görücü* visit was the first serious stop on an unknown road that would reach who knew where.[17]

Instead of the emissaries from the young *bey* of her dreams, she saw:

Fearful ogres of the dark tales that made up the neighborhood gossip . . . of a sister-in-law who gave a bride no peace, of a mother-in-law who compelled a beloved young bride to separate from her husband, a handsome *bey*, and made her take to her bed with tuberculosis. These tales destroyed her courage.

. . . Seniha longed to stay with her embroidery, but this *görücü* visit was a thing she could not avoid. She dressed in her rose silk clothing. Her feet stumbled over one another as, head bent and face flushed, she walked to the stool ready for her in the middle of the room and almost collapsed onto it.

The lip-smacking at every mouthful of coffee, drunk with such dignity, was as much of a torture to her now as a slap would have been. She was oppressed by the weight of the malignant looks she thought surrounded her everywhere and by the sorrow that arose at finding so thorny this *görücü* stool she had thought would be so sweet. She wanted to run, to weep.

All these women in front of her, what were they like? Seniha did not know them. When she'd entered the door, she had been able to discern only a wrinkle-faced old woman in a corner of the sofa, a woman who wore a dark kerchief like the one worn by that hag, Habibe Hanım, a neighbor she didn't like in the least; and in order to escape from the distasteful burden and to save herself as soon as possible from being examined for rosiness and plumpness, from having her eyebrows, her round eyes, and even her fingers scrutinized with disdainful looks, she persuaded herself never in her life to face another *görücü*.

Finally, after an inspection lasting centuries, the perspiring Seniha was released from this torture and hurried into the hall with obvious eagerness. As she got up and simply ran, she heard her mother discussing her leaving and apologizing that it was her first *görücü*, and how angry she became! Oh, why didn't her mother drive these women away? Well, she would behave this way every time.

Crying, she ran to her room and, untying her corset with nervous fingers, threw herself on the sofa. Had she dreamed these dreams, had she sewed these rose silks in order to appear before this treacherous-faced old woman with her hair bundled in a kerchief? She threw off the rich clothes violently, as if she would tear them to pieces, these rich clothes she had pulled over her shoulders so many nights when there had been no opportunity to wear them, so many days when she had so wholeheartedly wanted to wear them and had looked at their cut in the mirror to see if they were becoming. Her print *entari* that she wore in the house, how beautiful it had become to her now, how restful.[18]

Seniha, poor girl, either turned down or was turned down by every possible husband who came her way, so that 12 years later, at the age of 26, she was still being summoned for inspection.

Like a machine, without knowing what she was doing, Seniha got up, dressed and adorned herself. She sat down on the same stool in the same room that had wearied of seeing her years ago. While she awaited her fate on this stool whose rushes had worn thin by now, how many women had come and gone! . . . Doubtless even those suitors who had been rejected because the dreams had not come out well had children by now.

This made Seniha so despairing, and the jeering lip-smacking over the coffee made her so ashamed, she fled from the room without the permissive: "We have troubled the little lady." She fled with the longings that had grown old along with the clothes she put on and took off; she fled trying to hold back her tears, and with the firm resolve never again to subject herself to this endless shame.[19]

Seniha seemed well on her way to becoming an old maid, a fate that the system of arranged marriages had previously enabled a Turkish girl to avoid. For family connections were quite as important as personal beauty in the selection of a wife in Ottoman Turkey, and a girl's plainness could be compensated for by her family's influence.[20]

After a round of visits, the conventional procedure was for the boy's mother to report to her husband and son on the girls viewed, and then for the advantages and shortcomings of each possible match to be discussed in a family council.[21] The description of a particularly pretty girl might sway a man, and so might a childhood recollection of their youthful encounter.[22] Young children of both sexes had the run of the harem and *selâmlık* alike, and since it was the custom for married sons often to live under the patriarchal roof, a cousin remembered from childhood would be a likely candidate. In Istanbul, both the boy and the girl had probably been brought up in that city, for it was very rare for an Istanbul family to give its daughter to any but an Istanbul man, or at least one who had made good there. Old Istanbul families followed the same way of life; therefore, it was natural that they should intermarry. The way of life in the provinces was different.[23]

Once a particular girl had been selected by the boy's family, it remained for the girl's father to give his consent. Very often the families were known to one another, and the consent—or lack of it—came swiftly. In those cases where little was known about the boy's family, the girl's father made careful inquiries as to their resources and status. Meanwhile the girl's family had recourse to *istihare*, divination by dreams. If the suitor was to be rejected, this gave an easy excuse: "Our dreams did not turn out well."[24]

When the girl's family was satisfied with the character and family of the groom, a succession of visits ensued. Representatives of the two families met to agree on the trousseau and dowry[25] on mutually agreeable terms and to fix the dates for the engagement, or *nisan*, and the legal ceremony, or *nikâh*.[26] Then the boy's father and one or two male relatives called on the girl's father in order to get the promise of his daughter "at the command of God and the Prophet." They settled between them whether the couple was to live in the girl's home, *içeri*, or at the boy's, *dışarı*.

Next came the payment of part of the dowry by representatives of the boy's family. The dowry was a vestige of the bride-price paid by the nomadic Turks of Central Asia, fortified by the injunction of Islam.[27] Even its name was the same among Ottoman and Central Asian Turks: the latter called it *kalym*,[28] the former called it *kalın*,[29] as well as *mehr*.[30] They followed the Muslim practice of dividing the dowry into two parts. The first part, which the Ottomans called *ağırlık*,[31] was paid before the marriage contract was signed. Its purpose was to help defray the cost of the wedding and to contribute to the furnishing of the young couple's home. In the mid-nineteenth century it ranged from 5,000 to 20,000 gold piasters.[32] The main portion of the dower was the *nikâh* money, the sum the husband contracted to pay his wife in the event that he divorced her. This sum also came to her if he died while she was still his wife. The *ağırlık* was the *mihr-i muaccel*, or prompt marriage payment; the *nikâh* money the *mihr-i müeccel*, or deferred marriage payment.[33] No Muslim marriage was valid without a dowry.[34]

Once the *ağırlık* was paid, the couple were *nişanlı*, or engaged, at which time a contingent of the groom's female relatives, headed by his mother, called on the bride. They took with them several yards of red silk and a basket of bonbons. The red silk was eventually to be made into undergarments for the bride, but for the moment it was spread on the floor so that the girl might stand on it while she accepted her future mother-in-law's blessing and kissed her hand. From the candy the girl chose one piece, bit it in two, and handed half of it back to the older woman to be given to her son as a token of the girl's willingness to share her life with him.[35]

After this the girl sent the boy a *nişan bohçası*, or package of presents, for him and his family, and he reciprocated with presents of his own, the *nişan takımı*.[36] The bride's presents were conveyed by her *yenge*, who was an elderly woman relative or perhaps her nurse. They included a shawl, a shirt embroidered with pearls (perhaps by the girl's own hand), handkerchiefs and braces likewise embroidered, and a candy-filled box of mother-of-pearl set in tortoise-shell, all done up in a *bohça*. The girl and the boy also sent each other a variety of special foods.[37]

The *nişan takımı* was usually much more elaborate than the *nişan bohçası* and, among the rich, consisted of five trays carried on the heads of five servants. The first tray contained handsome *çitpit*, or house slippers, for the bride and for her female relatives, and *terlik*, less elegant slippers, for her family's servants; a silver hand-mirror; perfumes in tiny crystal bottles; and a filigree silver box, or *çekmece*, in which lay the *nişan yüzüğü*, the ring that would serve as both engagement and wedding ring.[38] It was usually set with a single large emerald, ruby, or diamond. The second tray carried flowers; the third baskets of fruit; the fourth baskets of sweets and spices, coffee, colored wax candles, and bags of Mecca henna. On the fifth were the material for the wedding dress and other fabrics, a pair of handsome *nalın* (clogs) inlaid with mother-of-pearl and equipped with pearl-embroidered straps, a small silver basin, and some elaborate combs for the bride's bath. These trays were each tied in muslin and decorated with ribbons.[39]

Meanwhile the local *imam*, for a fee, had secured from the local *kadı* the *izinname* or permission to marry.[40]

On the appointed day the *akit*, or signing of the contract, took place at the home of the bride.[41] This was done by the male parents or guardians of both the bride and groom, in the presence of the *imam* and male witnesses. The bride and her attendants usually occupied an adjacent room.[42] The *imam* read aloud the conditions of the contract, but with the difference that whatever the actual amount of the dowry, he announced it as one *kuruş*.[43]

The bride's only part in the ceremony was to answer "yes" three times when the *imam* asked her consent three times through an open door. Then the *imam* signed the contract and, as he did so, prayed that the couple would be as happy and prosperous as Adam and Eve, Abraham and Sarah, Joseph and Zuleikha, Muhammad and Khadija, and Ali and Fatima.[44] He later saw to it that the *nikâh* was registered in the *kadı*'s court.

The groom did not have to be present at this ceremony; it was necessary only for him to be represented by his *vekil* (representative). Sometimes a *vekil* acted for the girl also.[45] If a *vekil* acted for the groom, as soon as the *nikâh* contract was signed a *müjdeci* ran to his house to inform him that he was married.

The *nikâh* ceremony was concluded with a banquet for the families of the bride and groom. Although these two had had very little to do with the affair, their turn would come later with the *düğün*.

The climax of the marriage drama, the part for which families turned their houses—and their purses—inside out, was the *düğün*, the week-long feast that gave the marriage its social sanction.[46] It might follow the *nikâh* immediately, or it might be postponed for years. When, as sometimes happened, bride and groom had been legally pledged in their infancy,[47] the time lag was caused by the necessity of waiting for them to grow up. Sometimes the expense of the wedding festivities made delay unavoidable; at other times a postponement was caused by reluctance on the part of the bride to embark upon a life of matrimony, as was the case with Ayeşa, the daughter of Melek Hanım and Kıbrıslı Mehmet Pasha.[48]

When the *düğün* finally took place, it consisted of a week of feasting and celebrating. It was enjoyed by both sexes separately, in the harem of the bride's house and the *selâmlık* of the groom's, and proceeded day by day on a time-honored schedule. On Monday the trousseau passed in procession from the bride's house to the groom's,[49] a ritual supervised, like every phase of the *düğün*, by the *yenge*.[50] In the case of an imperial wedding, this procession was a magnificent affair which people lined the streets to observe. The articles were carried on the heads of slaves or servants, or in baskets that looked like huge gilded cages.[51] Over the baskets the branches of date palms (*nahil*) swayed.[52] The most spectacular procession, that of Fatma Sultan, the daughter of Ahmet III, was so enormous it demolished the balconies of the houses on the narrow streets through which it passed. The trousseau procession of Mihrimah, daughter of Mahmud II, was another splendid affair. Julia Pardoe describes it thus:

The band led the way, playing the Sultan's Grand March upon their wind instruments, and the military followed in good order.

The Troops were succeeded by fifty Field Officers, the General Staff of the Empire, well mounted and attended; and they, in their turn, gave place to twenty Great Officers of the Imperial Household. With these individuals commenced the interest and Orientalism of the spectacle; the flashing diamonds upon their breasts and hands, and the glittering housings of their horses, relieving the monotonous slowness with which they progressed. This splendid train was followed by fourteen led mules, laden with packages, covered with gold and silver stuffs of Broussa, and secured upon the animals with cords of silk. The packages contained the velvet and satin mattresses intended for the harem of the Princess, and all the minor articles necessary for her household; which are supplied by the Sultan, even to the feather-brush that beats aside the flies from the dinner-table.

Next came twelve beautiful white mules, magnificently housed, and led by pages dressed in a scarlet uniform: a present to the Princess from her Imperial Father.

Nine carriages of silver net-work, roofed and draperied with coloured silk, each drawn by four bay horses, followed next in line, and through the transparent lattices glittered the costly sofa-furniture of tissue and embroidery; the velvet cushions, and the gold fringes which were to adorn the saloons of the bridal Palace.

After these came three open droskeys, with pages running at the bridle-rein of the superb leaders... and these were overlaid with cloths of crimson velvet fringed with gold, on which was displayed a collection of richly-chased silver plate.

Then followed five other carriages... containing trunks covered with coloured velvets and gold and silver stuffs, and clamped and hinged with wrought silver, laden with the linen of the Imperial Bride.

Next came what, at first glance... seemed to be a moving tulip-bed... a train of one hundred and fifty men, each attended by a page, and bearing upon his head a basket of wicker-work, covered with gold tissue, and surmounted by a raised dome of coloured gauze, decorated with bunches of artificial flowers. Beneath these transparent screens might be seen the toilette of the young Princess: her golden ewers, and jewel-studded basins—her diamond-covered essence-boxes, and gemmed water-vases—her glittering porcelain, her emerald-mounted hair-brushes—and all the costly gauds which litter so magnificently the chambers of the great. Golden cages, filled with stuffed birds—inlaid caskets, heavy with perfumes—musical instruments, rich with laboured gold and jewels—salvers, heaped-up with gold coins—and ten thousand toys, if not without a name, yet almost without a use, followed in their turn; and then came pyramids of sweetmeats, glittering like fruits which had suddenly been hardened into gems; and trays of shawls, each one a fortune in itself, enveloped separately in wrappers of coloured gauze, tied with long loops of ribbon.

But the most gorgeous display was yet to come; embroidered handkerchiefs whose gold and silver threads were mingled with silks of many hues, and whose texture was almost as impalpable as the gossamer—jackets of velvet worked on the sleeves and breasts with precious stones—trowsers sprinkled with stars of gold and silver—anteries [entaris] of white silk, wrought with coloured jewels—robes of satin powdered with seed-pearl—slippers as diminutive as that of Cinderella, fringed with floss silk and powdered with rubies; and finally, sixteen bearers, balancing upon their heads cages of silver wire, resting on cushions of crimson velvet, whereupon were displayed the bridal diamonds. The sunshine was flashing on them as they passed us, and at times it was impossible to look upon them.[53]

Although a private procession could not rival an imperial one, the upper-class family nevertheless approximated it as closely as possible. The women of the family had been weaving and embroidering for this event since the birth of the bride. To their handiwork were added, in the case of a pasha's daughter, for example, all manner of expensive gifts from relatives and friends and people looking for advancement.[54]

Such a trousseau[55] included numerous silver trays, bowls, and pitchers. In the nineteenth century, it also contained vases made of *çeşm-i bülbül* (nightingale's eyes), a type of colored glass marked by spiral white stripes;[56] tulip vases called *lâledan*; crystal bowls; household items ornamented with *sırma*, an embroidery done with gold or silver thread,[57] in this case much of it by the bride's own hand; jewels protected by glass; two *oda takımları*, that is, sets of furniture for two rooms—such things as braziers, inlaid mother-of-pearl stools, rugs, and fringed *makat*s, divan covers, of the same material as the pillows and window curtains, in most instances a *sırmalı* red velvet; kitchen, eating, and ablution utensils. Even the dustpans were elaborate—of walnut inlaid with silver.[58] There might be as many as fifty sets of bedding.[59] And, of course, there was the girl's wardrobe, which consisted of everything from *gecelik*s (nightgowns) to *yaşmak*s (veils), much of it embroidered with *sırma* by the bride. All this display of opulence was often roped off as a matter of security, for not only relatives and friends of both families but also any woman of the bride's and groom's quarter and any chance female passerby was welcome to come in and admire it.[60]

These trousseau displays aroused as much envy as admiration and called forth many a catty remark. The story has come down about a governor of Baghdad who, being determined to give his daughter a trousseau so handsome that no one would dare criticize it, crowned his efforts by setting a solid gold brazier in the middle of the room. He then hid himself near the door so as to be able to enjoy the compliments, only to hear one old woman say as she went out: "All show, all show!" Furious, the pasha dashed after her and asked what she meant by such a remark. Imperturbably the old woman told him, "You forgot the tongs for the brazier."[61]

The trousseau was attractively arrayed in one of the rooms of the bride's suite in her new home by her female relatives and friends and her *aşkıcı*s (bridal attendants), who had followed the procession by foot or by carriage. When their job was completed, the trousseau room was gay with the colors of rugs, Bursa brocades, *makat*s, *bohça*s (bundle covers), and handkerchiefs, all of them decorated with variants of the floral motifs that are found throughout Turkey from the tiles of the great mosques to the head scarfs of peasant girls.[62] These motifs possibly hark back to the appliqué on the tents of the Altaic peoples of Central Asia.[63]

In a second room the *aşkıcı*s arranged the trousseau furniture and set up the tray and crystal bowl that would later be used for *hoşaf*, the stewed fruits which were offered to the guests. Also in one corner of the room they put together a bower (*aşkı*) of rose-colored gauze, embroideries, and crepe-paper flowers, under which the bride would later sit on her throne to receive her guests.[64] These labors took up most of Monday night. The two rooms were now ready for the bride's arrival on Thursday; they would from then on be her private apartment which she would share with her husband. If the family house was not large enough to permit setting aside two rooms for the young couple, a new wing was added.

On Tuesday the bride and her guests went to the *hamam* for the bridal bath, the expense of which was undertaken by the groom. For two or three hours she was soaped, pummeled, shampooed, scalded, and perfumed by the *usta* of the *hamam*. Her body hair was removed with depilatory paste in accordance with the Hanafi law on decency in women.[65] Then she spent a half-hour in the *soğukluk* (cool room) where her hair was braided in eight or ten tresses and entwined with strings of pearls and gold beads or coins, and her eyebrows blackened. Finally she was ready to return to the *camekân*, or dressing room, where her guests waited. Gypsy music heralded her entrance. She was led by her mother or the *usta* three times around the circle of guests, kissing each *hanım*'s hand as the lady offered her congratulations. Then she dressed in her preliminary wedding finery, which traditionally was borrowed and which she wore till Thursday morning, when she put on her bridal clothes.

Next she was seated on a throne of gauze, ribbon, and gilt from which she viewed the entertainment provided by the gypsies. It was frequently a play called "The Corsair's Daughter" ("Korsan kızı"),[66] which had to do with a Christian girl and her father whose ship was captured by Turks. In the course of the play the father becomes a Muslim and the girl the bride of a Turk. The gypsy girl who played the father dressed to imitate a corsair,[67] thrust a spoon and ladle into her belt for weapons, and used a kettle lid as a shield. At the conclusion of the performance, the bride showed her appreciation by throwing gold coins and candies onto the kettle lid as the gypsy held it out to her.

After the refreshments, which were a part of every *hamam* gathering, the party was over.[68]

On Wednesday, early in the afternoon, the bride received her bridegroom's female relatives and friends.[69] Up until then, only her own female relatives and friends had been participating in her festivities. The guests were met at the door by a double row of the bride's party, two of whom escorted each guest upstairs. The visitors were virtually lifted up by hands placed under their arms, a procedure which was a mark of honor. Once seated, they were served unsweetened coffee and cigarettes and left to themselves for half an hour,[70] for it was no part of the Wednesday afternoon ceremonies for the relatives of the two families to intermingle. At the end of the half hour they were further refreshed, this time with sweetened coffee, and then the bride appeared and was escorted around the room by two women, neither of whom had been married more than once. Starting with her mother-in-law, she performed the usual hand-kissing ritual. She stayed with her guests only a short time, sitting for a few minutes next to her mother-in-law while, as a mark of affection, the two exchanged pieces of candy from which each had eaten.[71] After the bride was led away, the guests were entertained with music and dancing. Though forbidden by Muslim law, music and dancing were nonetheless a standard practice at weddings[72] and other festivities in the Ottoman Empire.

As the guests were leaving, the bride came to the door for the farewells, and at this moment the guests threw coins over her head into the street. Street hawkers, beggars, and children who had been hopefully eyeing the door now scrambled for them. Guests and bride would all meet again that evening at the *kına gecesi*.[73]

The *kına gecesi*[74] (henna night) was the time when the bride said farewell to her girlhood. It is a very old Middle Eastern custom of unknown origin, practiced alike by Arabs, Persians and Turks.[75] As it was followed in Turkey, the young bride and her young unmarried friends dressed gaily and decorated their hair with flowers and jewels. Then, holding lighted tapers, they wound their way down the stairs of the house and out into the garden, lacing their way among the trees and shrubs while musicians accompanied them and dancing girls wove about them clicking their castanets and swirling their wide skirts.[76]

Such a procession was known among the Asiatic Turks, but there the custom of marrying outside the clan made it a sad event. The Kazak bride and her friends visited the yurts of her relatives and neighbors, all those familiar people with whom she had grown up and must now leave to go to the distant yurt of her husband. As the procession made its way from yurt to yurt, a dance took place called either the *synsu*,[77] from the verb to complain or whine, or the *gyz tanysu*, the bride's farewell. It was accompanied by these mournful words:

> A goose swims with the stream in a little brook.
> A young woman must now forsake her native home.
> If you drip blood into water, the water will carry it away speedily
> And if you are married, a stranger will carry you far away.[78]

But among sedentary Turks, the bride's farewell was a mere formality, for her new home was seldom far from that of her family, and the *kına gecesi* was, on the whole, a gay occasion. The dances were special. In one of them each girl held a lighted candle on a tray of henna; the henna began to burn as the dance ended. As they danced on this, the bride's night, the girls sang such songs as:

> The panes of the new room, My Night,
> Burn candles fancy with gold and silver, My Night;
> I had not hoped for this from you, My Night...
> May the wish of my night come true, My Night.[79]

After the dances came the application of the henna, a duty which the *kaynana*, mother-in-law, assumed. First the bride's right hand and then the left were daubed thick with the mixture, into which the guests pressed gold coins, and then each hand was covered with a small bag. Finally the gypsy dancers performed for the bride a last dance, which Lady Blunt calls *sakusum* and describes as "of the most unrestrained and immodest nature, terminating with the dancers taking extraordinary positions before each guest, sometimes even sitting on their knees to receive their reward, which consists of a small gold coin, damped in the mouth and deposited on their unblushing foreheads."[80] This was undoubtedly the belly dance that most nineteenth-century writers passed over in shocked silence.

After this display, the purpose of which was probably to put the bride in a nuptial frame of mind, the guests dispersed. The bride left the henna on long enough for it to deposit its dye but not long enough for it to turn black, which would have meant bad luck.

Ahmet Midhat, in a chapter of his novel, *Jön Türk*, published in 1908, describes a *kına gecesi* gathering in vivid terms. He tells the story from the viewpoint of the girl's foster mother and thus is able to contrast the old generation with the new one of the Young Turks' day:

The *kına gecesi* of Ahdiye Hanım took place on a Wednesday evening. It was hard to believe that things like bringing in a *çalgı* and having a dancing girl perform were really going to happen in the house of Dilşinas Hanım.

However, there can be no wedding without a *çalgı*. Besides, without paying any attention to the objections of Dilşinas, a handsome piano was brought in from a rich neighbor. In addition, some of the neighbor women had *ut*s and *keman*s, one of them had a mandolin, and many had tambourines . . . all of which provided instrumental music.

. . . Trays of fruit, set aside for this night, were prepared in the most sumptuous and perfect fashion. Dilşinas had thought of sherbets, candies, pastries, ice creams; of everything that exists. After those who wanted to perform their evening prayers had done so, the musical performance began. Because the women had each studied under a different teacher, it didn't occur to them that they ought to keep time with one another, and when five or six were performing at once, their neglect of the unity that music demands was tremendous. Yet because only a few women were aware of the subtleties of the music, this lack of keeping time made no difference to anyone. Was it the business of these women to bring about harmony between the piano and the other instruments? It was impossible for the thin instruments to be heard over the piano anyway.

The pianists played solos in turn. Some of their teachers taught nothing à la turka, saying it would spoil their fingers. So they played European marches, polkas, and waltzes. Some of the advanced ones could even play easy passages of operettas and operas. But there are time patterns in European music and who was to distinguish how these were treated and whether the false notes were few or many? All the women present considered European music to consist of tumult anyway.

As the evening progressed, it brought a desire to dance à la turka. Though the women who wanted to dance pretended reluctance, they put aside their coyness when they were coaxed by some of the older women. However, this time their lack of attention to the tempos of à la turka music was the obstacle. They could not dance in the traditional fast fashion. As a matter of fact the instruments could not give the right tempo for this, which brought on a quarrel. Words were had on all sides.

Finally one of the older women said, "Let the instruments be. Sing and clap hands, and dance to that."

At her words everything was set to rights for à la turka dancing.

They were having a very good time. Furthermore some of the young women proved this evening that they could do very good imitations of actresses like Peruz and Eleni, who were winning more fame among the women than among the men with the songs they sang in the theaters.

There could have been only one complainer about this entertainment, if any, and she would have been Dilşinas Hanım. . . . She found the imitations of those theater girls and those songs indecorous.

Well, changes cannot be prevented, no indeed. She must content herself with this . . . when she compared this *kına gecesi* with others, she considered this the most moderate, because it was truthfully a distinguished gathering. To make a comparison, the others were old-fashioned *kına gecesi*s and this one modern.

In the *kına gecesi*s of the old days comic performances with ad-lib lines were regularly put on by disgraceful persons called gypsies, performances so scandalous they made one ashamed of the spectacle. Although we were children, nothing escaped our notice. One of the gypsies entered in the costume of a man, a mustache outlined on her lips. The spectacle she made of herself with the girls and the women surpassed even the scandalous behavior of the *Karagöz* scenes of that time.

Don't inquire about some of the modern *kına gecesi*s. They may even have men *çalgı* players, yes indeed. And even though the *kına gecesi* is planned especially for women, some youths from relatives' or neighbors' houses may be found in the *selâmlık* just in order to listen from a distance, yes indeed! News has come to our ears about some of these things; we don't know what, but things are seen that are considered strange at non-Muslim let alone Muslim weddings.

Well, compared to those old and recent *kına gecesi*s tonight's was truly Ottoman and well-mannered. Nothing happened that could really be criticized. Everybody had a good time. . . . The children went to sleep about midnight. Each of those tiny, distressing annoyances brought on by successful women's gatherings like this vanished and the tumult disappeared. The fact that tomorrow was *yüz yazısı* put an end to the entertainment a little after midnight. The close neighbors, who had not been invited to spend the night, left. Those who were staying had no need to sleep three and four to a bed on the spread-out *yatak*s as at some *kına gecesi*s, because the *konak* was a little mansion and roomy. Since the number of Dilşinas Hanım's beds, plus those of the tenant women, was more than enough for friends and guests, everyone lay down very comfortably.[81]

On Thursday morning came *yüz yazısı*, literally the decorating of the bride's face, though it also included dressing her in her complete wedding outfit. Virtually everything she wore was ornamented. Her fine white tulle shirt was worked with tiny gold spangles and pearls, her *şalvar* with ribbons and *sırma*. The *entari* (dress) she wore over this was a handsome deep red—or sometimes purple—velvet, heavily embroidered in gold or silver and, in a family of high rank, with pearls. Pearls and *sırma* decorated her calfskin boots. A single-strand necklace, called *akarsu* (flowing water) and made up of precious stones, hung about her neck, and earrings of jewel clusters were fastened to her ears. Bracelets dangled at her wrists; rings, usually of large single stones, shone on her fingers. The front of her *entari* sparkled with gems.[82]

Her hair was elaborately braided in eight or ten small braids that hung down her back, and each braid was plaited with *tel*, strands of silver or gold tinsel. At the end of the braid both hair and *tel* were released in a tuft. On each temple a lock of hair was left to curl, the bride's curls. Her bridal veil was of crimson tulle worked with silver or gold thread and hung long over her *entari*. Long streamers of *tel* descended from the edge of her veil at her temples. On her head over the veil were fastened the bridal aigrette of finely cut glass in whatever color she chose and diamonds in a setting called *divanhane çivisi*. This last consisted of an elliptical gold cup, like the end of a tiny egg, into which small diamonds were set as if nailed.[83] Finally the decoration that gave the day its name, *yüz yazısı*, took place. The bride's face was whitened and rouged, and gold dust, spangles, and even diamonds were affixed to her forehead, cheeks, and chin.[84]

So arrayed and accompanied by her mother and sisters, if any, she went before her father to be invested with the girdle of a married woman. It was conventional at this point for the women to weep, but the tears were usually real and the father's eyes were also likely to be moist, for this short ceremony marked the release of a daughter from her father's care. The young girl knelt before him, kissed his feet and then his hands. He raised her and clasped about her waist the bridal girdle,[85] which might be a jeweled belt, a fine shawl, or, in late Ottoman times, simply a ribbon symbolic of the girdle.[86] He then withdrew.[87]

Meanwhile the groom's party had arrived, the ladies in carriages, the men on horseback. They had come to claim the bride. After refreshments in the harem and *selâmlık*, they escorted her to her carriage in which, with her *yenge* at her side, she rode to her new home. She wore no *yaşmak* on this trip but was completely covered by her wedding veil.[88]

The *vekils* (male family representatives), wearing silk scarfs, rode on horseback at the head of the procession. The ladies followed in elegant carriages, each carriage bearing a piece of cloth of gold or embroidery across its front. The procession was accompanied by jesters carrying small drums and intermittently capering and begging.[89]

The groom waited at the door to greet his bride,[90] who was handed to him by the *yenge* with the words: "Take my little one into your keeping, and may God give you happiness." He took one of the bride's arms and, with the *yenge* holding the other and calling out loud *maşallah*s, escorted her through the crowd of women upstairs to her room.[91] At this stage the women guests wore no veil, on the probably sound assumption that the groom had no eyes for them. On their way up the stairs the bride and groom played the little game of trying to step on one another's feet to determine who should be the more masterful.[92]

As the groom led the bride into the *hacle* (bridal chamber) and to her *aşkı*, or throne, the *yenge* stayed outside to give them a few minutes along together. This was the groom's opportunity to raise the veil for a brief glimpse of his bride's face, if he had the courage. But the *yenge* gave him very little time, and her knock on the door caught many a bridegroom still unacquainted with his bride's features. This first meeting of bride and groom was called the *koltuk merasimi*, the ceremony when the bridegroom gives his arm to the bride.[93] It was often the occasion for ribald remarks shouted by the women in the adjoining room, who admonished the young pair to wait till evening.[94]

The groom now had to return to his male guests, making his way through the crowd of women waiting outside the door. Scattering coins to distract them, he would manage to slip away.

Now the women guests swarmed into the bride's room, bringing with them *düğün saçisi*, or wedding gifts.[95] These women came from everywhere and anywhere to look at the bride and examine her trousseau. Each was met at the door of the house by a serving woman called *soygun kadın*[96] with an incense burner, or *buhurdanlık*, in one hand and a bottle of rose water in the other. Another *soygun kadın* took the guest's *ferace* and *yaşmak* and led her up to the bride's room. There the guest was served a kind of candy called *peynir şekeri* (cheese candy), so named not because it contained cheese but because it was soft and melted easily.[97] Slaves poured coffee from a silver jug resting in a *sitil*, an ornate silver bowl on chains.

After one or two hours of being on public display, the bride joined her personal wedding guests in another part of the harem where feasting and entertainments were going on.[98] Finally, she returned to the bride's room after the evening prayers to receive her bridegroom.

All this time the groom had been entertaining in the *selâmlık*. His guests, who were his relatives, friends, and the *imam* of the quarter, were plied with food, coffee, pipes and sherbet—and sometimes the alcoholic drink *rakı*. At the evening *ezan* (call to prayer) they all accompanied him to the mosque. After prayer they all returned to the house. There the groom kissed the hands of his elders, including his father and father-in-law, and shook hands with the others. "*Uğurlu kademli olsun! Allah mübarek etsin!*"

(Good luck to you! God bless you!")[99] they called out and pushed him toward the harem door, sometimes pounding him on the back. The *soygun kadınlar* then escorted him to the bride's door for the *zifaf*, the formal entry of the groom into the bride's room.[100]

The *yenge*, who was the bride's only familiar contact in these new surroundings, was with her. As the groom came in, the *yenge* led the bride to him, took their hands and said, "May God give you a harmonious life! May you grow old on one cushion!"[101]

Yet before he could see or touch his bride the groom still had a duty to perform. Taking off his shoes, he knelt on the prayer rug[102] laid out for him and performed two *rekat*s, namely, two complete sets of prayer positions.[103] Now he was at long last privileged to look at the features of his wife. He seated her again on her *aşkı*, lifted her veil, and, as a token of appreciation, presented her with the *yüz görümlüğü*, the present on first seeing the bride's face. Among the rich it was often a diamond, which was pinned to the hair.[104]

They then sat side by side on a divan while the *yenge* showed them their reflection in a mirror, their closeness now a symbol of their life ahead. They exchanged candies they each had bitten into to symbolize the act of sharing, drank some coffee, and then were left alone while the *yenge* went off to prepare their evening meal.[105]

Up until now these two had not exchanged a word with one another, but this was the moment when the groom must coax his wife to speak. Her married friends had advised her to stay silent as long as possible, the object being apparently to increase the bridegroom's curiosity. How long this period of coaxing lasted depended on the couple, but eventually the bride would give in. This meant that the groom could signal the *yenge* to bring in the food, and they had their first meal together. It usually consisted of sweets and eggs but no meat, for to eat meat on this night was to invite quarrels.[106] After the meal, the *yenge* assisted the bride out of her wedding finery and stayed nearby in case her advice was needed to enable the newly wedded couple to overcome the initial awkwardness of matrimonial intimacy.[107] Thursday night was usually considered the time when the marriage was consummated.[108]

On Friday morning, bride and groom appeared before the family hand in hand and were duly scrutinized to learn whether or not their stars had met.[109] Friday was the feast of *paça günü*.[110] Sheep's trotters cooked in a stew, *pilav* (rice), and *kaymak* (cream), and, among the rich, the *ince yemek*, delicacies of *börek*, sweets, *dolma*s, and *hoşaf*, were served. Friday afternoon the bride was again on display to guests. On Saturday both families again partook of a meal, this one a feast of sweets. This was the finale of the wedding festivities.[111]

In cases where the couple were to live with the bride's family, the foregoing arrangements were somewhat different. All the women's visiting took place at her house. While she was being girded by her father, the guests would begin to arrive to view the trousseau and would be greeted by the *soygun kadınlar*. The bride then joined the guests and stayed until the *bekçi*'s (watchman's) knock on the door told them that the bridegroom was coming. Sometimes the roll of drums served notice even before the *bekçi*.[112] At this moment the women hurried downstairs to the door to greet the groom, the bride with her face covered with her crimson veil and escorted by her *yenge*. The *koltuk merasimi* took place and then the groom went back to his own house, to return to the bride's after evening prayer at the mosque.[113]

These elaborate ceremonies were all for a virginal bride. If the girl had been married before, the arrangements were much simpler. The *nikâh* took place very much as described above, but once it was over and the *imam* had said a prayer and drunk some sherbet, the witnesses left and the groom went into the harem to his wife. There was no *yenge*, since her role was that of tutor to an inexperienced bride. There was also no *yüz görümlüğü*, since this was not the first unveiling of the woman's face. But there was plenty of visiting, which began the next day when the bride dressed in her most gorgeous robes, fastened a headdress of brilliants in her hair, and received guests the entire day.[114]

As has been said, if the young couple was to live in the house of the bride's family, the arrangement was called *içeri* (within); if the groom's, *dışarı* (without). In the *içeri* household the bride was called *gelin hanım* (lady bride) and her husband *küçük bey* (young gentleman). In some households the husband was *iç güveysi* (son-in-law within) and the bride *küçük hanım* (young lady) to distinguish her from her mother, who was *hanım efendi* (lady excellency). If there was a grandmother she was called *büyük hanım* (great lady) or, in the early days, *kadın efendi* (woman excellency).[115]

As Westernization progressed and the nineteenth century turned into the twentieth, European fashions took hold and the fashionable bride of Istanbul forsook the embroidered dark velvet wedding dress for pastel colors or for the Westerners' white satin.[116] She also abandoned the custom of face-decorating. Yet so long as the monarchy survived, so did the old formalities. Enver, when he was Minister of War during World War I, still kept, in a place of honor in his home, the gold chair that had been his wife's *aşkı*. Yet his wife, though an imperial princess, took no part in affairs of state. She had to satisfy whatever curiosity she had about the American ambassador by peeping at him through a doorway as he went to call on her husband.[117]

In the latter half of the nineteenth century criticism of the practice of arranged marriages and of the custom that forbade bride and groom to see each other until after their wedding grew steadily. The critics were literary figures, the new group of Western-oriented Turks. As early as 1860 İbrahim Şinasi (1824–1871) wrote a comedy, *Şair evlenmesi* (The Poet's Wedding), parodying arranged marriages. Slightly later, in 1873–4, Namık Kemal stressed the possibilities for tragedy in arranged marriages in his play *Zavallı çocuk* (Poor Child). At the same period he was extolling romantic love in *Vatan veya Silistre* (Fatherland and Silistria), a play in which a young girl masquerading as a man follows her lover to war.

These writers were far ahead of their time, but their work cut the first path through the underbrush of old marriage customs. Even sharper criticism came later when Celâl Nuri (1877–1939), in his *Kadınlarımız* (*Our Women*), published in 1915, undertook to review the question of women in Turkey. "When buying watermelon," he wrote, "your eye can have access to it. How come in getting a wife or a husband this right to look is not allowed?"[118] And in another place: "When looked at objectively we can see how ludicrous our marriage customs are. Oh God! When buying a ring for a wife we can see it, we can show it to an expert in that field, but we do not see the wife! Common sense is bankrupt in this country."[119]

At the turn of the twentieth century Fatma Aliye (1864–1924) laid down a set of conditions she thought to be necessary for a successful marriage. First of all, she wrote, the consent of both parties must be obtained. Second, she believed that physical and spiritual health are necessary. Third, she felt that affection must be shown by the man to his wife. Fourth, she emphasized that both the man and his wife must, with devotion, carry out their mutual duties: loyalty, confidence, respect, affectionate thoughts, and emotional support. For confidence, she held that household affairs must not be concealed and that there must be an awareness of each other's ideas and inclinations. Finally, she said that the wife must be obedient and economical in the management of the household.[120]

Yet even when restraints were relaxed it was not easy for young people to overcome the timidity bred by their lack of social contact with the opposite sex. An Englishwoman acting as go-between in the early twentieth century had far less success than did Melek Hanım almost a century earlier. The Englishwoman invited the prospective bridegroom, a poet named Filan Bey, to her house to meet an attractive, Westernized Turkish girl named Gülistan. Neither spoke a word to the other; they addressed themselves solely to the hostess. The meeting came to nothing. Gülistan married a Westernized Turk who gave her the sort of life she wanted, but poor Filan Bey, who had hoped to find an educated girl, married a simple one who divorced him when he tried to educate her.[121]

Marmaduke Pickthall, who, as previously noted, had become a Muslim and lived among the Turks, reported that girls were beginning to refuse to marry men they did not know.[122] By the time he wrote, during World War I, it had become fashionable to allow the young people a few brief face-to-face meetings. However, the meetings were held in the most formal circumstances without the opportunity for the young people to become more than perfunctorily acquainted with one another.[123]

The dilemma of a Turkish girl with a Western education, nourished on the romantic French novel of the late nineteenth and early twentieth centuries, was dramatized by Pierre Loti's famous novel, *Les Désenchantées*, published in 1906. The history of this novel and the furor it caused reflected the confusion of the times, when the urban Turkish woman was caught between old customs and new. The story is supposedly told to the author by three Western-educated Turkish girls whose lives have left them disenchanted.[124] It made female hearts palpitate for its tragic heroine caught in the grip of an arranged marriage and a polygamous household; but the real story behind it did not come out until almost two decades later.

Of the three girls who fed Loti the story, two were granddaughters of le Comte de Chateauneuf, a Frenchman who had settled in Turkey, turned Muslim, and taken the name of Reşat Bey. The girls' father, who was the son of Reşat and a Circassian woman, held a high government post. Djenane, the heroine of the story and the leader of the three girls, was in reality a French woman journalist masquerading as a Turk, a Marie Léra who wrote under the name of Marc Helys. Loti at the time was commander of the French *stationnaire* at Istanbul and already a well-known figure in that city by virtue of his *Aziyadé*[125] (a novel about a slave girl) and other works. The three girls made contact with him for the purpose of persuading him to write a novel that would publicize the dilemma of the Western-educated Turkish girl, who was still unable to live the kind of life she read and dreamed about. Mme. Léra allegedly kept her real identity from Loti, who thought her a Turk.[126] Though a foreigner, she managed to convey to him the dilemma some Turkish girls faced.[127]

Léra—and Pierre Loti—succeeded so well that when Celâl Nuri came to write his *Kadınlarımız* nine years later, he was careful to point out the importance of giving educated women the opportunity to emerge from their cloistered lives in order to avoid having a nation of *désenchantées*.[128]

Sir Edwin Pears, a close observer of the Ottomans, thought the picture Loti presented to be untrue,[129] and certainly the *désenchantées* must have been far fewer in number than the girls who accepted the old arrangements. Yet as we have seen from Pickthall's comments, times were changing. In the days of completely arranged marriages, husbands were found for all women. It was, in fact, a religious obligation to marry again when divorced or widowed.[130] Now, with more personal picking and choosing, the less attractive and less wealthy girls were beginning to be left out.[131] For the first time, the concept of the old maid, which had been unknown to the Ottomans, came into being.

NOTES

1. This account of the Turkish marriage has been taken largely from Musahipzade Celâl, *Eski İstanbul yaşayışı*, pp. 3–26, amplified and clarified from other sources which will be noted.

2. There is an old Istanbul proverb to the effect that marriage brings a miracle: *"Nikâhta keramet vardır"* (Şehbal Teilmann, personal communication; Mehmet Halit Bayrı, *İstanbul folkloru*, p. 38).

3. A variant for *görücü* used among Anatolian Turks is *dünürcü*, which comes from *dünür*, the word for in-law. Hence, *dünürcü* is one who searches for an in-law. İnan believes that the *görücü*, or viewer, was originally a spy sent out from a Turkic tribe to look for a bride and to prepare the opportunity for *kız kaçırma*, running off with her (Abdülkerim İnan, "Turk düğünlerinde exogamie izleri," *Türk dili ve tarihi hakkında araştırmalar*, 1, Ankara, 1934, pp. 105–113).

4. Fanny Blunt, *The People of Turkey*, II, pp. 96–97; Lucy M. J. Garnett, *Home Life in Turkey*, pp. 238–239.

5. In many cases the visit of the *görücü* was a mere formality or was even dispensed with, the families of the boy and girl having betrothed them or signed a marriage contract in their behalf when they were infants; Charles White, *Three Years in Constantinople; or Domestic Manners of the Turks in 1844*, III, pp. 197–198. In these cases both the boy and the girl had the right to annul the marriage at puberty (Sir George Young, *Corps de droit ottoman*, II, p. 218). It was quite natural in Ottoman times to arrange marriages between close relatives, even between first cousins. This seems to have been a custom the Turks took over with the adoption of Islam, for the nomadic Turks of Central Asia practiced exogamic marriage (İnan, "Exogamie izleri," pp. 105–113).

6. İrfan Orga, *Portrait of a Turkish Family*, p. 21.

7. Garnett, *Home Life*, p. 277.

8. Ibid., pp. 237–239.

9. Melek Hanım [Melek-Hanum], *Thirty Years in the Harem*, pp. 34–38. Melek, a person of mixed Istanbul Greek, Armenian, and French extraction, eloped at 15 with an English doctor in the employ of the *valide sultan*. She bore him two children, was divorced by him and packed off to Paris, where she made her way to the Ottoman embassy to ask for help in getting home. This was about 1828, and Kıbrıslı Mehmet, later to become grand vizier, was then a young military attaché at the embassy. He fell in love with her, sent her back to Istanbul, and soon married her there. They lived together about 20 years. By her own account she was shrewd and conniving. When one of her schemes backfired, Kıbrıslı divorced her. The two were embroiled in litigation for years, Melek pitting her not inconsiderable intelligence against Kıbrıslı's power and position. In the end she had to flee to Paris, where she wrote the story of her life under the Ottomans. Her book contains many firsthand accounts of Ottoman life and is a valuable source on the life of the upper-class woman during the early and middle nineteenth century.

10. Halide Edip, *Memoirs of Halide Edip*, p. 122.

11. Melek Hanım, *Thirty Years*, pp. 34–38.

12. Ibid.

13. Halide Edip, *Memoirs*, p. 122.

14. Celâl, *Eski İstanbul*, pp. 6–7.

15. Hüseyin Cahit Yalçın, "Görücü," from *Hayat-ı muhayyel* (Istanbul, 1899), quoted in Mustafa Nihat Özön, *Son asır Türk edebiyati tarihi*, pp. 249–252.

16. Yalçın, "Görücü."

17. Ibid.

18. Ibid.

19. Ibid.

20. Melek Hanım, *Thirty Years*, pp. 48–50. Marriage was a meritorious act for a Muslim man (Young, *Corps de droit*, II, p. 211), a point of view that resulted in few bachelors and in widowers remarrying very quickly (Melek Hanım, *Thirty Years*, p. 85).

21. Blunt, *The People of Turkey*, II, p. 80. It was not permissible for a Muslim girl to marry a non-Muslim man, although a Muslim man might marry a Christian woman (Marmaduke Pickthall, *With the Turk in Wartime*, pp. 96–97).

22. Garnett, *Home Life*, p. 239.

23. Personal interview with Belkis Erad, August 1966.

24. Celâl, *Eski İstanbul*, p. 7.

25. In Islamic countries the dowry is the responsibility of the groom or his family.

26. White, *Three Years*, III, p. 199.

27. In Islam the dowry became due on the wedding day (Young, *Corps de droit*, II, p. 219f).

28. Alfred Emmons Hudson, *Kazak Social Structure* (London, 1938), pp. 39–54; *see also* M. A. Czaplicka, *The Turks of Central Asia, in History and at the Present Day*, p. 50.

29. H. C. Hony, with the advice of Fahir İz, *A Turkish-English Dictionary* (Oxford, 1957), p. 179.

30. Hony, *TED*, p. 234. Among both pre-Islamic Turks and pre-Islamic Arabs the dowry was paid to the family of the bride and became her family's property. Muhammad, as part of his program to ameliorate the lot of the Arab woman, decreed that the dowry belonged to the bride herself. For Arabs, *see* Mansour Fahmy, *La Condition de la femme dans la tradition et l'évolution de l'islamisme*, p. 144. For Turks, *see* İnan, "Exogamie izleri."

31. White, *Three Years*, III, p. 119; Z. Duckett Ferriman, *Turkey and the Turks*, p. 212; Mehmet Ali Ağakay, *Türkçe sözlük* (Ankara, 1966), p. 13.

32. White, *Three Years*, III, p. 203.

33. Asaf A. A. Fyzee, *Outlines of Muhammadan Law*, p. 114; Hony, *TED*, p. 235 (*see* under *mehr*; in Hony the izafet has become adjectival). Celâl (*Eski İstanbul*, p. 7) has reversed the meanings of the two phrases. *See* also Mehmet Zeki Pakalın, *Osmanlı tarih deyimleri ve terimleri sözlüğü*, III, p. 44, and Mithat Sertoğlu, *Resimli osmanlı tarihi ansiklopedisi*, p. 211.

34. Young, *Corps de droit*, II, pp. 212, 219.

35. Blunt, *The People of Turkey*, II, p. 86; *see also* Garnett, *Home Life*, p. 240. The descriptions of marriage customs are so similar in the Blunt and Garnett books as to suggest that Garnett relied heavily on Blunt. Lucy Garnett had originally come to the Ottoman Empire as governess to Lady Blunt's son (*see* Fanny Blunt, *My Reminiscences*, p. 175).

36. White (*Three Years*, III, p. 203) thinks that the presents were exchanged after the *nikâh* on the same day as the trousseau procession, but Celâl (*Eski İstanbul*, p. 7) clearly states that they were sent before the *nikâh*, and this certainly seems more logical. *See* also Clara Erskine Clement (*Constantinople, the City of the Sultans*, p. 274), who says that these gifts were sent to the bride's home eight days before the *düğün* began.

37. White, *Three Years*, III, p. 203.

38. Celâl, *Eski İstanbul*, p. 7. Hâmit Zübeyr Koşay says that in İsparta the groom's women relatives take the ring with them when they pay their *nişan* call on the bride, and put it on her hand with a prayer for happiness for her and long life for her husband (*Türkiye Türk düğünleri üzerine mukayeseli malzeme*, p. 28).

39. The accounts of the *nişan bohçası* and the *nişan takımı* are taken from White, *Three Years*, III, pp. 203–204, and Celâl, *Eski İstanbul*, p. 7. When Mustafa III pledged his daughter, Şah Sultan, to the Grand Vizier Mehmet Emin Pasha, Şah Sultan was in only her ninth year, but nevertheless elaborate and costly presents were exchanged. Those from Mehmet Emin were carried first to the Sublime Porte and then to the palace, where they were delivered by the *kâhya* to the Ağa of the House of Felicity, who in turn delivered them to Şah Sultan. Meanwhile, through the same channels, she sent her betrothed the ceremonial handkerchief that was the custom of royalty on these occasions. Among the presents Mehmet Emin sent her were a diamond ring, two emeralds to be made into earrings, a veil embroidered with diamonds, emeralds, and pearls, a buckle ornamented with emeralds and pearls, a pair of bracelets and a belt set with diamonds, a mirror, a court costume sewn with pearls, slippers embroidered with pearls and rubies, fancy clogs, rich fabrics, and vases and cups containing flowers, fruits and sweets. According to Hammer, it was customary in such cases for the fiancé to send seven valuable gifts. In this case they were diadem, ring, collar, earrings, bracelet, foot ring(?), and belt. Mehmet Emin added various other things of value and made his gifts amount to two times seven. In addition he sent flowers, fruits, and sweets to the princess's two brothers and small sister (*see* Joseph de Hammer-Purgstall, *Histoire de l'Empire ottoman depuis son origine jusqu'à nos jours*, XVI, pp. 165–167).

40. A. Ziyaeddin Fahri Fındıkoğlu, *Zia Gökalp, sa vie et sa sociologie*, p. 130, n. 130.

41. This might occur soon after the *nişan* (Celâl, *Eski İstanbul*, p. 7).

42. Melek Hanım, *Thirty Years*, pp. 241–242.

43. Celâl says that one *kuruş* was the figure named in the Şeriat, by which he presumably means the Hanafi code the Ottomans followed (*Eski İstanbul*, p. 7). Fyzee (*Outlines*, pp. 115–116) gives ten dirhems as the minimum under Hanafi law. He also says the dower must be fixed with due consideration for the status of the girl's family and her personal qualifications. *See* also 'Alī ibn Abū Bakr Marghīnānī, *The Hedaya, or Guide: a Commentary on the Mussulman Laws*, p. 44, which says of the dowry: "The law enjoins a dower with a view to manifest respect for the wife, wherefore it must be fixed, in its smallest degree, at such a sum as may be respectable."

44. White, *Three Years*, III, p. 202.

45. Halide Edip was married to Adnan Adıvar by proxy. She was in Syria at the time, and her father represented her. *See Memoirs*, p. 450.

46. By the end of the Empire this had been shortened to one or two days (interviews with Belkis Erad and Seniha Moralı, July and August respectively, 1966).

47. Celâl (*Eski İstanbul*, p. 7) calls betrothing children while still in their cradle *beşik kertiği*. Hony (*TED*, p. 39) calls the person thus betrothed *beşik kertme nişanlı*. In such cases the *nişan* may or may not have been followed by a *nikâh* while the boy and girl were still children, but in any event the *düğün* would have waited until they were in their teens.

48. Melek Hanım, *Thirty Years*, p. 242.

49. The events described here were the conventional ones. There were, of course, variations. If the couple were to live with the bride's parents, there was obviously no trousseau procession. If the *düğün* was held in conjunction with the *nikâh*, the latter took place on a Monday.

50. White, Blunt, and Garnett all call both the *görücü* and the *yenge* a *kılavuz* (guide), which creates the erroneous impression that they could be one and the same person. This was not the case. The *görücü* was a representative of the groom, but the *yenge* was always an intimate of the bride.

51. Antoine-Ignace Melling, *Voyage pittoresque de Constantinople et des rives du Bosphore d'auprès les dessins de M. Melling*, II (there is no pagination in this work).

52. According to Celâl Esat Arseven (*Sanat ansiklopedisi*, III, p. 1496) *nahil* is a corruption of the Arabic *nakil*, "date tree." It was an artificial tree made of beeswax and decorated with sheets of gold and silver. It was carried in the bridal procession and installed in the bride's room as an ornament. Ignatius Mouradgea d'Ohsson (*Tableau général de l'Empire othoman*, V, p. 150) reports that it often bore figures of men and animals. The art of making these was called *nahilbendi*. According to Pakalın (*Deyimleri ve terimleri*, III, pp. 642–644), it was probably an old pagan custom that passed through the Arabs to the Turks.

53. Julia Pardoe, *The City of the Sultans and Domestic Manners of the Turks in 1836*, I, pp. 494–497.

54. Melek Hanım, *Thirty Years*, p. 241.

55. The description of the trousseau is taken from Melek Hanım, *Thirty Years*, pp. 246–247; Blunt, *The People of Turkey*, II, pp. 89–90; White, *Three Years*, pp. 204–205; Garnett, *Home Life*, p. 242; and Melling, *Voyage pittoresque*, II, plate of trousseau procession.

56. Arseven, *SA*, I, p. 390. The name came from the fact that the glass was dark like a nightingale's eyes. Decanters and bottles of *çeşm-i bülbül* were made in a glass factory established at Çubuklu on the Asiatic shore of the Bosphorus in 1848. There is an exhibit of this glass in the Topkapı Palace Museum in Istanbul.

57. Hony, *TED*, p. 317. There is an illustration of a *sırmalı* napkin in Celâl, *Eski İstanbul*, p. 12.

58. Clement, *Constantinople*, p. 275.

59. Blunt, *The People of Turkey*, II, p. 89.

60. Melek Hanım, *Thirty Years*, pp. 247–248.

61. Celâl, *Eski İstanbul*, p. 14.

62. Koşay's book contains several photographs of trousseaus hung for display in contemporary provincial homes where old customs are still followed (*Türk düğünleri*, pp. 99, 101, 103, 107, 109, 111).

63. Emel Esin, *Turkish Miniature Painting*, illus. 9, back of book. For a further discussion of embroideries, *see* pp. 341–344.

64. Melek Hanım, *Thirty Years*, p. 246.

65. White (*Three Years*, III, p. 305) describes one such depilatory paste as being made up of astringent herbs mixed with quicklime and perfumed with wood ashes. It was called *ot* (*see* A. Vahit Moran, *Türkçe-İngilizce sözlük*, Istanbul, 1945, p. 963).

66. White calls this "*Koosan Kizy*" and mistranslates it as "The Knight's Daughter" (*Three Years*, III, p. 207).

67. Celâl describes a galleon dance for which the gypsies were dressed in similar fashion. He saw it at a *sünnet düğünü* (circumcision festivity) (*Eski İstanbul*, pp. 8–9).

68. White (*Three Years*, III, pp. 207–208) had the *kına gecesi* taking place the same day as the bridal bath, at the *hamam* a little after sunset. Perhaps this sometimes happened, but other sources agree that it took place at the girl's home on Wednesday evening.

69. White omits these calls and terms Wednesday a day of repose (*Three Years*, III, p. 207).

70. Garnett (*Home Life*, p. 243) says that the guests were left to themselves a full hour.

71. Ibid., pp. 243–244.

72. D'Ohsson, *Tableau général*, IV, pp. 414–434.

73. Ibid., V, pp. 150–151.

74. Celâl (*Eski İstanbul*, pp. 8–10), Melek Hanım (*Thirty Years*, p. 248), Blunt (*The People of Turkey*, II, pp. 94–95), and Garnett (*Home Life*, pp. 244–245) all give interesting accounts of the *kına gecesi*.

75. For the use of henna in the Middle East *see* "Henna," *Encyclopaedia Britannica* (New York, 1911), XXXIII, pp. 271–272; also *see* Raphaela Lewis, *Everyday Life in Ottoman Turkey*, p. 102; Henri Massé, *Persian Beliefs and Customs*, p. 78.

76. Garnett, *Home Life*, pp. 245–246; Clement, *Constantinople*, pp. 276–277. There is an old Ottoman proverb, "to laugh as on the henna night" (E. J. W. Gibb, *History of Ottoman Poetry*, IV, p. 290n.).

77. *See* Talat Tekin, *A Grammar of Orkhon Turkic*, p. 368.

78. Thomas G. Winner, *The Oral Art and Literature of the Kazakhs of Russian Central Asia*, p. 39 and n. 34.

79. Koşay (*Türk düğünleri*, pp. 180, 182) notes that among the peasants of both Malatya and Muğla the bride is supposed to weep during the *Kina gecesi*.

80. Blunt, *The People of Turkey*, II, p. 95.

81. Ahmet Midhat, "Bir kına gecesi," from *Jön Türk* (Istanbul, 1908) in Vasfi Mahir Kocatürk, *Metinlerle edebiyat*, pp. 136–138.

82. White, *Three Years*, III, p. 208; Celâl, *Eski İstanbul*, p. 14; Melek Hanım, *Thirty Years*, p. 249.

83. The description of the *divanhane çivisi* comes from personal interviews with Şehbal Teilmann and Süphiye Gürün. The setting is also called *divanhane kakması*.

84. Celâl, *Eski İstanbul*, p. 14; Melek Hanım, *Thirty Years*, pp. 249–251.

85. For the girding ceremony, *see* Melek Hanım, *Thirty Years*, pp. 249–250, Celâl, *Eski İstanbul*, p. 13, and Blunt, *The People of Turkey*, II, p. 96.

86. Information on the use of ribbon for this investiture was supplied by Şehbal Teilmann.

87. Celâl (*Eski İstanbul*, p. 13) says the father also instructed the girl to jump over his sword and wished her well with the words, "May you bring up sons and grandsons who will use this sword as well as their forefathers did." According to him this was an old Turkic tradition. However, we have not found this sword

ceremony in any other work, nor do our personal sources have any knowledge of it.

88. White, *Three Years*, III, p. 211.

89. White, *Three Years*, III, p. 211; Blunt, *The People of Turkey*, II, p. 98; Clement, *Constantinople*, p. 279. Musahipzade Celâl omits the marriage procession. Apparently what he is describing is an *içeri* marriage.

90. Garnett, *Home Life*, p. 246; White, *Three Years*, III, pp. 211–212.

91. White (*Three Years*, III, pp. 211–212) says the bride and groom pressed each other's hand to try to establish supremacy.

92. Blunt, *The People of Turkey*, II, p. 99.

93. Celâl, *Eski İstanbul*, p. 14.

94. Celâl Nuri [İleri], *Kadınlarımız*, p. 192. The ribald remarks are one of the many old customs about which Celâl Nuri complains.

95. Celâl, *Eski İstanbul*, p. 14. Wedding gifts to the bride became her personal property (W. E. Grigsby, *The Medjelle or Ottoman Civil Law*, p. 171).

96. The *soygun kadınlar* here were the women who took the guests' wraps (Celâl, *Eski İstanbul*, p. 13).

97. The description of *peynir şekeri* is from Şehbal Teilmann.

98. Melek Hanım, *Thirty Years*, p. 251.

99. Celâl, *Eski İstanbul*, pp. 10–14.

100. Ibid., p. 17.

101. Ibid.

102. The wedding prayer rugs, among the rich, were elaborately embroidered and resembled spreads more than rugs; they were provided by the bride's family. That of Emine Foat Tugay's father was of dark red velvet embroidered in gold (personal interview with Emine Foat Tugay, July 1966).

103. Blunt, *The People of Turkey*, II, pp. 96–97.

104. Melek Hanım, *Thirty Years*, p. 253.

105. Blunt, *The People of Turkey*, II, pp. 96–97.

106. Ibid., pp. 96–98.

107. Personal interview with a Turkish woman.

108. In his novel, *Les Désenchantées* (Paris, 1906), Pierre Loti (Julien Viaud) says that a marriage of the upper classes was not consummated this first night but that the groom spent some days courting his bride so that she would feel at ease with him.

109. Garnett, *Home Life*, p. 247.

110. Turks believe this dish to be particularly healthy; Melek Hanım, *Thirty Years*, p. 254.

111. Celâl, *Eski İstanbul*, pp. 18–20.

112. White, *Three Years*, III, p. 308.

113. Celâl, *Eski İstanbul*, pp. 13–17.

114. Melek Hanım, *Thirty Years*, p. 32.

115. Personal communication from Seniha Moralı.

116. The information concerning the pastel wedding dresses is from Şehbal Teilmann, whose aunts wore such dresses at their weddings in Istanbul in the early twentieth century. The information regarding the white satin dresses comes from Sir Edwin Pears in his *Turkey and Its People*, pp. 59–60.

117. Henry Morgenthau, *Ambassador Morgenthau's Story*, pp. 114–115.

118. Celâl Nuri, *Kadınlarımız*, p. 186.

119. Ibid., p. 187.

120. Fatma Aliye, "İzdivaç dair," *Hanımlara mahsus gazete* (*Nisan* 24, 1319 A.H.), pp. 175–176.

121. Mary A. Poynter, *When Turkey Was Turkey*, pp. 163–181.

122. Pickthall, *With the Turk in Wartime*, p. 189.

123. Personal interview with Seniha Moralı, July 1966.

124. Loti, *Les Désenchantées*, passim. One of the Turkish girls was named Zeynep. She corresponded with the English writer, Grace Ellison, who collected her letters in a book, *A Turkish Woman's European Impressions* (London, 1913). For this information I am indebted to Naile Minay.

125. Pierre Loti, *Aziyadé* (Paris, 1895; this was the 27th edition).

126. However, the fact that Loti called the hero of his novel Lhéry (which sounds very much like Léra) might indicate that he was better acquainted with Marie Léra than is usually assumed.

127. Lucien Maury, "P.S. à 'Faut-il-tuer l'éditeur?' " *Revue bleue*, 5 (March 6, 1926), pp. 153–154.

128. Celâl Nuri, *Kadınlarımız*, p. 124.

129. Sir Edwin Pears, *Forty Years in Constantinople*, p. 320.

130. D'Ohsson, *Tableau général*, IV, p. 335.

131. Pickthall, *With the Turk in Wartime*, p. 189.

5

Polygamy and Concubinage

That there was polygamy among the Ottoman Turks is generally known, but it is less easy to ascertain how widespread its practice was. Several of the more astute Western observers thought its occurrence to be rare. D'Ohsson, for example, stated that it was not as common as usually imagined, that few men had two wives, and that four was a rarity. The want of means of support, the fear of troubling domestic peace, and the scruples of parents who were reluctant to give their daughters to men already married, all constituted a restraint on the indulgence of the law.[1] Pardoe[2] and Rycaut[3] believed polygamy to be limited in practice, Rycaut giving as the reason a man's reluctance to pay more than one dowry. Charles White believed that it was not indulged in by more than five percent of the men of Istanbul, and mostly by the richest and most powerful functionaries.[4] In this, he backed up Pardoe, who found that polygamy flourished among the higher ranks of society.[5]

It is precisely the women of these higher ranks of society, the rich and the powerful, who are the subject of this study, and it is the opinion of this writer that among this class the incidence of polygamy was high.[6] White found that polygamous men were usually those who owned large mansions where there was room for each wife to have a separate establishment.[7] Dr. Madden, whose practice appears to have been among the upper class, states: "There is hardly a Turk of my acquaintance . . . who maintains not three or four wives, and double as many slaves.[8] Sir Edwin Pears, who was writing in the period of Abdülhamit II, thought polygamy prevailed among the wealthy and was occasionally practiced by the poor.[9] There were legitimate reasons to account for its continuing practice: it prevented men with wives who were ill from patronizing prostitutes; it increased the population; it saved unmarried women and widows from a state of man-lessness and lack of protection.[10]

Polygamy was greatly increased by the practice of concubinage.[11] The law allowed a man as many female slaves as he could maintain and con-cubinage with as many as he liked. This was a recourse often preferred by both the men and their wives. The man was freed from the trouble of dickering with inlaws over a marriage settlement and from having to con-tend with an independent-spirited Turkish woman who had her family to go home to if the marriage did not please her. On the woman's part, the wife felt less of a threat to her position as mistress of the household from the slaves than from any additional legal wives. Pardoe found that usually a man married a woman of his own rank and then bought slaves from Georgia or Circassia, who had to obey the wife.[12]

Polygamy was already an accepted pattern of life among the Arabs in Muhammad's day.[13] There is no real evidence that he tried to abolish it; he merely sought to contain it. As for the Turks, Ziya Gökalp held the view that among the pre-Islamic nomadic Turks polygamy had not been practiced, that it came to the Turks with Islam,[14] but this does not stand up against the evidence. For example, Czaplicka found that the Yakut Turks had practiced polygamy until the Russians occupied their territories, and that some were still polygamous as late as 1914.[15] The Yakuts never joined the realm of Islam and, though nominally Christianized, they re-tained their old Altaic shamanism.[16] Evidence among the Kazak Turks shows that there too the practice of polygamy was not necessarily connected with Islam. Hudson found that a Kazak could marry as many women as he chose and could support, and was not limited to the Islamic four. The only restriction was that he provide a separate *kibit* (yurt) for each wife and her children.[17] Halide Edip has endeavored to bolster the argument for Turkic monogamy by stating that among the Yürüks of modern Turkey, who still cling to nomadic Turkic customs, "I have not come across any case of polygamy."[18] Yet a contemporary study of certain recently settled tribes of the Çukurova-Tarsus region shows polygamy as part of their pattern of living.[19]

It would seem that Gökalp—and his followers, such as Fındıkoğlu and Halide Edip—have confused monogamy with freedom for women. It is true that the nomadic Turk of Central Asia did not seclude his women and that the first wife of a Turkic ruler sometimes had a status equal to his.[20] However, it does not follow that he had only one wife.

In most cases where there was more than one legal wife among the Ottoman Turks, the second and any subsequent wives were likely to be freed slaves, a state of affairs which helped to insure harmony in the household. For the slaves would have been trained to obey the first wife, the *büyük hanım*, and would not be likely to dispute her position as mistress of the household. Very often a second wife was taken because of a desire for children. For example, Hüseyin Galip Pasha (at the turn of the twentieth century) had two wives, the first wife a Turk, the second a Circassian *saraylı*, who was 15 years younger than the first one, and whom the Pasha married because he wanted children. In this case the man had asked and obtained the permission of his first wife to marry again. The *saraylı* had a daughter, whom both wives brought up in the Westernized fashion of the time, providing her with lessons in French and the piano, although neither of them knew either. The two wives lived together throughout their lives, the younger under the firm rule of the elder. They were known throughout the family as *Büyük* and *Küçük Yenge*.[21]

Another who took a *saraylı* as second wife when his first wife was very old was the brother of Kâmil Pasha. This girl was an accomplished musician and added to the gaiety of the *yalı*[22] which the whole family occupied at Beylerbeyi.[23]

In some cases, when the first wife refused to countenance her husband's taking a second wife, the man contented himself with slaves. Such was the case of İskodralı Mustafa Pasha, who had been the quasi-independent governor of Albania. By the time Pardoe met him, he had been persuaded to yield to the Sublime Porte and was living in Istanbul. He had a daughter and a sickly son by his Albanian wife. Afraid his son would die, he wanted another. When his wife frowned on his taking a second wife, he bought four Circassian slaves. One bore him two sons, and thereby became the favorite of the harem. One bore a daughter. One was childless and devoted herself to the pasha's grown daughter. One died on the way to Albania. The women strictly observed the rules of precedence toward one another. In receiving Pardoe, the *büyük hanım* held the preferred place on the sofa, the pasha's favorite *odalık* (concubine)—the mother of the two sons—the second, and the mother of the little girl the third.[24] The childless slave was apparently not present.

Cemal Bey, governor in eastern Turkey, was another man involved in a childless marriage. His wife knew he was unhappy over their lack of issue and proposed to remedy the situation. She gave him her own Circassian slave girl, making only the stipulation that any children resulting from the liaison should call her "mother." The Circassian bore one son and two daughters, and all three called the *büyük hanım "anne"* (mother) till the day she died, even though she long outlived her husband and the children knew she was not their real mother.[25]

Not every polygamous man married an additional wife from the desire for children. Some simply desired younger women. Sami Pasha, a nineteenth-century man, installed two odalisques in another house when his wife grew old. She knew nothing about them. A separate house was a favorite device for keeping peace in the family.[26]

Another case in which the first wife was not consulted was that of Mithat Pasha. Mithat, married 20 years to a Turkish woman named Fatma Naime, the daughter of a judge, had only a daughter and very much wanted a son. When he was governor of Baghdad (1869-1872) and his wife was in Istanbul, he purchased and married a Circassian of great beauty and charm. But Mithat, who had the courage to point out his duties to the sultan, the shadow of God on earth,[27] did not have the courage to tell his first wife he had acquired a second one. When Mithat and his second wife, Şehriban Hanım, returned to Istanbul, the pasha drove directly to the palace and sent Şehriban to the family *konak* to meet Fatma Naime alone. Perhaps it was just as well that way, for both women were schooled in their roles. Fatma Naime was not after all unprepared, for the grapevine had given her the news of her husband's marriage. Also she had known that the pasha was returning and that undoubtedly his new wife would be with him.[28]

When Şehriban Hanım got out of the carriage and entered the *konak*, which was in Beyazıt, she bent to kiss the *büyük hanım*'s hand. Fatma Naime prevented this and instead raised the girl's head in her hands and kissed her on each cheek. Thus was set the pattern for the household, Şehriban accepting the preeminence of Fatma Naime, and Fatma Naime accepting the second wife into the household. The *konak* harem was then divided into two sections, with an apartment for each wife, but the overall management stayed in the hands of the first wife.[29]

Şehriban Hanım bore Mithat three children, a boy and two girls. Shortly after Mithat was executed, she died of tuberculosis. By this time, in fact after the imprisonment of Mithat, the two wives had taken separate establishments in Izmir, where Mithat was governor at the time of his arrest. But now Fatma Naime took the children into her household and brought them up as her own.[30]

Despite their parting after Mithat's arrest, the lives of the two women had been harmonious when they lived in the same household. It is said in the family that there was never any trouble between them. Each strictly observed the etiquette of her situation.[31] After Mithat was arrested, a letter to him from either of them did not fail to include a message of regard from the other one. On at least one occasion Mithat wrote them a letter in common.[32] He wrote about family financial concerns and the necessity of having a man look after such matters in Istanbul, since the family was now in Izmir.[33] At one time he gave his wives power of attorney over some of his business interests.[34] He obviously trusted them not to work at cross-purposes with one another.

Mithat's wives were both exceptional women. Both were literate;[35] both possessed a high degree of charm and a sense of propriety. In some polygamous households the women were more simple, and yet in these, too, the situation sometimes worked harmoniously. When Melek Hanım was exiled to Konya in the early 1850s, she was taken as a guest into the household of the governor there.[36] The governor had four wives, all of whom accepted their situation with a resignation that infuriated Melek.

Countess Belgiojoso met her there in 1852 and found her trying, unsuccessfully, to arouse a spirit of independence among the pasha's wives. They
sensibly told Melek that it was one thing for a woman of the world like
her to take an independent attitude toward polygamy, and quite another
thing for those who knew no life outside the doors of their husband's
harem.[37]

Also unaware of her husband's polygamous activities was Benli Ayşe,
the beautiful daughter of Hacı Mehmet Ağa, the *ayan* (notable) of Eski
Zagra (a Balkan town) in the early nineteenth century. Her father had
brought her up to accompany him about his lands much as a son would
have done. She was even skilled in the use of a *yatağan* (a curved knife).
In fact, so dauntless as well as fetching is she reputed to have been that
the local youths hesitated to ask her in marriage for fear they would count
for too little in the ensuing ménage. So she was past 20 when her father
finally gave her to the handsome Çubuktar Mehmet Pasha, a follower of
the Balkan notable, Alemdar. They lived in a huge *konak* in Eski Zagra
and had a son, Emin, and a daughter, Fatma. One day little five-year-old
Emin came to his mother where she sat embroidering and teased her for
her belt, which he wound twice around his small waist. He then picked up
three *sırmalı* napkins from the nearby table, tucked them into his belt to
resemble a three-paneled *entari*, and proceeded to give an imitation of a
woman swaying across the room. His mother, laughing, asked him what
he was doing. He answered: "There are beautiful girls, mother, very beautiful girls."[38] Suspicious now, Benli Ayşe rushed to the *mabeyn*,[39] found it
locked, and firmly demanded admittance. Once inside she saw four handsome girls in three-paneled *entari*s, obviously living there. Fearing her
anger, the girls fell at her feet.[40]

Benli Ayşe kept command of herself and told the girls not to be afraid.
She had four *bohça*s and purses of gold made up and told the women she
would send them to Istanbul immediately or, if they chose, they could
remain with her. Two of the women, the daughter of the Greek gardener
and a Circassian called Çerkes Afet, elected to stay with her at the *konak*.
They had children by Çubuktar Mehmet, and his wife accepted them into
her household. The other two girls went to Istanbul, where presumably
they were resold into other houses. Benli Ayşe divorced Çubuktar, but
later, after his death, she also took in a child he had had with a *hamamcı*
(bath attendant).[41]

After he was found out, Çubuktar never came back to the *konak*, and
the gardener's daughter never became reconciled to losing him. She used
to say to Çerkes Afet, "Ah, Afet, how do you bear it?" Her attitude
illustrates the fact that concubines were less concerned about sharing their
man than was a free-born Turkish woman.[42]

There were even instances in which polygamous wives seemed to like
their fate. Kenan Bey was a *şeyh* (sheikh) of the Mevlevî order who had

a *konak* at Fatih and a house at Sarıyer.[43] He knew many languages, played the violin, was a healer, and was considered saintly by many. He used to hold literary discussions for women in his house at Sarıyer. This man, who must have had a compelling personality, had four wives, all of whom adored him.[44]

According to Ottoman custom each wife was supposed to have her husband's amorous attentions once a week. If a husband faltered in his attentions to a legal wife, she had the right to complain and demand divorce.[45] Yet it is not likely that an upper-class woman, secluded as she was, would take her complaint to a *kadı* (judge). Whatever the law, it is very possible that such household arrangements were made privately. Legal wives were known simply to ignore their husband's attentions to slave concubines. Such was the case with the mistress of the slave girl Kanarya, whose history is discussed in the next chapter. Emmeline Lott, who lived in Egypt as governess to the khedival family, reported that İsmail's wives simply did not deign to notice his attentions to his slaves.[46]

Yet not all polygamous households were as peaceful as the ones we have described here. There were often powerful rivalries between the children of different mothers, even when the mothers lived in relative harmony with one another. Halil Halit gives a realistic account of polygamy in the household of his uncle, a member of the 1876 Parliament. His uncle had at first married a woman from a family socially on a par with his own and, while she lived, he had remained monogamous. But once she died he bought, freed, and married three Circassians, each of whom had her own apartment in his house. The result was a tumultuous household, because although the wives observed strict etiquette toward one another, their children and servants quarreled loudly.[47]

Other Turks, like Admiral Slade's friend, the *kaptan paşa* Pabuçcu Ahmet, found the quarrels that went with two wives in the same house insupportable. Therefore his *büyük hanım* lived in Istanbul, and his *ortak* (second wife), a beautiful Georgian, resided at Büyükdere on the Bosphorus, close to where his flagship was stationed. However, such were the pasha's notions of propriety that he visited the latter only after dark. Though the Georgian was said actually to dislike him, she was nevertheless jealous of a Circassian slave who had subsequently caught his eye.[48] Such were the hazards of polygamy.

Halide Edip tells of the emotional storms which her father's second marriage had unleashed in his household and how he had to divide his home into two separate apartments to bring about a measure of serenity.[49]

There were some men who, because of the ease of divorce or of concubinage, or both, carried polygamy to extremes. Such was Damadzade Murat Molla, a *kazasker* (chief military judge) of the late eighteenth century. De Tott relates how he was having coffee with the *molla* one day when a barefoot, badly clothed child came up to the latter and kissed his hand. The *molla* caressed the boy and asked, "Who is your father?"

"It is you," the child answered.

"What is your name?"

"Yusuf."

"Who is your mother?"

"Hatice."

"Ah yes, Hatice.[50]

According to d'Ohsson, Murat Molla, though he came from a family of *müftü*s (jurists), was censored for his sensual excesses, as well as for his love of luxury and ostentation. D'Ohsson considered him to be an exception.[51]

A progressive outlook in political affairs did not always preclude polygamy in private life. Thus it was with Mithat Pasha and his two wives, and with the nineteenth-century Minister of Education, Suphi Pasha, an enlightened man who did much to advance education in Turkey, yet who kept a *konak* in Fatih inhabited by ten wives and concubines.[52]

However, as the nineteenth century progressed and the Turks became more Westernized, there grew a body of opinion opposed to polygamy, and with that came an attempt to explain it as contrary to the spirit of Islam. As far back as 1880 the writer Şemseddin Sami, in *Kadınlar*, pointed out that although polygamy is permitted in the Koran it is not recommended. He then added: "It must not be forgotten that there is a sentence that consists of the meaning, 'to be satisfied with one wife is better'. . . . The passages which declare that everything in the world is in pairs, and yet that one man does not have two hearts, can be considered just witness against polygamy."[53]

Osman Bey, a late nineteenth-century writer, also reported the rumor that the Divan (Imperial Council) had held a discussion of polygamy led by one "R"—probably Reşit Pasha—who called polygamy a cancer, but thought it incurable because of the Koran and the Şeriat (body of Islamic law). It was believed that, desirable though monogamy was, public figures would certainly lose their portfolios and perhaps their lives if they advocated it. According to the rumor, the Divan agreed to leave it a private matter, but the statesmen would, on their own initiative, limit themselves to only one wife, the "diplomatic" wife, who would exchange visits with the wives of the foreign diplomats of Pera, the European quarter of Istanbul. Actually, according to Osman Bey, some of the men had more than one wife, but kept the fact hidden. "R" was bossed by his "diplomatic" wife, who was the mistress of his house, but when she died three others appeared, some with children, whose relationship to the pasha had not been known.[54]

Pears, in the late nineteenth century, believed that polygamy was decreasing. It was considered too expensive, though not wrong.[55] Garnett, writing in the early twentieth century, found it still practiced. She mentioned a visit to a Mevlevî şeyh at Magnesia in whose household there were two wives. As often happened the second one was married because of the childlessness of the first.[56] Garnett found that there were limits to polygamy and largely agreed with d'Ohsson as to what they were: the expense of more than one wife, the fact that most parents wanted their daughters to be büyük hanıms and would, therefore, not give them in marriage to men who were already married, and a paucity of available women. By the time Garnett was writing, the sources of Caucasian slaves were drying up. Previously, especially after the Circassian exodus to Turkey, it was probably true that there had been a superabundance of women. Garnett thought, like d'Ohsson, that it was unusual for a man to have four wives, two being the general limit.[57]

Pickthall agreed with Garnett. Writing during the Balkan Wars, he found that polygamy was little practiced, and believed it was indulged in only when the first wife was childless. He thought too that the independence of the Turkish wife, who sometimes refused to leave Istanbul when her husband was sent as governor to some far-off place like Baghdad or Damascus, was a reason for polygamy, for then the husband took along a Circassian slave.[58]

This was the case with Hasan Hayrullah, the şeyhülislâm. When he was exiled to Mecca, his wife stayed in Istanbul. He then bought a slave in Mecca who lived with him during his exile and stayed close to him when he was imprisoned with Mithat in Tâif.[59]

By the twentieth century, some people were speaking out strongly against polygamy. Among them was Celâl Nuri, who thought that concubinage and polygamy undermined the family, which was the basic unit of civilization.[60] "The needs of today," he wrote, "make monogamy a necessity."[61] He felt that the custom of polygamy was dying out because of its cost, as well as because of the growing maturity of women. He too believed Islam was essentially against polygamy and had simply been misinterpreted.[62]

Throughout the period under discussion, there were factors which discouraged polygamy, even among the upper classes. But monogamy could also be legally guaranteed. Under Islamic law the husband had the power to waive his right of divorce, and he could bind himself to monogamy by inserting in the marriage contract a clause that authorized his wife to divorce him if he married a second wife without her consent.[63] When the Young Turks enacted the Family Code of 1917, they confirmed the woman's right to contract to be the sole wife,[64] thus codifying a practice that had long been in existence.

Polygamy ended in Turkey with the change in point of view that Westernization brought about and with the loss of the lands of the Empire and the consequent decline in wealth. Though a Suphi Pasha could choose to have, and could afford to support, ten wives and concubines, his children chose monogamy.

NOTES

1. Ignatius Mouradgea d'Ohsson, *Tableau général de l'Empire othoman*, IV, p. 343.

2. Julia Pardoe, *The City of the Sultans*, I, p. 102.

3. Sir Paul Rycaut, *The History of the Present State of the Ottoman Empire*, II, pp. 288–289.

4. Charles White, *Three Years in Constantinople*, III, p. 7.

5. Pardoe, *The City*, I, p. 102.

6. Halide Edip (*Memoirs of Halide Edip*, p. 41) says that polygamy was rare in households that had no slaves. It might therefore be argued, conversely, that it was prevalent among slave-holding families.

7. White, *Three Years*, III, p. 39.

8. R. Robert Madden, *Travels in Turkey, Egypt, Nubia and Palestine in 1824, 1825, 1826 and 1827*, I, p. 25.

9. Sir Edwin Pears, *Turkey and Its People*, p. 68.

10. Peyami Safa, *Türk inkılâbına bakışlar*, pp. 61–62.

11. Adolphus Slade (*Records of Travels in Turkey, Greece, etc.*, II, p. 9) points out that the argument that polygamy tended to decrease the population makes no sense.

12. Pardoe, *The City*, I, p. 102.

13. Polygamy must also have been prevalent in pre-Turkic Asia Minor. In the first century of the Christian era Paul placed great importance on the bishops' and deacons' having only one wife, which would hardly have been necessary to do had there been no polygamy (*see First Epistle of Saint Paul to Timothy*).

14. Gökalp argued that the ancient Turks of Central Asia were not actually polygamous because the *kuma* (the second or third wife) was really a concubine (*see* A. Ziyaeddin Fahri Fındıkoğlu, *Zia Gökalp, sa vie et sa sociologie*, pp. 128–129). In this work Fındıkoğlu suggests that Gökalp was mistaken, but in a later work one finds him saying that the Turks of Central Asia did not know polygamy (*Essai sur la transformation du code familial en Turquie*, p. 19). Gökalp promoted the view of Central Asian Turkic monogamy at a time when polygamy was losing favor among the Ottoman Turks, and he was perhaps influenced by his desire to lead his people away from the custom.

15. M. A. Czaplicka, *Aboriginal Siberia*, pp. 53–57.

16. Ibid., p. 167.

17. Alfred Emmons Hudson, *Kazak Social Structure* (London, 1938), pp. 39–54.

18. Halide Edip, *Conflict of East and West in Turkey*, p. 251.

19. Joseph S. Szyliowicz, *Political Change in Rural Turkey: Erdemli*, p. 51.

20. Hudson, *Kazak Social Structure*, pp. 39–54.

21. Personal interview with Beraet Bulayır, Hüseyin Galip Pasha's grandniece, August 1966. In this instance *büyük* means "old" and *küçük* "young."

22. A house that overlooks the water.

23. From the reminiscences of Perihan Arıburun, Kâmil Pasha's granddaughter (personal interview, November 1967).

24. Pardoe, *The City*, I, pp. 233, 240-241.

25. Personal interview with Saide Tanriover, the grandniece of Cemal Bey, August 1966.

26. Personal communication from Seniha Moralı, 1966.

27. "Our wish, by means of the promulgation and announcement of the constitution, is to remove despotism and arouse the royal person to his duties. . . . " (From the letter of Mithat Pasha to Abdülhamit II cited in Ali Haydar Mithat, *Hatırlarım 1872–1946*, pp. 26–27).

28. Personal interview with Mithat Akçit, Mithat Pasha's grandson, June 1966.

29. Personal interview with Mithat Akçit, June, 1966.

30. Ibid.

31. Ibid.

32. İsmail Hakkı Uzunçarşılı, *Midhat Paşa ve Tâif mahkûmları*, p. 45.

33. Ibid.

34. Ibid., pp. 43-44.

35. Personal interview with Mithat Akçit, June, 1966.

36. Melek Hanım [Melek-Hanum], *Thirty Years in the Harem*, pp. 165–168.

37. Princess Christina Trivolzio de Belgiojoso, *Oriental Harems and Scenery*, p. 134. Belgiojoso found Melek passing herself off in the harem as a widow. The governor, however, knew her real story. Belgiojoso who, like other observers, noted that the less wealthy Turks were monogamous, told the touching story of a simple provincial Turk who brought his blind wife to her because he had heard she had medical knowledge. The old couple had lost their only son in childhood, and when Belgiojoso asked the old man why he had never taken another wife in order to have children, he answered, "It would have grieved the poor creature there, which would have prevented me from being happy with another wife, even with children. . . . We cannot have everything in this world. I have loved her for over forty years, and I will not take another wife." Yet near Ankara Belgiojoso found an old *müftü* whose many wives, each quickly replaced when she died, had provided him with so many children he had lost track of most of them (*Oriental Harems*, pp. 110ff).

38. Reşat Ekrem Koçu, "Benli Ayşe Hanım," *Türk düşüncesi*, 2 (*Eylül* 1, 1954), pp. 254–256, and "Çubuktar Mehmet Paşa," *Türk düşüncesi*, 2 (*Ekim* 1, 1954), pp. 326–328.

39. The *mabeyn* is the portion of the house between the harem and the *selâmlık*.

40. Koçu, "Benli Ayşe Hanım" and "Çubuktar Mehmet Paşa."

41. Ibid.

42. In "Meddah Yusuf ve Ayşe Reis hikâyesi" (*Türk düşüncesi*, 2, *Ağustos* 1954, pp. 170–173) Koçu tells how Meddah (storyteller) Yusuf, when a small boy in Eski Zagra, met a *kahveci* (coffee server) on the road and became his apprentice and

eventually his heir to the *kahvehane* (coffee house) which he owned in Istanbul. At a time when the coffee houses were closed by the government, Yusuf took up *meddahlık* (story telling). Among the tales which he told was one about a female corsair named Ayşe Reis whose character he built on that of Benli Ayşe of the Eski Zagra of his childhood.

43. Fatih is a district in Istanbul and Sarıyer a town on the European shore of the Bosphorus.

44. Personal interview with Seniha Moralı, August 1966.

45. White, *Three Years*, III, p. 8; Rycaut, *Present State*, II, pp. 288–289.

46. Emmeline Lott, *Harem Life in Egypt and Constantinople*, p. 308.

47. Halil Halit [Khalil Khalid], *The Diary of a Turk*, pp. 39–41.

48. Slade, *Records of Travels*, I, pp. 353–355.

49. Halide Edip, *Memoirs*, pp. 143–148.

50. Baron de Tott, *Mémoires sur les Turcs et les Tartares*, I, p. 52.

51. D'Ohsson, *Tableau général*, IV, pp. 342–343.

52. Personal interview with Seniha Moralı, July 1966.

53. Tezer Taşkıran, "Şemseddin Sami ve kadınlar," *Türk yurdu*, 1 (*Haziran*, 1955), pp. 946–950.

54. Ibid.

55. Pears, *Turkey and Its People*, p. 68.

56. Lucy M. J. Garnett, *Home Life in Turkey*, pp. 222–223.

57. Ibid., pp. 221–222.

58. Marmaduke Pickthall, *With the Turk in Wartime*, p. 91.

59. Uzunçarşılı, *Midhat Paşa ve Tâif mahkûmları*, p. 201, n. 1. Hasan Hayrullah had a son by her, in addition to his children by his first wife.

60. Celâl Nuri, *Kadınlarımız*, pp. 129–138.

61. Ibid., p. 139.

62. Ibid., p. 140–141.

63. Asaf A. A. Fyzee, *Outlines of Muhammadan Law*, pp. 104–105; 134–135.

64. Fındıkoğlu, *Essai*, pp. 37–38.

6

The Woman Slave

If age can lend respectability, then slavery in the Ottoman Empire can be said to have become a respectable institution. Certainly it was a venerable one.[1] Long before Istanbul became an Ottoman city, it was a flourishing way station and market for the Caucasian slave trade. Throughout the Middle Ages slaves were purchased in the Crimea and the ports of the Taurus Peninsula for transport to *Mamlûk* Egypt, then the slave-trader's best customer. Some came by land, but most were carried across the Black Sea and through the Straits by the ships of the Christian city states of Italy.[2] Though the Pope issued repeated edicts against the slave trade and threatened slave merchants with excommunication, Venice, Genoa, and Florence continued to enrich themselves through its pursuit.[3] In fact, so lucrative was the slave trade that the *Mamlûk* sultans decided to take their cut. In 1290 the Egyptian sultan obtained permission from the Byzantine emperor to allow a certain number of his own ships each year through the Straits to the slave ports on the Sea of Azov and the mouth of the Don. In 1431 Sultan Barsbay negotiated a treaty that allowed his agents to buy slaves in the Genoese port of Kaffa. Very soon thereafter a Genoese merchant of the d'Imperiali family was appointed the *Mamlûk*'s slave agent. On the eastern and northern shores of the Black Sea, Christian merchants searched for boys to be sold to Egypt as eunuchs and soldiers, and for girls for Egyptian harems.[4] Even little Armenia took the slave trade in stride. In 1285 it allowed Egypt right of transit for slaves of both sexes, along with horses and mules.[5]

Yet not all slaves went to Muslim Egypt. It is known that women were sent to Venice and Genoa for domestic service;[6] there is evidence of slave purchases in Venice as late as the end of the fifteenth century.[7] This is not to say that the Turks learned about the enslavement of women from the West. They had certainly known the enslaved woman war captive in their nomad days in Central Asia.[8] They had been familiar with the *cariye* in the harems of Sassanid Persia and the Abbasid Caliphate.[9] But it was only when the Ottoman dynasty gained power and wealth that the institution of the *cariye*, the slave girl as handmaiden, concubine, and source of prestige, took hold among the Ottoman Turks.

The world came late to moral indignation about slavery. In the Middle Ages it was an accepted institution. The Turks, finding it established in the Middle East, recognized it and regulated it. Slavery in the Ottoman Empire had none of the debasing qualities the word connotes to the Westerner today. In the Ottoman family the woman slave, whether concubine or *kalfa*, was an accepted member of the household, to be taken care of as long as she remained in the household, and frequently thereafter.[10]

In the early days of the Empire the woman slave, or *cariye*, was often a war captive and might therefore have been Russian, like Süleyman's Hürrem,[11] or Italian like Safiye,[12] or Greek or Balkan. As the Empire ceased expanding, women captives became less plentiful. By the eighteenth century the *cariye* was usually a purchased Circassian or Georgian. She may have been kidnapped in her homeland, or sold by her parents, or she may have voluntarily put herself in the hands of a slave merchant in order to get to Istanbul.[13] She may even have been bred for sale. There is some evidence that members of the Circassian slave class were encouraged to breed children for their owners to sell, some say as a means of buying the parents' freedom, others merely for the owners' profit.[14] De la Motraye, who investigated Circassia in the early eighteenth century, found that the *myrsa*s (nobles) sold the children of their subjects and even sometimes their own. The people of the district brought their children to the *myrsa* for this purpose. Fathers and mothers taught their daughters to guard their virginity, for in that lay a good part of their value. A man who violated the virginity of a girl was forced to buy her from her parents.[15] There is, however, another school of thought which holds that only the slave class sold their children, and that when daughters of noble families sometimes reached the slave market they got there as a result of raids, or had gone to the slave ports of their own free will.

After the Russian conquest of Circassia in 1864 and the subsequent Circassian exodus to Turkey, the trade in Circassian girls still went on. Selling children was a very old practice in Circassia and Georgia. Far from having compunctions about it, the parents thought they were insuring a better future for their daughters, who might thereby enter the household of a rich pasha or even the confines of the palace. And when the Circassian émigrés settled in the Empire, the need for money in a new country was an added incentive.[16] Thus we find that at the end of the nineteenth century the slaves in an Ottoman household were almost wholly Circassian,[17] some still coming from Circassia, others from within the Empire.

Freygang, who did considerable research on the Circassians, said they were divided into three classes: prince, noble, and slave. The princes governed; the princes and nobles made war and plundered; the slaves and women did the work.[18] Therefore it must have been the princes and nobles who profited from the sale of captives, and also, as evidence shows, from the sale of slave children, however acquired.

De Fonton thought that the principal instruments of slave commerce were the mountaineers.[19] Habesci asserted that most of the raiders were Turks,[20] but it is well established from other sources that Circassian tribes raided one another. Spencer, for example, noted that the girls who became *cariye*s were often booty from raids made by Caucasian tribes for the express purpose of garnering beauties for sale.[21] However, Habesci, anti-Turkic though he was, admitted that Georgian and Circassian females were sold by their parents. He furthermore stated that inoculation against smallpox, which was developed in the Caucasus, was practiced there as a means of preserving beauty for sale.[22] Yet even while the parents or masters were inoculating the girls' bodies against smallpox, they were careful not to inoculate their minds against a change in religion. According to Adolphus Slade, an extremely perspicacious observer of affairs in the Ottoman Empire, Christian Circassian families avoided giving their girls a Christian upbringing so they might adapt more easily to the Islam of their buyers.[23]

We know much about the slave trade between the Caucasus and Istanbul, for we have descriptions of it not only from foreign observers but also from some of the girls themselves. At the beginning of the twentieth century there were still many ex-slaves living in Istanbul, a good part of them married to Turks. One Circassian used to recall how she had been playing with other children when a horseman appeared and asked her whether she would like a ride. Captivated by the idea as any child might be, she was easily captured by the man and then taken to a slave dealer in a coastal town. Another, sold by her parents, came eagerly to Istanbul in the hope of marrying a pasha. She did the next best thing. She married a pasha's son, an uncle of Seniha Moralı. Seniha Hanım describes her thus:

Aunt Mail or Mail Yenge, as we called her, was one of the kindest and sweetest women I knew. She was a Circassian and always spoke Turkish with a marked accent. She was quite illiterate and did not even know the date of her birth. She was born in the middle of the nineteenth century when Circassians still sold their daughters as slaves. She remembered her native country quite well, and she told me she had wanted to be sent to Istanbul because she had heard Circassian girls married pashas there. She was sold to the house of Suphi Pasha, who married her to his eldest son, Ayetullah. Ayetullah had been offered a more beautiful Circassian bride, but he preferred Mail.

Their only child, a boy, died in infancy. Ayetullah was an essayist and a poet. He associated with the poets Namık Kemal and Ziya Pasha. Because of his liberal opinions he was suspect to the authoritarian government and appointed to a government office in the far eastern province of Erzurum, where he died in 1878 at the age of thirty.

Mail Hanım married again and was widowed for the second time. Having no other means of subsistence than a government pension, she returned to the *konak* of her late father-in-law, Suphi Pasha. Many of his children and grandchildren lived there, and they all loved her very much. There she spent the rest of her life. She was especially fond of children, and whenever there was a birth in the family she was there to help. She was always ready to help the needy. She was very pious and strictly observed the rules of praying and fasting. When my brother was fighting at the Dardanelles she was quite concerned about him as we were, and when I was writing to him she said, "Give him my love and tell him I would write myself if I knew how to write."

We all loved her dearly and mourned when she died of old age, in the first quarter of this century.[24]

Julia Pardoe reported a Georgian child sold by her mother for 6,000 piasters in about the year 1834. Another, bought for 7,000 piasters, was sold by her parents at her own request.[25] Far from being a tragedy, the prospect of being sold was often looked upon as an opportunity to enter into a more glamorous and prosperous world.

There were times when ex-slaves returned from Turkish or Persian harems adorned with fine clothes and elaborate jewels. To attain so enviable a state, Circassian girls were known to go down to the slave ports of their own free will and jump aboard ship, impatient to be off to Istanbul, the city of opportunity.

Until Russia won control of the Caucasus and the Taurus Peninsula in the 1860s, girls were openly transported across the Black Sea. After 1860, Russia stepped up efforts to stop the slave trade, with the result that girls were clandestinely taken to Istanbul in ships that sailed only by night or during the winter months when patrols were few because of the roughness of the sea. Even the ones who came through safely often experienced hardship. One Circassian, purchased as an *odalık* for a pasha in the late nineteenth century, a slave to whom motherhood gave the status of wife, told her children that there had been a shortage of water aboard the ship that carried her, and all the girls had suffered from thirst.[26]

By the eighteenth century, most of the girls were taken directly to the Esir Pazarı (Slave Market), located near the Covered Bazaar.[27] Before it was built, slaves were sold in certain streets, which became so congested that at times they had to be closed off. Because the *esirci esnafı* (slave-dealers' guild) complained of the consequent loss of business, in 1609 Ahmet I had the Esir Pazarı constructed. It has been described as a quadrangular building with a central court. Negro women from Africa were displayed on a platform in the center of the court, but white girls were concealed in separate rooms behind latticed windows and brought into special salons when displayed to customers.[28] Since virginity was a major factor in their value, they were carefully guarded and held for two or three months after arrival to give time for possible pregnancy to manifest itself. The market had the services of a *şeyh* (Muslim preacher) and a *kethüda* (steward);[29] it also had a small mosque, now gone, the Esirpazarı Mescidi.[30]

The slave trade was a strictly regulated business; the female merchandise had to be accurately described. In one case a *tutsakcı* (slave dealer) not only had to return the 215 *kuruş* which he had received for selling a Persian woman as a Georgian (Georgians apparently being worth more than Persians) but was also imprisoned.[31]

Some highly placed Ottoman women were slave traders of a sort, buying very young girls, teaching them accomplishments which increased their value and, when they reached marriageable age, reselling them at a profit.[32] It must, however, be stated that profit was not the only motive here. To be attended by handsome, cultivated slave girls was a mark of rank in Ottoman society.[33] Nor were the girls sold to just any willing buyer, but rather to families of high position with whom a link was politically and socially desirable. The girls were, in fact, trained to take a high place in Ottoman society.

Admiral Slade, in his capacity as British naval adviser to the Sublime Porte, came to know Istanbul well. He thought the slave trade tragic only in the cases of war captives, noting that Circassian and Georgian girls, who made up the bulk of the slave trade, were treated with special consideration.

In the market they are lodged in separate apartments, carefully secluded, where in the hours of business—between nine and twelve—they may be visited by aspirants for possessing such delicate ware. . . . The would-be purchaser may fix his eyes on the lady's face, and his hand may receive evidence of her bust. The waltz allows almost as much liberty before hundreds of eyes.[34]

A different picture, that of a war captive, is given by Madden, a British doctor practicing in the Ottoman Empire, whose profession gave him access to the Slave Market. At the time of the Greek-Ottoman War of 1829 he noted a Greek war captive

of about fifteen, brought forth to exhibit her gait and figure to an old Turk, whose glances manifested the motive for her purchase; he twisted her elbows, he pulled her ankles, he felt her ears, examined her mouth, and then her neck; and all this while the slave merchant was extolling her shape and features, protesting that she had only turned thirteen, that she neither snored nor started in her sleep, and that, in every respect, she was warranted.[35]

The price of these girls naturally varied from year to year, depending upon the availability and quality of the merchandise. Slade found that in his time, the first half of the nineteenth century, a white girl usually brought 100 pounds. Especially beautiful girls sold for more but, he thought, were likely to be picked up by the Ağa of the House of Felicity for the palace. Melek Hanım, who was in a position to know, since she herself bought slaves, found the price to be from 4,000 to 20,000 francs, or 160 to 800 pounds.[36] Beauties brought the most money. Homely slaves, purchased for duties that did not entail an appearance before the master of the house, sold for not over 1,500 to 2,000 francs. Samuel S. Cox, American Ambassador to the Sublime Porte in the late nineteenth century, put the price in American terms: a girl under ten was sold for $100, one from 12 to 16 from $3,500 to $5,000, "if she be attractive and can play on the zither," and from $4,000 to $6,000 if a rare beauty with blond hair and black eyes. A girl well educated in the French language and the social graces was worth twice an ordinary girl.[37] Thus it can be seen that there was money to be made in buying these girls young and training them.

In some cases the price of a girl depended on whether or not the girl snored, and individual slave dealers were known to let a girl sleep in a prospective customer's house a night or two so that her sleeping habits might be tested. Physical defects lowered a girl's value. A flat-footed girl was thought so unlucky she was fortunate if she could be sold at all.[38]

Girls were usually sold between the ages of six and 13.[39] Some were mere infants, and in such cases either the baby's *sütnine* (wet nurse) went with her or a substitute was provided.[40] In the purchaser's behalf each girl was examined by a midwife to make sure she was a virgin.[41]

In 1680 Mehmet IV issued a regulation forbidding slave merchants to powder and rouge the faces of their merchandise. He also required that the merchants sell the girls with the clothing "with which they have clothed them." Mantran says the guild of the slave dealers then had 2,000 members, which indicates the extent of their activity.[42]

In 1854 the Slave Market was closed as a concession to Western pressure, but the commerce in slaves went on unhindered. The slave merchants, who had formerly lived near the Market, simply moved. Those dealing in Circassians tended to live in Tophane, others in Fatih. Lucy Garnett describes the situation thus:

Since the abolition of the public slave-market, the private trade in slaves has become much more general and widely spread than formerly. This traffic is carried on to a great extent by women of rank, some of whom are themselves emancipated slaves; and the profits they realize are said to be very considerable, especially when their operations are on a large scale. On the arrival in the capital of a fresh batch of children, a broker is dispatched by the consignees to the houses of these women dealers, who, if they desire to add to their stock-in-trade, either drive to the establishments of the slave merchants, or have the girls brought to their own house for inspection. Children of from six to ten years of age are the most sought after by these connoisseurs, who pay large prices for them in the expectation of receiving perhaps ten times that amount when the girls are about seventeen.[43]

In addition to the slave markets—they existed in the provinces as well as in Istanbul—there were the *esircis* or *esir tuccarıs*, men and women slave dealers who brought their wares to the customer. They not only sold girls newly arrived in Istanbul, but also resold those whose owners wanted to dispose of them for some reason, or those girls who themselves wanted new quarters. In cases of resale the merchant was allowed a broker's fee (*dellâliye*), and also a maintenance fee (*nafaka*), for each day he lodged the slave. In 1826 the *nafaka* was fixed at 50 or 60 *para* per day, though the *ihtisap ağası* (local tax official) had the authority to lower it as he saw fit.[44] There was also a tax, the *pencik*, on the sale of each slave, collected by a *pencik emini*.[45] On payment of the tax, which was one-fifth the value of the slave, a title-deed was delivered to the owner. If the slave was resold, the title-deed passed to the new owner. If the slave was freed, it was endorsed and registered and given to the ex-slave as proof of manumission.[46] In 1800 the *pencik* on the sale of women slaves was increased as a method of raising revenue for Selim III's war-depleted treasury. The increase produced more revenue than anticipated.[47]

The slave dealer usually regaled the buyer with a lively sales talk. If the buyer was the lady of the *baş kalfa* (head servant) of a private house, the dealer might say: "What a strong girl she is, from top to toe! Would I bring you a bad slave, my lady? We make a sparrow into a nightingale and a nightingale into a sparrow, according to the customer. Furthermore, there hasn't been an epidemic in the lot." And so on.[48]

Once the girl was purchased, her mistress took her into the family home. A new name was given her, usually a fancy one such as Gülbahar (Rose of Spring), Neşedil (Gay-Hearted), Nazikemsal (Example of Courtesy) and Servetseza (Worthy of Riches). Slave names exemplifying grace or beauty were traditional in the Ottoman Empire. In the seventeenth century a diligent scribe compiled a list of names suitable for slaves, most of them combinations containing such words as *can* (soul), *gül* (rose), *nev* (new), and *nur* (light).[49] When these girls married, they usually added an Islamic name such as Ayşe or Fatma.[50]

While the girl was learning the elaborate etiquette of an Ottoman household she stayed below stairs, where she practiced her duties by waiting on the *kalfas*, or fully trained slaves. She learned to sew and embroider and very likely to crochet the fine lace called *oya*. She learned to speak and to read Turkish, but in many cases she was not taught to write lest she be tempted to write love letters. On the one hand she was taught the tenets of Islam, on the other instructed in the art of playing Turkish musical

Figure 1. Turkish Lady and Slave in the Harem

instruments and in the dance.[51] Furthermore, she was taught the art of enhancing her charms.[52] If the girl had a special talent, such as in calligraphy, it was cultivated. If she had been bought with the idea of future resale or if she was considered suitable to marry into the family, she did nothing that might spoil her hands. In fact, white slave girls usually had no manual work to do; the hard work was done by Negresses. Instead, the white girl learned to stand in an attitude of respect with her hands folded, to attend her mistress, to sit according to rank, and to display all the niceties of manners. An important part of her duties was the ceremony of waiting on guests, serving sherbet and coffee or full meals.

Julia Pardoe describes the ministrations of a slave girl to guests in Istanbul in the 1830s:

As we rose from the table, a slave girl presented herself, holding a basin and a strainer of wrought metal, while a second poured tepid water over our hands, from an elegantly-formed vase of the same materials; and a third handed us embroidered napkins of great beauty.[53]

In addition to all this, she of course learned to dress in the accepted Ottoman fashion.

Girls whose talents were intellectual learned to write (these, apparently, could be entrusted not to indulge in love letters, at least not extracurricular ones). Some learned to read Persian and Arabic. Some were trained to become nursemaids (*dadı*) or instructors of the children of the family.[54] Many, either because of their charm, their cultivation, or both, were married to sons of the family[55] or into families with whom a connection was desirable. The slave girl continued her relationship with her foster family much as an actual daughter would have done.

A Circassian girl's marriage could mean a connection favorable both to her foster family and to the family into which she married. So it was with Şehriban who was brought up in the household of one Nazif Pasha. When 17, she was married to Mithat Pasha, then 50 and governor of Baghdad. How Şehriban came to Istanbul and got into the household of Nazif Pasha is not known; she was too young at the time to remember. Her foster family must have had some knowledge of her parents, however, because she grew up with the impression that she came from a noble family of the Ubykh tribe, which migrated to Turkey in its entirety in 1864.[56] Perhaps they settled with many other Circassians around Bandırma, Gönen, or Adapazarı, all near enough to Istanbul so that it would not have been difficult to take her there. In any event, she was a singularly beautiful and talented girl whom her foster family took pains to educate. Şehriban was chosen for Mithat by his sister, who visited harems as his *görücü*. In return for her, Mithat paid her foster family 2,000 *altın* (a gold coin), an extraordinarily high amount, and she was sent to him in Baghdad with a fine trousseau and a large retinue, as befitted a daughter marrying a man of rank.[57] But whatever pleasure she derived from her marriage was short-lived, for Mithat Pasha was arrested and exiled in 1881 and she was never again to see him.

Other cases turned out more auspiciously. When Âli Pasha was grand vizier, his Circassian wife presented their daughter-in-law, Cemile Sultan, who was the sister of Abdülhamit II, with a charming Circassian slave. When Abdülhamit was still a prince he became so taken with this girl on his visits to his sister that Cemile gave her to him. On his accession, this slave became *baş kadın* (head wife or concubine). She still retained her affection for her former mistress, invited her to the palace, and freely admitted it was to this woman that she owed her good fortune.[58]

Also relatively fortunate was Lâyıka Hanım, the fourth wife of Kâmil Pasha, who was four times grand vizier in the latter years of the nineteenth and the early twentieth century. Lâyıka, a Circassian whose parents had sold her in order to better her lot in life, was brought up by a family that specialized in training girls for the palace and the great houses. She grew up to be very beautiful and dignified in manner, and was sought in marriage by two men, a prince and Kâmil Pasha. Kâmil Pasha was a widower 39 years older than Lâyıka, but she chose him because he had always been monogamous (though he had married three times) and had a reputation for kindness. Lâyıka lived with him happily until the end of his life, bore him ten children, and earned for herself an important place in the family. Comparing her children with those of her husband's former wives, she used to say, "I brought beauty to this family."[59]

Some families preferred slave girls for daughters-in-law. Some men preferred them as wives.[60] They were thought to be more tractable than girls from Turkish families, for they had no family to which to return. Furthermore, a large part of their training consisted of learning how to please their men. Perhaps the old nomadic practice of exogamy made it easy for Turkish men to accept the idea of a foreign wife.

White estimated that 500 Circassian *cariye*s a year were being imported into Istanbul when he wrote in 1844, and that 30 to 40 percent of them would be married off.[61] Of the remainder, a certain number would become concubines, and, if they had children, gain the status of *'umm-al-walad*,[62] which meant that they could not be resold.[63] The rest would help to run the big households of which they would become a part. Though marriage was the goal of most *cariye*s, it was not unknown for a girl to prefer her servitude. In the household of Emine Foat Tugay's grandfather, Ahmet Muhtar Pasha, there was such a woman. She eventually became *baş kalfa* and was taken care of by the family for life.[64]

That a great many did marry is attested to by the large number of Circassian grandmothers and great aunts recalled by today's older generation. And history tells us about others. For example, Mustafa Bayraktar,

the general who tried to reinstate Selim III on the throne, took four *cariyes*
as concubines and had children by them. Whether or not he ever married
them is not recorded, but since he had precisely the legal number of four,
it is probable that he did. In any event, each had the status of *'umm-al-
walad* and on his death was allotted a pension by the government.[65]

Even in the late nineteenth century the large *konaks* of Istanbul had a
great many slaves. Of the hundred inhabitants of the 60-room *konak* of
Sami Pasha, Suphi Pasha's father, a large proportion were Circassian slaves.[66]
The same is true of the 100-room *konak* of Hasan Hüsnü Pasha, Abdülhamit's Minister of the Navy.[67] And in Kasr-i Ali, the Cairo palace of the
valide kadınefendi (mother of the khedive) of Egypt, there were 300 Circassian slaves. Twenty of them were supervising *kalfas*, 40 served meals,
some were musicians, others dancers. A few were purchased as children
to be companions for the *valide*'s grandchildren.[68] It was largely the pashas—the administrative and officer class—who took Circassian girls as
wives and concubines, rather than the members of the *ulema*.[69]

The fate of the *cariye* clearly depended on the family that purchased
her. We have already indicated that if she became pregnant by a member
of the household, she could no longer be sold or given away, for she then
had the legal status of *'umm-al-walad*, or mother of a child, and became
free on her master's death. Once the man acknowledged the child as his,
it was free and inherited equally with the children of the legal wives.[70]

The grapevine between Istanbul and Circassia or Georgia was sufficiently
active for the slave girls to have definite ideas of what they wanted—well-
to-do homes in the Ottoman capital with considerate mistresses. Sometimes
they balked when the slave dealer tried to send them to far-off places, as
when purchased for the princes of Egypt or the beys of Tunis. Some girls
objected to becoming an *ortak*. With these the slave dealer used the argument that their youth and superior training would soon give them the
ascendancy in the household.[71] This, however, could never be wholly true,
so firmly was Ottoman society ruled by rank.

Occasionally, a wife resold a *cariye* of whom she was jealous.[72] She had
the right to do this only if the slave had been bought as her attendant, not
her husband's. Other wives, more subtle, like Melek Hanım, married off
the girls as soon as they became old enough to interest a man sexually.[73]
There were times when a wife's *cariye*, finding the master's attentions
embarrassing, asked to be sold.[74] Occasionally a harsh mistress was the
motive for a girl's desire to be sold.

Not every *cariye* found life smooth. The story of Kanarya was related
to the author by Merzuka Nayır in August 1966. Some time before Kanarya's birth in the Bandırma region, in the early 1870s, there had been a
fight between her mother's Circassian émigré clan and another Circassian
émigré clan. When the fight was over, Kanarya's mother found herself the
only person left in her village; all the others had either been killed or driven

off. Her husband, to whom she was newly married, was nowhere to be found. At this time a man came up to her, the slave of some local person of importance. He took her to his master, at whose place they married, and she too became the master's slave. The couple had two girls, one of whom was Kanarya. Because he thought the children would be a burden to his household, and also undoubtedly because girls were ready money, the master sold them. The girls were taken to Istanbul. In later years Kanarya had a faint memory of being jostled about in a basket strapped to the side of a donkey, while her sister bounced back and forth in the basket on the other side of the animal. Their mother escaped from her household and accompanied them to Istanbul to insure their safety and well-being. Kanarya thought they had all been taken to Tophane, which is likely, since that was the district of Istanbul where Circassian girls were being sold. Her younger sister, a baby of nine months, was bought for the palace, where she was later trained for the service of Yusuf İzzeddin, a son of Sultan Abdülaziz. Eventually she became this prince's *baş kahveci* (chief coffee-server) and spent her life in his service, dying just before the women of the palaces were freed at the beginning of the Republic.

Kanarya was bought by Abdülaziz' *kuşbaz* (man in charge of the sultan's birds), Hurşit Bey, and her mother went to the same household as a maid. Kanarya was four or five when Abdülhamit II ascended the throne and immediately banished many of those who had been in the service of his predecessors. In the middle of the night, Hurşit Bey was informed that he was to depart at once, by a ship waiting off Sirkeci at the entrance to the Golden Horn. Fond of his little slave girl, he bundled her up and took her with him to the Sirkeci quay, where they set out in a small boat for the ship that was to take him into exile. Kanarya recalled that they were hoisted aboard by a winch.

She remembered too that there was a *şeyhülislâm* aboard, very probably Hayrullah Hasan Efendi who had given the *fetva*s (legal sanctions) for the deposition of Abdülaziz and Murat V and whom Abdülhamit, with his persistent fear of being deposed, exiled to Madina. Kanarya did not recall exactly where she and her master disembarked, but thought it might have been at Iskenderun. She did recall that the *şeyhülislâm* was kept shut up in his cabin at the start of the voyage until, at the protest of the passengers, the captain let him out, since he could hardly escape on the high seas.

Kanarya enjoyed the voyage. She was the only child on board and the recipient of a great deal of attention from her elders. Even the captain took a fancy to her.

Wherever it was that Hurşit Bey first settled, he was dependent on money which his son sent to him from Istanbul. A little later, when Kanarya was 11 or 12, he was appointed governor of a province in eastern Anatolia, perhaps Mardın or Dıyarbakır. Kanarya went with him and was his constant companion, even when he sat up drinking all night. When she was about

15 he sent her to his son in Istanbul, perhaps with the thought that the son would find her a suitable husband. The move was an unfortunate one for Kanarya. The son's wife was jealous of her, relations were difficult, and Kanarya asked to be sold.

She was taken to a slave merchant named Bedestanlı Ali Bey and sold to a high official. This man had only one wife, but it was his practice to buy slave girls to be his *odalık*s but introduce them into the household as his wife's attendants. He bought Kanarya for this purpose, lodging her first at his sister's house until he could prepare his wife. Finally he took her to his wife, who accepted her and named her Kanarya. What her name or names were before is not known.

Though she shared her husband with concubines, the pasha's *hanım* ruled the household; even the pasha was a little afraid of her. She disliked make-up and refused to let the *cariye*s use it. If a *cariye* aroused her ire, she banished her downstairs to the servants' quarters. When Kanarya entered the household there was another *odalık* named Dilfüruz. The pasha seemed to prefer her, but his wife had a liking for Kanarya, perhaps because Kanarya was clever enough to defer to her. In any event, at one point Dilfüruz was banished downstairs, while Kanarya was privileged to eat at the table of the pasha and his lady. No doubt Dilfüruz did not forget this.

When the pasha wanted Dilfüruz or Kanarya to enliven his bed, he simply sent for her. The *hanım* pretended not to notice, but she laid down one rule: there were to be no children by concubines, and there were none during her lifetime. However, he had children by his wife, one of them a daughter.

In time the *hanım* grew ill, and Kanarya attended her till she died. Now the daughter became mistress of the household. Now, too, Dilfüruz took advantage of the pasha's preference for her and became extremely difficult to get along with, so much so that the pasha's daughter encouraged Kanarya to stand up for herself. There came a day when Dilfüruz pushed Kanarya too far. She took Kanarya's clothes out of a washtub and put her own in. Dilfüruz had long hair down to her waist, and Kanarya pulled it, after which the two girls got into a brawl. The result, undoubtedly a surprise to Dilfüruz, was that the pasha was angry at both of them and decided to sell them. It was only through the intercession of his daughter that he changed his mind and set them free instead.

A free, unmarried slave had no means of support, so Kanarya was put into an *araba* and taken to the household of an aide of the pasha, one Hacı Pasha, who had a house near Fatih. It was not long before a widowed official asked for her in marriage. The fact that she had been another's concubine was not a disadvantage; in fact her former master's high position probably gave her status. Her husband changed her name, this time for life.

Now that she had her own household, her whereabouts became known to her sister in the palace. The younger woman, who had become Nem'i Kalfa, drove out of the *saray* with an escort of six to pay a call on her. The girls, apart from babyhood, did not even know what one another looked like. But, whether they had little to talk about or whether they felt restrained by *saray* etiquette, the visit was short. They were to see each other only once more. On one of the rare days when the *saraylıs* were allowed outside visitors, the erstwhile Kanarya went to Dolmabahçe Palace to visit Nem'i Kalfa.

The rest of the story concerns their mother. For seven years she had had no news of her children. The younger one was shut away in Dolmabahçe; the older one had disappeared. People told her the children were dead. She took to visiting cemeteries and searching for their names on tombstones. Finally she went back to Bandırma whence she had fled—to find that her husband had just remarried. Delighted by her return, her husband at once divorced his new wife. Still, from time to time, Kanarya's mother returned to Istanbul to visit a woman in whose household she had once served and, on one of those trips, she somehow learned that her daughter was in a certain pasha's house. She told her story to the pasha's servants, who smuggled Kanarya downstairs for a reunion made all too brief by Kanarya's being missed by the *kalfa* and ordered back upstairs again. Whether the mother ever made contact with her younger daughter is not known.

Aside from disappointing reunions with her sister and her mother, Kanarya's story had a happy ending, which is more than Turkish novelists allowed their slave heroines. Slavery was a natural theme for the sentimental novel of the turn of the century, and Samipaşazade Sezai (1850-1936) squeezed every teardrop out of it in his *Sergüzeşt* (*Adventure*), the story of a runaway slave named Dilber. She was sold the first time for 40 gold liras, a few years later for 60 liras, and finally for 150. The slave merchant who sold her the last time said that if she had been more beautiful her price would have been 200 liras.[75]

The typical runaway slave of Ottoman fiction followed a set procedure. She took nothing that did not belong to her; she carried her belongings in a *bohça*, she left her slippers beside the door or garden gate as a sign of her departure; and she betook herself to a slave merchant for resale, often to the one who had previously sold her.[76] This, Sezai described step by step—the departure of Dilber, a child of nine, from the clutches of a cruel mistress and a cruel Negro slave, Taravet:

Taking off the dress the woman had given her in a highly majestic manner, she opened the cupboard. She took out the Circassian kalpak and coat cast into a corner.... The light of the oil lamp, weak and thin like her star of hope, showed a child's coat thrown onto a cushion, a torn *entari*, and Taravet plunged in heavy slumber. She must decide what to take with her. Opening the *bohça* into which she used to put her school things, she first of all placed in it her little doll . . . then an apple, and two little pieces of iron that resembled rings . . . all the possessions she owned in the world.[77]

But she remains unlucky. After two more unhappy experiences with her owners, she throws herself into the Nile.

Sergüzeşt was written at the end of the nineteenth century, by which time considerable feeling had been aroused against the slave trade. Though it had long since been prohibited by law, slavery was still an issue because of its continuing practice. Pressure for interfering in the trade came first from the West. In 1850 the British Ambassador, Sir Stratford Canning, persuaded the Sublime Porte to forbid the transport of slaves on Turkish ships.[78] Yet so old and established a practice could not so easily be ended. In the following years the Porte issued a succession of orders restricting the slave trade. In 1854 it addressed a *ferman* (imperial edict) to the pasha of Batum on the Black Sea, commanding him not only to enforce with vigor the order against the buying and selling of women and children, but also to ferret out the victims of the slave traffic and restore them to their families. At the same time instructions were given to the pasha of Trabzon and officials of other Black Sea districts to forbid the debarkation of slaves. These orders were obviously Western-inspired, overlooking as they did the fact that most slaves did not want to be returned to their families.

There was now the question of what to do with the slaves who had been purchased before the embargo. In 1869 an *emirname* (written command) was issued to Izmir allowing trade in slaves bought before the prohibition on their importation, provided they had been purchased for a specific reason. Only two years later the Porte reversed itself and sent a circular letter to the *vali*s (governors) of all the *vilayet*s (provinces) demanding the closing of all slave markets and ordering prison terms for anyone engaging in the slave trade.[79]

Yet the trade went on, tolerated though illegal. The constitution forced on Abdülhamit II by Mithat Pasha in 1876 provided that all subjects of the Empire, including slaves, be free. Since it was very soon suspended, it had no effect on slavery until revived by the Young Turks in 1908.[80]

European efforts to stop the slave traffic did more harm than good, for the trade simply went underground. It was then that the girls were shipped during the winter months, herded into unsafe little vessels that sometimes sank, with the result that more girls were shipped out in order to replace the losses. Yet the Westerners kept on trying. In 1856-1857 Lady Blunt's brother and brother-in-law made a trip into the Caucasus with the aim of persuading parents to stop selling their children. They equipped themselves with presents of *lokum*[81] and finery, only to have their gifts refused. Mothers were indignant at what they felt were attempts to keep their daughters from getting to Istanbul and advancing themselves. Each had a vision of her daughter entering the *saray* and becoming *valide sultan*.[82]

Some Ottoman families themselves took a hand in mitigating slavery by liberating their slaves after a certain period, usually seven years.[83] Ahmet Vefik Pasha (1823-1891), and his father before him, refused to have slaves in their household.[84]

In any case, since there was no social stigma connected with being a slave in the Ottoman Empire, slave girls were quickly absorbed into the population. Yet as the ideas of the French Revolution spread in the Empire and men became more concerned with individual rights, the institution of slavery came to be looked upon with disfavor. The Turks who grew up in the great houses at the turn of the twentieth century remember the attendants in their households as being free. The slaves they knew belonged to the generation of their grandparents.[85]

At the end of the nineteenth century Ottoman writers took up the anti-slavery cause, not only in novels like *Sergüzeşt*, but in tracts as well. By the time the Young Turk movement was in full force the institution of the *cariye*, except for the palace and perhaps in certain other instances, was just about over. Celâl Nuri, writing in the period of the Balkan Wars (1912-1913), castigated concubinage and slavery as immoral and injurious to the institution of the family. He quoted a certain Cenap Bey, who had called the Caucasian countries *harar*s (stud farms) for the production of *cariye*s.[86]

In any case, by then the sources of *cariye*s had dried up. With the absorption of the Circassians into the population, there must have been very few of them available for the slave market. Moreover, Russian ownership and surveillance of the slave ports of the Caucasus inhibited the flow of slaves from that direction.

The Young Turks took the final step in the outlawing of slavery in 1908.[87] Though two years earlier a doctor in Izmir had reported examining five slave girls for sale within a month,[88] and five years later U.S. Ambassador Morgenthau was to complain about what he called the white-slave trade,[89] the institution of the *cariye*, whether concubine or attendant, was quickly fading. In many of the *konak*s and *yalı*s the girls had for some time been legally free. A change in attitude made slavery seem decadent rather than fashionable. Even more important, a change in the way of life was forced on the Ottoman grandees by the loss of land and income upon the contraction of the Empire, which made the large patriarchal household, with its numerous *cariye*s, an economic impossibility.

NOTES

1. Johann Schiltberger, *The Bondage and Travels of ——, a Native of Bavaria, in Europe, Asia, and Africa, 1396-1427*, p. 178, translator's note 11a, which says that the Circassians had been known to Strabo and Procopius as slave dealers.

2. G. I. Bratianu, *Recherches sur le commerce génois dans la Mer Noir au XIIIè siècle*, pp. 228-230.

3. Georges Bernard Depping, *Histoire du commerce entre le Levant et l'Europe depuis les Croisades jusqu'à la fondation des colonies d'Amérique*, II, pp. 171, 104-105, 208-209, 230-231. *See* also Bratianu, *Recherches*, p. 226, for slave markets in Nice and Montpellier.

4. Depping, *Histoire*, II, pp. 208-209.

5. Ibid., II, pp. 171, 296.

6. Wilhelm Heyd, *Histoire du commerce du Levant au Moyen-Âge*, II, pp. 555-563.

7. Depping, *Histoire*, II, pp. 321-322.

8. Vilhelm Thomsen, "Inscriptions de l'Orkhon déchiffrées," *Mémoires de la Société Finno-Ougrienne*, V (Helsinfors, 1896), pp. 99, 107, 113.

9. Carl Brockelmann, *History of the Islamic People with a Review of Events, 1939-1947*, p. 118; Aly-Akbar Mazahéri, *La Famille irannienne au temps anté-islamiques* (Paris, 1938), p. 135.

10. Emine Foat Tugay, *Three Centuries, Family Chronicle of Turkey and Egypt*, pp. 303-312. As Samuel S. Cox emphasizes (*Diversions of a Diplomat in Turkey*, pp. 541-544), there was no resemblance to the situation portrayed in *Uncle Tom's Cabin* in the Ottoman treatment of slaves.

11. Edward S. Creasy, *History of the Ottoman Turks*, pp. 182-183.

12. İsmail Hakkı Uzunçarşılı, *Osmanlı tarihi*, III, pp. 2, 138.

13. Tugay (*Three Centuries*) and Seniha Moralı (personal interview, July 1966) make the point that girls often voluntarily gave themselves up to be sold.

14. Mehmet Ziki Pakalın, "Esir tuccarı," *Osmanlı tarih deyimleri ve terimleri sözlüğü*, I, pp. 554-555; Essad-Bey, *Twelve Secrets of the Caucasus*, p. 81.

15. Aubrey de la Motraye, *Travels Through Europe, Asia, and into Parts of Africa*, II, p. 76.

16. When Fanny Blunt visited a Circassian camp in Bulgaria, men and women came up to her party offering to sell their children (Fanny Blunt, *The People of Turkey*, I, p. 146).

17. Lucy M. J. Garnett, *Turkish Life in Town and Country*, p. 78.

18. Wilhelm von Freygang, *Letters from the Caucasus and Georgia*, pp. 150-152.

19. Félix de Fonton, *La Russie dans l'Asie Mineure*, pp. 124, 136, 138.

20. Elias Habesci, *The Present State of the Ottoman Empire*, pp. 157-158.

21. Edmund Spencer, *Travels in Circassia, Krim Tartary, etc.*, II, p. 373; Schiltberger, *Bondage and Travels*, p. 50: "Item, a country called Starchas, which lies by the Black Sea, where the people are of the Greek faith; but they are a wicked people, because they sell their own children to the Infidels, and steal the children of other people, and sell them." *See* also p. 177, n. 11, where Starchas people are identified as Cherkes or Circassians. *See* also Hurşit Paşa, "Cariyeler hakkında, saray hatırları," *Hayat tarih mecmuası*, 5, (*Haziran*, 1965), p. 60.

22. Habesci, *The Present State*, p. 175; Freygang, *Letters*, p. 175.

23. Adolphus Slade, *Record of Travels in Turkey, Greece, etc.*, II, pp. 240-241.

24. Personal communication from Seniha Moralı.

25. Julia Pardoe, *The City of the Sultans and Domestic Manners of the Turks in 1836*, I, p. 312.

26. Personal interview with Seniha Moralı, July 1966.

27. The girls were housed in a large, 300-room *han* (inn) in the Slave Market (Pakalın, "Esir tuccarı," p. 555). For a detailed description of the Slave Market in the 1840s, *see* Charles White, *Three Years in Constantinople*, II, pp. 279-284.

28. İbrahim Hakkı Konyalı, "Cariyeler ve esir pazarı," *Türk dünyası* (15 *Mart*, 1960), pp. 72-74, which quotes *Muhimme defteri* #78, Başbakanlık Arşivi.

29. De la Motraye, *Travels*, I, p. 189; Rev. R. Walsh, *A Residence in Constantinople*, II, p. 2; White, *Three Years*, II, p. 317; Konyalı, "Cariyeler"; R. Brunschvig, " 'Abd," *EI²*, I, p. 28.

30. Tahsin Öz, *İstanbul camileri*, I, p. 52 and p. 52, n. 109.

31. Cevdet Türkay, "Esircilerle ilgili bir belge," *Belgelerle Türk tarihi dergisi*, 2 (*Auğustos* 1968), p. 60.

32. Pakalın, "Esir tuccarı," pp. 553-554; Tugay, *Three Centuries*, pp. 303-312; Melek Hanım, *Thirty Years in the Harem*, pp. 124-128.

33. Lady Mary Wortley Montagu, *Letters*, pp. 129-131, 133, 148, 156; Slade, *Records of Travels*, II, pp. 316-317.

34. Slade, *Records of Travels*, II, p. 242.

35. R. Robert Madden, *Travels in Turkey, Egypt, Nubia and Palestine in 1824, 1825, 1826 and 1827*, I, p. 41. *See* 'Allī Marghīnānī, *The Hedaya, or Guide*, p. 600: "It is permitted to a man to touch a female slave when he has an inclination to buy her, notwithstanding he may be apprehensive of lust."

36. Melek Hanım, *Thirty Years*, p. 125. Fifty years later Leylâ Saz gave the price of a *cariye* as from 300 to 600 lira. *See* Pakalın, "Esir pazarı," *Deyimler ve terimler*, I, pp. 553-554. White (*Three Years*, II, p. 285) gives more detail: "The average price of newly imported slaves at Yessir Bazary is as low as 1500 piastres (not £14), and never exceeds 2500. The ordinary price for second-hand slaves, clean, healthy, and well instructed, averages from 2500 to 3000, and never exceeds 5000. White women sold in this bazar, when young and without defects, average from 10 to 15,000 piastres. The maximum according to the dellâl [*tellâl*, or broker] was 45,000; but this is rare, and only in cases of great beauty, extraordinary accomplishments, and virginity, as sometimes occurs when death of proprietors, or other circumstances, throw the whole contents of a harem on the market." Z. Duckett Ferriman (*Turkey and the Turks*, p. 110) writes that a child sold for £40 to £80, but that a full-grown girl brought ten times as much. He was writing after slavery was officially abolished, but when it was still secretly practiced.

37. Samuel S. Cox, *Diversions of a Diplomat*, p. 543.

38. Pakalın, "Esir pazarı." Samuel Cox thought the Circassian girls came from inferior tribes after the Russian conquest of Circassia. He recounts: "A captain of a Black Sea steamer has insisted that out of a thousand girls and women whom he carried to the capital, the great majority were ugly, most of them half famished, and all of them dirty" (*Diversions of a Diplomat*, p. 541). Their half-famished condition gives a clue as to why they were sold, and they may have been dirty because of the lack of water aboard ship. However, in view of the great number of handsome Circassians who entered the households of Istanbul in the late nineteenth century, we doubt the captain's statement that most of them were ugly, although deprivation and lack of care may have made them seem so at the time.

39. Melek Hanım, *Thirty Years*, p. 125.

40. Pakalın, "Esir pazarı," pp. 553-554. On the sale of infants, *see* Marghīnānī,

The Hedaya, p. 279: "It is abominable to separate two infant slaves (or an infant and an adult) related within the prohibited degrees, by a sale of one of them."

41. By the early twentieth century male doctors were examining the girls (Sir Edwin Pears, *Forty Years in Constantinople*, p. 336).

42. Robert Mantran, *Istanbul dans la seconde moitié du XVIIè siècle*, pp. 334, 506-509.

43. Garnett, *Turkish Life in Town and Country*, pp. 79-80. This was at the turn of the twentieth century. In earlier times the girls would certainly have been resold at a younger age.

44. Pakalın, "Esir pazarı," p. 553.

45. Mithat Sertoğlu, "Pencik," *Resimli osmanlı tarihi ansiklopedisi*, pp. 264-265.

46. Brunschvig, " 'Abd," *Encyclopaedia of Islam*, second edition, I, p. 29.

47. Pakalın, "Pencik," *Deyimler ve terimler*, II, pp. 366-367. Pakalın ("Pencik kanunu," *Deyimler ve terimler*, II, pp. 767-768) gives an account of this law. It was originally formulated at the end of the fifteenth century to regulate the disposition of slaves taken in raids. According to Sertoğlu ("Beççe," *Resimli osmanlı tarihi ansiklopedisi*, p. 38), there were six classes of women war captives:

Şirhor - nursing babies

Duhterek - girls from three to eight

Duhter - girls from eight to twelve

Umm-ül-velet - girls who had reached adulthood

Mariye - women past their prime

Fertute - very old women

To these Pakalın adds *ma'yube* (with a defect), *bimare* (sick), *yekdest* (with a single hand), *yekçeşm* (with a single eye), and omits *şirhor*.

48. Pakalın, "Esir tuccarı," pp. 554-555.

49. İsmail Mevlevî, *Mecmua-ı esamı-ı cariye*, Belediye kütüphanesi, M. Cevdet collection, K63. The writer is indebted to Dr. Necat Göyünç for calling this work to her attention.

50. Personal communication from Seniha Moralı, 1966.

51. Tugay, *Three Centuries*, p. 308; personal interview with Nazli Tektaş, August 1966; Melek Hanım, *Thirty Years*, pp. 51, 168; personal interview with Seniha Moralı, July 1966.

52. De la Motraye writes that slaves were "taught to please, to excite desire by dancing wantonly, singing amorous songs and playing instruments. It is the Turkish fashion for women to caress men, call them emperors or kings of their hearts, souls, etc. Merchants give slaves this amorous education, but take care they don't put it into practice before they are sold" (*Travels*, I, p. 189).

53. Pardoe, *The City*, I, p. 25.

54. Pakalın, "Dadı," *Deyimler ve terimler*, I, p. 388.

55. The ladies of James E. P. Boulden's party (*An American Among the Orientals*, pp. 93-94) were received into the harem of Fuat Pasha, then Foreign Minister. There they were entertained, in the presence of Fuat's wife, by a young

Circassian slave who played Italian and Turkish airs for them on the piano. This girl was later married to Fuat's son.

56. S. A. Tokarev, "The Caucasus," multigraphed translation from the Russian by Aert Kuipers (Columbia University, n.d.), p. 72.

57. Information on Şehriban Hanım from her grandson, Mithat Akçit.

58. Tugay, *Three Centuries*, p. 310.

59. Personal interview with Perihan Arıburun, November 1967.

60. Halide Edip, *Sinekli bakkal*, p. 22.

61. White, *Three Years*, II, p. 321.

62. *'umm-al-walad*, an Arabic term meaning "woman who has borne a child."

63. White, *Three Years*, II, p. 349.

64. Tugay, *Three Centuries*, p. 50.

65. "Alemdar 'ın evlât ve torunları," *Tarih dünyası*, Tarih kütüphanesi No. 3, p. 39.

66. Personal interview with Seniha Moralı, July 1966.

67. Personal interview with Nazli Tektaş, August 1966.

68. Tugay, *Three Centuries*, p. 192.

69. Personal interview with Fahir İz, June 1966.

70. Brunschvig, " 'Abd," p. 28.

71. Pakalın, "Esir tuccarı," pp. 554-555.

72. Pardoe, *The City*, II, p. 121.

73. Melek Hanım, *Thirty Years*, pp. 84-95.

74. Pakalın, "Esir tuccarı," pp. 554-555; personal interview with Merzuka Nayır, August 1966.

75. Samipaşazade Sezai, *Sergüzeşt*, passim; excerpts from the unpublished anthology of Turkish literature of Fevziye Abdullah Tansel, 1960. For a novel of a slave girl, *see* also Pierre Loti, *Aziyadé*.

76. Pakalın, "Esir tuccarı," pp. 554-555.

77. Samipaşazade Sezai, excerpts from *Sergüzeşt*, Tansel anthology.

78. Pears, *Forty Years*, p. 366.

79. Grégoire Aristarchi Bey, *Législation ottomane*, II, pp. 35-36. A mixed commission was set up in 1870 to inspect for slaves all ships of the Egyptian Aziziye Company (pp. 36-37).

80. Brunschvig, " 'Abd," p. 37. According to Ali Haydar Midhat (*The Life of Midhat Pasha*, p. 112), Mithat wrote a draft of the *hat-i hümayun* for the inauguration of Abdülhamit II which proclaimed the abolition of slavery. Abdülhamit excised the whole paragraph.

81. The candy called "turkish delight."

82. Blunt, *My Reminiscences*, pp. 44-46.

83. Tugay, *Three Centuries*, p. 304.

84. Austin Henry Layard, *Autobiography and Letters*, II, p. 47.

85. Personal interviews with Emine Foat Tugay and Seniha Moralı, July-August, 1966.

86. Celâl Nuri, *Kadınlarımız*, pp. 139-141. The Cenap Bey whom he mentions is perhaps Cenap Şahabeddin (1870-1934), a teacher, poet, and contributor to the *Servet-i Fünun*, the distinguished literary magazine.

87. Pakalın, "Esir tuccarı," p. 555.

88. Pears, *Forty Years*, p. 366.

89. Henry Morgenthau, *Ambassador Morgenthau's Story*, p. 156.

7

Divorce

An Ottoman marriage could be dissolved in various ways under Islamic law.[1] The most frequently employed was *talâk*, divorce by repudiation. There were two types of *talâk*: repudiation according to the Sunna, which was both approved and legal; and repudiation according to *bid'at* (innovation), which was disapproved but nonetheless legal. Approved *talâk* could be categorized as *ahsan* (very good), or *hasen* (good). To obtain an *ahsan* divorce the husband needed only to pronounce his wife divorced during the time when she was canonically free from impurity, and then abstain from marital relations with her for the next three months, the period called *iddet*.[2] During these three months, he could change his mind and take her back; otherwise, at the end of *iddet*, the divorce became final and irrevocable. To obtain a *hasen* divorce the husband had to pronounce his wife divorced during each of three successive but not necessarily consecutive periods of purity. If only one or two declarations of repudiation had been made, the husband could resume his marriage during the *iddet* without any formality. If the *iddet* had expired, he had to go through another *nikâh* (marriage ceremony). The marriage was irrevocably dissolved upon the third pronouncement, after which the husband could remarry his ex-wife only if she first married another man, consummated the marriage, was divorced by him, and then observed three months of *iddet*.[3] If the wife turned out to be with child during a period of *iddet*, there could be no divorce until after the birth of the baby.

The wording of the divorce pronouncement was simple. The man had only to say, in the presence of two male Muslim witnesses, "*Seni boşadım*" ("I divorce thee") or "*Boşsun*" ("Be divorced").[4] If he said it thus clearly, he did not need to give any further explanation of intent. He was, however, allowed to use more ambiguous phraseology if he chose, such as "Cover thy face, thy *nikâh* is in thy hands,"[5] but this required an accompanying declaration of intent. The words did not have to be pronounced face to face. Divorce was equally legal upon the delivery of a *boş kağıdı* (divorce paper) by mail or by telegraph.[6] It was not necessary to let the woman state her side of the case, as Melek Hanım found out. Kıbrıslı divorced her without even a talk with her.[7]

The *bid'at*, or disapproved-of repudiation, was less frequently used. Such a divorce could be obtained by making a triple declaration of divorce during one period of purity, or by making a single declaration stated as irrevocable, either verbally or in writing. Both were regarded as sinful but allowable under Hanafi law. In certain cases Hanafi law allowed the husband to pronounce a divorce during a period of impurity. All *bid'at* divorces were irrevocable from the moment of pronouncement.

A man of sound mind never needed to state his grounds for divorce, but a woman seeking divorce did, and very few grounds were allowed her, especially by the Hanafis. Under Hanafi law, as practiced in the Ottoman Empire, a woman had the right to petition the court to dissolve her marriage only if her husband failed to support her or was impotent.[8] There may have been cases where she was allowed a divorce on the grounds of desertion or maltreatment, if the courts applied the rules of other schools of law.

Hanafi law gave women one other possibility of freeing themselves from an unhappy marriage through the rule that "a divorce pronounced under compulsion or under the influence of intoxication" was valid. In the Ottoman Empire women used this provision to get rid of dissolute husbands by producing witnesses to swear before a *kadı* that their husbands had divorced them when drunk.

Islam also allowed divorce by mutual consent. But there was a difference of opinion among the *ulema* as to whether or not a woman had to relinquish her dowry in this type of divorce.[9]

In addition, there was the provision that the wife was able to get a divorce by virtue of her husband's having delegated his right of divorce to her in the marriage contract. Such a divorce was known as *talâk-ı tevkil*, repudiation by deputy.[10]

Finally, Islamic law permitted dissolution of a marriage by means of what Fyzee terms judicial process, which could take two forms. First: If a husband swore in court that his wife had been unfaithful but was unable to prove his charge, the wife was entitled to dissolve the marriage.[11] Second: It was at least theoretically possible for a wife to get an annulment of the marriage. Annulment was granted when a woman who had been married as a minor desired to annul the marriage on reaching majority, as well as in cases of an obvious mismatch, such as that of a woman of good family having eloped with a servant.[12]

Whatever her grounds, it seems clear that in most circles it was socially unacceptable behavior for a woman to initiate a divorce. Such action was resorted to only by women of position, mainly the sisters and daughters of the sultan.[13]

The ease with which a man could divorce his wife could lead him to act rashly and on flimsy evidence. Such was the case of an Ottoman diplomat who stood up at the table one day, pronounced "I divorce you" to his wife, and stalked out of the house, never to return. He thought that she had put poison into his coffee, but what she had actually done was to pour in a love potion in the hope of strengthening his love for her. The diplomat was Kâzim Bey, one-time ambassador to Washington, and his wife was Lûtfiye Hanım, daughter of the Minister of Education, Zühtü Pasha.[14]

Lûtfiye was a remarkable woman who, though her life bridged the change from Empire to Republic, clung to the old ways. She held court in her father's *konak* on the Asiatic shore of the Bosphorus, gradually selling off her property in order to maintain the old-time tradition of hospitality. Her house was always full of servants, relatives, and friends. She had nine devoted grandchildren who visited her frequently. Friends sometimes came for long periods, one of them prolonging a visit to four years. Each evening she insisted upon being served her *rakı* and *mezeler* (assorted appetizers). Yet she was modern to the extent of discarding the veil after World War I and receiving men with her head uncovered. In her later years, when her family was scattered, she was persuaded by her friends to marry a rich provincial who had come courting. By now it was the days of the Republic, and she went through a civil ceremony. But when the bridal party got back to her house and she saw her new husband in the garden, gathering olives in a red bandanna like a peasant, that proved too much for the sensibilities of an Istanbul-born lady. She decided then and there she didn't want him for a husband, and to illustrate her determination not to go through with the marriage she threw herself down a stairway and broke her leg. The bridegroom went home to the country; the marriage was annulled.[15]

As to Kâzim Bey, who had made the hasty decision that changed their lives, his suspiciousness can perhaps be understood in light of the fact that he was close to Abdülhamit II and spent much time in the palace, with its atmosphere of fear and intrigue.[16]

Sometimes a wife's family would decide that divorce was necessary, as did Halide Edip's grandfather. Halide's mother's first husband had been a Kurd, who was fond of shooting off guns just for the fun of it. They were living *içeri* (with the wife's parents) and when the Kurd accidentally wounded someone Halide's grandfather arranged his daughter's divorce. Halide doesn't tell us what grounds he used. Her mother soon married the man who was to become Halide's father, a palace secretary by the name of Edip Bey. After her death, Edip Bey for a time lived polygamously with two wives, a situation that taught Halide first hand the anguish that polygamy could bring to a woman.[17] Later on, when her own husband took a second wife, Halide insisted on divorce, though she had been married nine years and had borne two sons, and her husband agreed to it reluctantly.[18]

Some women succeeded in divorcing husbands who neglected them. Seniha Moralı has communicated such a case to the author:

Hayriye Hanım was probably born in 1868. She came of a family of sheikhs. Her father's right to the administration of their *tekke* and mortmain estates was contested, and they were very poor. After her father's death she lived with her mother and grandmother in a house also of mortmain estate on a street sloping up the hill of Kanlica on the Bosphorus.

She was educated in a girls' school and learned music. She married an officer in the army. Their only child, a boy, died in infancy. Her husband was sent to Crete, and he neglected her. She sued for divorce.

One day she met a man on the street who said, "I love you!"

She answered, "How very sudden! I have been married now for seven years, and my husband is still hesitating about whether he loves me or not."

She finally obtained a divorce and married a man younger than herself, of a very good family but very poor, who had some small office in the municipality. She had another son.

They had very limited means, but life was easy in those days. In the middle class, harems were not as secluded as in the upper class. Men and women made calls together, went out together, had gatherings and parties together. Women covered their hair with veils. Hayriye Hanım attended to business herself and took legal proceedings to obtain her rights to the mortmain estates of her family. She hoped her son might become a sheikh in the *tekke* and to prepare him for that purpose asked the village *imam* to instruct him in Arabic.

Hayriye Hanım was very amusing and witty and had access to the houses of influential officials who helped her in her pursuit. Rich ladies had plenty of leisure and liked to receive women who could entertain them. Hayriye Hanım was a perfect mimic and related in a very amusing manner her experiences in the Ministry of Mortmain Estates.

After much trouble she obtained her rights to, and the accumulated revenues of, the mortmain estate, but her son refused to become a sheikh.[19]

The type of divorce which Westerners most often noted was the three-repudiation approved variety. There were many stories circulating about husbands who had changed their minds after repudiating their wives three times and then had to hire temporary husbands, sometimes *imams*, in order to fulfill the requirement of an intervening marriage. It was said that at times the temporary husband liked his duties so well he refused to give the woman up.[20]

The most frequent cause of divorce appears to have been childlessness.[21]

Whatever other reasons there may have been, Western observers generally agree that infidelity on the part of the woman was rarely one of them, for she was too restricted in her movements to have much opportunity for extramarital activity.[22]

The Turks themselves held a different view of women, believing them to be essentially amoral creatures forever looking for an opportunity to be naughty. Fazıl Bey, a Turk writing at the start of the nineteenth century, thought there were plenty of women who liked to dress up and go out, principally to the bazaar to carry on with the merchants.[23] He thought a man inclined to amiable pleasures soon discovered that women were more disposed to bad actions than to good.[24] Since Fazıl Bey's *Zenan-name* (*Book of Women*) was one of the most popular works in Turkey, it may be supposed that many Turks shared his opinion.[25] He portrayed the ideal Turkish woman of Istanbul as one who foreswore such illicit pleasures, who was "unaccustomed to appearing in public... her locks of hair never free to the caresses of the zephyr nor her face to the glances of the sun: solicitous of the honor of her reputation, she left her house neither night nor day."[26]

The woman able to carry on a love affair must indeed have been ingenious, for the whole neighborhood in which she lived guarded her virtue. The mere presence of an unfamiliar male in the harem was cause for suspicion. Neighbors could call in the local *imam* and, with him, invade the house in order to arrest the culprit.[27] Such a raid is described by Yakup Kadri Karaosmanoğlu in his short story, *Baskın* (*Raid*). The story starts with a lonely young man and a young widow carrying on an innocent flirtation by means of notes. Then, one snowy evening, the widow invites him in, and the young man, his loneliness and longing overpowering his good sense, obliges. The two are scarcely in one another's arms when the street door is pounded upon. A group of people force their way in and the young man, in terror, jumps out a window and is killed.[28]

The bleakness of this story points up the dangers facing adulterers in Ottoman Turkey. The law condemned them to stoning.[29] Istanbul had its favorite form of punishment: drowning in the swift waters of the Bosphorus. But this was frowned upon during the period in which Yakup Kadri Karaosmanoğlu was writing, namely, the last years of the Empire. Yet had the woman not been a widow, her husband would have had the right to kill her, although she would have had no such right over him in the event of his infidelity.[30]

This double standard set off a revolt that bore its first legal fruit in 1911, after the constitution had been reinstated and Parliament convened by the Young Turks. The members of Parliament who stood for women's rights questioned the fairness of the article of the Turkish Penal Code which gave a husband the right to kill an adulterous wife. Shouldn't the man caught in adultery also be punished? Wasn't he the more guilty, since social custom gave him opportunities for emotional satisfaction denied to women? The Parliament of 1911 thought so and made the adulterer liable to two years in prison and a fine of from five to 500 Turkish lira.[31]

By the beginning of the twentieth century, the state of the Turkish family and the legal disabilities of women were favorite topics of discussion among Turkish intellectuals, both in exile and at home. Ahmet Rıza and Sabaheddin both wrote on the subject.[32] Gökalp was instrumental in showing up the disadvantages of Ottoman marriage customs in a nation endeavoring to become modern and European. [33] It may be, as Fındıkoğlu thinks, that the tension generated by the transformation of the traditional Islamic society into a modern one resulted in an increase in the divorce rate.[34] At any rate, it resulted in forcing attention on the disadvantages of women in the matter of divorce.

In 1916 the feminist group made another breach in the Hanafi code. It succeeded in granting a woman the right of divorce in cases where the husband was suffering from certain incurable maladies. The question was put to the şeyhülislâm: "Should a woman whose husband has been seized, after marriage, with mental alienation, leprosy, elephantiasis, and certain other maladies be in a position to claim divorce?" To this, Mustafa Hayrı Efendi, the şeyhülislâm at the time, answered an unqualified "yes."[35]

The ferment over women's rights was a result of the stepped-up Westernization under the Young Turks. Magazines and newspapers increasingly carried articles about women, and periodicals, such as *Mehâsin* (*Beauty*) and *Süs* (*Ornament*),[36] were published especially for women readers. During this period, Celâl Nuri wrote his *Kadınlarımız*. We have already seen how he spoke out against polygamy. He was equally opposed to the ease and unfairness of divorce. He quoted from the Koran and from Hanafi scholars in an attempt to show that the ease with which divorce was obtained was contrary to the spirit of Islam. He had been much impressed by Sir Edwin Pears' book, *Turkey and Its People*, which castigated the three evils of polygamy, concubinage, and divorce as detrimental to the stability of Turkish family life.[37] This is a criticism one frequently runs into in books by Western observers.

Celâl Nuri agreed with Sir Edwin Pears that the Ottoman family lacked a solid foundation and thought this kind of instability put the Turk at a disadvantage in the competition with the West because "the government is based on the nation, the nation is based on the family, and the family is based on marriage."[38] That many women felt insecure in their marriages there can be no doubt. Even Melek Hanım's antic action of fraudulently producing a son (see below) was motivated by this feeling.

Celâl Nuri recommended a new divorce law which would conform to what he considered to be the true spirit of the Şeriat. Such a law would prohibit a man from divorcing his wife for trivial reasons, such as anger or whim, and would take into consideration the rights of the children. Even if divorced for good reasons, he thought the wife should receive more compensation than simply the amount of her dowry.[39]

Under Islamic law a husband was liable for the maintenance of his wife, an allowance called *nafaka*.[40] *Nafaka* was still due a wife during the three months of *iddet* after repudiation.[41] The amount was set according to the means and status of husband and wife, and among the upper classes it was usually a substantial sum. There were, however, cases in which the husband gave only token support: bread and a candle would be left at the door of the woman's room or apartment each day in order to abide by the letter of the law.[42] Whatever the amount of the *nafaka*, the husband was no longer liable for it after the *iddet*. He still had to continue to provide sustenance for any children by the divorced wife, for sons until they attained puberty and daughters until they married.[43] As for the repudiated wife, she had only her dowry money to live on for the rest of her life. If her family were without the means or the inclination to support her, she could be destitute.

Celâl Nuri also wanted to see marriage taken out of the hands of the *imams* and placed under civil jurisdiction, and he urged that civil records be kept. He thought the *düğün* a foolish expense:

Many a fortune goes for this purpose. Many people . . . sell their farms and borrow money, and all this money and effort is gone in one night. . . . I think it would be much better if the wedding were celebrated by only a dinner or such and the remainder of the money given into the hands of the wife and husband to begin life with some comfort.[44]

He wanted the age for marriage raised, so that the bride and groom might be physically mature enough for marriage and mentally mature enough to realize the seriousness of the step they were taking.[45]

A good deal of what Celâl Nuri called for was included in the Young Turks' Family Code of 1917. It allowed the bride and groom to contract for monogamy. It set the age limit at 17 for the bride and 18 for the groom, allowing for younger marriage only with the consent of the judge and, in the case of the bride, confirmation by her family that she had reached puberty. It upheld the right to immediate divorce if the husband had an incurable malady or had disappeared. It provided for a family council in case of disagreements, so that the wife might have the benefit of consultation with her relatives.[46] Perhaps most important of all, it made marriage subject to the jurisdiction of the Ministry of Justice, whereas it had been formerly under the jurisdiction of the *Mesihat*, the office of the *şeyhülislâm*. Therefore, in order to be legal, marriage now had to be performed by a magistrate or his substitute before two witnesses. No longer was solemnization by an *imam* sufficient.[47]

As Fındıkoğlu has pointed out, the new law was a compromise between the modern and the old Islamic concepts of marriage. With the *ulema* still a part of the state apparatus, this was as far as the reformers dared to go. It remained for public opinion, in a society that still tolerated the *baskın*, to catch up with the reformers.

Meanwhile divorce was resorted to, especially by the rich and powerful. One of the most notorious was that of Melek Hanım and Kıbrıslı Mehmet Pasha. Following the murder of a eunuch in Melek's household and the revelation that she had adopted a baby boy and passed him off as her own son, Kıbrıslı divorced her, handed her back her dowry, and confiscated her personal property. Reşit Pasha, who was grand vizier and had fallen out with Kıbrıslı, took Melek under his protection. She succeeded in getting a decision forcing Kıbrıslı to return her personal property, but before the *fetva* to seal it could be issued, Reşit fell from the vizierate and Kıbrıslı was appointed in his place. At this the *şeyhülislâm* refused to issue the *fetva*. This was by no means the end of the feud between Melek and Kıbrıslı. Kıbrıslı's daughter by Melek Hanım, Ayeşa, though married to the son of her father's second wife, fled from his household and joined her mother, which was a source of considerable embarrassment to Kıbrıslı. As a consequence, Ayeşa was, in turn, divorced by her husband. Finally, in 1866, to escape imprisonment, mother and daughter fled to Western Europe.[48]

A later divorce that stirred Istanbul was that of Abdülhamit II's daughter, Naime, and Mehmet Kemaleddin. It seems that Mehmet Kemaleddin had involved himself with Murat V's daughter, Hatice. Both he and Hatice were divorced by their respective spouses around 1900 as a result of the ensuing scandal.[49]

NOTES

1. Material on the dissolution of Islamic marriage is taken from A. A. Fyzee, *Outlines of Muhammedan Law*, pp. 128-144. *See* also 'Ali Marghīnānī, *The Hedaya, or Guide*, pp. 72-73. When other sources are used, they will be noted. Turkish orthography is used for Islamic terms in place of Arabic.

2. Fyzee (*Outlines*, p. 89) defines *iddet* as "the period of continence imposed on a woman on the termination of a marriage in the interest of paternity"; that is, the period required by law for a possible pregnancy to show itself. For the free woman the *iddet* was for three months, for the slave woman two months (Mansour Fahmy, *La Condition de la femme dans la tradition et l'évolution de l'Islamisme*, pp. 89ff).

3. One frequently reads that the reason for this provision was to make divorce more difficult. Fyzee says Muhammad decreed final dissolution of a marriage after three repudiations in order to prevent the Arabs from keeping a wife in the constant turmoil of being repudiated and taken back and thus without the protection of a steady husband (*Outlines*, p. 134). The intervening marriage was called *hülle* (H. C. Hony, with the advice of Fahir İz, *A Turkish-English Dictionary*, Oxford, 1957, p. 149).

4. A. Ziyaeddin Fahri Fındıkoğlu, *Essai sur la transformation du code familial en Turquie*, p. 8.

5. Lady Fanny Blunt, *The People of Turkey*, II, p. 81. *See* also Marghīnānī (*The Hedaya*) for other pronouncements by implication, such as "Be united unto your people" and "Veil yourself" (pp. 84-85).

6. Fındıkoğlu, *Essai*, p. 8. Also the writer knows of an instance of a woman, mother of two children, having been divorced by telegram. The incident was related to her in Istanbul in 1957 by a middle-aged woman who had been one of the two children. Fındıkoğlu thinks that repudiation, along with polygamy, is a non-Turkic institution that the Turks took over along with Islam. As evidence he points out that Mongol law forbids repudiation, and he considers the Uygurs the source of Mongol law (*Essai*, pp. 14-15).

7. Melek Hanım, *Thirty Years in the Harem*, p. 157.

8. Fındıkoğlu, *Essai*, pp. 8-9. If the husband was impotent he had to be allowed a year's probation before the divorce was granted, during which time sexual intercourse, if it occurred, barred the divorce. If the divorce went through, the woman was entitled to her entire marriage portion (Marghīnānī, *The Hedaya*, pp. 126-127).

9. Lucy M. J. Garnett (*Home Life in Turkey*, p. 219) says a woman could be released from marriage on grounds of her husband's desertion, cruelty, or neglect to maintain her according to status, and still receive her *nikâh* money; but if she left her husband without due cause, she forfeited her dowry.

10. Fyzee, *Outlines*, p. 134.

11. If a man charged his wife with adultery, he had to swear an oath to that effect, for which he was liable to the curse of God if it was false; the wife had the right to deny the charge on oath, and if she swore falsely she was subject to the wrath of God. When both parties had made their statements on the subject, they were divorced. However, in Hanafi law, if the husband admitted that he was wrong, he might marry his wife again (*see* Marghīnānī, *The Hedaya*, pp. 123-125).

12. Fyzee, *Outlines*, p. 92.

13. M. Abdolonyme Ubicini, *Letters on Turkey*, I, p. 153.

14. Interview with Nezih Manyas, Lûtfiye Hanım's grandson, April 1967.

15. Interview with Nezih Manyas.

16. Interview with Nezih Manyas.

17. Halide Edip, *Memoirs of Halide Edip*, pp. 128, 142-148.

18. Ibid., p. 308.

19. Personal communication from Seniha Moralı.

20. Blunt, *The People of Turkey*, II, pp. 84-85; Garnett, *Home Life in Turkey*, p. 220.

21. Princess Christina Trivolzio de Belgiojoso, *Oriental Harems and Scenery*, pp. 113ff.

22. An exception to this view was held by Lady Mary Wortley Montagu, who wrote in the early eighteenth century (*Letters from the Right Honourable . . . 1709-1762*, p. 116).

23. Fazil Bey [Fazıl Hüseyin Enderunlı], *Le Livre des femmes (Zenan-name)*, pp. 75-76.

24. Ibid., p. 83.

25. According to the translator of *Zenan-name*, this and another of Fazil Bey's

poetic works were suppressed by Mustafa Reşit Pasha, who "took pride in austerity" (Fazil Bey, *Le Livre*, p. 5).

26. Fazil Bey, *Le Livre*, pp. 75-76.
27. Ignatius Mouradgea d'Ohsson, *Tableau général de l'Empire othoman*, IV, pp. 347-348.
28. Yakup Kadri Karaosmanoğlu, "Baskın," *Bir serencam*, pp. 24-58.
29. D'Ohsson, *Tableau général*, IV, p. 352.
30. Fındıkoğlu, *Essai*, p. 32.
31. Ibid.
32. Ahmet Rıza (1859-1930), a member of the Young Turk movement, was the son of an Austrian mother and a Turkish father. A liberal, he fled to Paris where for some years he edited a publication called *Meşveret* (*Consultation*). Prince Sabaheddin (1877-1948) was the son of Sultan Abdülhamit II's brother-in-law, Damat Mahmut Pasha. He fled to Paris with his family because he could not persuade the sultan to restore the constitution (*see* Ernest Edmondson Ramsaur, Jr., *The Young Turks, Prelude to the Revolution of 1908*, pp. 22-26 and 54ff.). Ahmet Rıza published *La Crise de l'Orient* in Paris in 1907 and Sabaheddin "Les Turcs et le progrès" in *Revue* (Paris, 1905, série 4, pp. 433-448).
33. Fındıkoğlu, *Essai*, pp. 16-17.
34. Ibid.
35. Ibid.
36. Information supplied by Fevziye Abdullah Tansel.
37. Celâl Nuri, *Kadınlarımız*, p. 129.
38. Ibid., p. 193.
39. Ibid., pp. 154-155.
40. Fyzee, *Outlines*, p. 181. According to Mehmet Zeki Pakalın (*Osmanlı tarih deyimleri ve terimleri sözlüğü*, III, p. 642), *nafaka* literally means the means of subsistence for children, wife, and self, but in connection with divorce it is understood to mean food, clothing, and dwelling for children and wife.
41. Fyzee, *Outlines*, p. 162.
42. Melek Hanım, *Thirty Years*, p. 284.
43. Fyzee, *Outlines*, p. 183.
44. Celâl Nuri, *Kadınlarımız*, p. 192.
45. Ibid., pp. 191-193.
46. Fındıkoğlu (*Essai*, p. 44) seems to think that giving the wife the benefit of a family council was something new. It may have been new in Ottoman practice, but substantially the same thing is prescribed in the Koran (iv:35): "And if ye fear a breach between them twain, appoint an arbiter from his folk and an arbiter from her folk...."
47. Fındıkoğlu, *Essai*, p. 34ff. Fındıkoğlu, both in this work and in his study of Gökalp, attributes this law to Gökalp's influence. Yet it followed Celâl Nuri's recommendations so closely, he too must have had an influence on Parliament. The Family Code of 1917 was actually in effect a little less than two years and was abrogated in 1919 in a decree issued during the period of intervention of the Allied High Commission after World War I (*see* Mehmet Hıfzı [Timur], *Le Lien de mariage à travers l'histoire juridique turque*, p. 104). The Allied argument was that a purely civil marriage interfered with the privileges of the non-Muslim communities.
48. Melek Hanım, *Thirty Years*, pp. 188-193, 261-267, 321-324.

49. A. D. Alderson, *The Structure of the Ottoman Dynasty*, Tables XLIX, n. 7 and L, n. 11; Melek Hanum and Grace Ellison, *Abdul Hamid's Daughter*, passim. There was some opinion to the effect that Hatice was endeavoring to revenge her deposed father by intriguing against Abdülhamit's daughter.

8

Social Life Outside the Home

The daily life of the upper-class Ottoman woman was enlivened and enriched by a variety of diversions, many of which took place in the harem, but some of which took her outside the home. We shall here first discuss her out-of-the-house amusements. Of these, the most popular the year round throughout the centuries was the weekly visit to the *hamam*.

The institution of the public bath has a very long history that goes back at least to the Babylonians;[1] its Islamic version started with the Umayyads.[2] Of the Ottomans, it has been said that they took over the institution from the Byzantines,[3] but this is an error. In fact, baths were built in Turkic lands long before Fatih took Istanbul. For example, the Selçuks of Iran built baths and probably took as their models those of the Syrians whose baths, in turn, were based on the *thermae* of antiquity.[4] The Ottoman baths may go back, by an independent route, to the same sources as do the Byzantines'. The Ottomans often built their baths on Byzantine sites, owing to the availability of water there. Mamboury indicates that the Turks heated their baths rather more thoroughly than did their predecessors.[5] They also, according to Sourdel-Thomine, put emphasis on the steam room (*sıcaklık*) and the dressing room (*camekân*), which became a focus of social activity.[6]

In Istanbul, as in other Islamic cities, there was at least one *hamam* for each quarter (*mahalle*). Some were large, some small, depending on the clientele; some were single, having but one set of rooms devoted to men and women at different hours; some were double (the *çifte hamam*s), having a full set of rooms for each of the sexes. Among the *çifte hamam*s, one of the most notable is the bath known variously as the Ayasofya or the Haseki Hürrem Sultan Hamamı, which is situated at one corner of the park that lies between the Sultanahmet and Ayasofya (Santa Sophia) mosques. The entire structure is erected on one axis, the women's bath at one end, the men's at the other. It was built by the great Ottoman architect Mimar Sinan (1490-1588), and displays the satisfying sense of proportion for which he was famous.[7]

Though the large mansions and palaces were provided with private baths, the public bath had its own attractions. It was likely to be more evenly heated, and there a woman could enjoy the society of others of her kind. Women usually went in groups, taking with them their small children, including little boys up to nine.[8] The *hamam* day was particularly important as a diversion in the times before the *araba* and the tramway made more frequent visits possible.

The upper-class woman came to the bath equipped with her *hamam takımı* (bath set): towels (*peştemal* and *havlu*), purse (*kese*), bathing basin (*hamam tası*), and comb. This might be supplemented by a rug and cushions.[9] Raised above the wet floors on her inlaid *nalın* (clogs),[10] she went through the tepid room (*ılıklık*) to the warm room (*sıcaklık*). This was the bathing place. It might be a large, octagonal hall, like the one Julia Pardoe visited, where eight jets of water (*fiskiye*) splashed nearly 300 women wearing nothing but fine linen, which became so saturated it clung to the figure. Slaves stood about, naked from the waist up, their arms folded across their breasts and piles of embroidered and fringed napkins or towels balanced on their heads. The room was undoubtedly domed for light, and had a pool (*havuz*) in the center. A woman might bathe either in that pool or at one of the basins (*kurna*), which were situated along the wall in small compartments separated by low dividers and equipped with marble seats over which a rug might be thrown to soften the surface.[11]

Although often quoted, Lady Montagu's description of the Turkish bath is worth repeating, for it gives in words a picture as effective as the Ingres paintings of the Turkish bath that hang in the Louvre.[12] According to her, the *hamam*[13]

is built of stone, in the shape of a dome, with no windows but in the roof, which gives enough light. There were five of these domes joined together, the outmost being less than the rest, and serving only as the hall, where the portress stood at the door. Ladies of quality generally give this woman the equivalent of a crown or ten shillings. . . . The next room is a very large one paved with marble, and all around it, raised, two sofas of marble, one above the other. There were four fountains of cold water in this room, falling first into marble basins, and then running on the floor in little channels made for the purpose, which carried the streams into the next room, something less than this, with the same sort of marble sofas, but . . . so hot with streams of sulphur proceeding from the baths adjoining it. . . . The other two domes were the hot baths, one of which had cocks of cold water turning into it, to temper it to what degree of warmth the bathers have a mind to. . . .

The first sofas were covered with cushions and rich carpets, on which sat the ladies;

and on the second, their slaves behind them, but without any distinction of rank by their dress, all being in the state of nature . . . so many fine women naked, in different postures, some in conversation, some working, others drinking coffee or sherbet, and many lying negligently on their cushions, while their slaves (generally pretty girls of seventeen or eighteen) were employed in braiding their hair in several pretty fancies. In short, it is the women's coffee-house, where all the news of the world is told, scandal invented, etc. They generally take this diversion once a week, and stay at least four or five hours. . . .[14]

The *hamam* was the woman's beauty parlor. Here her hair was dyed with crushed laurel berries or henna, and her nails tinted with henna. Her hair was then braided. Her eyebrows were tweezed and dyed. The hair was removed from every part of her body with a yellow paste depilatory made of quicklime and perfumed wood ashes (*ot*), as was required of a Muslim woman. Her body was scrubbed with a serge glove and lathered with perfumed soap.[15] Lady Craven expressed the point of view of many Westerners when she said that the continual bathing of Turkish women was bad for them. She thought it made them look old.[16] Pardoe believed it brought on exhaustion.

In the *camekân*, the customer lounged, lunched, and listened to musicians, often joining in the singing. At times she watched dancing. Always she talked and gossiped. This was her day out. Yet there were Ottoman ladies who felt that their social position forbade them this type of relaxation and intimacy with other women, and who did their bathing in the family *hamam*, which usually consisted of three small rooms. (The imperial women, of course, used the palace harem *hamam*s exclusively). For them the *camekân*, instead of being a club room, became a boudoir where they were attended by their slave girls.[17]

The upper-class *hamam* became a victim of Westernization, but the old *mahalle* (neighborhood) *hamamı* still lingers in the poorer quarters of Istanbul and other cities.

The freeing of the Ottoman woman from her cloistered harem was effected not entirely by the spread of Western social ideas, but also by the development of new means of transportation. Foremost among these was the introduction of the *araba* (carriage) in the seventeenth century.

The word *araba* was used for many kinds of vehicles, from the simple cart to the fancy coach.[18] The original *araba* or *arba* seems to have been the high two-wheeled cart of the Turco-Mongols of Central Asia, and of the Scythians before them. Its floor was made of wicker, which gave it a spring-like resilience. It was often covered with a kind of hood, more or less decorated, and was drawn by one horse between shafts or, sometimes, by an ox or camel.[19]

The Ottomans not only elaborated on the simple *araba*, but also adopted the Hungarian coach, called *koçu*.[20] The latter was at first reserved only for royalty, but gradually this restriction was lifted and the upper classes began using the conveyance. Sultan İbrahim gave a highly ornamented *koçu* to one of his *kadıns*.[21] This was the first coach for ladies that has come to our attention. During this period, the seventeenth century, the *araba* was in such general use in Istanbul that the sultan complained of the clogging of the streets and banned it. His orders were not strictly heeded until one day, finding his way blocked by an *araba*, he flew into a rage, sent for the grand vizier, Salih Pasha, and ordered him strangled for failing to carry out his wishes. For a time after this the sultan's ban on the *araba* was strictly enforced, but gradually the authorities grew lax and the vehicles became plentiful again. This history of restriction and relaxation concerning the use of the *araba* was to be repeated several more times during the following two centuries.

By the time of the Lâle Devri (the Tulip Period) of the eighteenth century, *araba*s had proliferated and were very elaborate, being lined with multicolored silks and drawn by as many as three pairs of horses. Upper-class women paraded in them around Sadabad on the Golden Horn and in other places.[22] Lady Montagu, who was in Turkey during the reign of Ahmet III, took note of the painted and gilded lattices, the floral decorations, and the embroidered and fringed cushions of their interiors, but thought them too hot. She remarked that the ladies peeped through the lattices.[23] Some *araba*s, as a matter of fact, were made of latticework. Among the most handsome vehicles of this period was the four-horse bridal coach of Ahmet III's daughter, Fatma Sultan. Its iron frame, wheels, and rims were brought from Paris, but its body, with its elaborate decorations, was Ottoman-made. Unlike most of the early carriages, it was hung on springs in order to diminish the shaking that was characteristic of the ordinary *araba* as it rumbled over Istanbul streets.[24]

The Patrona Halil rebellion (1730) suppressed the use of the *araba* for a time, but by 1751 the reaction against this puritanism had set in and women were so frequently seen driving about Üsküdar, Çamlıca, and other pleasure places, that once again the authorities intervened and the grand vizier issued a *hüküm* forbidding the *araba* in public places. In that year there were 665 *koçu*s in Istanbul alone.[25]

However, by the end of the eighteenth century, *araba*s had once more become a favorite means of locomotion by upper-class Ottoman women, especially to reach excursion places. Lady Craven, supercilious as usual, said the women "hire what they imagine to be coaches, called *arabat*s—a vile machine like a covered cart, with rows of benches in the inside. There are no springs in them, and one day in a valley called 'Echelle du grand Seigneur,' I got into one, but chose rather to get out and walk six miles, than to be jolted unmercifully."[26] She appears to be describing the vehicle Melling depicted in one of his views of Büyükdere, in which women are seen riding in a Conestoga type of wagon.[27] Davey, in 1810, saw such vehicles issuing from the gate of Topkapı Palace. He called them "farm wagons with umbrella-shaped awnings of silk or satin embroidered with gold." He noticed that the Turks turned their backs when the *araba*s of the court ladies passed.[28] Şehsüvaroğlu shows a picture of the "farm wagon" type of vehicle, a four-wheeled wagon with low, decorated sides and an awning top. It is drawn by oxen and carries women in *feraces* (dustcoats) and *yaşmaks* (veils).[29]

In the nineteenth century, as Western influence became more pronounced, the types of *araba* became more varied. Charles White, writing in 1844, says that he used to watch the great men of the Empire returning home along the Divan Yolu (then Istanbul's principal avenue) in heavy open carriages brought from Vienna, low, "modern" phaetons and something he calls a chariot. But the ladies, even those of the sultan's family, often still used the old ox-drawn *araba* or the closed coach called *talika*.[30]

Europeans opened carriage-making shops in Istanbul. Abdülhamit II set up a factory for the manufacture of landaus and other carriages, which once more became so numerous they began to choke the streets. According to Rodinson, the two most popular types in this century were the *talika* and the *uzun araba*, or "long carriage." The former was "a sort of open fiacre, without a door, with a footboard surmounted by a small dais," and was generally used along the Bosphorous shore. The latter was "a sort of *char à banc*, also open, with doors at the back, furnished with curtains and two longitudinal banquettes."[31]

Pardoe, needless to say, took a ride in an *araba*:

Its form was that of a small covered waggon; its interior was all crimson cloth, blue silk fringe, and tassels; and its exterior precisely resembled a wedding cake of gilt gingerbread. Four round looking-glasses, just sufficiently large to reflect the features, were impannelled on either side of the doors; and in place of the windows we had gilt lattices, so closely made that our position was the very reverse of cheerful; and, as I found it, moreover, quite impossible to breathe freely, these lattices were flung back despite the cold, and this arrangement being made, I established myself comfortably on the satin cushions, with my feet doubled up under me *à la Turque*, amid the piled-up cushions of *duvet* and embroidery.[32]

This was a period when women drove about relatively freely. During the Rev. Walsh's stay in Turkey from 1820 to 1836 he saw the women going about in long "*arrhubas*," enclosed by curtains, eight to ten women sitting on the floor.[33] In 1834 the ladies of the marriage procession of Mahmut II's daughter, Saliha Sultan, rode in carriages and coaches decorated with stars.[34] White, a decade later, reports that "ladies drive in *araba*s drawn by oxen or in the *teleka*, a French style closed coach with curtained windows." He thought that the carriages and their bright *ihram*s (cloth coverings) gave "to the places of public resort an air of brilliancy and originality that defies description."[35]

Nevertheless, there were times when a husband objected to so much going about. Kethüdazade Arif Efendi was a learned man who gathered around him some of the most progressive men of his time, the first half of the nineteenth century. He married Esma Hanım, the daughter of the former *sadrazam* Koca Yusuf Pasha, who, as part of her trousseau, provided her with four Georgian slaves and a coach lined with starred red fabric. With this conveyance at her disposal, Esma Hanım took to visiting her mother and aunts so frequently that her husband objected. He urged her to stay home with him in their *konak* and, when she ignored his protests, divorced her.[36]

In Abdülmecit's period the women drove about in open landaus, guarded by eunuchs on horseback. Two women, daring too much for their time and place, threw kisses to a French officer as they passed him on Galata Bridge. No doubt thinking a gentleman could do no less, he threw kisses back, whereupon a eunuch struck him in the face. As the kisses had been too much for his gallantry, the insult was too great for his pride, and he pulled his sword and ran it through the eunuch. The result was an international incident. The French, however, maintained that their officer had been provoked, and the crisis subsided.[37]

In the mid-nineteenth century the pavements of Istanbul were so rough that they made "the use of carriages almost impossible," according to Nassau Senior, but still the *araba*s with their cargo of women traversed them.[38] Gautier, about 1875, heard merry voices as the gilded, painted, and curtained *araba*s passed, and sometimes glimpsed a lovely face with the veil thrown back. He noticed small girls too young for the veil sitting on the box in front, and thought their almond eyes, penciled brows, slightly aquiline noses, oval faces, and lips like parted pomegranates hinted at the harem ideal.[39]

This was the period when Edmondo de Amicis watched the carriages of the ladies "of the high aristocracy" as they came to the Dolmabahçe mosque on Fridays, when the sultan arrived there in procession to pray. He found them "guarded by gigantic eunuchs on horseback, motionless, on either side."[40]

During Abdülhamit II's time, despite his promotion of the carriage-making trade, *araba*s were in less general use for women than earlier, for social life was stifled under his oppressive rule.

In the 1870s the tramway was introduced, with its curtained-off section for women, and this greatly enhanced the mobility of women. Watching them in 1875, de Amicis thought they now had a new liberty, which they were using to the full:

It is amusing to watch one of them from a distance, and following her footsteps from afar, observe how she prolongs and spreads out the pleasure of vagabondizing. She enters a mosque near by to say a prayer, and stays a quarter of an hour under the portico chattering with a friend; then to the bazaar to look in at a dozen shops and turn two or three upside down in search of some trifle; then she takes the tramway, gets out at the fish market, crosses the bridge, stops to contemplate all the braids and wigs in the hair dresser's windows, in the streets of Pera, enters a cemetery and eats a sweet meat, sitting on a tomb, returns to the city, goes down to the Golden Horn, turning a hundred corners, and glancing at everything out of the corner of her eye—shop-windows, prints, placards, advertisements, people passing, carriages, signs, theatre doors—buys a bunch of flowers, drinks a lemonade, gives alms to a poor man, crosses the Golden Horn in a caique, and walks about Stamboul; there she takes the tramway again, and arriving at her own door, is capable of turning back, to make the tour of a small group of houses.... Any poor corpulent *efendi* who should try to follow his wife to spy out her actions, would be left behind before half the journey was accomplished.[41]

Despite the tramway, the great families still kept their *araba*s. As late as 1917 there were so many of them, and their passengers were deemed so arrogant, that the newspaper *Tasvir-i efkâr* complained about it in an editorial.[42]

For transportation round and about Istanbul, very likely the oldest method, older than the *araba*, was the boat. In our period boats were of two kinds: either a ferry that plied the Bosphorus, its canvas-covered rear deck reserved for women,[43] or a *kayık* (caique). The caique was a twin-prowed craft, steered by a rudder and manned by oars, and so sensitive to movement that it easily tipped. "But," said American Ambassador Samuel B. Cox, "the Turkish lady has a cautious step, and an immobility when seated, which exactly suit the humor of the caique."[44]

Upper-class women favored a slim and elegant caique known as the lady's needle (*hanım iğnesi*),[45] but the most impressive were those known as swallows (*kırlangıç*), used by the imperial women.[46] Charles White saw the *valide* of his time, Besm-i Âlem, descend the Golden Horn in a richly ornamented, 14-oared craft in which she was seated on embroidered cushions atop a purple velvet carpet fringed with gold. Her *kethüda* and *haznedar* sat opposite her, their backs to the *kayıkcıs* (boatmen). Two eunuchs were on the after-deck, a third at the bow. Lesser imperial women followed in similar caiques, each caique attended by only two eunuchs and rowed by ten oars.[47] The caiques of "ladies of quality" were smaller and manned by fewer boatmen. When such a lady used a hired caique, "a crimson or dark blue *ihram*, fringed with gold, is spread over the cushions, and a part is left hanging over the side as a mark of distinction. Ladies of the higher classes are generally attended by a servant, or by a lalla (black slave), who sits cross-legged upon the after-deck, and shelters them from wind and sun with an umbrella."[48]

Melling has done an engraving of a party of two caiques at Büyükdere on the European shore of the Bosphorus in the early nineteenth century, showing women with white-swathed heads in one, men in turbans in the other.[49] Pardoe, in her time, found the caique the most comfortable way of getting from Pera to Yeni Kapı. It eliminated the joggling of the *araba* trip.[50] Boulden, in mid-century, saw caiques in the evenings at Sarayburnu, the women in them sometimes pushing aside their *yaşmaks*.[51] Senior reported hundreds of them at the Sweet Waters of Asia, carrying the *beau monde* of Istanbul. Women and children would be rowed along the Bosphorus shore summer evenings to listen to the song of the nightingale. The route took them past the valley of Balta Limanı on the European shore and across to the Bay of Kanlıca and the Sweet Waters of Asia, where the echo of the nightingale came through particularly well.[52] In the late afternoon the ladies of the family of the grand vizier, Kâmil Pasha, would go out on the Bosphorus from their Beylerbeyi *yalı* in *kayıks* rowed by stalwart Albanians. The *kayıkcıs* wore *şalvar* (baggy trousers), full-sleeved shirts, and boleros, and rowed with their heads to one side so as not to look at the women. The women took advantage of the plenitude of *kayıks* to visit with one another on the water.[53]

During the *mehtap* concerts (moonlight concerts on the water) the Bosphorus swarmed with caiques, some belonging to members of the upper classes who participated, some hired by people who came to look and listen.[54] The great families owned their own caiques and kept private *kayıkcıs*.[55]

The *kayıkcıs* were usually Greek, and always colorful-looking. Pardoe reports that in the summer they "wore shirts of silk gauze, of about the thickness of mull-muslin, with large, hanging sleeves, and bordered round the breast with a narrow scallopping of needlework; their ample trowsers were of white cotton, and their shaven heads were only partially covered by small skull-caps of red cloth, with pendant tassels of purple silk; their feet were bare."[56]

With ladies as well as with men, the number of pairs of oars allowed was fixed by rank. The *haznedar usta* (woman treasurer), who was one of the most important women in the imperial harem, was allowed three pairs, the sultan's daughters and *kadıns* five pairs, and the *valide* (if White counted correctly) seven pairs. Some caiques had small kiosks at the stern, some were entirely open. The caique was used for solemn occasions as well as for pleasure. When her son, Abdülmecit, died and Besm-i Âlem had to move to Topkapı (by then the Old Saray) she traveled by caique.[57]

An occasional mode of transportation was by sedan chair, or *sedye*. This was used in Istanbul chiefly by Christian and foreign women, but on a long overland trip it could be the means of conveyance of a great Ottoman lady. Melek Hanım traveled in one in the provinces when she was Kıbrıslı Mehmet Pasha's wife. She and her daughter fled by sedan chair to the boat that would take them to Western Europe, no doubt because it was unlikely that the authorities would have looked for Muslim women in that conveyance.[58]

Long journeys posed a problem for women until the end of the Empire. When Melek Hanım left Jerusalem, where Kıbrıslı Mehmet Pasha had been governor, she traveled back to Istanbul by a variety of conveyances—four days by litter to Akka, again by litter to Beirut, and, finally, by steamship to Istanbul. On board ship the entire salon was reserved for the pasha's harem. When he was appointed governor of Belgrade, his entourage took a packet boat from Istanbul to Varna, a smaller steamship to Vidin, flat boats drawn by oxen over the shallows of the Danube, and then a small river steamer to Belgrade.[59] As far as possible, journeys were made by water, since ships afforded the most comfort. They carried the traffic to Egypt, the provinces of the Black Sea coast, and the Adriatic littoral. Mary Mills Patrick once encountered the harems of prominent Turks aboard a Black Sea steamer.[60]

Even the building of railroads did not always solve the problem of a trip to a far-off place, since the rails did not reach outlying districts. Halide Nusret Zorlatuna tells of traveling from Mosul to Kirkuk, where her father was sent as governor in the early twentieth century. They had to spend days on the road in a crowded carriage and nights in congested village guest houses. When they reached a certain bridge called Altın Köprü (Golden Bridge), which dated from the time of Murat IV, they had to get out and walk, its arch being so high that it made the road too steep for safety. And traveling meant taking many things along.[61] The late Emine Foat Tugay describes the luggage her family carried with them, even to Europe: carryalls containing bed linen, pillows, blankets, and quilts, a thin mattress, and towels. They were accompanied by a retinue of people that included governesses, maids, and a valet.[62]

Even the move of an upper-class family from winter to summer konak was not easy. Lucy Garnett said they transported a minimum of belongings on these journeys, yet along went two bohças of clothing for each person, a few lamps and candlesticks, a couple of brass jugs and basins, some copper cooking pots, a coffee pot, and a modest array of glasses and crockery.[63] Both Garnett and Halil Hamit reported that the roads were "awful," and Lucy Garnett further said that in mountainous districts roads were often only torrent beds, bridges were few, and fording was often necessary.[64] Traveling was further complicated by the fact that a woman could not travel alone but had to be accompanied by her husband or a close relative.[65] It is clear why a guest, after the ordeal of her trip, expected to make her visit a prolonged one.

At the beginning of the eighteenth century, when the means of transportation were still rudimentary, home visits were rare. D'Ohsson said that when a woman came to visit she brought her small children and slaves along and usually stayed from fifteen to twenty days. Visits then were almost exclusively to relatives, and some women of large families spent the whole year continuously visiting.[66] There are no Turkish records available of early visits. However, we have the accounts of those wide-eyed Englishwomen, who have provided us with other descriptions.

Lady Montagu, the earliest of our period, called on the *kâhya's* (steward's) wife in Edirne in the spring of 1717, when the court was located there. She wrote an account of the visit to her sister:

I was met at the door by two black eunuchs, who led me through a long gallery between two ranks of beautiful young girls, with their hair finely plaited, almost hanging to their feet, all dressed in fine light damasks, brocaded with silver.... [I] entered into a large room, or rather pavilion, built round with gilded sashes, which were most of them thrown up, and the trees planted near them gave an agreeable shade.... On a sofa, raised three steps, and covered with fine Persian carpets, sat the *kiyaya's* lady, leaning on two cushions of white satin, embroidered; at her feet sat two young girls, the eldest about twelve years old, lovely as angels, dressed perfectly rich, and almost covered with jewels.... She stood up to receive me, saluting me after their fashion, putting her hand upon her heart with a sweetness full of majesty.... She ordered cushions to be given to me, and took care to place me in the corner, which is the place of honour....

She told me the two maids were her daughters, though she appeared too young to be their mother. Her fair maids ranged below the sofa, to the number of twenty. ...She made them a sign to play and dance. Four of them immediately began to play some soft airs on instruments, between a lute and a guitar, which they accompanied with their voices, while the others danced by turns.... When the dance was over, four fair slaves came into the room with silver censors in their hands, and perfumed the air with amber, aloes-wood, and other scents. After this they served me coffee upon their knees in the finest japan china, with soucoupes [*zarfs*] of silver, gilt. The lovely Fatima entertained me all this time in the most polite agreeable manner, calling me often *Guzel sultanum*, or the beautiful sultana....

When I took my leave, two maids brought me a fine silver basket of embroidered handkerchiefs; she begged I would wear the richest for her sake, and gave the others to my woman and interpretress.[67]

A less pleasant picture is given in 1786 by Lady Craven, who seems never to have liked what she saw. She called on the *kaymakam's* sister in Bahçesaray, Istanbul, where she was served sherbet, coffee, and sweets. She found her hostess's face badly painted, and disliked her eyebrows, which were joined over the nose. Another time she paid a visit to the wife of the *kaptan paşa* outside the city. Again, she disliked the women's makeup, and surmised that their teeth were black from smoking. She found herself being asked simple, direct questions: "Are you married?" "Have you children?" As she and her companions were about to get into their carriage to leave, her hostess sent a messenger asking if they would drive two or three times around the courtyard so that the women in the harem might observe them. She wrote that she refused the request, adding haughtily, "as you may imagine."[68]

According to Dr. Madden, it was usual for the Ottoman woman to send advance notice of her intention to call, so that the men of the house could leave the harem. Once there, the visitor took off her veil, was salaamed, smoked a pipe or two and ate the fruit, candy, and lump sugar her hostess offered her, meanwhile talking dress and scandal.[69]

Julia Pardoe paid a call at the harem of Mustafa Pasha of Skodra, who had recently been deprived of his *paşalık* by Mahmut II. Negro slaves seated Pardoe and her interpreter on a sofa "whereon lay a mandolin and a tambourine. . . . "

A female slave shortly afterwards appeared to conduct us to the apartment of the Buyuk Hanoum, which, when we entered, was half full of attendants, some standing in a semi circle around the mangal, the others squatted on the carpet at the extremity of the room.[70]

This was the first polygamous family Pardoe had visited, and she took note of the etiquette observed:

The Buyuk Hanoum occupied the upper end of the sofa, against which the tandour [heater] was placed; she was a plain woman, with a cold and somewhat stern expression of countenance: and there was more haughtiness in the bend and smile with which she welcomed us, than I had yet seen exhibited by a Turkish female; when we entered, she was amusing herself, as is common with both sexes in this country . . . in rapidly passing through her fingers the beads of a chaplet, that rested on the gold-embroidered covering of the tandour. . . .

[It] was of fine pearls, beautifully matched, and each the size of a pea, the divisions being formed by emeralds similarly shaped and sized, and the whole string secured by one pear-shaped emerald the size of a hazel-nut.

At the angle of the sofa sat the favourite Odalique of the Pasha, a short, slight, unattractive woman of about thirty years of age; with common, and rather coarse features, but with a shrewd and keen expression that almost made them interesting. Close beside her was seated a third lady, who, although certainly not pretty, was nevertheless tall, graceful and delicate, with fine, full eyes, and an exquisite complexion; when we entered, she was employed in fondling a sweet little child of between one and two years old. A pile of cushions, carefully and comfortably arranged, was prepared immediately opposite to the seat of the Buyuk Hanoum, for her fair daughter, but the lovely Heymine had not yet left the bath.[71]

Unlike Lady Craven, Julia Pardoe found many things attractive about Turkish women. She thought that their hair dyes were particularly good, much better than similar products in Europe, and found Emine, the Büyük Hanım's daughter, especially lovely. They were entertained at dinner, which was served in European fashion, with cutlery and a table with chairs. Afterwards she was invited to Emine's apartment, "when the young beauty, freed from the restraint of her mother's presence, clapped her hands, and

ordered her pipe, which she smoked with as much grace and gusto as any
Moslem of the Empire."[72] When she was with Emine, Pardoe met the
Pasha's third *odalık*, who came to pay the girl a good night visit:

She was slight and beautifully formed, with a soft, low voice which was almost
music. She appeared much attached to the lovely Heymine, and hastened, after
the first salutations were over, to replenish the pipe that rested beside the young
beauty, and to hand it to her; a mark of attention and respect which was acknowledged by the object with the graceful salutation common to the East—the pressure
of the fingers of the right hand to the lips and brow.[73]

Later the Büyük Hanım led Pardoe into the presence of the Pasha, where
they were joined by Emine and the favorite *odalık*.

A motion of his hand invited both to take their places upon the cushions already
alluded to [where the Büyük Hanım was already seated]; and then I remarked the
ascendancy of the latter [the odalık] over the spirit of the Paşa—an ascendancy
due probably as much to her being the mother of his two sons, as to her natural
shrewdness of intellect. Be that as it may, however, it was easy to perceive that
she was a woman of great natural talent, and wonderful quickness of perception;
and very likely to retain the supremacy she had gained.[74]

Pardoe spent the night in the harem as visitors frequently did. Emine
Foat Tugay gives a description of the extensive overnight hospitality of her
family home in Moda in the early twentieth century. It was called Mermer
Konağı, the Marble Mansion. She tells how mattresses were spread on the
floor, for the women in the harem, and for the men in the *selâmlık*, which
at her home was a separate building. Then she gives an amusing description
of the *dalkavuk*, a person who nods his or her head (*lit.* turban) approvingly
at the remarks of his or her patron. Such people made themselves welcome
by their "witty conversation" and their "tidbits of gossip." Though hospitality was the rule, rank was carefully observed, the humble seating
themselves near the door.[75]
Emine Foat Tugay's home provided cupboards for guests who came
frequently. In these they kept their sheets, towels, slippers, dressing gowns,
and whatever else they might need, all wrapped up in *bohça*s. Each guest
had her own cup, which was put away between visits.[76]
From the latter part of the nineteenth century on, certain Istanbul ladies
paid calls on the wives of important Europeans. Two wives of pashas came
to call on Mrs. Hornby, the wife of the British judge of the Consular Court,
attended by two slave girls and an old Negro woman. They gave full rein
to their curiosity, and while they smoked their *çubuk*s (pipes), they examined their hostess's clothes and parlor, and then asked if they might see
some men. It was finally arranged that they would look through a doorway
at Mrs. Hornby's male cousin, which they did for half an hour, keeping

themselves well veiled in the process.[77] During World War I, a pasha's widow and daughter visited Lady Poynter, bringing with them a black female slave, Snowdrop, and a smooth-faced eunuch who saw to it that the hostess's husband stayed out of the harem until the guests had left.[78]

By this time certain women from very progressive families were entertaining mixed groups, men and women, Turkish and foreign. The first to do this was the wife of the general, Hilmi Pasha. Emine Foat Tugay's mother entertained men, but only her husband's closest friends.[79] On the other hand, Seniha Moralı's mother saw no men except the members of the family, although her husband, Sami Bey, was one of the great hosts of the Bosphorus. That does not mean, however, that she had no social life, for she entertained many women visitors, and even occasionally tasted *rakı*.[80]

The Turks in those days ate but two meals per day: breakfast (*kavaltı*), taken about 11 a.m., and another meal (*yemek*), taken at sunset. Since the men usually partook of *kavaltı* away from home, the women often invited in their friends. Covers, consisting of a long spoon and a piece of bread, were laid on *sofra*s, circular trays on stands about eight inches from the floor. If the guests were of lower rank, the hostess was the first to pick up her spoon, which was for the *hoşaf* of stewed fruits cooled in ice. The *pilav* of rice was eaten with the fingers. At the end of the meal, slaves carried around pitcher and basin, *ibrik* and *leğen*, and poured water over the guests' hands. After this the guests ranged themselves on the sofa in order of rank and were served coffee in the *kahve fincanı* (small, often handleless cups) set in *zarf*s (containers of silver or gold filigree or latticework).[81] With their coffee they smoked their pipes—or, in the twentieth century, cigarettes held in amber mouthpieces.[82]

One of the small revolutions made possible by a more general use of the *araba* was going out to shop. Before this time the upper-class woman's purchasing had been confined to the goods brought to the harem by the itinerant tradeswoman, the *kıra* or *bohçacı*, the latter so called because she carried her wares on her back in a *bohça*.

The itinerant woman merchant had a long history in the Ottoman Empire. The term *kıra* goes back several centuries to a period when the best known of these merchants was a Jewish woman named Esther Kıra, an agent for Süleyman's mother, Hafise Valide Sultan.[83] In return for her services, Süleyman granted her and her heirs immunity from certain taxes. Her life and contact with the palace extended through the reigns of succeeding sultans into that of Mehmet III, when she became an agent of the unscrupulous *valide*, Safiye. She eventually became a Muslim and took the name of Fatma.[84]

In 1600 she was murdered by the *sipahi*s (cavalrymen) in front of the *konak* of the *kaymakam* as an act of vengeance against the *valide*, who was notorious for accepting bribes. There was also hostility against Esther

Kıra because she was Jewish; for the Jews, together with *valide*s Nurbanu and Safiye, were blamed by the military for the debasement of the currency which made soldiers' pay worthless.[85]

Despite Esther Kıra's fate, the institution of the *kıra* continued. Though the majority of them were Jewish women, Greek, Armenian, and eventually French women engaged in the trade. They sold jewels and "precious stuffs," and various kinds of embroidery and other handwork, as well as articles of clothing, cosmetics, and perfumes. They were sufficiently important in the daily life of the palace women that Topkapı had a special room set aside for them in the harem. Being, as they were, one of the few links between the sequestered woman and the outside world, they were often the agents of intrigue of one sort or another. Because of their entry into many harems they often acted as *görücü*.[86] They were also thought to possess medical knowledge and were in demand for that reason too.[87]

Itinerant women merchants were still active in the last period of the Empire. Emine Foat Tugay speaks of them as *bohça kadınları* and tells how, in her youth, these women came to her family's Marble Konak and "dealt in every kind of material that could be used in the house or for clothes." There was one woman in particular who sold *yazma*s (material with a hand-printed pattern).[88]

Emine Foat Tugay's mother, the Princess Nimetullah, seems never to have gone shopping herself,[89] but with the advent of the *araba* many other upper-class and even *saray* women drove to the bazaar, where they had the opportunity to view a wider variety of merchandise, along with enjoying the pleasure of an outing. This was a nineteenth-century innovation, for at the end of the eighteenth century d'Ohsson was writing that Ottoman ladies were not to be seen in shops or markets and that non-Muslim women went from door to door selling various articles.[90] Yet by the 1830s Julia Pardoe found women fairly buzzing about the bazaar and flirting with bazaar merchants. For the latter pastime, the routine was to select a shop that employed a young and handsome man, and then to get him to show a number of pieces of merchandise. These all elicited objections, so that it became necessary to make several trips and view many articles before making a purchase. Mahmut's sister, Heybetullah Sultan, was considered to be most adept at this practice.[91]

In the latter years of the nineteenth century the Ottoman lady was not necessarily limited to the bazaar in old Istanbul, but made her way to the shops of Galata and Pera. This was considered a little naughty, and stories were rife about flirtations with bazaar merchants there.[92]

On her shopping expedition the Ottoman woman was accompanied, in the earlier days, by a slave, and, in later times, by a servant, who carried her purchases in the ubiquitous *bohça*.[93] Despite the more relaxed attitude in regard to women going about, there were certain upper-class families

whose women continued to shop from itinerant tradeswomen until the end
of the Empire.

Another form of amusement that depended on the *araba* was the celebration of *hıdrellez günü* (Ilyas Day, the 40th day after the spring equi-
nox),[94] a celebration of spring. It was a day of picnics when the ladies of
the family drove out into the country in open carriages drawn by oxen. It
was a day for calling on grandparents, wearing new shoes, and eating special
foods, such as whole roasted lamb, thin white onions, romaine lettuce, and
a special helva called *irmik helvası*.[95] Many went to Kağıthane and pic-
nicked in its meadows.[96]

A favorite diversion of Ottoman women, the making up of little four-
line poems called *mani*s,[97] is connected with *hıdrellez günü*. These poems
would be written on any and every subject, and when *hıdrellez günü* came,
they would be put into a bag, the *mani torbası*, and buried under a rosebush.
The next day the women unearthed the bag, blindfolded a girl, and had
her pick out, one by one, the slips of paper on which the *mani*s were
written. The woman who, before the paper was opened, offered to sing
its *mani* would have her future foretold by that poem. The poems tended
to be simple, and more attention was generally given to rhyme than to
meaning. Here, without benefit of rhyming, are literal translations of a
few.[98]

> The nightingale is a very small bird,
> Its song is pleasant in the city;
> The Creator of the earth and sky
> Will bring me together with my beloved.

> Remove the wine from the cup,
> Remove the curls from the fez;
> If you are truly my love,
> Come, remove me from mourning.

> Today my head is full of poison,
> Laughing is not for me;
> Like the peddler's goods,
> My sorrow is in heaps.

> A star walks in the sky,
> My eye sees the beloved;
> It is something unbearable
> [But] My Lord gives me patience.

There were other, occasional festive days: celebrations of a royal wedding with the pomp of its procession; of the circumcision of princes, when
acrobats and tightrope artists and other performers entertained the public;
of a victory, the launching of a new ship, or a royal birth, when women

drove out in their carriages to see the sights of the *donanma*, the "decking-out" of the streets with pennants and floats; of the acceptance of a new ambassador when his procession made its way to the palace.[99]

A characteristic of summer celebrations was the illuminations. From a caique on the Bosphorus, Julia Pardoe watched the illumination of the shore palace (*sahil sarayı*) of Esma Sultan on the occasion of the marriage of Mahmut's daughter, Saliha Sultan:

There must have been many hundred caiques wedged together in front of her terrace, and not less than fifty of them contained musicians.

She told of bright lights of many colors mixed with boughs and exotic flowers. Apparently, on this occasion, a girl might enjoy a little freedom, for Pardoe "saw more than one light and fairy figure, that even the feridjhe failed wholly to conceal." Later, when she was rowed over to the palace of the bride, she found it "bright with festooned fires."[100]

Illuminations continued up to the end of the great houses. Emine Foat Tugay tells us that on the sultan's birthday, summer dusk was made bright by little lamps lit around the gardens and the facades of the houses, and the gardens were opened to the public. People went out in boats along the Bosphorus to view the illuminations.[101]

The Prophet's birthday was similarly celebrated. On that occasion, the rich distributed candy in little silk and satin bags painted in vari-colored floral motifs. A great house would give out as many as two hundred such bags, all of which had been patiently made in the harem.[102]

A review of troops was also a great occasion. About 1830, Adolphus Slade watched a parade that seemed more a celebration of spring than a military affair, and found that the sexes were permitted to mingle in the throngs, though "the fairer is usually veiled."[103] (These were very likely middle-class women.) Charles White saw a review for which tents, surrounded with ten-to-twelve-foot screens, had been put up for the imperial harem. The *valide*'s was at the extreme right of the group, and part of its front had been left open to permit the ladies a view.[104]

There were other processions. Julia Pardoe watched a dazzling one when Mahmut II went to pray at Sultanahmet Mosque on *kurban bayramı*,[105] wearing a fez with an aigrette of diamonds. She noted that officers flirted with women in carriages.[106]

The Lâle Devri[107] (the Tulip Period) of the 1720s was a time when entertainments of many sorts took place. Although most of the private entertainments that have been described were for men, it is not to be supposed that Nevşehirli İbrahim Pasha's wife, who was Ahmet III's daughter, Fatma Sultan, and his daughter, who was the poet Nedim's wife, did not have entertainments of their own. D'Ohsson has written that in the harem women put on comedies in which they made fun of Christian dress and manners, and even of Christian religious practices.[108] Baron de Tott has written of his wife and mother-in-law being entertained at the palace of Esma Sultan, a daughter of Ahmet III, where women, pretending to be men, acted out a kind of joust.[109] Melek Hanım saw a striking impromptu play at the *saray* of the Princess Nazli of Egypt, in which one of the slave girls acted the part of Nazli's lover.[110] At some of the festivities of the imperial harem, the youngest slaves, who were after all little more than children, turned the gaiety into a romp. Meanwhile, at his pleasure, the sultan watched the harem entertainments from behind a grilled window, but did not necessarily show himself. When he visited his sisters, however, it was usual for dancing girls to perform for him.[111]

Among the most popular and enticing of Ottoman entertainments were the *mehtap*s, or moonlight concerts on the Bosphorus. The season for them was of course the summer, when the fashionable world was at the *yalı*s along the shore, some time between June 15 and September 15. The moon had to be full, the Bosphorus calm, and the sky cloudless. This severely limited the number of these concerts, especially as it was customary to have only one per evening to limit the amount of confusion as the water procession advanced. The result was that there were only three or four *mehtap*s per summer.[112]

In the time of Abdülaziz, thousands of boats assembled for these concerts, and the route was longer, reaching down to Leander's Tower. By the period of which Abdülhak Şinasi Hisar was writing, the early years of the twentieth century, the boats numbered in the hundreds, and the route had been fixed by tradition to reach from the Bay of Kalender to Bebek. By now the concerts were generally given by one of the following three persons: the Dowager Khedive of Egypt, known as the *valide paşa* to distinguish her from the *valide sultan*, whose *yalı* was at Bebek; Sait Halim Pasha, a Prince of Egypt and sometime Ottoman grand vizier, whose summer residence was at Yeniköy; and Sami Bey, a son of the famous Minister of Education and scholar, Suphi Pasha, who had a handsome *yalı* at Kanlıca, on the Asiatic shore.[113]

The guests would assemble in caiques, those of the ladies having *ihram*s (coverings) of fringed cloth or velvet which trailed from the stern. Some of the ladies were in *sandal*s, the heavier boats with higher seats that came in in Abdülhamit II's time. The concert boat was large and tall, with a deck for the musicians and singers, who embarked at the *yalı* of the host.

The party would gather at Kalender where, as the concert commenced, the guests' boats would cluster around the concert boat. The boatmen knew how the currents ran and where the echoes were strongest and clearest. As a rule, the procession made its way to Yeniköy and Istiniye and then across the Bosphorus to the Bay of Kanlıca in Asia. There, where the moonlight was especially beautiful, the singers would sing their songs of romantic melancholy, and the echoes would answer them. Between the songs there were instrumental interludes played on the lute, the violin, and the dulcimer. *Mehtap*s provided the occasion for romance, for despite the men and women being in separate boats, a certain amount of discreet flirting went on. Should a man's boat come too near a lady's, however, her boatmen carefully shoved it off with their oars.

From Kanlıca onwards the concert boat, followed by its audience, might stop at the *yalı*s of relatives of the host, or at especially important houses, such as the *yalı* of the deposed Khedive İsmail at Emirgân. Here the concert boat would float in silence to give an opportunity for the Khedive's band of a thousand girl slaves to play and sing.[114] It is said that one particular girl's voice was so strong it produced echoes across the water in Kanlıca. Toward morning the procession would reach Bebek, and there it disbanded.

Ramazan evenings were another time when women could escape from the tedium of harem life. Garnett describes how, after the *teravi* (the evening Ramazan prayer) during the time of Abdülaziz (1861-1876), women went out in their carriages and coaches and drove about the broad esplanade of Süleymaniye "which, at that hour, would be crowded with elegant equipages containing Turkish *hanum*s, or high dignitaries of state, and also with throngs of pedestrians of every rank—a gathering which partook somewhat of a carnival character, petty missiles being thrown and other liberties indulged in at the expense of the occupants of the carriages which would not at any other time have been ventured on."[115] Lane-Poole also found women at Süleymaniye, and thought that they were likely to be pinched by passing male admirers.[116]

During Ramazan evenings women were allowed to go to the mosques to pray, at least in the latter years of the Empire. Before 1850 this seems not to have been true, for both Melek Hanım during Ramazan and Julia Pardoe on an unnamed religious holiday in the 1830s disguised themselves as men to go into a mosque.[117] On the other hand Lane-Poole, in the 1870s, once dressed as a woman and went to Sultanahmet Mosque, where he found the women chattering gayly, although the men were praying earnestly.[118]

Halide Edip remembered being taken as a child to Süleymaniye Mosque for evening prayer the first night of Ramazan, and her sensitive pen has given us a vivid description of Istanbul on a Ramazan evening:

The streets were lighted by hundreds of . . . moving lanterns. Men, women, and children flickered forward like a swarm of fireflies, drums were sounding in the distance, and from every minaret the muezzin was calling, *Allah Ekber, Allah Ekber*. . . . The grand harmony came nearer or grew more distant as we moved on. Then suddenly above the dimly lighted houses, above the mass of moving lights, a circle of light came into view high over our heads in the dark blue air. The tiny balcony of some dim minaret was now traced out as though by magic in a slender illusive ring of light. These circles multiplied into hundreds, standing out in the bluish heavens, softly lighting up the picturesque masses of the wooden buildings below them, or the melting lines of the domes. And now in the same air, hanging in fact between minaret and minaret, other beautiful lines of light as if by a miracle interlaced and wove themselves into wonderful writing: "Welcome, O Ramazan!"[119]

Kadir gecesi, the 27th day of Ramazan and the anniversary of the date when the Koran had first been revealed to Muhammad,[120] was the night of all nights when people went to the mosque, and preferably to Ayasofya (Santa Sophia), for that is where the sultan prayed on that evening. One witness found its interior "wrapped in a golden haze" from the oil-lit chandeliers overhead. Holy men chanted the Koran.[121] Melek Hanım also found masses of people in Ayasofya, its crowds "almost too dense for entry."[122]

Pardoe, at the same period as Melek, was carried away by the sight of the illuminated mosque:

Far as the eye could reach upward, circles of coloured fire, appearing as if suspended in mid-air, designed the form of the stupendous dome of Santa Sophia; while beneath, devices of every shape and colour were formed by myriads of lamps of various hues: the Imperial closet, situated opposite the pulpit, was one blaze of refulgence, and its gilded lattices flashed back the brilliancy, till it looked like a gigantic meteor![123]

At the end of Ramazan came the *şeker bayramı* (sweets holiday), when for three days the streets became a carnival and the women went visiting, taking pains to call only on those of higher rank. The greatest ladies postponed their social calls until eight days after the *bayram* had ended.[124] But as with other social activities, it was the advent of the *araba* that made a wider range of *bayram* calling possible.

NOTES

1. Charles White, *Three Years in Constantinople; or Domestic Manners of the Turks in 1844*, III, p. 309.
2. J. Sourdel-Thomine, "Hamam," EI², IV, pp. 139-144.
3. N. M. Penzer, *The Harem*, p. 212.
4. Sourdel-Thomine, "Hamam."
5. Ernest Mamboury, *The Tourists' Istanbul*, p. 210; Celâl Esat Arseven (Djelal Essad), *Constantinople de Byzance à Stamboul*, p. 224.
6. Mamboury, *The Tourists' Istanbul*, p. 211; Sourdel-Thomine, "Hamam"; Ali Saim Ülgen, "Hamam," İA, V, pp. 174-178. A detailed account of these arrangements will be found in the *İslâm ansiklopedisi*.
7. Celâl Esat Arseven, "Hamam," *SA*, II, p. 681 and illustration; Ülgen, "Hamam."
8. Halil Halit [Khalil Khalid], *The Diary of a Turk*, p. 231f.
9. Arseven, "Hamam," *SA*, II, p. 683; Penzer, *The Harem*, p. 217 (quoting Bassano de Zara, *I Costumi et i modi particolari de la vita de Turchi*, pp. 2-4).

10. According to White (*Three Years*, II, p. 124), "The naelingee look upon our Savior as their patron. The origin of the use of naelins, according to common tradition, was the inconvenience suffered by our Savior, when performing his ablutions at the bath at Nazareth. The heat of the floor blistered his feet, whereupon Joseph, whom Moslems call 'the beloved carpenter,' fell to work and made for him a pair of wooden pattens. The model of these pattens was preserved, and is supposed to have continued unchanged until the present day. . . . It is probable that the patten or wooden clog generally used in England was imported by the Crusaders, or brought from Spain, where it was introduced by the Arabs." Penzer (*The Harem*, pp. 217-218) thought it possible that the Venetians introduced the *nalın* to the Ottomans, but this overlooks the fact that *nalın* is of Arabic derivation, contracted from *naleyn*, the dual of *nal*, meaning patten or clog. *Nalın*s were often very elaborate, being inlaid with mother-of-pearl and silver, and their straps richly embroidered (Arseven, *SA*, III, p. 1498).

11. Julia Pardoe, *The City of the Sultans and Domestic Manners of the Turks in 1836*, II, pp. 129-137.

12. There are two Ingres (1780-1867) paintings of the Turkish bath in the Louvre. One, "Le Bain Turc," shows many nude women lying about, most wearing necklaces. One white woman plays a musical instrument resembling a mandolin, while a negro woman shakes a tambourine. Some of the women dance. The other painting, "La Petite Baigneuse," dated 1828, shows a young, dark-haired girl, nude, her back to the viewer.

13. This bath is in Edirne, and seems to differ from the usual Turkish bath in the number of rooms and in the arrangement of domes.

14. Lady Mary Wortley Montagu, *Letters from the Right Honourable . . . 1709-1762*, pp. 104-105.

15. Lucy M. J. Garnett, *Home Life in Turkey*, pp. 273-274; Ignatius Mouradgea d'Ohsson, *Tableau général de l'Empire othoman*, II, pp. 59-66; White, *Three Years*, III, pp. 300-313; Edward William Lane, *The Manners and Customs of the Modern Egyptians*, pp. 343, 379; Lady Dorina Neave, *Romance of the Bosphorus*, p. 38; Pardoe, *The City*, II, pp. 55-56; Penzer, *The Harem*, pp. 219-229.

16. Lady Elizabeth Craven, *A Journey Through the Crimea to Constantinople (1786)*, pp. 263-264; Pardoe, *The City*, II, p. 137.

17. D'Ohsson, *Tableau général*, II, pp. 59-66; Lane, *The Manners and Customs*, pp. 343, 379; Pardoe, *The City*, II, p. 137; White, *Three Years*, III, p. 176. The great Ottoman traveler and writer Evliya Çelebi (1614-1682) wrote that there were 14,838 *hamam*s in Istanbul in his time, including the *konak* and palace *hamam*s (Ülgen, "Hamam," *İA*, V, pp. 174-178).

18. Sir James W. Redhouse (*A Turkish and English Lexicon*, Constantinople, 1921, p. 1292) calls the *araba* "any kind of wheeled carriage."

19. Maxime Rodinson, "Sur l'araba," *Journal asiatique*, 216 (1957), pp. 273-280. Rodinson says there were two types in Central Asia. In one the driver sat in the carriage; in the other he rode the withers of the horse. The former was used in Kwarezm, the latter in Kashgar.

20. Géza Bárczi, *Magyar szófetjö szótár* (Budapest, 1941), *s.v. kócsi*, p. 167. A *koçu* seems to have been a particular kind of large carriage.

21. A. Cemal Erksan, "Saltanat arabaları," *Tarih dünyası* (Istanbul, 15 *Haziran* 1950), pp. 184-187.

22. Rodinson, "Sur l'araba;" Halûk Y. Şehsüvaroğlu, "Arabalar," *Asırlar boyunca İstanbul*, pp. 97-100.

23. Montagu, *Letters*, p. 104.

24. Erksan, "Saltanat arabaları."

25. Şehsüvaroğlu, "Arabalar."

26. Craven, *A Journey*, p. 213.

27. Antoine-Ignace Melling, *Voyage pittoresque de Constantinople et des rives du Bosphore d'auprès les dessins de M. Melling.*

28. Richard Davey, *The Sultan and His Subjects*, pp. 200-201.

29. Şehsüvaroğlu, "Arabalar."

30. White, *Three Years*, III, pp. 78-79. According to White (III, p. 167), over the "tilt" of the *araba* was usually draped a length of wool, an *ihram*, bright-colored and gold-fringed. It is not clear whether he means the canopy or something over the canopy. Purple *ihram*s were reserved for the sultan, green for descendants of the Prophet.

31. Rodinson, "Sur l'araba."

32. Pardoe, *The City*, I, pp. 35-36.

33. Rev. R. Walsh, *A Residence in Constantinople*, II, p. 483.

34. Şehsüvaroğlu, "Arabalar."

35. White, *Three Years*, III, pp. 79, 167.

36. İsmail Hakkı Uzunçarşılı, "Nizam-ı Cedit ricalından Valide Sultan Kethüdası meşhur Yusuf Ağa ve Kethüdazade Arif Efendi," *Belleten*, 20 (*Temmuz*, 1965), pp. 485-525. Arif Efendi was the grandson of Yusuf Ağa, the *kethüda* of Selim III's *valide*. He was born in Istanbul in 1777 and died in 1848. He was associated with the Bektaşîs but was saved by his friends when Mahmut II suppressed this dervish order in 1826.

37. Joan Haslip, *The Sultan: The Life of Abdul Hamid*, p. 35.

38. Nassau W. Senior, *A Journal Kept in Turkey and Greece in the Autumn of 1857 and the Beginning of 1858*, p. 14.

39. Théophile Gautier, *Constantinople*, p. 141.

40. Edmondo de Amicis, *Constantinople*, p. 193. During the period of financial retrenchment following Abdülaziz's deposition, the *saray* carriages were tied up with chains in the imperial stable so that the women could not drive about the city in them (Şehsüvaroğlu, "Arabalar").

41. De Amicis, *Constantinople*, pp. 213-214.

42. Rodinson, "Sur l'araba."

43. Mary Mills Patrick, *Under Five Sultans*, p. 12; Senior, *Journal*, p. 13.

44. Samuel S. Cox, *Diversions of a Diplomat in Turkey*, p. 405.

45. Mehmet Zeki Pakalın, *Osmanlı tarih deyimleri ve terimleri sözlüğü*, I, p. 730. He quotes the late eighteenth-century poet, Sümbülzade Vehbi: "What fezzed oar propels the twinned caique, a lady's needle, unique among small craft!"

46. Halûk Y. Şehsüvaroğlu, "Kayıklar," *Asırlar boyunca İstanbul*, pp. 105-108.

47. White, *Three Years*, III, p. 4.

48. White, *Three Years*, I, pp. 37–38, 49–50; III, pp. 4-5. He gives a full discussion of the caique and the *kayıkçı* in I, pp. 35–69. According to White, the use of the umbrella for any but royalty and the grand vizier was an innovation, and it was necessary to furl it when passing a palace where the sultan was in residence. Old-fashioned people still used fans (*yelpaze*) of goose or swan's feathers,

and sometimes of black ostrich feathers, with a small mirror in the center. They were purchased from the Arab merchants who plied the Bosphorus in caiques (*Three Years*, I, p. 38).

49. Melling, *Voyage pittoresque*.

50. Pardoe, *The City*, I, pp. 216-217.

51. James E. P. Boulden, *An American among the Orientals*, pp. 150-151.

52. Senior, *Journal*, p. 37.

53. Personal interview with Perihan Arıburun, November 1967.

54. Abdülhak Şinasi Hisar, "Moonlight on the Bosphorus," unpublished condensation and translation by Nesrin Moralı, p. 10.

55. Cox, *Diversions*, pp. 102-110.

56. Pardoe, *The City*, I, p. 217.

57. H. Y. Şehsüvaroğlu, "Saray kayıklarında geçen tarihi vakalar," *Asırlar boyunca İstanbul*, pp. 107-111. There seems to have been some variation in the number of oars allowed. According to Şehsüvaroğlu (ibid.), Abdülmecit gave the father of the woman poet, Leylâ Hanım, two caiques, one with four pairs of oars, the other with seven. It is, therefore, likely that the lady *sultan*s and *kadın*s were sometimes rowed by more than five pairs of oars, especially inasmuch as some of the imperial caiques had very many pairs.

58. Melek Hanım, *Thirty Years*, pp. 107, 323; Şehsüvaroğlu, "Sedyeler," *Asırlar boyunca İstanbul*, p. 127.

59. Melek Hanım, *Thirty Years*, pp. 54, 103-107, 108-109. Varna seems an unlikely place to transship en route from Istanbul to Belgrade, but this is the information she gives.

60. Patrick, *Under Five Sultans*, p. 14.

61. Halide Nüsret Zorlatuna, "Meslek hatırları, Musul'dan sonra Kerkuk," *Türk yurdu*, 50 (*Ocak*, 1960), pp. 45-46.

62. Emine Foat Tugay, *Three Centuries*, p. 185.

63. Garnett, *Home Life In Turkey*, p. 73.

64. Halil Halit, *The Diary of a Turk*, p. 75; Garnett, *Home Life in Turkey*, p. 73.

65. D'Ohsson, *Tableau général*, IV, p. 267. According to him even a woman slave had to be accompanied by a male, although this had not always been so. It was the "corruption" of the eighteenth century that made the precaution necessary for slaves too.

66. D'Ohsson, *Tableau général*, IV, p. 325.

67. Montagu, *Letters*, pp. 131-134.

68. Craven, *Journey*, pp. 181f., 223f.

69. R. Robert Madden, *Travels in Turkey, Egypt, Nubia and Palestine in 1824, 1825, 1826 and 1827*, I, pp. 11-12.

70. Pardoe, *The City*, I, p. 230. Iskodralı Mustafa Paşa, of an old Albanian family, had joined the Albanian revolt against the Porte, but, after a time, he had capitulated and turned his stronghold over to Reşit Paşa. At the time of Pardoe's writing he was out of favor, but eventually regained Mahmut's graces. Under Abdülmecit he held various Asiatic *paşalık*s. His wife was from the family of Tepedelenli Ali (M. Cavit Baysun, "Mustafa Paşa," *İA*, VIII, pp. 727-730).

71. Pardoe, *The City*, I, pp. 231-233.

72. Ibid., I, p. 238.

73. Ibid., I, p. 242.

74. Ibid., I, pp. 250-251.

75. Tugay, *Three Centuries*, pp. 250-251.

76. Interview with the late Emine Foat Tugay and with the late Belkis Erad, August 1966. There were no guest rooms in the *konak*s or even in the palaces.

77. Senior, *Journal*, p. 92.

78. Mary A. Poynter, *When Turkey Was Turkey*, pp. 163-181.

79. Tugay, *Three Centuries*, p. 224.

80. Personal interview with Seniha Moralı, August 1966. The harems of the middle class were by this time not as secluded as those of the upper class. Middle-class men and women made calls together and had mixed parties, at which the women covered their heads with veils.

81. Garnett, *Home Life in Turkey*, p. 274; Arseven, *SA*, II, p. 904. Some of the old *fincan*s had verses inscribed on them. In early times certain of them were made of pipemaker's red clay, but most were of china or porcelain, from İsnik or Kütahya. In the nineteenth century the Turks began to import Saxon ware. *Zarf*s, besides gold and silver, were made of gold-plated copper or sometimes of ivory.

82. Garnett, *Home Life in Turkey*, p. 274.

83. The provenance of the word *kıra* has not been settled. Bernard Lewis (lecture notes, April 6, 1960) considers it a Greek word meaning "harem go-between." J. H. Mordtmann ("Die jüdischen Kira im Serai der Sultans," *Mitteilungen des Seminars für orientalische Sprachen auf der K. Friedrich-Wilhelms Universität zu Berlin: West asiatische Abteilung, Januar*, 1955, pp. 1-38) points out that it was occasionally used as a personal name, and that it may come from the word *kıra* which means "rent," inasmuch as Esther Kıra had leased the right to collect taxes. Jan Reychman and Ananiasz Zajaczkowski (tr. Andrew S. Ehrenkreutz, *Handbook of Ottoman-Turkish Diplomatics*, The Hague, 1968, p. 98) cite V. D. Smirnov ("Vostochnya zametki," *Gramota sultana Osmana semeistvu Kiry*, Moscow, 1895), who presents letters from Osman II to the Kıra progeny, thereby using it as a surname.

84. Mordtmann, "Die jüdischen Kira"; John Sanderson, "Sundrie the Personall Voyages Performed by John Sanderson of London, Merchant, Begun in October 1584. Ended in October 1602. With an Historical Description of Constantinople," *Hakluytus Posthumus or Purchas His Pilgrims*, pp. 412-485.

85. Mordtmann, "Die jüdischen Kira."

86. Garnett, *Home Life in Turkey*, p. 277; Halil Halit, *The Diary of a Turk*, p. 70; Barnette Miller, *Beyond the Sublime Porte*, pp. 10-11.

87. Mordtmann, "Die jüdischen Kira."

88. Tugay, *Three Centuries*, p. 217. Colorfast vegetable dyes were employed. The technique of *yazma* was usually used to decorate the borders of *yemeni*s (scarfs to bind around the hair), quilt-coverings, and prayer-rugs. *See* Yakup Kadri Karaosmanoğlu, *Hep o şarkı*, pp. 60-63, for a scene between a *bohça kadın* and a *hanım efendi*. Armenian women used to sell *yazma* at the *yalı* of Kâmil Pasha at Beylerbeyi. Also a female jewelry merchant regularly appeared to show her wares, from which a selection would be made. Lâyıka Hanım, Kâmil Pasha's wife, was fond of fine embroidery and ordered beautifully worked bed linen and table cloths from the itinerant women merchants (Personal interview with Perihan Arıburun, November 1967).

89. Tugay, *Three Centuries*, p. 217.

90. D'Ohsson, *Tableau général*, IV, pp. 321-322, 326.

91. Pardoe, *The City*, I, pp. 34-35. In his novel *Aşk-ı memnu* (*Love of the Forbidden*), Halit Ziya Uşaklıgil describes a typical shopping expedition by upper-class women.

92. Melek Hanım mentions the elopement of a young *saraylı* (palace woman) with a young Greek bazaar merchant (*Thirty Years*, pp. 28-30). Gerard de Nerval relates a story of an intrigue between a merchant and a fair shopper that he says was told to him by an old man who, when young, had kept the accounts of an Armenian woman merchant who had a shop in Galata. One day several *saraylı*s came in, well covered, and purchased some jewelry which needed cleaning and repairs. When this was done, the man delivered the pieces to the Beşiktaş palace. It transpired that the purchaser was a lady *sultan*, who ordered him into her presence. He was paid and then invited by an attendant to view an exhibition of tightrope dancers. He was given dinner and later led into a room where the lady *sultan* sat on a sofa. There he was served coffee and a *nargile* (water pipe) while musicians played on a balcony. He had just gathered enough courage to take the princess's hand when the Janissaries arrived at the palace, whereupon he and the tightrope dancers were pushed through a trapdoor into the Bosphorus, where they swam to safety (*The Women of Cairo [1842-1843]*, II, pp. 186ff). The tale may well be apocryphal since it is unlikely that the Janissaries, for all their unruliness, would have dared to intrude on an imperial princess. Yet the story is an example of the kind of gossip that was making the rounds at that time.

93. White, *Three Years*, III, p. 165.

94. *Hıdrellez*, according to Redhouse (*TEL*, p. 833), is the vulgar form of Hızır Elyas, the Old Testament prophet Elijah. He is mentioned in the Koran as "of those sent [to warn]" (XXXVII, 123-130). He has also, by some means, become identified with St. George. *Hıdrellez günü* is the day of the spring feast, May 6, or St. George's Day (A. Vahid Moran, *Türkçe-İngilizce sözlük, a Turkish-English Dictionary*, Istanbul, 1945, p. 473). H. C. Hony (with the advice of Fahir İz, *A Turkish-English Dictionary*, Oxford, 1957, p. 143) and Redhouse (*TEL*, "Khızr," pp. 851-852) call it the first day of summer.

95. Tugay, *Three Centuries*, p. 286, and personal interview with Emine Foat Tugay and Belkis Erad.

96. Mithat Sertoğlu, "Hıdrellez," *Resimli osmanlı tarihi ansiklopedisi*, pp. 141-142.

97. The *mani*, which is very similar to the quatrain known as *tuyuğ*, was especially developed among the Eastern Turks. According to M. F. Köprülü ("Tuyuğ," *Türk dili ve edebiyatı hakkında araştırmalar*, Istanbul, 1934, pp. 204-240), N. Samoilovich found the *tuyuğ* in Çağatay and in the *Kutadgu Bilig* under the name *mani*.

98. Ignácz Kúnos, "A törők nök nyelve és költészete," *NYK*, XXIII (Budapest, 1893), pp. 424-431. Kúnos collected a number of *mani*s from the mother of Nigâr Hanım, who recited them from memory. He considered them "example of purely feminine folk poetry." The writer is indebted to E. Halasi-Kun for the translation of this article from Hungarian into English, and to Şehbal Teilmann for assistance in deciphering the transcription of the *mani*s. Mehmet Halit Bayrı (*İstanbul folkloru*, pp. 60-72) gives a long list of *mani*s.

99. M. Münir Aktepe, *Patrona isyanı (1730)*, p. 60; Ahmet Refik [Altınay], *Lâle devri*, p. 72; d'Ohsson, *Tableau général*, IV, pp. 408-412.

100. Pardoe, *The City*, I, pp. 484-485.

101. Tugay, *Three Centuries*, pp. 226-227.

102. Personal interview with Mesut Koman, August 1966.

103. Adolphus Slade, *Records of Travels in Turkey, Greece, etc.*, II, p. 212.

104. White, *Three Years*, III, p. 40.

105. The Muslim festival of sacrifice.

106. Pardoe, *The City*, I, p. 179. According to Pardoe, officers "were constantly passing and repassing, and making frequent pauses in our immediate vicinity; incited thereto, as I have no doubt, by the presence of two lovely young Turkish ladies, who had quitted their carriage, and established themselves on the footboard behind."

107. In the time of Ahmet III the celebration of spring was added to the fêtes for *bayram*s, which included the birth of princes, the exposition of the mantle of the Prophet, the departure of the caravan for Mecca, and victory celebrations. *See* Joseph de Hammer-Purgstall, *Histoire de l'Empire ottoman depuis son origine jusqu'à nos jours*, XIII, pp. 196-197.

108. D'Ohsson, *Tableau général*, IV, pp. 412-413.

109. Baron de Tott, *Mémoires sur les Turcs et les Tartares*, I, pp. 80, 87.

110. Melek Hanım, *Thirty Years*, p. 94. Nazli is reputed to have served up to her husband the head of a slave to whom he had paid some attention and of whom she was jealous (ibid., p. 95). Also, Tugay, *Three Centuries*, p. 117. Male clothing was apparently at times worn by some of the slaves of Esma Sultan, the sister of Mahmut II (Pardoe, *The City*, I, p. 319).

111. D'Ohsson, *Tableau général*, IV, pp. 412-413; Melek, *Thirty Years*, p. 27; Pardoe, *The City*, I, p. 308.

112. The material on the *mehtap* is taken from an unpublished English translation by Nesrin Moralı of Abdülhak Şinasi Hisar's *Mehtap*. It is used with the permission of the translator, who was the granddaughter of Sami Bey, one of the *mehtap* hosts.

113. The personal information concerning Sami Bey is from his daughter, Seniha Moralı.

114. Abdülhamit II put an end to this part of the *mehtap* by forbidding Muslim girls to sing in public (Personal interview with Seniha Moralı, July 1966).

115. Garnett, *Home Life in Turkey*, pp. 145-146. She points out that this sort of frivolity vanished under Abdülhamit II. White, who visited Turkey in the 1840s, writes that at that time the ladies preferred to congregate on Serasker Square (also called Beyazit Square) between midday and sunset prayer during Ramazan (*Three Years*, III, pp. 118-119).

116. Stanley Lane-Poole, *Turkey*, p. 283.

117. Melek Hanım, *Thirty Years*, pp. 25-26; Pardoe, *The City*, II, pp. 375-381.

118. Lane-Poole, *Turkey*, p. 283.

119. Halide Edip [Adıvar], *Memoirs of Halide Edip*, pp. 70-71.

120. Hony, *TED*, p. 176.

121. Tugay, *Three Centuries*, p. 263.

122. Melek Hanım, *Thirty Years*, pp. 25-26.

123. Pardoe, *The City*, I, p. 378.

124. Melek Hanım, *Thirty Years*, p. 137.

9

Social Life Within the Home

Probably the most frequent diversion inside the home was the receiving of visitors, the counterpart to paying visits, which has been covered in the preceding chapter. Many upper-class Ottoman women had a weekly at-home day called *kabul günü* (reception day) which was reserved for that purpose. Other home diversions included the playing of games, music and dance, the Karagöz (shadow theater), and the tales of the *masalcı* (woman storyteller). Of all these perhaps music was the most important, the most widely enjoyed.

Though there had always been controversy about the lawfulness of music in Islam, it was a favorite Ottoman diversion. One tradition had it that Ayesha claimed Muhammad had listened to singing girls in her house. Yet the schools of canon law usually opposed music, and Hanafi law refused to accept testimony from wailing women, singing women, and people who sang to the *tambur* (a kind of guitar or lute with a long neck and six strings) or who sang in public.[1] Eastern music was derived from Sassanian music, which in turn was based on some still older, perhaps Semitic source,[2] and was also influenced by Greek music. It had its aficionados in all Islamic lands. For a time *'ilm al-musiki* (knowledge of music) was part of the *medrese* curriculum. Al-Ghazali quoted a philosopher as saying, "There is in the heart a glorious excellence; the force of speech is not able to elicit it with words, but the soul can do it with melodies."[3]

The Ottoman Empire, along with other Islamic lands, had religious as well as secular music. The *tekke* (dervish lodge) music of the Mevlevî convents is well known, but there was also privately sponsored religious music in the great houses. Âdile Sultan (daughter of Mahmut II), Seniha

Sultan (Abdülmecit's daughter), and Nazime Sultan all had performers of religious music play in their palaces.[4]

There were families who specialized in music. A famous early eighteenth-century composer of both religious and secular music, İsmail Dede, had a daughter, Fatma, who was not only a singer but a collector of *şarkı*s (songs). İsmail was taken into the palace by Selim III, and acquired a *saraylı* wife. We have a record of at least one woman musician, Mevlevî Şeref Hanım, who wrote *methiye*s (hymns of praise).[5]

Evliya Çelebi has told us something about the organization of musicians in Istanbul in the seventeenth century, and this situation must have lasted through the eighteenth. It was not until the abolition of the Janissary band and the introduction of Western music under Mahmut II that a change could have taken place.

According to Evliya[6] there were more than 6,000 musicians in Istanbul in the seventeenth century, organized into two official and many private groups. One official group, quartered near the palace, had the job of awakening the palace people for morning prayers and also of performing a morning serenade for the sultan and such high dignitaries as were about to be promoted. The other group was quartered at Yedi Kule and played each morning and evening on the walls of the city and in each *mahalle* (quarter). These two groups were headed by the *mehterbaşı* (head of the band). Other groups were headed merely by a *sazendebaşı* (head musician). In all, 71 corps of string, wind, and percussion instruments played at either public or private functions.

The Turks were very fond of music and used it for virtually all ceremonies, public and private.[7] When the sultan chose a girl to share his bed for the first time, she was led to his bedroom in procession with music and singing.[8]

The palace was always a patron of music. Even in the days of rigorous seclusion music was so important that *cariye*s were sent to the houses of *usta*s (masters) to take lessons on such musical instruments as the *keman* (violin), *tambur*, *ney* (flute), or *çöğür* (a kind of lute).[9] Their teachers were the most eminent musicians of their time.[10] Especially during the time of Selim III (1789-1807) and Mahmut II (1808-1839), both of whom particularly enjoyed music, *cariye*s were sent out from the *saray* to the houses of male music teachers for lessons.[11] Later in the nineteenth century the teachers came to the palace. Modesty was acknowledged by the girls wearing a strip of muslin over head and shoulders.[12]

These musically trained *cariye*s made up the corps of girl musicians in the palace and in some of the great houses. Other houses had individual girl musicians, such as Julia Pardoe heard while visiting Esma Sultan, Mahmut's sister. Nazıp Hanım, Esma's adopted daughter, "sent a slave for her zebec, and played and sang with considerable sweetness and execution."[13] Later that day another girl accompanied a slave who sang. Nazıp

Hanım then played "the theorbo, and, while another of the party beat the tambourine, half a dozen voices pealed out the ballads of the Sultan, who is a poet."[14] Melek Hanım also heard Nazıp play "on a kind of guitar," to which other girls danced. In the palace of İbrahim Pasha of Egypt, she heard slave girls sing to a kind of mandolin she called a *derbouka*.[15] Altınlı Kadın, lady treasurer of the above Esma Sultan, was a fine lute player to whom Mahmut liked to listen. She married one of the notables Mahmut ordered to Istanbul, who occupied himself with spending her money.[16]

Inasmuch as in the nineteenth century musicians came to the palace to give lessons, it is not surprising that romance sometimes bloomed. During the time of Abdülmecit, a musician named Arif Bey became enamored of a 15-year-old Circassian *cariye* and composed music for her. Her name was Çeşm-i Dilber (Eye of the Beloved). The palace buzzed with gossip about the two, which resulted in the sultan retiring Arif on a pension and giving him permission to marry the girl. Arif's leaving was a great disappointment to the other girls, who were all a little in love with him. This was perhaps unavoidable; they saw so few men.[17]

Unfortunately, Arif and Çeşm-i Dilber did not live happily ever after. It is said she was so beautiful that she was expected to become an *ikbal* of the sultan, and that she didn't enjoy settling down to a less grand estate. She had flirted with Arif only because it was forbidden, and now she left him after two years and two children. Some time later Arif was reappointed teacher to the palace *cariye*s. He seems to have been a susceptible man, for again he fell in love with one of his students, another Circassian named Zülf-ü Nigâr (The Lovelock of the Beauty), and again he was pensioned off and permitted to marry the girl. This wife died, and once more he came back to the palace as *ser hanende* (head singer) and teacher. There, he continued his amorous activities, this time with a girl belonging to Valide Pertevniyal. He married her too, but was finally banished when he showed signs of conceit and caprice to Abdülaziz, who was by then on the throne. He was brought back by Abdülhamit II, who made him *kolağası* (adjutant major), although his impertinence once brought him imprisonment for 50 days. However, in his last years he was again *persona grata* in imperial circles and paid visits to Pertevniyal and Abdülhamit's *valide*, Perestû. His son became a famous violinist.[18]

The performance standards for girl musicians were high, and a girl who made a mistake could be in for trouble. Abdülhak Şinasi Hisar related that a mistress once broke a lute over a girl's head for her musical carelessness, though she was fond of the girl.[19]

In the late years of the Empire, women who had been trained in music in the palace and had left to marry sometimes gave private lessons. Gülüzar Hanım, who had been first flutist of the palace all-girl ensemble and had been taught by an Italian, gave flute lessons to Ali Ekrem Bulayır, Namık Kemal's son, when he was a child.[20]

The private all-girl ensembles got their start with the imperial harem group organized by Giuseppe Donizetti, brother of the opera composer. Mahmut II brought him to Istanbul in order to train an imperial band in the playing of Western music. (That was when Mahmut abolished the Janissary band.)[21] Mahmut's successor, Abdülmecit, greatly encouraged this group, which now consisted of 40 slave girls attired in male costume.[22] We have already mentioned the all-girl group of the Khedive İsmail; another was the band of 48 slave girls in the household of Sadeddin Pasha, onetime military commander of Istanbul.[23]

Abdülaziz is said to have been less interested in Western music than his predecessors, but it regained favor under Abdühamit II, who understood and enjoyed it. Both his daughter, Ayşe Sultan, and Murat V's daughter, Hatice Sultan, were accomplished pianists.[24]

The first person to have Turkish music written in the Western system of notation was Prince Halim of Egypt, a son of Mehmet Ali. When he was exiled from Egypt, he settled on the Bosphorus and gave private concerts. His children were taught to play musical instruments so that they could give family concerts.[25] At the turn of the twentieth century, an old woman, Hanende Hanım, who had been a slave of Mehmet Ali of Egypt, was still singing in the Bosphorus yalıs.[26]

During the early years of the twentieth century, Ziya Pasha, who had been ambassador to Washington and was later a senator in the Istanbul Parliament, opened a girls' music school in Istanbul, the Darülelhan (House of Musical Notes), in an old palace or mansion in the center of the old city. It taught Eastern classical and folk music, which the girls sang and played on violins, lutes, and tamburs.[27] In the last days of the Empire, according to Duckett Ferriman, the most popular instruments were still the lute, the tambur, the dulcimer, and "a small viol about a foot long, having three strings, and played with a short, slightly arched bow," plus the flute. The tambourine, he said, was used for dancing. Among foreign instruments were the mandolin, the zither, the violin (which was played on the knee), the violoncello, and the piano (which was to be found in many upper-class harems).[28] The piano, in particular, had become a token of Western sophistication.

Dancing was a frequent accompaniment of music in the harem. In the palaces and konaks, girls who belonged to the household were trained in dancing. This persisted, so that even as late as the early twentieth century Duckett Ferriman could say, "Song and dance hold the chief place in the recreation of the harem."[29]

In addition to the dancing by members of a household, there were dances put on by troups made up of 12 dancing girls or çengis, under the supervision of a manager, or çengi kolbaşı, and her assistant, all of whom could be hired for an occasion.[30] Mme. de Tott was entertained by such girls in the garden of Esma Sultan, daughter of Ahmet III and sister of Mustafa III, who was then reigning. De Tott gives us this vivid account of what his wife saw:

Some new troups of slaves had been disposed near an extremely beautiful kiosk where the company was supposed to go. This richly furnished and decorated pavilion, built in a large pool of water, occupied the middle of the garden where the espaliers of roses on all sides and hid from the eyes the walls that formed the prison. . . .They were scarcely seated there when the eunuchs, who had preceded the march, ranged themselves in a row at some distance from the kiosk in order to make room for the musicians of the princess. The troup was composed of ten women slaves who performed different concerts, during which a band of dancers, not less richly but more indecorously dressed, came to execute different ballets sufficiently agreeable because of the figures and variety of the steps. The dancers were of the best troup, for they ordinarily performed in private houses: soon a new band of twelve women, dressed as men, arrived, without doubt to add to this tableau the appearance of the sex the festivities lacked. These feigned men commenced then a sort of joust, in order to contend for and secure the fruits which the other slaves came to throw into the pool. A little boat conducted by female boatmen, equally disguised as men, gave the foreigners the pleasure of a promenade on the water, after which, rowed to the sultan, they prayed leave of her with the ceremonies of usage. . . .[31]

Like Mme. de Tott, Western observers have not, in most cases, described the dances themselves. Lady Craven came near to it. She watched a girl and boy dance in the courtyard of a judge's wife in the Crimea and said the woman danced with her feet on the ground and moved all parts of her body. Lady Craven found the dance improper.[32] The dancing did not, however, shock the intrepid Julia Pardoe, who describes a dance given by a judge's *odalık* to entertain guests gathered to pay their respects to his wife on the birth of a child:

she twirled the tambourine in the air with the playfulness of a child; and, having denoted the measure, returned it to one of the women, who immediately commenced a wild chant, half song and half recitative, which was at times caught up in chorus by the others, and at times wailed out by the dancer only, as she regulated the movements of her willow-like figure to the modulations of the music. The Turkish women dance very little with their feet; it is the grace and art displayed in the carriage of the body and arms which form the perfection of their dancing; the rapid snapping of the fingers, meanwhile, producing the effect of castenets.[33]

Pardoe was also entertained by dancing girls in the palace of another Esma Sultan, this one a sister of Mahmut II. As did Mme. de Tott, she found some of the dancers in male dress, but tells us nothing about their movements.[34]

Lady Ramsay, on a visit to a judge's wife in a town near Konya in the early twentieth century, gave details of the dance she saw. The dancers were not a trained troop but guests at a party. They danced in twos to a tambourine, their arms high, clicking spoons like castanets, advancing and retreating and circling one another in short, staccato steps.[35]

The eighteenth-century artist Levnî has painted an attractive Ottoman dancing girl in one of his miniatures. She has one arm raised and one lowered, and her hands and shoulders are gracefully bent to her right side. Her step seems a small one, so it is likely, as we have seen, that the dance did not cover much ground.[36]

Neither Julia Pardoe nor Lady Ramsay saw the belly dance, although Lady Craven probably did. An evocative description of it is given by Yakup Kadri Karaosmanoğlu in "Bir kadın meselesi" ("The Matter of a Woman"), a short story having to do with an *oturak âlemî*, a male drinking party at which a girl dances. In this case it was the host's concubine:

Every part of her oscillates, so to speak, from her fingers to the strands of her hair. Her arms emerge from wide sleeves and lock together above her head. As she snaps her fingers to accompany herself... she sometimes shows the rakish shape of her hips, sometimes the amorous form of her breasts. Withdrawing from mankind under the sublimity of the long black hair that covers her naked shoulders like a silk shawl, she seems to turn into an angel.[37]

Lady Montagu's impression, as she watched the girls dance in the harem of the *kâhya*'s lady, corroborates Yakup Kadri's description. "Nothing," she wrote, "could be more artful, or more proper to raise certain ideas. The tunes so soft—the motions so languishing—accompanied by pauses and dying eyes! half-falling back, and then recovering themselves in so artful a manner, that I am positive the coldest and most rigid prude upon earth could not have looked upon them without thinking of something not to be spoken of."[38]

Lady Montagu wrote in the early eighteenth century. Emine Foat Tugay, writing her recollections of life in the ruling family of Egypt in the late nineteenth and early twentieth centuries, says that in her day the "navel" dance was considered indecent and not performed in the palace.[39] She tells us that the slaves in her family's residences were fond of old Circassian dances, but she does not give any information on how these dances were performed. She does, however, say that in later years the dancers of the Khedive's mother performed a sort of simplified ballet. At a party given by the Khedive's mother at her *yalı* in Bebek, she remembers seeing girls in pink satin and gauze, their hair girt with garlands of roses and their hands holding roses, whirl and dip in an old Turkish flower dance.[40]

Dancing, like music, eventually became Westernized, but still in some circles the old dances continued to have an appeal.

A form of entertainment periodically enjoyed in the harem by the upper-class woman, particularly during Ramazan, was the Karagöz, a kind of theater generally characterized by considerable vulgarity.[41] On Ramazan evenings and on special occasions, such as circumcisions and weddings, a *karagözcü* (puppeteer) would be summoned. He would set up his stage, a cloth screen on which shadows were thrown by a light from behind, and line up his puppets as if on a clothes-string. These were cut-out figures of colored camel skin, translucent so that the light of an oil lamp showed through them, and articulated so that they could be moved by strings. The *karagözcü* held the figures upright against the screen and, as the performance got under way, worked each one by means of a slender stick which was inserted into a small hole in the leather.[42] According to the poet Hüseyin Seyit Vehbi (died 1736), Karagöz performances were put on on four separate screens during the wedding festivities of Ummetullah Sultan.[43] Of these four screens, it is very likely that at least one must have been placed in the harem for the benefit of the imperial women, including the bride, then seven years old.

The Karagöz was also known as the *hayal-i zıl*, the "shadow specter." According to the diary of his *sırkâtibi* (private secretary), Selim III, who enjoyed all forms of entertainment, had a *hayal* play performed in the *mabeyn* of the palace on December 21, 1792.[44] Although the diary does not indicate so, the fact that the performance took place in the *mabeyn* may mean that a curtained area was set aside from which the women could watch from behind a screen. Such a dispensation would fit in very well with Selim's characteristic thoughtfulness toward his mother and sisters. The performance in question was probably in connection with the wedding of Zeynep Sultan, since the clerk noted that in the same month of that year Selim held an entertainment to celebrate that event.[45]

Though the Karagöz was brought into the harem as a means of entertainment,[46] it also served as an eye-opener for the imperial women. The type of low life that the Karagöz pictured must have been largely unknown to the denizens of the royal and upper-class harems. The Karagöz also served to educate women politically, at least such women as were sufficiently alert to understand the point of the political satires which were sometimes depicted. That there were such women, the intrigues of the Ottoman Empire bear witness.

Nevertheless the Karagöz never played as important a role in the leisure life of the Ottoman lady as the story-teller. There were two types of story-tellers during the Empire, the *meddah* and the *masalcı*. The former, a man, carried on his profession in public places, and hence to an audience of men. It was the *masalcı* who entertained the women in the harem. Julia Pardoe made the acquaintance of one while visiting in an Ottoman household during Ramazan. Though she gives no inkling of the *masalcı*'s tale, she describes the scene:

A very pretty old maddalijhe, or tale-teller, had been invited to relieve the tedium of the evening with some of her narrations. This custom is very general during the

Ramazan, and is a great resource to the Turkish ladies, who can thus recline in
luxurious inaction, and have their minds amused without any personal exertion.[47]

Melek Hanım mentions a story-teller whom she had been in the habit of
employing but, like Pardoe, gives no information about the type of stories
she told.[48]

Mehmet Tevfik, in the chapter "Tandırbaşı" ("At the *Tandır*")[49] in his
novel, *İstanbul 'da bir sene* (*A Year in Istanbul*), shows the *masalcı* to be
an important personage in the harem. The story takes place in the harem
of one Süleyman Ağa, who was Chief of Scales and who had a *konak* on
the Sea Road at Eyüp. His harem housed a number of women: his wife,
his mother, his mother-in-law, his daughter, and the three or four slaves
who were in their service. In addition there were several women who often
stayed there for long periods of time: the wife of the *hoca*, Süleyman Ağa's
old *sütana* (wet-nurse), a neighbor woman, and a *masalcı* famous for her
tales and for her pearls—the latter the favorite of them all and the most
pampered. Following is Mehmet Tevfik's description of a winter evening
in Süleyman Ağa's harem:

When, on cold and snowy nights, the women arrange themselves around the *tandır*
and the heat spreads to their bodies, how their chins wag! Now nonsense is cheap.

The talk of a chatterbox . . . the old *hamam* woman who creates preposterous things
like tales of ogres . . . if the door of the cupboard is open, the mouth of the enemy
will be open . . . if one comes upon one's shoes, one will go out into the street . . .
if one's eyes stare in preoccupation or if a cat scratches itself and puts its feet over
its neck, it is a sign that guests will come. If one were to write down the talk like
this around the *tandır*, it would make a big book.

When the family sat down around the *tandır* with all this nonsense, everyone had
his special place, and the nights were decked out with all kinds of fruits and glasses
of *boza*[50] and cups of roasted chick-peas, and they enjoyed games such as "Is it
odd or is it even?" and seemed to consider true the tales the old woman related.

On winter evenings the family of Süleyman Ağa was quite a world. In January,
when it was stormiest, the ladies arose for coffee after eating, then left their coffee
cups on the *tandır*, and each played music at the hour of the *sofra* (meal). . . . After
a little watery snow had fallen, bird's head snow in big flakes began. . . . No sound
could be heard except the clattering of the wind in the cypresses of the graveyards
on the Sea Road. When the sky became dark and gloomy, Süleyman Ağa's wife
and harem, in order to mitigate the gloom as much as possible, requested a longish
story from the pearl-decorated lady.[51]

She recited for them a tale of three poor girls who sewed for a living in
a country where a cruel ruler had forbidden candles. The listeners inter-
rupted frequently to comment in pity or in indignation. The story had
familiar ingredients: the protagonists were poor, the antagonist an op-

pressive ruler, and the denouement satisfying, for romance led the girls
out of their troubles, after due suffering.[52] It must have been a typical
masalcı tale.

When, in the nineteenth century, the upper-class woman learned to read
and novels became available, there was less need for the *masalcı*. She
either disappeared from the harems of the great houses or was hired to
entertain the less educated among the slaves. One finds no mention of her
at all in Emine Foat Tugay's family history.

We note that Mehmet Tevfik had his women playing a guessing game.
Other games were also popular. Draughts, backgammon, and a game with
seashells called *peçiç* were played. In the summertime, the women amused
themselves with blind man's buff and swinging.[53] European influence brought
in dominoes and card games.

Smoking pipes, often set with precious stones, was another time-honored
pastime of the Ottoman woman. The pleasure of tobacco was introduced
to Istanbul in 1009 A.H. (1600/01). At first it was recommended simply as
a cure for certain diseases, but soon became an addiction and a source of
considerable controversy. Besides giving rise to what was to some the
noxious smoke, it was considered to be the cause of many fires. At times
the *ulema* forbade its use but usually without success. Finally in 1634 the
chief *müftü*, in accordance with the principle that all that was not forbidden
in the Şeriat was permissible, ruled in its favor.[54] We do not know when
tobacco entered the harems, but probably it was no later than the *müftü*'s
ruling. Women must have learned of the pleasure of smoking from the
men of their families. Certainly by the eighteenth century it was one of
women's favorite pastimes.

In the first half of the nineteenth century, Julia Pardoe found older
women smoking the *kadın çubuğu* (woman's pipe) at Göksu,[55] and a very
young woman, the daughter of İskodralı Mustafa Pasha, not only smoking
her *çubuk* but using it "coquettishly."[56] She found the *büyük hanım* (great
lady) of the Reis Efendi (Foreign Minister) of her time "stretched out on
the sofa . . . propped with cushions, glittering with diamonds, and busy with
her chibouk."[57] In Bursa, joining the childbirth reception of the wife of
the *kadı*, she noticed "half a dozen stately Hanoums . . . seated on the
crimson velvet sofa, leaning against its gorgeous cushions, and some of
them engaged with the chibouk."[58] White stated that almost all elderly
Turkish ladies smoked.[59] He also noted that perfumes were used to add
fragrance to the tobacco.[60] Cox was impressed by the amount of tobacco
consumed in the harems.[61] Writing at the end of the nineteenth century,
Clara Erskine Clement found that the Turkish lady still smoked but had
switched to cigarettes; she began her day with them and had them again
with her coffee after dinner.[62] Lucy Garnett, following in the early twentieth century, stated that pipe-smoking had gone out of fashion and had
been replaced by cigarette smoking. With pipe-smoking had gone "the

ancient ceremonial of pipe distributing and lighting. Cigarettes are now handed on a tray to each lady separately, and when she has adjusted one in her amber mouthpiece, another slave approaches with a glowing charcoal ember on a little brass dish from which to light it. When the cigarettes are all alight, the slaves retire to the lower end of the apartment where, ranged in a line, they stand with arms crossed on their bosoms and eyes modestly cast down until their services are required again."[63]

NOTES

1. James M. A. Robson, *Tracts on Listening to Music*, pp. 1-13.

2. Arthur Christensen, *Iran sous les Sassanides*, p. 484; H. G. Farmer, "Musiki," *Encyclopaedia of Islam*, first edition, III, pp. 749-755. Eastern music's octave has varied through the centuries, but in the eighteenth century the Ottomans settled on one based on a 24-tone scale, partly major and partly minor, whose tones were divisible into quarter-tones. The Ottoman octave allowed for unusual intervals. Ottoman music, even the classical music played by the bands, was monophonous, consisting simply of the melodic line, with infinite variations but without harmony or counterpoint (Farmer, ibid.). Westerners remarked on its melancholy (Baron de Tott, *Mémoires sur les Turcs et les Tartares*, I, pp. 157-158).

3. Robson, *Tracts*, pp. 1-13.

4. Sadeddin Nüzhet Ergün, *Türk müziki antolojisi*, I, pp. 444, 487, 567.

5. Ibid., I, p. 640, n. 1.

6. Robert Mantran, *Istanbul dans la seconde moitié du XVIIè siècle*, pp. 500-501.

7. Charles MacFarlane, *Constantinople in 1829*, II, p. 172.

8. İsmail Hakkı Uzunçarşılı, *Osmanlı devletinin saray teşkilâtı*, p. 151.

9. According to Gian-Battista Toderini (*De la littérature des Turcs*, I, pp. 231-233), who made a study of Ottoman music, the chamber instruments the Turks played were the following:

Keman (violin)

"Ajakalı" keman (a type of violin with a pedal, played on the knee)

Sine keman (Toderini calls it a viola d'amore)

Rebap (a kind of guitar, with two strings)

Tambur (Toderini says it has eight strings, seven steel and one brass; *see* above for a different description.

Ney (flute)

Girift (a small *ney*)

"Le neí à octaves"

Mescal (pipes)

Santur (dulcimer or psalter)

Kanun (dulcimer or zither, played by the *saraylıs*)

Daire (tambourine)

10. Ibid., I, p. 150, n. 1; according to *Tarama sözlüğü* (II, p. 243), the *çöğür* is a popular stringed instrument. *Tarama* quotes the *Bürhan-ı katı tercümesi* as saying it was used especially by shepherds, and cites Naima as mentioning the Janissaries playing it.

11. In the latter half of the seventeenth century, in the time of Mehmet IV, some of the musicians who taught the *cariye*s were also puppeteers (Uzunçarşılı, *Saray teşkilâtı*, p. 151).

12. Samuel S. Cox, *Diversions of a Diplomat in Turkey*, p. 524.

13. Julia Pardoe, *The City of the Sultans and Domestic Manners of the Turks in 1836*, I, p. 311.

14. Ibid., I, p. 314. Pardoe goes on to say: "The part taken in this concert by Nazip Hanoum and the Secretary was intended as a high compliment to their Frank visitors; for the Turkish ladies hold it as a degradation to exhibit a talent which is made an object of speculation and profit by hired performers."

15. Melek Hanım [Melek-Hanum], *Thirty Years in the Harem*, pp. 27, 99; Edward William Lane (*The Manners and Customs of the Modern Egyptians*, p. 373) shows a picture of a *darabukkeh*, as he spells it.

16. Reşat Ekrem Koçu, *İstanbul ansiklopedisi*, I, p. 460.

17. Yılmaz Öztuna, "Büyük bestekâr Hacı Ârif Bey," *Hayat tarih mecmuası*, 2 (*Temmuz 1*, 1966), pp. 20-26.

18. Ibid.

19. Abdülhak Şinasi Hisar, "Moonlight on the Bosphorus," p. 73.

20. Selma Ekrem, "Flutist of Old Istanbul," *Christian Science Monitor* (November 26, 1966). Selma Ekrem is Namık Kemal's granddaughter.

21. Ayşe Osmanoğlu, *Babam Abdülhamit*, p. 26.

22. Hisar, "Moonlight," p. 14.

23. Osmanoğlu (*Babam Abdülhamit*, p. 17) says that this band played at the celebration of the marriage of Abdülmecit to Perestû. However, M. Çağatay Uluçay (*Haremden mektuplar*, pp. 167-171) says that the girl Abdülmecit legally married was not Perestû but was Bezmâra, *evlatlık* of İsmail Pasha, son of Kavalalı Mehmet Pasha, and that the sultan later abandoned her because of her jealousy. Charles White (*Three Years in Constantinople*, III, p. 10) mentions one of Abdülmecit's *kadın*s as having been purchased by Rıza Pasha and given to Esma Sultan. A. D. Alderson (*The Structure of the Ottoman Dynasty*) in his Table on Abdülmecit does not list Bezmâra among his *kadın*s. Yet the letter in the Uluçay collection is signed "Cariye-i ahirin Bezmâra Hanım" (Lady Bezmâra, your humble slave).

24. Osmanoğlu, *Babam Abdülhamit*, p. 25; Enver Behnan Şapolyo, *Mustafa Reşit Paşa ve Tanzimat devri tarihi*, p. 191; Tahsin Tunalı, "Türk bestekârlarının asıl meslekleri," *Hayat tarih mecmuası*, 1 (*Haziran 1*, 1965), pp. 27-33.

25. Emine Foat Tugay, *Three Centuries, Family Chronicle of Turkey and Egypt*, p. 103.

26. Hisar, "Moonlight," p. 14.

27. Muftizade K. Ziya Bey, *Speaking of the Turks*, p. 223.

28. Z. Duckett Ferriman, *Turkey and the Turks*, pp. 315-316.

29. Ibid., pp. 311-312. Cox (*Diversions*, p. 524) has also given an account of a pantomimic dance. His authority was Clara Clement Walker, a painter who had access to the harems. Unfortunately, those who witnessed singing and dancing in the harems—such as Julia Pardoe, Melek Hanım, Clara Erskine Clement, Fanny

Blunt, and Lucy Garnett—give little information about the dances and none at all about the songs. On the other hand, Ferriman (*Turkey*, pp. 313-314) has translated the song of a man from Adana, which he calls "The Plaint of the Daughter-in-Law":

O friends, what shall I do?
To whom shall I tell my woes?
Ah! the chin of my husband's mother is never still.
On the shelf there is honey, mother-in-law.

Why do you look unkindly at me?
Your son loves me right well,
Burst and split, mother-in-law.

The hearth cowl is cracked.
My mother-in-law is angry with me.
Let her be angry!
Her son embraces me.

30. Ignatius Mouradgea d'Ohsson, *Tableau général de l'Empire othoman*, IV, pp. 425-426; Mehmet Zeki Pakalın, "Çengi," *Osmanlı tarih deyimleri ve terimleri*, I, pp. 349-350. Along with the dancing troop sometimes went a four-person group of girl musicians. The instruments were the violin, a set of small double drums, and two tambourines.

31. De Tott, *Mémoires*, I, pp. 86-88.

32. Lady Elizabeth Craven, *A Journey Through the Crimea to Constantinople (1786)*, p. 171. Clara Erskine Clement agreed. She witnessed a gypsy dance at a *kına gecesi* and termed it "a most immodest and revolting dance . . . accompanied by indecent songs and gestures" (*Constantinople, the City of the Sultans*, p. 277).

33. Pardoe, *The City*, II, p. 101.

34. Ibid., II, pp. 318-319.

35. Sir W. M. Ramsay, *The Revolution in Constantinople and Turkey*, pp. 275-276.

36. A. Süheyl Ünver, *Levnî*, Plate No. 8.

37. Yakup Kadri Karaosmanoğlu, "Bir kadın meselesi," *Bir serencam*, pp. 141-149.

38. Lady Mary Wortley Montagu, *Letters from the Right Honourable . . . 1709-1762*, p. 133.

39. Tugay, *Three Centuries*, p. 308.

40. Ibid., p. 288.

41. Lady Fanny Blunt (*The People of Turkey*, II, p. 74) reports that even though the Karagöz was indecent, the Turkish women loved it. Hellmut Ritter, whose study (*Karagös, türkische Schattenspiele*, Hannover, 1924 and Lipzig, 1941, 2 vols.) is based on a *saray karagözcüsü*, also believes the exhibitions were definitely lewd. However, Sabri Esat Siyavuşgil points out that there was a vast difference between the burlesque farce exhibited in the coffee houses and the Karagöz performances that took place in the sultan's palace and in the houses of the dignitaries of the Empire. The latter, he says, were put on "by well educated and cultured exhibitors who organized performances of a much more refined type, wherein they brought

into play all the literary, philosophical and musical accomplishments, as well as the gift of satire" (*Karagöz*, p. 7). Seniha Moralı agreed that the performances in the harems were not vulgar, although those put on in the *selâmlık*s "used a language that was considered shocking in those days." She remembered a Karagöz performance put on in her home in her childhood (personal communication, October 1966).

42. Celâl Esat Arseven, *SA*, II, pp. 955-957. Arseven says that the figures were usually nine inches long, but the author has in her possession two old Karagöz figures which measure 12 and 13 inches, respectively. Edmond Saussey explains that the orthodox theologians tolerated Karagöz figures because they were mutilated with holes and moved by rods, which kept them from being considered forbidden representations of human figures ("Le Théatre populaire," *Etudes orientales*, 4, Paris, 1936, p. 74).

43. Siyavuşgil (*Karagöz*, p. 7) says that she was Ahmet III's daughter; but this is unlikely since, according to Alderson (*Structure*, Table XI), his daughters named Ummetullah—there were two—died in infancy. It is more likely that she was Ummetullah, the daughter of Mustafa II, who was born in 1700.

44. Tahsin Öz, "Selim III.ün sırkâtibi tarafından tutulan ruzname," *Tarih vesikaları*, 13 (*Ağustos*, 1944), pp. 26-43.

45. Ibid., 14 (*Ekim*, 1944), pp. 102-116. The same source tells about a European "joking" entertainment called opera put on at the *ağa yeri* for Selim III—and enjoyed. The date for this was May 3, 1797. The *ağa yeri* was the court in the palace gardens where the sultans watched games and displays of horsemanship.

46. Théophile Gautier (*Constantinople*, pp. 163-173) saw, on a Ramazan evening, a "censored" performance of Karagöz. At another time, in a garden behind a café in the Tophane district of Istanbul, he saw an "uncensored" production. Of this he said: "The garden was full of people when we arrived. Children and little girls were there in particular abundance; and their appreciation and enjoyment of a performance too gross for description, was by no means the least singular part of the exhibition . . . Karagheuz is often sent for to perform in the harems; the females witnessing the exhibition from curtained and latticed 'boxes' or enclosures." Gautier thinks that allowing women to see these lubricious performances indicates that the Turks degraded women to the purely animal.

47. Pardoe, *The City*, I, pp. 25-26.

48. Melek Hanım, *Thirty Years*, p. 179. She also said that the Karagöz was used to communicate to the sultan and other great personages what no one would dare to tell them face to face (ibid., p. 99).

49. A kind of table with a brazier underneath it.

50. A fermented drink.

51. Mehmet Tevfik, "Tandırbaşı," *İstanbul'da bir sene*, pp. 12-13.

52. Ibid., pp. 13-38.

53. D'Ohsson, *Tableau général*, IV, p. 412; Musahipzade Celâl, *Eski İstanbul yaşayışı*, p. 104.

54. Bernard Lewis, *Istanbul and the Civilization of the Ottoman Empire*, pp. 133-136.

55. Pardoe, *The City*, II, p. 245.

56. Ibid., I, p. 238.

57. Ibid., II, p. 218.

58. Ibid., II, p. 101.

59. White, *Three Years*, II, p. 128.
60. Ibid., II, p. 80.
61. Cox, *Diversions*, p. 529.
62. Clement, *Constantinople*, pp. 252-253.
63. Lucy M. J. Garnett, *Home Life in Turkey*, pp. 276-277.

10

Intrigue

When authority is granted as a personal favor, there is inevitably a fertile field for intrigue. Moreover, it was natural that the women of the Ottoman Empire, with freedom outside the walls of the harem denied to them, should look for areas within the household in which to further their interests, therefore indulging in what we call "harem intrigue." This type of activity often had as a goal the promotion of their husbands' careers. Several of the more astute Western observers were struck by this point. Adolphus Slade wrote in 1832 that *saraylıs*, in particular, advanced the careers of their husbands and "more pashaliks have been gained by petticoat interest than is supposed."[1] Melek Hanım, writing 40 years later, says: "The promotion of officers is independent of any fixed rule; favor and caprice dictate their selection; the women also employ themselves actively in the matter, on behalf of their sons, their brothers, and their husbands. As they visit a good deal, they try to ingratiate themselves with the wives of the ministers or the generals in chief, and these speak in favor of their protégées when they find themselves alone with their husbands, and, by dint of importunity, obtain from them the steps which they desire."[2] The men seem not to have been so sure of the old Ottoman adage that women are long in hair and short in intelligence after all. Sir Edwin Pears, in his book of reminiscences, which spans the years from 1873 to 1915, reports: "An efficient Turkish officer and gentleman . . . told me that his one chance of promotion was through the connection of his wife with one of the palace ladies."[3] The *saraylıs* were valued as wives for their palace connections, and in general, according to the historian Mehmet Zeki Pakalın, married officials.[4]

The period in which women, especially palace women, had the greatest influence was, of course, the seventeenth-century *Kadınlar Saltanatı*, or Women's Sultanate. However, even when the rule of women had come to an end it did not mean that they no longer counted in matters of state. They simply had to be more subtle in their activities. Women close to the sultan, in particular the *valide*, were always cultivated as a source of power. The same was true of the women of the viziers' families. Since the manners of the time made it impossible for a man seeking office to pay court to the wife of a vizier or the mother of the sultan, either his wife, sister, or mother danced attendance for him, or else he carried out his objectives through the intermediary of a *kethüda* or *harem ağa*. Nassau Senior thought that the fall of a ministry could sometimes be traced to harem intrigue,[5] and Fanny Blunt believed that "the number of viziers and pashas who have attained such high rank solely through the interest and influence of their wives is very great; a fact which, if better known in Europe, would disabuse them of the idea that a Turkish wife of every rank is the slave of her husband."[6] Emine Foat Tugay, writing of the last days of the Empire, speaks of a woman whose husband owed his success to his wife's talent for witty conversation and to her fine voice with which she kept the ladies of important houses entertained.[7] Seniha Moralı was acquainted with a woman who, though poor, had access to the great houses because she came from a family of *şeyh*s and entertained the ladies of high estate with her mimicry of officials.[8]

Because of her closeness to the sultan, the *valide* was both the source and the object of much intrigue. As we have mentioned above, she was the one person who was on near-equal terms with the ruler. Her identification with him was so complete, even in the late nineteenth century, that Murat V's mother, Şevkefza, in speaking about her son's nervous illness at the time of Abdülaziz's suicide, could say, "Everyone knows in what condition *we* were at that time"[9] (italics the author's).

At the beginning of our period Râbia Gülnûş, the mother of both Mustafa II (1695–1703) and Ahmet III (1703–1730), was *valide*. We have numerous examples of her influence. Like all *valide*s she had her agents in Istanbul, from whom she learned of the rising dissatisfaction with her son Mustafa II. The court was then at Edirne, which contributed to the problem, for the populace of Istanbul resented the sultan's absence from their city. At Edirne the *valide* persuaded Mustafa to sacrifice the *şeyhülislâm* and his family in order to save his throne. He signed a *hat* (decree) to that effect, but it failed to quell the unrest. When Râbia Gülnûş realized this and understood that Mustafa would be dethroned, she switched her loyalties to her other son, Ahmet III.[10]

In the days of Mustafa II, as a result of Râbia Gülnûş's influence, her *kethüda*, Hasan Pasha, who had been brought up in the palace, became governor of Egypt, commander of Chios, grand vizier, and governor of Baghdad.[11] Hasan married Hatice Sultan, the daughter of Mehmet IV, and it was shortly after this that he became commander of Chios. Unfortunately, Chios had to be surrendered to the Venetians, as a result of which Hasan was imprisoned. Because of his high connections he was soon pardoned and sent to command the Azak stronghold. Meanwhile, because of his relationship to the imperial family, he became a *rikab-ı hümayun*,[12] *kaymakam*,[13] and, sometime later, governor of Aleppo. Finally, in 1703 when he and his wife were guests of the sultan's niece, Fatma Hanım Sultan, who lived across from the Imperial Gate of Topkapı Palace, Hasan became grand vizier. He received the royal seal at his wife's *yalı* in Ayvansaray, but lost the post the next year because of the intrigues of the *valide*'s *ağa*, Uzun Süleyman, whose appointment as Ağa of the House of Felicity he had blocked. He was then exiled to Izmit. However, his wife was allowed to go with him, which was an extraordinary favor. In 1707 he was appointed governor of Egypt, where his wife was not permitted to go.[14]

Incidentally, after the fall of Hasan in 1704, the *valide*'s *ağa* gained the coveted appointment as Ağa of the House of Felicity (*kızlar ağası*).[15] Hasan was supplanted as grand vizier by Kalaylıkoz Ahmet Pasha, who had the support of the *valide*'s *ağa*. This fact would seem to show that a harem eunuch, because of his day-to-day contact with the *valide* or with the sultan, would be in a better position to promote his desires than a former favorite who had gone out into the world.[16]

Ahmet Pasha did not last long as grand vizier either. In 1706 he was appointed *sancakbeyi* (governor general) of Hanya (the capital of Crete), whence complaints against him were lodged with the Porte. As a result he was removed to the island of İstanköy, from where he appealed to the *valide sultan*. Since Uzun Süleyman had been made *kızlar ağası* during Ahmet Pasha's vizierate, the *ağa* undoubtedly helped to promote his former benefactor's cause. At any rate, in 1710 Ahmet Pasha was awarded the governorship of the *eyalet* (province) of Candia. Once again, he aroused complaints, this time concerning his wish to convert the silver objects from the churches into sets of silver animals, and once again he was sent to İstanköy. Writing of him in *Osmanlı tarihi* (*Ottoman History*), Uzunçarşılı says that he was generous and sincere, but ignorant. His advancement undoubtedly came more from intrigue than from ability.[17]

When Nevşehirli İbrahim Pasha became grand vizier in 1716, his strength of character clipped the influence of the *kızlar ağası*, and the *valide sultan* was by now dead.[18] Yet Nevşehirli İbrahim was susceptible to the special pleading of his wife, Ahmet III's daughter, Fatma Sultan. In 1729 it happened that a French consul along the west coast was attacked by Janissaries while protecting the captain of a Genoese ship that had had an accident. The French consul journeyed to Istanbul to lodge a protest with the Porte, but instead of apologies he received imprisonment. Furthermore, the *kaptan paşa* (head of the navy) abolished the French consulates in the Aegean Islands and Canakkale, which played havoc with French commercial interests. The French ambassador, Villeneuve, tried to straighten things out with the grand vizier, but was unable to make contact with him. However, Villeneuve was acquainted with a Genoese woman who was teaching Fatma Sultan lacemaking, and he decided to make use of this relationship. The woman told the story to Fatma Sultan. The French were popular in the palace at that time—the Tulip Period—and Fatma had the whole story written down and brought to her. She passed it on to her husband, and in a few days İbrahim received Villeneuve. Villeneuve sent Fatma Sultan three diamond buttons in gratitude.[19]

Not all women's influence was so benign. When the Patrona Halil rebellion broke out at the end of Ahmet III's reign, Ahmet's sister, Hatice Sultan, came to the palace to advise him.[20] He was at Edirne, and his advisers had decided he should return to Istanbul in procession, the sacred standard in front of him and the court and princes following him. Hatice suggested that he bring all his ministers along, so that if the mob demanded satisfaction, he could save his life and his throne by sacrificing them. This is very nearly what happened. First Ahmet gave up the *kaptan paşa* and the *kethüda* to the rebels but tried to save the life of İbrahim. The mob offered to let the *şeyhülislâm* go into exile, but was firm in its demands for the life of the grand vizier. And so Nevşehirli İbrahim, who had been responsible for so much of both the accomplishment and the follies of Ahmet III's reign, met his end.[21]

On the accession of Mahmut I to the throne in 1730, his *valide*, Saliha, filled the vacuum left since the death of Râbia Gülnûş and became a power. In the past, families who had wanted to place their sons in imperial service had got them in via the Janissaries; now they sent the boys directly to the *valide sultan*. The rabble-rouser Patrona Halil, though he was riding high at the time, nevertheless thought it necessary to have an interview with both the Ağa of the House of Felicity and the *valide sultan*.[22] Soon after Saliha was installed in the *valide*'s suite in Topkapı, the bailo (the Venetian resident at the Porte), Angelo Emo, sent her 24 robes, along with perfumes, mirrors, and other feminine fripperies.[23]

In the early years of Mahmut I's reign the sultan changed grand viziers often, supposedly on the advice of Ahmet III who thought he had made a mistake in keeping Nevşehirli İbrahim in office so long. The result of this new policy—there were five grand viziers in four years and four months— was necessarily, and without doubt purposefully, the absence of a forceful personality in the post. During this period there were complaints of excessive influence wielded by the *valide*, and it was said that Kabakulak İbrahim Pasha, grand vizier in 1731, had to pay a considerable sum to the Ağa of the House of Felicity and the *valide* in order to secure his position. This constant changing of grand viziers left the door open for intrigue, and even the support of his powerful patrons did not help Kabakulak İbrahim keep his post very long.[24]

There were also strong-willed and powerful women outside of the palace. Take, for example, Âdile Hanım, the wife of Mızraklı Süleyman Pasha, known as Ebu Leyle (Abū Laylā), who was governor of Baghdad during the reign of Mahmut I (1730–1754). Âdile was the daughter of Ahmet Pasha, a governor of Baghdad, and granddaughter of the famous Hasan Pasha, a governor, who founded a ruling dynasty there. Her father married her to his *kâhya*, Süleyman, a Georgian who had been a slave, which was an asset to him in Baghdad where Caucasian slaves had long enjoyed a high status. Although Süleyman was a tough general and an efficient administrator, Âdile seems to have dominated him. She held audiences herself, receiving both men and women, interfered in affairs of state, and even organized her followers into an association in which their mark of distinction was a silk badge. On Süleyman's death Ali Pasha, who had been his *kâhya*, succeeded him as governor. But Âdile resented having the power pass from her hands and conspired to get rid of him. Ali Pasha was forced to flee Baghdad, dressed as a woman, but was killed before he reached safety. Âdile then conspired to have her younger sister's husband, Ömer Pasha, appointed in his place. Ömer turned out to be a weakling, and chaos reigned under him.[25] Âdile is also implicated in the death of a former enemy of her family, Selim Pasha Baban.[26]

Several men attained high rank through marriage to Saliha, sister of Mustafa III (1757–1774). The best known of her husbands was Ragıp Pasha, called by Hammer the last of the great grand viziers. After Ragıp's death, she married once again, this time Tursu Mehmet Pasha, who was then raised to the rank of *kaptan paşa* for the second time, and honored by the title of Melek (Angel) for being willing to marry the much-widowed and no longer young Saliha Sultan.[27]

After the death of Ragıp Pasha the ensuing grand viziers' authority was nominal, and Mustafa ruled largely by himself. One of these powerless grand viziers, Muhsinzade Mehmet, was married to Esma Sultan,[28] a cherished sister of Mustafa III. By this connection, as well as by his submission to the will of Mustafa, he was able to keep his post.[29] A niece of Mustafa III had particular influence during his reign. He so much admired her youth and beauty that she was able to get a slave she had known in the palace, one Bekir, first appointed to the post of *reis-ül-küttap* and later made a vizier. She was married to the governor of Rumelia who later became *kaptan paşa*. She kept her influence at court until 1757, when she refused to reveal where her husband had hidden his valuables.[30] De Tott tells of successfully using the influence of a *hanım sultan* in behalf of a candidate for the Patriarchate. It may well have been the same *hanım sultan*.[31]

One of the most active intriguers of the late eighteenth and early nineteenth centuries was Ahretlik Hanım, or Dür-ü-Şehvar, who was a daughter of Abdülhamit I (1774–1789), born to him while he was still a prince. Somehow in this instance the rule that the princes would be given only barren *cariye*s too old for childbirth went awry. She was credited with being a great favorite of her father's and took full advantage of her position to indulge in intrigue. She was married to Ahmet Nazif Efendi, a statesman who rose in rank thanks to her efforts. Ahretlik was also thought to have had a hand in the dismissal of Halil Hamit Pasha, although Uzunçarşılı credits Abdülhamit I's sister, Esma Sultan, with having been the person who learned of Halil Hamit's plan to depose Abdülhamit and put the far abler Selim on the throne.[32] Ahretlık Hanım's interference in this matter brought on her head her husband's wrath, and she was shut up in her *konak* during the execution of Halil Hamit and not heard of again until the deposition of Selim III. But she gained the favor of Mahmut II, who assigned her to accompany his mother from the Old Palace to Topkapı.[33]

The women of the imperial harem took sides passionately in disputes concerning the throne. Peyk-i Dil, a *kadın* of Mustafa IV (1807–1808), looked on and made no attempt to rescue Selim III when he was killed in the harem in Topkapı Palace. She was later executed by Mahmut II (1808–1839).[34]

Melek Hanım, Kıbrıslı Mehmet Pasha's Levantine wife, tells a story of intrigue a little later in the nineteenth century in which women played their part. At the time Kıbrıslı was a young officer under the command of Mehmet Ali Pasha, son-in-law of Mahmut II and commander of the To-phane armory. Mehmet Ali and Minister of War Rıza Pasha persuaded the sultan to purge the army of 12 generals who were out of their favor. Kıbrıslı was one of them. He had to give up his sword and his diamond decorations, the emblems of his rank. His income was much reduced and Kıbrıslı and his wife lived close to poverty for two years until Melek, by catering to Rıza's favorite wife, who was a *saraylı*, obtained his appointment to the governorship of Acre.[35] Later, when Kıbrıslı wanted the post of ambassador to London, he sent Melek to negotiate with the wife of Reşit Pasha (the great Tanzimat statesman). This maneuver was supposed to save Kıbrıslı's face in the event that he failed to get the nomination. As it happened, he was appointed, and the first news of their success came via Reşit's wife's message to Melek Hanım.[36]

Melek Hanım also writes about a *kadın* of the late Mahmut II. The lady, who was probably Hûşyar Hanım, wanted Kıbrıslı to use his influence with Reşit Pasha in behalf of her son-in-law, Sait Pasha. Reşit Pasha was then grand vizier and Kıbrıslı his protégé. The ruling group at the time was roughly divided into conservatives, who thought that all the difficulties of the Empire stemmed from lack of adherence to the early Muslim virtues and who abhorred the *gâvur* (unbeliever), on the one hand, and the re-formers, led by Reşit Pasha, on the other. Sait Pasha belonged to the conservative element. According to Melek Hanım, Sait Pasha told Sultan Abdülmecit (1839–1861) that the result of Reşit Pasha's policy would be the loss of provinces to England and France. His remarks were reported to the grand vizier and Sait Pasha was exiled. Melek Hanım heeded the *kadın efendi*'s pleas to take up Sait Pasha's cause with Kıbrıslı, who in turn took it up with Reşit Pasha. Sait Pasha was given the *valilik* (governorship) of Damascus, an appointment which had the virtue of giving him a position in keeping with his station and of getting him out of the way, at one and the same time.[37]

Hûşyar Hanım had long been a partisan of her son-in-law. Shortly after his marriage to her daughter, Mihrimah Sultan, Sait Pasha had incurred Mahmut's displeasure and been exiled to the provinces, to his wife's and mother-in-law's distress. At this time, as Mahmut's second *kadın*, Hûşyar had felt sufficiently sure of her influence to petition the padishah directly, and did so in a letter. She followed this up with two letters of thanks, one when Mahmut granted her request and ordered Sait Pasha brought back to Istanbul, the other when the young pasha actually arrived.[38]

At the time Melek Hanım knew Hûşyar, the latter was an unhappy woman. Her daughter had died in childbirth, and with the death of Mahmut she had lost her influence at court. Hence her recourse to Kıbrıslı.[39]

Kıbrıslı Mehmet Pasha, despite the complexities of his private life, was an able public servant. He continued to rise in the service of the state and by 1860 was grand vizier, which gave him more women problems, for now he had to contend with the corruption of Abdülmecit's *valide*.[40]

In the days of Abdülmecit another kind of intrigue went on, which, while it did not directly involve women, involved their habitat. Henry Layard has written of the information-collecting missions he was sent on by British Ambassador, Sir Stratford Canning. These missions frequently landed him, late at night, in some harem up the Bosphorus or in an out-of-the-way corner of Istanbul. There he had interviews with various members of the Reform Party in otherwise empty harem rooms, where no opposition spies could lurk.[41]

The final illness of Abdülmecit in 1861 started a spate of rumors that there was a group in the palace who wanted Murat to succeed to the throne instead of Abdülaziz. There seems to have been no truth in these allegations, but they nevertheless worried Abdülaziz and especially his mother, Pertevniyal. On the night when Abdülmecit died and the grand vizier, the *kaptan paşa*, and the commander-in-chief of the Army conducted Abdülaziz (1861–1876) from the heir's suite to the ruler's suite in Dolmabahçe, Pertevniyal thought they were taking him prisoner. They waited in the sultan's suite until the imperial caiques were ready, and then escorted Abdülaziz to Topkapı, the palace of his forebears, to await the gathering of the council of ministers, some of whom had to be summoned from their homes up the Bosphorus. Pertevniyal, to reassure herself, followed him there.[42]

Abdülaziz's reign was rife with intrigue, partly owing to the pervasive influence of Pertevniyal and to the ruler's instability of character. He was known to have strange desires, such as a craving for the company of rare animals and birds. After the death of his able grand vizier Ali Pasha, who had exercised a stabilizing influence over him, his government became increasingly capricious.[43] The fact that the sultan's hold on mental health was insecure was known by the women of his entourage and suspected by the public. The *saraylı*s and the *valide* suspected that a spell had been cast on him and hired *şeyh*s to counteract it. At the time the *valide* had a special prayer read for him in some of the imperial mosques during the Friday sermon (*hütbe*), a circumstance which increased uneasiness about his mental condition.[44]

When Abdülaziz took his trip to Europe, his mother was anxious about him the whole time he was away. On his way home he stopped at Rusçuk, where Mithat was governor, with the intention of staying a month and acquainting himself with the Balkan country. But Pertevniyal, a possessive and short-sighted woman, wrote him to come home immediately. Sultan of Turkey though he was, he obeyed his mother's command.[45]

Pertevniyal contributed to the instability of her son's rule by meddling in affairs of state. Especially unwise was her alliance with Mahmut Nedim Pasha, the sycophantic grand vizier whose recklessness and incompetence led to further financial chaos.[46] There was such an outcry against Mahmut Nedim that he finally fell from power in 1876 and was succeeded by Mithat Pasha, who did his best to get the Empire on a sounder financial footing. There was a sum of 100,000 Turkish lira unaccounted for in the budget, and Mithat discovered that it had been appropriated by Mahmut Nedim. Privately Mahmut Nedim disclosed that the money had not been spent by him but had gone to the palace, presumably to the *valide sultan*. Mahmut Nedim was exiled from the capital for a while, but with the *valide*'s powerful backing was soon able to return. Mithat's efforts at financial reform were blocked, and he was replaced by Mahmut Nedim.[47] Finally, when talk of Abdülaziz's deposition was in the air, Pertevniyal sent a harem *ağa* to Mithat requesting him to prepare a document giving his advice on how her son could save his throne. Mithat carefully composed such a document which was approved by the *valide*, but neither she nor anyone else had the courage at this point, with the sultan in a highly nervous state, to submit it to him.[48]

By now the die was cast. Hüseyin Avni Pasha, the Minister of War, was rallying important men to his project of deposing Abdülaziz. Among others, he enlisted Mithat, and plans were made for the coup on May 31, 1876. Mithat had an informant in the palace, a *saraylı* who kept in touch with him, doubtless through his *büyük hanım*, the extremely capable Fatma Naime. Shortly before the appointed date, the *saraylı* sent word that the palace was suspicious and alarmed, and so the date was moved one day ahead.[49]

On that fateful night of May 30 warships converged on Dolmabahçe, and two battalions surrounded it on the land side. Those on duty in the palace, the *nöbet kalfa*s and the *ağa*s, awoke the *valide*, telling her it looked as if there were a fire. She, viewing the warlike assemblage through a window, knew that what she feared was about to happen: the deposition of her son. She herself awakened him, warned him of the approaching crisis, and said, "It is the will of God."[50]

"Have they then," he asked, remembering the fate of Selim III, "transformed me into Sultan Selim?" Outside of his bedroom window the warships met his eye, and he turned to his mother and confessed he had dreamed of this event many times.[51]

The intrigue that had whirled about Abdülaziz did not cease with his dethronement, nor even with his death a few days later. Çerkes Hasan, the brother of Abdülaziz's second *kadın*, broke into the *konak* of Mithat Pasha during a cabinet meeting and killed Minister of War Hüseyin Avni Pasha, the Minister of Foreign Affairs, and several attendants. Mithat escaped only because he happened to be standing near a door to the harem and disappeared through it. It has never been clear to what extent, if any, Hasan's attack was instigated by his sister, or by Abdülaziz's son, Yusuf İzzeddin, whose aide-de-camp Hasan had been.[52]

On the night of the day Abdülaziz committed suicide—with nail scissors given him by his mother—the new *valide*, Murat V's mother, Şevkefza, when questioned as to how those around Abdülaziz had been appointed, imperially answered, "I cannot call to mind the reason why I should suffer the responsibility for these names."[53]

That might have ended the matter had Murat V (1876) remained sultan. But Murat's mental condition being even worse than that of Abdülaziz, Mithat and the other king-makers engineered a second *coup* and installed Abdülhamit II (1876–1909) on the throne before a year was out. However, Mithat had taken the precaution of securing Abdülhamit's assurance that he would promulgate a constitution, and there is certain evidence that he had received Abdülhamit's pledge, in writing, to abdicate should Murat regain his health. Mithat Pasha's son, Ali Haydar Mithat, published a letter from Mithat Pasha to Mme. Mithat, instructing her to send to London for safe-keeping as soon as possible a certain letter she would find in a blue paper envelope. "That letter, relative to the future of the Sultan, ought to be sent later to the heir presumptive," Mithat Pasha wrote his wife. "If it is not possible to send it to London, destroy it to keep it from falling into the hands of the present government." According to Ali Haydar Mithat, the letter comprised Abdülhamit's pledge.[54]

When Ali Haydar Mithat speaks of Mme. Mithat, as he does throughout his life of his father, he undoubtedly means his father's first wife, Fatma Naime. He never says "my mother," for his mother was Şehriban Hanım, Mithat Pasha's much younger second wife. Although Mithat Pasha was very devoted to Şehriban Hanım and her children, it is clear from his letters from prison in Tâif that he turned to Fatma Naime Hanım in practical matters.[55] Therefore, it was undoubtedly Fatma Naime not only to whom the above letter was addressed, but who hid all the incriminating papers in the cradle of Şehriban Hanım's youngest baby, then only 40 days old, the night the authorities came to Mithat Pasha's official residence in Izmir to arrest him.

The personal war that Abdülhamit carried on against Mithat after the ruler suspended the Constitution of 1876—a document into which Mithat had put his heart—is well known. What is less well known is that Abdülhamit's officers continued to harass Mithat Pasha's family long after Mithat Pasha himself had been killed and, in fact, until Abdülhamit's abdication.[56]

The harassment began when the order to arrest Mithat Pasha reached Izmir. Mithat Pasha, warned by a personal agent, fled to the French Consulate for protection, but later gave himself up. Meanwhile, troops ransacked his house and even broke into the harem. Fatma Naime finally sent for the commander, Hilmi Pasha, and threatened to open the windows and call to the people for help if the troops did not leave. Hilmi forthwith pulled them out, stationing only one or two soldiers as guards.[57]

One night the family was turned out of the official residence and had to spend the rest of the night in a neighboring garden. The next day they were able to find living quarters. Interestingly, the two wives, though remaining friendly toward one another, each took a house of her own.[58]

Abdülhamit used the death of Abdülaziz as a pretext for getting rid of Mithat Pasha and, as we know, staged a fake trial in which fabricated evidence was presented that led to the pasha's conviction, exile, and death. Some of this evidence was presented by the wife of one Münir Bey, who pressured her into giving it and, as his reward, was made a pasha.[59] Although the plot originated in the mind of Abdülhamit, it is not unlikely that he ended up believing it. He tried to pry evidence out of Murat's mother, but she adhered to her story, saying in her final statement: "Neither I nor my son has any information about the appointees to the suite of the late ruler. On the first day of the deposition, everything having to do with Sultan Aziz and the palace was the duty of Hüseyin Avni Pasha, and Nuri was his representative. . . . As for the order given regarding the late ruler, it was to look after and strive for his rest and repose."[60] Yet, in his memoirs, Abdülhamit implicated a *kalfa* of the royal harem named Ebru Nigâr, who was a frequent visitor to the *konaks* and *yalıs* of Hüseyin Avni and Murat and "others of the seditious great, and was an intriguer," along with Cevher Ağa (the Ağa of the House of Felicity), Murat's mother, and Hüseyin Avni.[61]

What happened to Abdülaziz was very well established, both from the evidence given by his mother at the time and by the depositions of Western doctors who were brought in to examine him. He had cut an artery in his arm with the scissors that his mother had given him, and his body was found very shortly after the suicide. Yet all sorts of gossip persisted, and people who should have known better were wont to elaborate on the story. Lady Blunt in her *Reminiscences*[62] said she talked about Abdülaziz with a woman who maintained they heard him cry for help and found him dead the next morning. According to her, the women of his entourage denied he had committed suicide and said a fortune in gems disappeared that day. There may have been a natural unwillingness on the part of his women to admit the suicide. The Western press, however, published the sworn statements of the doctors and the statement Abdülaziz's mother made before Abdülhamit's people got hold of her and talked her into changing her story. In that statement she blamed herself for having given him the scissors.[63]

Mithat Pasha was the only important person whom Abdülhamit had executed, but he persecuted others. A military aide of his, İsmail Fazıl Bey, was exiled to Erzincan in the late nineteenth century, whereupon his wife, Zekiye, wrote the sultan that if her husband was not released she would run off to France and spread word of Abdülhamit's despotism. When she received no answer, she made arrangements with the captain of a French ship to take refuge in his cabin, where she locked herself in. Abdülhamit sent a messenger to tell her that her husband would be brought back to Istanbul if she returned to shore, but the captain advised her not to leave the cabin and informed the messenger that the ship was French territory over which the Porte had no jurisdiction. The ship then went to Izmir, where the same thing happened, but Zekiye held out and sailed to France. Finally she received word that her husband had been forgiven, but she still refused to return until she had a letter in his own handwriting telling that he was free.[64]

Zekiye was part German. Her father had been a German named Karl Detroit, who was converted to Islam and became Mehmet Ali Pasha. He was a protégé of Âli Pasha, went to military school in Turkey, fought in the Crimean War, and was commander of the Ottoman army in the Russo-Turkish War of 1877–78, where he was forced to retreat and was replaced. He was mobbed and killed by Albanian insurgents in September, 1878.[65]

His daughter Zekiye was married at 14 and was about 30 when she fled to France. She is said to have been very religious. Perhaps her religious education was emphasized because she had a foreign parent, as was the case with her daughter-in-law, Leylâ Cebesoy. Zekiye and her husband were the parents of the famous Turkish general, Ali Fuat Cebesoy (1882–1968).[66]

Abdülhamit II's heir was his brother, Reşat, who became Mehmet V (1909-1918). Pears reported that all the women of Reşat's harem, even to the scullions, were appointed by Abdülhamit and acted as his spies.[67] İsmail Kemal further wrote that a Greek girl, who was supposed to have been a favorite of Reşat's, was murdered because she was suspected of acting as intermediary between Reşat and certain foreigners. One does not know whether this is true. İsmail Kemal himself was suspected of having some sort of understanding with Reşat via his Circassian servants and Reşat's Circassian women.[68] It was a time of guilt by association.

The harem *ağa*s were frequently the center of intrigue. İsmail Kemal maintained that the Porte refused to go to the aid of Egypt during an uprising in Alexandria because a certain eunuch, Bayram Ağa, claiming to have special knowledge of the situation via a woman connected with the British Embassy, advised against such an excursion.[69] It is interesting how often a woman's influence was involved in these tales, whether they were true or not. To add to the confusion, men writers often shielded themselves from the sultan's wrath by using women's names. Ahmet Rasim, for example, signed his work Leylâ Feride.[70]

During the reign of Abdülhamit II there were two kinds of intrigue going on in the Ottoman Empire, one in behalf of the sultan and the other against him. Women were involved on both sides. In the early days of the Young Turk movement, as well as during the 1908 Revolution, women carried messages for the Young Turks because police agents were not allowed to search them.[71] But these agents could, nonetheless, make life very difficult for the women they suspected of indulging in illicit political activity. One of their favorite targets was the family of Mithat Pasha. These people, forbidden to return to Istanbul, had continued to live in Izmir. By the time of the Young Turks, Mithat's younger wife had died of tuberculosis, and her children were being brought up by Fatma Naime, the elder wife. Mithat's and Şehriban's son, Ali Haydar, had been smuggled out of the country because the family felt his life was in danger. From Europe, Ali Haydar sent messages for the Young Turks to his sister, Mesrure, who had been only 40 days old when Mithat was arrested and only four years old when he was strangled. Since her house was searched every six or eight months by the sultan's men, she had to be careful where she put the letters. Sometimes she hid them under the tiles of the roof. Once, when they came to arrest her husband and take him to Istanbul for questioning, Mesrure was caught with very little notice. This time she hid the letters in the cradle of her son, even as, in earlier years, papers had been hidden in her own cradle.[72]

This, the elder of her two sons, she had named after his grandfather, but so obsessive was Abdülhamit's fear of Mithat that it extended even to his name, and one day an emissary of the palace arrived at Mesrure Hanım's home to inform her that the sultan insisted that the boy's name be changed. So for a time, until the Revolution of 1908, the boy Mithat was known as Numan.[73]

Mesrure Hanım received the letters from her brother via the French Consulate and a priest in Izmir, and used her children's French governess as her courier to pass them on. She had a good measure of her father's energy and determination, and involved herself in politics when still very young. Sometimes she was followed by soldiers on the street, but her purpose—to advance the liberal and constitutional principles of her father—did not waver.[74]

Ali Haydar returned to Turkey after the Young Turk Revolution, and had the amazing experience of being offered in marriage a daughter of Vahideddin, the last sultan (1918–1922). The Young Turks, who ruled the country, thought that they would thus heal the breach between the imperial family and that of Mithat Pasha, but the breach was too deep and Mithat's family had suffered too much. Ali Haydar refused the honor.[75]

When the Young Turks took power they found that every department of government was top-heavy with employees, many of whom had been appointed through the influence of the imperial harem.[76] Now, however, that influence had waned. But not so the need of a wife to protect her husband. During the counter-revolution of 1909, among the liberals whose lives were in danger was Emine Foat Tugay's father, Mahmut Muhtar Pasha. A general, he personally fought the rebellious troops in Beyazit Square, and, when he finally returned to his home in Moda, was attacked there. He managed to escape across a neighboring Frenchman's yard to the house of Sir William and Lady Whittall, which gave his wife time to arrange for him to get out of the country. This she did by obtaining a German Embassy launch to transport him from the Whittalls' pier to a British ship. He disembarked at Piraeus and made his way back to Istanbul after the rebellion had been crushed.[77]

As the Empire drew to its close, the part played by women became more open, and we find direct action replacing behind-the-scenes intrigue. What would have been unthinkable a few years before happened on June 6, 1919, when Halide Edip stood unveiled in Sultanahmet Square and asked the people to swear that they would not bow down to the Greek invasion of Izmir.[78]

NOTES

1. Adolphus Slade, *Records of Travels in Turkey, Greece, etc.*, II, pp. 316–317.

2. Melek Hanım, *Thirty Years in the Harem*, pp. 33–34.

3. Sir Edwin Pears, *Forty Years in Constantinople*, p. 222.

4. Mehmet Zeki Pakalın, *Osmanlı tarih deyimleri ve terimleri sözlüğü*, III, p. 127.

5. Nassau W. Senior, *A Journal Kept in Turkey and Greece in the Autumn of 1857 and the Beginning of 1858*, p. 83.

6. Lady Fanny Blunt, *The People of Turkey*, II, p. 100.

7. Emine Foat Tugay, *Three Centuries, Family Chronicle of Turkey and Egypt*, p. 251.

8. Personal interview, August 20, 1966.

9. Halûk Y. Şehsüvaroğlu, *Sultan Aziz, hususi, siyasi, hayatı, devri ve ölümü*, p. 192.

10. Joseph de Hammer-Purgstall, *Histoire de l'Empire ottoman depuis son origine jusqu'à nos jours* XIII, p. 119.

11. Clément Huart, *Histoire de Baghdad dans les temps modernes*, p. 136.

12. Member of the sultan's suite, literally imperial stirrup.

13. Representative of the grand vizier.

14. İsmail Hakkı Uzunçarşılı, *Osmanlı tarihi*, IV, pp. 273–274, 274 n. 3, and 279.

15. Hammer, *HEO*, XIII, p. 256.

16. Uzunçarşılı, *Osmanlı tarihi*, IV, p. 277.

17. Ibid., p. 279.

18. Râbia Gülnûş died toward the end of 1715 (Hammer, *HEO*, XIII, p. 288).

19. Ahmet Refik [Altınay], *Lâle devri*, pp. 110–111.

20. Ibid., p. 148.

21. Hammer, *HEO*, XIV, p. 222; Uzunçarşılı, *Osmanlı tarihi*, IV, p. 312. According to Mary Lucille Shay (*The Ottoman Empire from 1720 to 1734*, p. 32), after her husband's death and her father's deposition, Fatma worked to restore Ahmet to the throne, but her only reward was imprisonment. We have not seen this corroborated and have some doubts as to the likelihood of a woman *sultan* being imprisoned.

22. Ahmet Refik, *Lâle devri*, pp. 154–155; Shay, *The Ottoman Empire*, pp. 30–32.

23. Emo, of course, also sent gifts to the grand vizier, among them a robe. The *reis efendi* saw the robe and requested one like it for his wife. Emo sent her four robes and a small gold watch and chain. The former *kaptan paşa* asked for a piece of green and gold brocade for a dress for his wife, but refused the material offered because it was the wrong color and in two pieces (Shay, *The Ottoman Empire*, pp. 51, 54).

24. Shay, *The Ottoman Empire*, pp. 320–321; Uzünçarşılı, *Osmanlı tarihi*, IV, p. 319.

25. Stephen Hemsley Longrigg, *Four Centuries of Modern Iraq*, pp. 169–174; Clément Huart, " 'Adile *Khātūn*," *EI²*, I, p. 199; Huart, *Histoire de Baghdad dans les temps modernes*, pp. 153–154. There are some differences in the stories as told by Huart and Longrigg; we have followed Longrigg.

26. Longrigg, *Four Centuries*, pp. 169, 179.

27. Hammer, *HEO*, XVI, p. 153.

28. Esma Sultan was 33 at the time of the marriage, which was her second (*see* A. D. Alderson, *The Structure of the Ottoman Dynasty*, Table XLI; Uzunçarşılı, *Osmanlı tarihi*, IV, p. 400).

29. Hammer, *HEO*, XVI, p. 163.

30. Ibid., p. 19. He does not give her name.

31. According to de Tott, the Patriarch Kirlo of Istanbul and Kalinico, Archbishop of Amalfie, had had a fight over the issue of baptism by immersion. De Tott hid Kalinico until de Tott's brother-in-law, who had connections with the *hanım sultan*, was able to secure a *hat-ı şerif* deposing Kirlo and appointing Kalinico to the Patriarchate. When the vizier's men came to escort the new Patriarch to his palace, he was at first afraid to emerge from his hiding place but was finally compelled to do so by de Tott (*Memoires sur les Turcs et les Tartares*, I. pp. 91–97).

32. Uzunçarşılı, *Osmanlı tarihi*, IV, pp. 434, 496.

33. Reşat Ekrem Koçu, *İstanbul ansiklopedisi*, I, p. 311.

34. Alderson, *The Structure*, Table XVV, n. 3.

35. Melek Hanım, *Thirty Years*, pp. 45–48, 52–53.

36. Ibid., pp. 140–141.

37. Ibid., p. 130.

38. M. Çağatay Uluçay, *Haremden mektuplar*, pp. 139–143.

39. Melek Hanım tells a story concerning Hûşyar's reluctance to become Mahmut's concubine, a story that may have been true in view of the fact that it meant being shut off from the world during his lifetime. However, Melek Hanım adds that Mahmut wooed Hûşyar for about ten days and had nothing further to do with her (*Thirty Years*, p. 130), a tale manifestly untrue. In the first place, the status of *kadın* she gained by giving birth to a child would have placed her among those honored by a *nöbet gece*, and second, it is of record that she had another child, Zeynep Sultan, who died young (Uluçay, *Haremden mektuplar*, p. 138). Reşit Pasha and Kıbrıslı Mehmet Pasha fell out in later years, Melek Hanım said as a result of Reşit's wife and Kıbrıslı's second wife not getting along. Here one must make allowances for Melek Hanım's resentment of Kıbrıslı's second wife. On the other hand, Melek Hanım had been close to Reşit Pasha's wife, which may have in itself caused a gulf between this lady and Kıbrıslı's second wife. However, although Kıbrızlı's loss of petticoat influence may have had something to do with it, Melek Hanım oversimplifies the reasons for the differences between him and Reşit Pasha. The old protector-protégé relationship gave way to one of political rivalry (Melek Hanım, *Thirty Years*, p. 185).

40. Enver Ziya Karal, *Osmanlı tarihi*, VI, p. 107.

41. Sir Austin Henry Layard, *Autobiography and Letters*, II, pp. 56–57.

42. Sehsüvaroğlu, *Sultan Aziz*, pp. 24–25.

43. Roderic H. Davison, *Reform in the Ottoman Empire, 1856–1876*, pp. 268–270.

44. Sehsüvaroğlu, *Sultan Aziz*, p. 32.

45. İsmail Kemal, *The Memoirs of İsmail Kemal Bey*, pp. 36–37. İsmail Kemal Bey was an Albanian in the service of the Porte and was a member of the imperial entourage on this trip.

46. Davison, *Reform*, p. 282.

47. Ali Haydar Midhat [Mithat], *The Life of Midhat Pasha*, pp. 64–65; Ali Haydar Midhat Bey, *Midhat-Pacha, son vie—son oeuvre, par son fils*, pp. 29–30. There is certain information in the French edition that the English edition does not carry. *See* also Clément Huart, "Midhat Pacha," *Revue du monde musulman*, 8 (1909), pp. 419–430.

48. Şehsüvaroğlu, *Sultan Aziz*, p. 72.

49. Ali Haydar Midhat, *Midhat Pasha*, p. 83.

50. Şehsüvaroğlu, *Sultan Aziz*, p. 95.

51. Davison, *Reform*, p. 335; Şehsüvaroğlu, *Sultan Aziz*, pp. 95–96.

52. Davison, *Reform*, p. 346; George Washburn, *Fifty Years in Constantinople and Recollections of Robert College*, p. 106; personal interview with Mithat Akçit, Mithat Pasha's grandson, July 1966.

53. Şehsüvaroğlu, *Sultan Aziz*, pp. 189–192.

54. Ali Haydar Midhat Bey, *Midhat-Pacha*, p. 65. This letter is not in the English

edition, Ali Haydar Mithat explained, because he found it only after publication of that book. His father had written the letter after his arrest by Abdülhamit's men in Izmir. *See* also Davison, *Reform*, pp. 353 and 419–421.

55. Personal interviews with Mithat Akçit, July-August, 1966.

56. Personal interviews with Mithat Akçit and the late Mesrure Akçit, Mithat Pasha's daughter, July-August, 1966.

57. Ali Haydar Midhat, *Midhat Pasha*, pp. 200–204.

58. Personal interviews with Mithat Akçit, July-August, 1966; İsmail Hakkı Uzinçarşılı, *Midhat Paşa ve Tâif mahkûmları*, pp. 45, 182, 195.

59. Ali Haydar Midhat Bey, *Midhat-Pacha*, p. 192, n. 1.

60. Şehsüvaroğlu, *Sultan Aziz* pp. 189–192.

61. Abdülhamit II, *Abdülhamit'in hatıra defteri*, pp. 154ff.

62. Lady Fanny Blunt, *My Reminiscences*, pp. 159–160.

63. *See* Ali Haydar Midhat, *Midhat Pasha*, pp. 219–220, where he quotes the *Times of London* for July 7, 1881.

64. Interview with Leylâ Cebesoy, Zekiye's daughter-in-law, August 1966.

65. Ibid.

66. Ibid.

67. Pears, *Forty Years*, p. 287.

68. İsmail Kemal, *Memoirs*, pp. 283–284.

69. Ibid., p. 229.

70. *See* Fevziye Abdullah Tansel, *Ziya Gökalp külliyatı, II.*

71. Pears, *Forty Years*, p. 288; Sir Edwin Pears, *Turkey and Its People*, p. 65.

72. Personal interviews with Mesrure Akçit and with Mithat Akçit, Mithat Pasha's daughter and grandson, respectively, July-August, 1966.

73. Ibid.

74. Ibid.

75. Ali Haydar Mithat, *Hatırlarım 1872-1946*, pp. 233–236.

76. Pears, *Forty Years*, p. 244.

77. Tugay, *Three Centuries*, p. 60.

78. Halide Edip, *The Turkish Ordeal*, p. 32.

11

Costume

The Ottoman lady of the eighteenth and nineteenth centuries dressed much as her forebears did in the sixteenth and seventeenth. As d'Ohsson has pointed out, the changes in fashion that the European woman followed did not attract her. In fact, it was not until the late nineteenth century that she was even aware of them. So the dress we shall describe here is the traditional dress of the upper-class Ottoman lady before Western influence set in. In doing so, it seems best to begin with lists of the items she habitually wore, the costumes differing only in minor details.[1] We shall start with articles that covered the trunk of the body,[2] then list head and foot coverings, and finally accessories.

BODY COVERINGS

Cepken (*Çepken*)—a short jacket with slit sleeves, often heavily embroidered.[3]

Çarşaf—a two-piece, dark-colored outer garment for street wear that covered a woman from head to foot. One piece was a skirt, one a sort of cape that started at the top of the head and came down over the skirt. It was introduced into Istanbul from Syria during the Tanzimat.[4] At first it incurred official displeasure, but it came to be the accepted feminine outer garment.[5] A short history of its use in Istanbul is given below.

Dizlik or *Don*—drawers that reached halfway down the leg and were tied with a drawstring called *uçkur*. The leg opening was frequently ornamented with lace edging.[6]

Entari—the dress proper. It was long, reaching to the floor and sometimes trailing,[7] low of neck, open in front from the waist down, and above the waist closed here and there with buttons, often jeweled. Its skirt consisted of segments: in the earlier periods, three of them that flowed freely from the hips; as time went on, two; and finally only one piece of material that surrounded the lower body. The sleeves were sometimes long and tight, but at other times they reached only to the elbow so that the sleeves of an undergarment hung beneath them. The *entari* was girded at the waist by a jeweled silver or gold belt, or a shawl. *Entari*s for special occasions were often made of heavy brocaded material.[8] When the skirts were very long, they were looped up at the belt for walking.[9]

Ferace—a long, loose coat that reached from the shoulders to the ground. It had long sleeves and, usually, a wide collar. It was made in various colors and in fabrics such as satin, taffeta, fine merino, and other woolens. The collar and sleeves were frequently trimmed with ribbon, lace, braid, or even feathers. The width of the collar and the amount of trimming were matters with which the government concerned itself and about which it issued sumptuary decrees. Although the *ferace* was gradually replaced by the *çarşaf*, some women continued to wear it. Musahipzade Celâl, in his *Eski İstanbul yaşayışı*, has reproduced a photograph of the poet Nigâr Hanım in a *ferace* that is made very like a fancy late Victorian coat, buttoned on the left front with three buttons and having what looks like a ribbon boa attached to the collar. Its skirt has slits at the sides into which three tiers of ruffles have been inserted. Its sleeves are long and wide.[10]

Gecelik entarisi—nightgown.[11]

Gömlek—a long shirt made of fine, transparent material, through which the form of the breasts showed. It was closed at the throat with a jeweled button. These shirts often had long sleeves which hung, wide and loose, below the sleeves of the *entari*.[12]

Hırka—a short, lined coat.[13]

Kaftan—a robe worn over the *entari*, usually of a rich material and in winter frequently lined with fur.[14]

Libade—a short, quilted coat.[15]

Maslah—a loose, light coat for summer.[16]

Salta—a jacket, sometimes short, sometimes hip length.[17]

Şal—a shawl. Kashmir was the most popular material and was widely imitated. The best Turkish shawls were products of Bursa and Gürün. They resembled Lahore shawls in design, but were finer and more brilliant. Shawls had many uses: as a girdle about the waist, as a *bohça*, as a turban, or as a wrap. Shawls were also used to swaddle babies and to face jackets. They were usually striped and in bright colors.[18]

Şalvar—baggy trousers, usually made of heavily embroidered silk, and tied at the waist and ankles with a string.[19]

Yeldirme—a light summer cloak with attached head covering.[20]

Yelek—a vest. There is a certain amount of confusion among sources as to this garment. The *yelek* is usually a fancy sleeveless vest of rich material, often elaborately trimmed, and open in front. Lucy Garnett, who was well acquainted with late Ottoman costume, says the *yelek* was worn directly over the *gömlek* and *şalvar*, but adds that it was "a sort of long coat tight-fitting above the waist, and buttoned from the bosom to below the girdle, but open on each side from the hip downwards, and trailing a few inches on the floor." This seems to describe the *entari*. Yet the Levnî miniatures show women wearing a vest under the *entari*, very much in the manner Garnett described except that it reaches only to the hips. The Levnî vests have sleeves that are sometimes tight at the wrist and sometimes flow out from under the *entari* sleeves.[21] Perhaps the *yelek* was different in different periods.

HEAD COVERINGS

Başlik—a head covering, a bridal crown.[22]

Baş örtüsü—a head covering.[23]

Fes—a fez, often decorated with coins or embroidery.[24]

Hotoz—called by sources a bonnet, but actually a kind of loose pillbox; a very old headgear of varying shapes, sometimes jeweled.[25]

Namaz bezi—a piece of white muslin worn over the head while praying.[26]

Peçe—the black or dark veil that covered the face from below the eyes, usually made of fine horsehair. This was worn with the *çarşaf*.[27]

Takke—basically a skullcap.[28]

Tarpuş—a fez, red and tasseled.[29]

Tepelik—a piece of openwork metal sewed to a fez, and ornamented with gold and silver embroidery and pearls.[30]

Yaşmak—a two-piece veil, one part oblong, one part square, often made of some fine, transparent white material. The oblong piece covered the hair and forehead down to the eyebrows. The square piece was folded diagonally and placed so that the widest part came over the face, covering it from directly below the eyes to below the chin. Both pieces were tied in the back.[31]

Yemeni—a colored cotton kerchief worn over the head and tied above the forehead, sometimes wound about a *hotoz*. Its edges were frequently trimmed with *oya* or some other fancywork.[32] There were two types, *kundak* and *salma*. A *kundak* left the neck free; a *salma* hung down the neck a short distance.[33] There was also the *dallı* (ornamented) *yemeni*, which was a square of transparent material with floral designs printed by hand. It covered the face and fastened the head portion of the *çarşaf*.[34]

FOOT COVERINGS

Cedik pabuç—a slipper, yellow for Muslin women, for indoor wear.[35]

Çizme—boots.[36]

Çorap—stockings woven of wool, mohair, or silk.[37]

Mest—a light, soleless boot worn in the house or with overshoes.[38]

Nalın—the high clogs worn in the bath, often inlaid with silver or mother-of-pearl.[39]

Pabuç—a shoe or slipper.[40]

Şipşip—a slipper without a back.[41]

Terlık—house slippers, usually embroidered.[42]

ACCESSORIES

Ben—a mole or beauty-mark on the face. Women who lacked moles affixed false ones.[43]

Çamaşır—underwear.[44]

Kemer—a belt, often of gold or silver, with a jeweled clasp.[45]

Kına—henna, used to color the palms of the hands, the fingers, the fingernails, the toes, the toenails, and the hair.[46]

Korse—a corset, worn only in the later period.[47]

Kürk—fur, of which the following were the most popular: *samur*, sable; *kakim*, ermine; *elma kürk*, fur made from the cheek pieces of fox skins; *vasak*, lynx; and *zerdeva*, marten.[48]

Kuşak—a belt or girdle, wound around the *entari*.[49]

Oya—a tatting-like lace, usually in flower shapes and very popular for edging.[50]

Rastık—a cosmetic for blackening the eyebrows.[51]

Sırma—the raised metal-thread embroidery used on many garments, especially brides' dresses.[52]

Sorguç—a jeweled aigrette attached to the headpiece of a bride.[53]

Şemsiye—a parasol. In the days before men and women could meet openly, there was a code of flirtation in the manner in which it was used.[54]

Uçkur—the waistband or waist-string, often embroidered, that holds up *dizlik* or *şalvar*.[55]

Yazma—literally "writing," in this instance a floral pattern imprinted on cloth. The printing was done by wooden blocks which were carved by hand. *Yazma* was used in several ways: to decorate *bohça*s, as the border of head *yemini*s, as an all-over pattern for quilts, and on prayer rugs.[56]

Jewels were worn in great quantities, according to Castellan:

Diamonds constitute the principal wealth of the women: they are set in bracelets, ornaments for the corset, egrettes, and ear-rings. They have many other jewels, such as watches, snuff-boxes, and cases. The turban, of embroidered muslin, painted or printed, is adorned with several rows of pearls, bouquets of flowers, formed of precious stones of different colours, and butterflies mounted on pins, which seem to flutter around the heads of the wearers.

Women employ all their ascendency over the men to obtain jewels of as great value as possible, because they are always left in peaceable possession of them when they lose their husbands: nay, they have no other resource, when the effects of their families are confiscated by the sultan, which is no uncommon circumstance with persons in office.[57]

In the eighteenth and most of the nineteenth centuries the upper-class woman's clothes and the slaves' clothes were often made within the *konak* by the women slaves, Ottoman women having always been adept with the needle. Such was the case, for example, in Suphi Pasha's *konak*. Even later, when there were maids instead of slaves, some of the maids were hired specially to sew the clothes for the entire staff. This must have absorbed a considerable amount of time, for it was not unusual for the great houses to have 50 or more maids. There were also women who came in by the day to sew; they were called *gündelikçi*.[58] According to the late Emine Foat Tugay, "It meant dressmakers and their assistants would bring materials to the houses of their clients."[59]

By the end of the nineteenth century, professional ateliers had been established, owned and staffed by women of the minorities. Istanbul had Calivrusi, who was Greek, Fegara and the Shaki sisters, who were Jewish, and two Frenchwomen, the Demilville sisters, who had a fashionable atelier in Beyoğlu (Pera). They copied Parisian styles, took pictures of them to the court for the women to choose from, and then came back for the fittings. Other ladies, not of the court, went to the ateliers rather than have the dressmakers come to their houses. Some women ordered their clothes direct from Paris. By this time, the Ottoman lady had become as fashion-conscious as her Western counterpart.[60]

Facial makeup was an art much practiced by the Ottoman lady, with results not always pleasing to the eye of the Western observer, who was unaccustomed to so liberal a use of it.[61] Lucy Garnett tells us: "Oriental women are much addicted to the use of cosmetics, and faces are blanched and rouged, eye-brows and lashes touched up with *sürme*, and numerous other little coquetries resorted to, which, toned down by the semi-transparent *yashmak,* are calculated to 'put beholders in a tender taking' ."[62] There was a brisk trade in the products used for makeup, and Adolphus Slade saw, in the Egyptian Bazaar in Istanbul, kohl for the eyes, henna for the fingertips, and a powder to give hair a "golden hue," blonde hair being much desired by Ottoman women.[63]

Until modern times, the best descriptions of the Ottoman woman's dress have been given by Western observers. This is natural, since the Turks did not write about women, and in any case would not have been likely to describe what was to them commonplace. Perhaps the most quoted one is the following, given in 1717 by Lady Montagu, who owned and sometimes wore a Turkish costume:

The first piece of my dress is a pair of drawers, very full, that reach to my shoes, and conceal the legs more modestly than your petticoats. They are of a thin, rose-

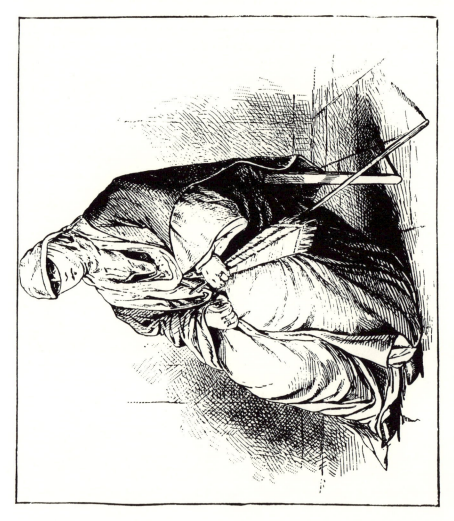

Figure 2. A Turkish Lady of 1851

coloured damask, brocaded with silver flowers; my shoes are of white kid leather, embroidered with gold. Over this hangs my smock[64] of a fine white silk gauze, edged with embroidery. This smock has wide sleeves, hanging half-way down the arm, and is closed at the neck with a diamond button; but the shape and colour of the bosom very well to be distinguished through it. The *antary*[65] is a waistcoat, made close to the shape, of white and gold damask, with very long sleeves falling back, and fringed with deep gold fringe, and should have diamond or pearl buttons. My *caftan*, of the same stuff with my drawers, is a robe exactly fitted to my shape, and reaching to my feet, with very long straight falling sleeves. Over this is the girdle, of about four fingers broad, which all that can afford have entirely of diamonds or other precious stones; those who will not be at that expense, have it of exquisite embroidery on satin; but it must be fastened before with a clasp of diamonds. The *curdee* is a loose robe they throw off or put on according to the weather, being of a rich brocade (mine is green and gold), either lined with ermine or sables; the sleeves reach very little below the shoulders. The head-dress is composed of a cap, called *talpock*,[66] which is in winter of fine velvet embroidered with pearls or diamonds, and in summer of a light shining silver stuff. This is fixed on one side of the head, hanging a little way down with a gold tassel, and bound on, either with a circle of diamonds (as I have seen several) or a rich embroidered handkerchief. On either side of the head, the hair is laid flat; and here the ladies are at liberty to show their fancies; some putting flowers, others a plume of heron's feathers, and, in short, what they please; but the most general fashion was a large *bouquet* of jewels, made like natural flowers; that is, the buds of pearl; the roses, of different coloured rubies; the jessamines, of diamonds; the jonquils, of topazes, etc., so well set and enamelled, 'tis hard to imagine any thing of that kind so beautiful. The hair hangs at its full length behind, divided into tresses braided with pearl or ribbon, which is always in great quantity.

I have counted a hundred and ten of the tresses of one lady's head, all natural. . . . They generally shape their eyebrows; and the Greeks and the Turks have the custom of putting round their eyes (on the inside) a black tincture, that, at a distance, or by candlelight, adds very much to the blackness of them. . . .[67] They dye their nails a rose-colour.

No woman, of what rank soever, being permitted to go into the streets without two muslins; one that covers her face all but her eyes, and another that hides the whole dress of her head, and hangs half way down her back, and their shapes are wholly concealed by a thing they call a *ferigee*, which no woman of any sort appears without; this has straight sleeves, that reach to their finger-ends, and it laps all round them, not unlike a riding-hood. In winter 'tis of cloth, and in summer of plain stuff or silk.[68]

Later Lady Montagu went to call on Hafise, *kadın* of the late Sultan Mustafa II. The description she gives of Hafise's dress shows the richness of court costume:

She wore a vest called *donalma*,[69] and which differs from a *caftan* by longer sleeves, and folding over at the bottom. It was of purple cloth, straight to her shape, and thick set, on each side, down to her feet, and round the sleeves, with pearls of the best water, of the same size as their buttons commonly are . . . about the bigness of a pea. . . . This habit was tied, at the waist, with two large tassels of smaller pearl, and large diamonds; her shift fastened at the bottom with a great diamond, shaped like a lozenge; her girdle as broad as the broadest English ribbon, entirely covered with diamonds. Round her neck she wore three chains, which reached to her knees; one of large pearl, at the bottom of which hung a fine coloured emerald, as big as a turkey-egg; another, consisting of two hundred emeralds, close joined together, of the most lively green, perfectly matched, every one as large as a half-crown piece, and thick as three crown pieces; and another of small emeralds, perfectly round. But her earrings eclipsed all the rest. They were two diamonds, shaped exactly like pears, as large as a big hazel-nut. Round her *talpoche*[70] she had four strings of pearl, the whitest and most perfect in the world, at least enough to make four necklaces . . . fastened with two roses, consisting of a large ruby for the middle stone, and round them twenty drops of clean diamonds to each. Besides this, her head-dress was covered with bodkins of emeralds and diamonds. She wore large diamond bracelets, and had five rings on her fingers, all single diamonds. . . . Her whole dress must be worth above a hundred thousand pounds sterling.[71]

Lady Montagu's descriptions are of the dress of the period of Ahmet III. About 70 years later, in 1786, another English ambassador's wife, Elizabeth Craven, went to call on the wife of the *kaptan paşa* at her *konak*, a league from Istanbul. The *kaptan paşa*'s wife was a middle-aged woman dressed in "petticoat and vest," over which she wore a satin robe with short sleeves, embroidered "in the finest colors and gold and diamonds." Under the robe was a jeweled girdle from which an embroidered hand-kerchief hung. Over the robe hung a large ermine cape that came down to her hips. On her head she wore a turban adorned with diamonds and pearls. All the other women of the household were similarly, if less richly, dressed. They wore their hair either down their back in multitudinous small braids or tied up to the turban. They used what Lady Craven thought was an excess of makeup, lined their eyes with black, and accented their eye-brows. She found the teeth of some of them black, she believed from smoking (it may have come from chewing nuts), and noticed they were stoop-shouldered, a posture she decided came from sitting tailor-fashion.[72]

From this account, it can be seen that the style of dress had not changed to any great extent. Nor did it change until Mahmut II brought in European fashions. Yet Julia Pardoe found the old dress still in use in 1836. The everyday house outfit she describes as follows:

[The women] all wore chemisettes or under garments of silk gauze, trimmed with fringes of narrow ribbon, and wide trousers of printed cotton falling to the ankle: their feet were bare, save that occasionally they thrust them into little yellow slippers, that scarcely covered their toes, and in which they moved over the floor with the greatest ease, dragging after them their anterys, or sweeping robes. . . . Their upper dresses were of printed cotton of the brightest colours—that of the daughter had a blue ground, with a yellow pattern, and was trimmed with a fringe of pink and green. These robes, which are made in one piece, are divided at the hip on either side to their extreme length, and are girt about the waist with a cashemire shawl. The costume is completed in winter by a tight vest lined with fur, which is generally of light green or pink.[73]

The beginnings of change, however, had come in court costume. On Pardoe's visit to Esma Sultan, Mahmut II's aunt, she paid particular attention to the dress of Nazip Hanım, Esma's adopted daughter:

Her costume was an odd mixture of the European and the Oriental. She wore trousers of pale blue cotton flowered with yellow; and an antery of light green striped with white, and edged with a fringe of pink silk floss; while her jacket, which was the production of a Parisian dress-maker, was of dove-coloured satin, thickly wadded, and furnished with a deep cape, and an immense pair of sleeves, fastened at the wrists with diamond studs. But the most striking feature of the costume in the Imperial Palaces is the head-dress. Nothing can be imagined more hideous! A painted handkerchief is bound tightly around the brow, and secured by jeweled bodkins: the back hair is crepé until it becomes one high dishevelled mass, when it is traversed across the top of the head by a corner of the handkerchief: a number of slender plaits of false hair hang down the back, frequently differing very materially from the colour of the natural tresses: the front locks are cut square across the forehead, and left a couple of inches longer at the sides, where they lie quite flat, and are stuck full of roses, or gems; or overhung by the deep fringe of the handkerchief, wrought to resemble a wreath of flowers. To this head-dress, such as I have described it, Nazip Hanim had added, in common with the other females of the household, a star and crescent of sticking plaster between her eyebrows, which were stained a deep black, and destroyed the natural softness of her expression. But her hands and arms were lovely! White, and round, and soft, as though they had been moulded in wax; and her slight elastic figure looked as if it had been modelled by the Graces.[74]

European fashion had not yet made much headway in the first half of the nineteenth century, even in imperial circles. Enver Ziya Karal says that changes in costume and customs came in under Abdülmecit. Then underclothing, corsets, and gloves were imported from Europe. The palace took them up first, and from there the fashions spread to the families of the pashas.[75] The period in which one finds an actual mélange of the European and the Oriental is the latter half of the nineteenth century.[76] By then there were no more şalvar among the fashionable, the old three-skirted entari had turned into a European gown, and high heels had been adopted. But the love of lavish jewels was still strong and was probably never more manifest than in the Khedive İsmail's court, which was known for its extravagance. By 1912 we have the startling phenomenon of a bride, Atiye, a daughter of the Khedive Abbas Hilmi, appearing in a wedding dress of white satin. Emine Foat Tugay was a bridesmaid at Atiye's wedding and wore a dress of ivory satin with an overshirt of net and lace that would have been suitable for any fashionable Western wedding.[77]

This metamorphosis from Eastern to Western costume was not accomplished without a good deal of travail. We know that the Ottoman Empire considered clothing a mark of rank in society and had rigid laws as to who might wear what. The costumes of government officials were set in the time of Mehmet II so that, as Babinger has pointed out, "the charge and the rank of each functionary were easily recognizable by the color of his clothing . . . by the cut of his sleeves, by the fur that decorated his garb, but above all by the shape of his turban . . . and the cut of his beard."[78]

The dress of women was regulated not so much so that women could be distinguished by rank or religious affiliation, although that was part of it, as it was to protect their modesty. The Ottoman Empire was not alone in its purpose of denoting rank and protecting modesty by means of a dress code. Switzerland took a lively interest in regulating women's attire. The sumptuary laws there were strictest during the sixteenth century, as they were in the Ottoman Empire under Süleyman.[79] They remained in force for more than two centuries, and in 1727 we find the Chamber of Basel meeting 41 times on matters of women's dress.[80]

As in Switzerland, in the Ottoman Empire the frequency with which the decrees on women's dress were promulgated shows their lack of effect, thus exemplifying the old Turkish proverb, "The prohibition of the ruler lasts three days."[81] The basis of the Ottoman proscriptions on dress was the Hanafi law which, though it allowed a more elaborate dress to women than to men, frowned on ornament and ostentation.[82] Though these strictures were little followed among upper-class Ottomans, from time to time the government took measures against innovation or too much ornamentation in dress. In 1725, though the Tulip Period was at its height and the government largely concerned with pleasure, Ahmet III issued an order forbidding women to go on the streets with wide collars or head scarfs with wide braid.

. . . and if they do, it is warned that the collars will be cut off. . . . The *imam* of the quarter is strongly and repeatedly ordered to punish them with banishment and by forbidding them to be received in the houses of the quarter, and the tailors and makers of braid who are factors in the immorality of innovation are also strongly warned. If they are not vigilant after this, the collars and headpieces will be cut from the *feraces*, lest the harm of the good-for-nothing spread to the chaste ladies, and their garments will be torn off and burned in fire according to the degree that the curtain of chastity is violated. And you who are the Janissary *ağa* and the *bostancıbaşı*, if there is heard any sort of negligence in the performance of this illustrious imperial order of the Caliph regarding the immoral women you come upon, know that each will be taken to task.[83]

That this command had a lasting effect is doubtful, considering the temper of the times, which was inclined toward every sort of luxury. It is possible that this *hüküm* was promulgated to satisfy the reactionary people who were clamoring that life was altogether too free.[84]

Later in this century Osman II (1754–1757) issued a whole series of sumptuary decrees. Women were forbidden to go out of doors on Fridays or to cross the Bosphorus with men, and when they did cross they had to choose boatmen with long beards. They were forbidden to wear what Castellan calls the *sarye*, "a kind of Tartar cap in the shape of a horn, which was then in fashion, and which has been succeeded by a close cap of coloured woolen stuff, fringed." Furthermore, their *ferace*s had to be made of coarse cloth in a dull color instead of the gay Kashmir they had been using. Dark green, dark red, or dark brown were the colors recommended. To complete their displeasure, they were forbidden to go shopping and were ordered to leave these outings to their husbands and male relations. Osman insisted that his decrees be respected, but fortunately for the women his reign lasted only three years.[85] However, several of his successors issued similar decrees.

A sumptuary decree was issued during the reign of the liberal sultan, Selim III, but this had as at least part of its purpose the protection of native industry. Selim forbade women to have their *ferace*s made of English alpaca. However, Ankara alpaca was also forbidden because it was too thin. The tailor who did not heed this order was to be hanged at the door of his shop.[86]

The period of Abdülhamit II was a strict one, since he did not share the relatively liberal outlook of the Tanzimat sultans who preceded him. In a memo (*mâruzat*) submitted to the sultan, the distinguished statesman Ahmet Cevdet Pasha wrote about the general extravagance of the times:

In the governorship of Abbas Paşa, very many pashas and *bey*s and *hanım*s have emigrated from Egypt to the Darüssaadet [Istanbul]. *Konak*s and *yalı*s are bought at high prices. The Istanbul ministers and the rich are extending themselves with wasteful expense and foolish squandering to copy Zeynep Hanım, the daughter of Mehmet Ali Pasha. As for the *sultan*s, they are in such debt because they have begun to spend without reckoning, in order to be in any case and deservedly superior to the wives of the ministers, and their allowances are not sufficient. The *kadın efendi*s, who since days of old have concealed and hidden themselves in the imperial palace, have begun to go about in carriages in conformance with the tenor of the times, and they have naturally plunged into outlay and expense in order to be superior to the city dwellers. . . .

The family of a pasha takes up a fashion each month in imitation of the madames and thus these families have ruined chaste women and the morals of Islam.[87]

In Abdülhamit II's time the all-enveloping *çarşaf* replaced, except among court and a few highly placed women, the more graceful *ferace*, but the *çarşaf*, concealing though it was, was at first looked upon as a dangerous innovation. Seniha Moralı has pointed out that in his youth Abdülhamit was familiar with the *ferace*, but after he shut himself up in Yıldız Palace he was oblivious of the fact that the *çarşaf* mode had appeared. Then one day, when he was on one of his rare outings, two women dressed in *çarşaf*s stopped to salute him on the street with a very low bow. "The padishah ordered his aide-de-camp to find out who these foreign women in mourning were who bowed à la turka."[88]

According to another source, in 1890 Abdülhamit, while returning to Yıldız Palace via Teşvikiye after a Friday *selâmlık*, noticed some women on Silâhhane Street wearing black *çarşaf*s and extremely thin veils. Being unaccustomed to viewing this garb, the sultan thought that they were Christian women in mourning, but then he recalled having heard that a man had dressed himself in the all-enveloping *çarşaf*, stealthily entered a house, and stolen some articles. For this reason, and because he did not consider the *çarşaf* suitable for Islamic women, on April 1,[89] 1892, he issued a decree forbidding the wearing of it. He later rescinded this.

The *çarşaf* came to Istanbul from Syria, it is said, brought by the ladies of Suphi Pasha's family when he was governor there in 1871.[90] According to another source, Abdülhamit at first disapproved of the *çarşaf* as an innovation, but later changed his mind and issued an order forbidding *yaşmak*s and *ferace*s. This came about because two women of the aristocracy were molested and had their *yaşmak*s and *ferace*s torn by street rowdies in the neighborhood of Süleymaniye. For a time after this command, women accustomed to the *yaşmak* and *ferace* did not go out of the house in order to avoid wearing the *çarşaf* and *peçe*, but gradually they became accustomed to the new fashion.[91]

From the modern vantage point the adoption of the *çarşaf* and the *peçe* appears to have been a step away from modernization and Westernization. Yet by degrees the *çarşaf* changed from a voluminous, formless wrap to a covering that to some extent followed the form of the figure. The earliest *çarşaf*s made a woman look like a bundle. "What a shapeless costume that!" says Seniha Moralı. "A *çarşaf* that consists of a skirt in two pieces instead of the elegant *ferace*, a one-piece skirt, the under part, gathered at the waist, the upper part a cape covering the head and shoulders as far as below the waist. In place of the white tulle that left the eyes clear, a thick printed (*dallı*) *yemeni* covered the face. Women appeared like headless phantoms."[92]

According to Seniha Moralı, this garment was at first called *zar*, meaning "integument" or "envelope," and only later became known as *çarşaf*.[93] Pakalın says it was also called *torba* (bag) and *dolma* (something stuffed).[94] Seniha Moralı thinks the reason it came into vogue may have been that it was comfortable and generally useful.[95]

At first the *çarşaf* was made of serge or alpaca, but later European silks

Figure 3. A Turkish Lady of 1887

came into vogue. The conservative favored dark colors like navy blue, purple, dark red, and black, but virtually all colors could be seen, many of them light and gay.[96] The upper portion of the garment was gradually shortened to become a cape, and in the time of the Young Turks some women discarded the skirt portion altogether and wore simply the cape. *Bekçis* (watchmen) knocked at the doors of the houses of their quarters with the announcement, "The skirt of the *çarşaf* must be full and long," but stylish women paid attention neither to the command of the government nor to the whisperings of the old women who disapproved of the new modes.[97]

Women even took to wearing the corset, and in 1894 Emine Semiye wrote an article for *Hanımlara mahsus gazete* (*Gazette for Ladies*) pointing out that changes in style were commonplace among European women who accepted innovations that pleased them and rejected the others, and hinting that Ottoman women should do the same. She warned her readers against the corset, even going so far as to say that one not accustomed to a corset could be made ill by wearing it. It was particularly the metal stays that worried her, and she recommended a locally made "sport corset" that did not have any. It supposedly gave a woman the desired figure without afflicting her with indigestion.[98] The hour-glass figure was in vogue at the time, and the magazine carried in successive issues an advertisement of ready-made dresses sold at a "fixed and reasonable price" in Galata.[99] It was illustrated with women in leg o' mutton sleeves and with wasp waists. One of the figures, amazingly, wore a hat. On the subject of hats, Seniha Moralı told the author a delightful story about Seniye Cenani, a fashionable woman of the early twentieth century when Seniha Moralı was a child. One day Seniye's mother took her to visit her great grandfather, Sami Pasha (1795-1878), who was also the great grandfather of Seniha Moralı. He lived in a large house of 60 rooms housing 100 people, "many of them beautiful young Circassian slaves, tall and slim, and as dignified as princesses." Sami Pasha was a distinguished statesman and a mystic, and far too conservative to appreciate the broad-brimmed Parisian hat little Seniye wore. Her mother knew this and, as they were driving to his *konak*, she recommended: "Remember, you are not to go into grandfather's room with your hat on." It would never have entered Seniye's mind to do so, but now she thought it a splendid idea. She ran straight to the old gentleman's room. He was sitting by a window overlooking the garden. He eyed his great granddaughter critically and said: "Oh! Bonjour, mademoiselle." She, delighted with the impression she had created, ran to him and kissed his hand. He pointed to the pond in the garden. "See this pond?" "Yes sir." "You go right there and throw your hat in it." "Yes sir." She immediately complied with the request, and thought it all delightfully exciting, although her mother did not.[100]

Yet so far did the pendulum of style swing toward Europe that in 1911 one Western observer, Duckett Ferriman, was bemoaning the absence of the charm and the color of the women's dress of old:

The outdoor costume of the Turkish lady at present consists of skirt, and cape drawn up over the head, and the *charchaf*,[101] a short veil, black, or a dark tint. . . . The *yashmak* is now only worn by ladies of the Imperial harem. . . . The short veils at present worn conceal the feature more effectually than either the *yashmak* or the semi-transparent long veils worn during the closing years of the last century, but it can be raised at any moment, whilst both the long veil and the *yashmak* were fixtures . . . but the *yashmak* was certainly far more becoming. A filmy cloud, it really enhanced the charms it pretended to conceal. . . .
The tendency to tone down color is perhaps the most noticeable feature in the dress of the Turkish ladies of the present day. In the seventies of the last century, the *feridgees* were apple-green, cherry-red, bright blue, full yellow, intense violet, or even pure scarlet. . . . When Murad V drove through the streets to his first selamlik, balconies, stands, and pavements resembled gorgeous parterres. This infantile delight in primary colours was succeeded by the taste for shades of helio-trope and *eau de nil*, peacock-blue, old gold, coppery bronze, ruby and garnet, and with these came greater richness in material. The *broche* silks of the close of the last and the beginning of the present century have never been surpassed, and at that period, too, the veils were of varied tints, and delicate floral patterns were woven into their fabric.
Now, the short veil is black or dark brown, and the dress is of the same colour or a very dark blue. Sometimes—but this is exceptional—it is of discreet grey, and this, for the moment, seems to be the only excursion the ladies allow themselves out of the sombre tones in which fashion decrees that they shall appear. . . . This applies only to their outdoor costume. Indoors, they avail themselves of all the latitude of the West.[102]

Yet as time went on, the *peçe* became thinner and lighter in color, and came increasingly to resemble the *yaşmak*. Though the hat continued to be frowned upon, the *hotoz*, which was very like a hat, grew in popularity, along with the turban.[103] In 1919 the Istanbul woman might be found wearing a pink dress, donning a hat, and carrying a parasol, her face covered with only a transparent blue *yaşmak*.[104] The fashionable women of Istanbul had set the pace that other urban women of the country would soon be following in Westernized clothing.

NOTES

1. In studying costume, we have relied on observation of actual articles of clothing, pictorial reproductions, and descriptions in the works cited. Clothing was observed in the Belediye (Municipal) Museum in Istanbul, the Ethnological Museum in Ankara, and the Koyunoğlu Museum in Konya. Reproductions of costumes were found mainly in Levnî's incomparable miniatures of the early eighteenth century; Antoine-Ignace Melling, *Voyage pittoresque de Constantinople et des rives*

du Bosphore, plates; Emin Cenkman, *Osmanlı sarayı ve kıyafetleri*; Reşat Ekrem Koçu, *Türk giyim kuşam ve süslenme sözlüğü*; and A. Süheyl Ünver, *Geçmiş yüzyıllarda kıyafet resimlerimiz*. The author does not claim to have compiled a totally complete list.

2. In addition to the list given here, Charles White (*Three Years in Constantinople; or Domestic Manners of the Turks in 1844*, III, p. 191) gives *seiman* as a wadded jacket for winter use. We have found no other reference to a garment by this name.

3. Koçu, *Türk giyim*, pp. 51–52.

4. Mehmet Zeki Pakalın, *Osmanlı tarih deyimleri ve terimleri sözlüğü*, I, pp. 327–329.

5. Musahipzade Celâl, *Eski İstanbul yaşayışı*, pp. 133, 138, 139; Koçu, *Türk giyim*, pp. 65–68.

6. Koçu, *Türk giyim*, pp. 94–95; N. M. Penzer, *The Harem*, p. 169; White, *Three Years*, III, p. 191.

7. At the Friday *selâmlık* the *entari*s of the women *sultan*s might have trains that swept the floor, but it was not etiquette for other women to have trains or to wear their hair uncovered (Melek Hanum and Grace Ellison, *Abdul Hamid's Daughter*, pp. 46–49).

8. Koçu, *Türk giyim*, pp. 102–105; A. Süheyl Ünver, *Levnî*, plates 2–6, 8; Melling, *Voyage pittoresque*, plate of Hatice Sultan's salon; White, *Three Years*, III, p. 191.

9. Penzer, *The Harem*, pp. 169–170; Enise Yener, "Eski Ankara kadın kıyafetleri ve giyiniş tarzları," *Ankara Üniversitesi dil ve tarih-coğrafya fakültesi dergisi*, 13 (*Eylül*, 1955), pp. 21–37, plate II.

10. Musahipzade Celâl, *Eski İstanbul*, pp. 130–133. There are several interesting *ferace*s in the Belediye Müzesi, among them a cream-colored one elaborately embroidered and with braid at the neck. *See* also Antoine Laurent Castellan, *Turkey, Being a Description of the Manners, Customs, Dresses and Other Peculiarities Characteristic of the Inhabitants of the Turkish Empire*, pp. 77–78. For *ferace*, *see* also Koçu, *Türk giyim*, pp. 108–111.

11. Koçu, *Türk giyim*, p. 103.

12. Ünver, *Levnî*, plates 3–5, 8; Ünver, *Kıyafet resimlerimiz*, picture 39. The album of costumes reproduced in the latter-named work, though dated 1720, is, according to Ünver, a copy of an album of 1688. Thus the costumes are 30 years earlier than the Levnî costumes but, in view of Ottoman conservatism, were unoubtedly still in vogue in the beginning of the eighteenth century. The figures lack the grace of Levnî's. *See* also Penzer, *The Harem*, pp. 168–169; White, *Three Years*, III, p. 191.

13. *See* illustration in Koçu, *Türk giyim*, p. 130.

14. White, *Three Years*, III, p. 191.

15. Musahipzade Celâl, *Eski İstanbul*, p. 125.

16. Ibid., p. 124; Seniha Sami Moralı, "Çarşaf modası bize Suriye'den geldi," *Hayat* (30 *Eylül*, 1960), pp. 4–5; Pakalın, *Deyimler ve terimler*, II, p. 145. Şemseddin Sami (Koçu, *Türk giyim*, p. 170) said it was worn in a carriage.

17. Koçu, *Türk giyim*, p. 201; Yener, "Eski Ankara kadın kıyafetleri."

18. Nurettin Yatman, *Türk kumaşları*, pp. 57–59. For a full discussion, *see* Koçu, *Türk giyim*, pp. 51–52.

19. Koçu, *Türk giyim*, pp. 215–216; Ünver, *Levnî*, plates 6, 8, 10; Ünver, *Kıyafet resimlerimiz*, picture 51.

20. Seniha Moralı says that the *maslah* and *yeldirme* were worn by village women. Pakalın says that both were generally worn in the summer time (*see* Pakalın, *Deyimler ve terimler*, III, p. 615). Koçu (*Türk giyim*, p. 242) has an illustration of a *yeldirme*.

21. Lucy M. J. Garnett, *Home Life in Turkey*, p. 278; Koçu, *Türk giyim*, pp. 242–243; Ünver, *Levnî*, plates 3–4, 6, 8, 10. The Belediye Müzesi has a short *yelek* with a trimming of tiny balls.

22. *New Redhouse Turkish-English Dictionary* (Istanbul, 1968), p. 1393; Koçu, *Türk giyim*, p. 29.

23. Musahipzade Celâl, *Eski İstanbul*, p. 123.

24. Belediye Müzesi.

25. It was originally a Çağatay word, *kotaz* or *kaytaz*, and signified a tassel hanging as decoration from the neck of a horse (Koçu, *Türk giyim*, pp. 131–132).

26. Ibid., p. 180.

27. Pakalın, *Deyimler ve terimler*, II, p. 765.

28. The Belediye Müzesi has a small headpiece in this shape marked *cakke*. According to Koçu (*Türk giyim*, p. 220), quoting from Şemseddin Sami, *takke* comes from the Arabic word *tak*, meaning vault or dome, and was originally *takiye*. Sir James W. Redhouse (*A Turkish and English Lexicon*, Constantinople, 1921, p. 1225) gives it as *taqye*. See also Pakalın, *Deyimler ve terimler*.

29. Koçu, *Türk giyim*, p. 222.

30. Ibid., pp. 227–228; also personal observation.

31. Musahipzade Celâl, *Eski İstanbul*, pp. 131, 132; White, *Three Years*, III, p. 191. An excellent description of the *yaşmak* is given by Clara Erskine Clement in *Constantinople, the City of the Sultans*, p. 247: "The *yashmak* consists of two parts. One is bound about the head, covers the forehead to the eyebrows, and is tied at the back of the neck; the other covers the lower part of the face up to the eyes, and the two are so folded together that they seem to be but one.... The ladies of Constantinople wear the flimsiest of gauze, and put them on so loosely that they are no inconvenience in any way." Actually, there were two kinds, the closed *yaşmak* of opaque material and the open *yaşmak* of transparent fabric (Koçu, *Türk giyim*, pp. 240–241).

32. Musahipzade Celâl, *Eski İstanbul*, p. 130.

33. For illustrations of these, *see* Koçu, *Türk giyim*, pp. 160 and 201.

34. Information from Seniha Moralı.

35. Koçu, *Türk giyim*, p. 69.

36. H. C. Hony, with the advice of Fahir İz, *A Turkish-English Dictionary*, Oxford, 1957, p. 69.

37. Koçu, *Türk giyim*, pp. 78–81.

38. Hony, *TED*, p. 258. For an illustration, *see* Koçu, *Türk giyim*, p. 173.

39. Koçu, *Türk giyim*, pp. 179–180.

40. Hony, *TED*, p. 281.

41. *New Redhouse*, p. 1061; Hony, *TED*, p. 335.

42. Koçu, *Türk giyim*, p. 228; White, *Three Years*, III, p. 191.

43. Koçu, *Türk giyim*, p. 33.

44. Hony, *TED*, p. 60.

45. Ibid., p. 194.

46. Koçu, *Türk giyim*, p. 157.

47. Hony, *TED*, p. 208.

48. Ibid., pp. 97, 177, 218, 304, 385, 412; *kürk* is also used to mean a furred caftan (White, *Three Years*, III, p. 191).

49. Koçu, *Türk giyim*, pp. 160-161.

50. Belediye Müzesi; also personal possession.

51. Hony, *TED*, p. 294.

52. Ibid., p. 317; Belediye Müzesi.

53. Koçu, *Türk giyim*, p. 208.

54. Ibid., pp. 217–218.

55. Ibid., p. 236; Penzer, *The Harem*, p. 169; White, *Three Years*, III, p. 191.

56. Emine Foat Tugay, *Three Centuries, Family Chronicle of Turkey and Egypt*, p. 217; Belediye Müzesi.

57. Castellan, *Turkey*, pp. 79–80.

58. Personal communications from Seniha Moralı and the late Emine Foat Tugay, January 1968.

59. Tugay, *Three Centuries*, p. 217.

60. Personal communications from Seniha Moralı and Emine Foat Tugay, January 1968.

61. *See*, for example, Lady Craven's remarks on the makeup of her hostess (Lady Elizabeth Craven, *A Journey Through the Crimea to Constantinople [1786]*, p. 216).

62. Garnett, *Home Life in Turkey*, p. 272.

63. Adolphus Slade, *Records of Travels in Turkey, Greece, etc.*, II, p. 219.

64. This is the *gömlek*.

65. Lady Montagu uses the terms of dress differently from other descriptions. What she calls *antary* seems to be a *yelek*, *caftan* the *entari*, and *curdee* a *kaftan*. (The *kurdi* was "a kind of woollen cloth or garment of kurdish make"; Redhouse, *TEL*, p. 1587. It was undoubtedly a kind of cloak.)

66. She probably means *takke*.

67. This was of course kohl.

68. Lady Mary Wortley Montagu, *Letters from the Right Honourable . . . 1709–1762*, pp. 114–115.

69. She may mean *dolama*, a long garment tied with a belt (Koçu, *Türk giyim*, pp. 92–93).

70. Perhaps she means *tarpuş*, which is a skullcap decorated with tassels (Pakalın, *Deyimler ve terimler*, III, p. 413).

71. Montagu, *Letters*, pp. 153–154.

72. Craven, *A Journey*, pp. 223–224.

73. Julia Pardoe, *The City of the Sultans and Domestic Manners of the Turks in 1836*, I, pp. 19–20.

74. Ibid., I, pp. 305–306.

75. Enver Ziya Karal, *Osmanlı tarihi*, VI, pp. 278–279.

76. Emmeline Lott, *Harem Life in Egypt and Constantinople*, pp. 276–277.

77. Tugay, *Three Centuries*, pp. 297–299. In Halide Edip's novel, *Sinekli bakkal* (p. 210), there is a discussion of what is to be the heroine's bridal costume. A young friend wants it to be a modern white *entari* and veil, but the elderly woman

who is the girl's benefactor decides on an old-style purple velvet *entari* embroidered with gold and silver flowers.

78. Franz Babinger, *Mahomet II le conquérant et son temps, 1432–1481* (Paris, 1954), p. 526.

79. In his household, Kanunî Süleyman so regulated costume that each class of persons could be recognized by costume, headdress, or both (Albert Howe Lybyer, *The Government of the Ottoman Empire in the Time of Suleiman the Magnificent*, p. 135).

80. The same sort of thing went on in Zurich, where in 1728 the city council announced that uncovering the neck was "highly offensive . . . very displeasing to God and the respectable world." *See* John Martin Vincent, *Costume and Conduct in the Laws of Basel, Bern and Zurich, 1370–1800* (Baltimore, 1935), pp. 126–130.

81. Seniha Sami Moralı, "Çarşaf modası."

82. 'Alī ibn Abū Bakr Marghīnānī, *The Hedaya, or Guide*, p. 597: "Women may dress in silk; but men must not"; and "Men are not to wear ornaments of gold or silver, except signet rings, girdles, and swords." There is no prohibition against ornament for women. In fact (p. 598) the law says: "It is proper . . . that men, wearing rings, turn the setting or beazel toward the palm of the hand, and women otherwise, because, with respect to them, rings are considered an ornament." Also (p. 598), the Hanafi code says: "Vain superfluities are not allowable." Even handkerchiefs are considered abominable if used not from necessity but for ostentation.

83. Ahmet Refik [Altınay], *Hicrî on ikinci asırda İstanbul hayatı*, pp. 86–88, No. 118.

84. In the early eighteenth century these sumptuary laws were frequently promulgated. In 1703, when Daltaban Mustafa Pasha took over the vizierate from Amcazade Hüseyin Köprülü, he issued an order on dress which forbade women to wear narrow street garments or thin veils (*see* Joseph de Hammer-Purgstall, *Histoire de l'Empire ottoman depuis son origine jusqu'à nos jours*, XIII, p. 81). In 1732, when the puritanical effects of the Patrona Halil rebellion were still being felt, another order was given with the same proscriptions plus regulation of the length of collars on women's coats. At this time a number of women were drowned, accused of having sought to corrupt orthodox Muslim women (ibid., XIV, p. 265).

85. Castellan, *Turkey*, p. 80.

86. Reşat Ekrem Koçu, *Tarihimizde garip vakalar*, pp. 62–66.

87. Ibid.

88. Seniha Sami Moralı, "Çarşaf modası."

89. Rukiye Bulut, "İstanbul kadınlarının kıyafetleri ve II. Abdülhamid'in çarşafı yasaklaması," *Belgelerle Türk tarihi dergisi*, 8 (*Mayıs* 1968), pp. 34–36.

90. İbrahim Alâettin Gövsa, *Türk meşhurları ansiklopedisi*, p. 358.

91. Seniha Sami Moralı, "Çarşaf modası."

92. Ibid.

93. Ibid.

94. Pakalın, *Deyimler ve terimler*, I, pp. 327–329, quoting Mehmet İzzet.

95. Seniha Sami Moralı, "Çarşaf modası."

96. Pakalın, *Deyimler ve terimler*, I, pp. 327–329.

97. Seniha Sami Moralı, "Çarşaf modası." The *çarşaf* continued to be worn

longer than the veil. Seniha Moralı tells about an aunt of hers, wife of the master of ceremonies (*teşrifatcı*) of Abdülhamit II, who, while working at the Red Crescent (Kızılay) during World War I, wore the *çarşaf* but not the veil.

98. Emine Semiye, "Moda ve korse," *Hanımlara mahsus gazete*, 59 (11 *Nisan*, 1312 A.H.), pp. 1–2.

99. *Hanımlara mahsus gazete*, 59 (11 *Nisan*, 1313 A.H.), p. 4 (second p. 4) and other issues.

100. Personal communication from Seniha Moralı.

101. He is confused here; he means *peçe*.

102. Z. Duckett Ferriman, *Turkey and the Turks*, pp. 271–275.

103. Seniha Sami Moralı, "Çarşaf modası."

104. Watercolor by Messour İzzet, Belediye Müzesi, Istanbul.

12

House and Furnishings

The furnishings of the upper-class Ottoman home were rich but, from the Western point of view, sparse.[1] At the end of the seventeenth century, they consisted largely of divans, a few chests, plentiful rugs, and an array of the small articles mentioned below. The windows of the harem usually jutted out and were protected by wooden lattices called *kafe*s, but at that date were undraped. There were no chairs until the nineteenth century, and the plethora of tables and ornaments that filled Western rooms was yet to come. There were no bedsteads until Westernization took hold. People slept on mattresses (*yatak*, "bed") kept in cupboards during the day and laid out on the floor at night. Clothes were kept in chests, which were often decorated.

The earliest description we have of an Ottoman house from a Western observer comes as usual from Lady Montagu. In 1717 she and her ambassador husband were lodged in a house belonging to the sultan at Edirne, which prompted her to make the following observations:

Every house, great and small, is divided into two distinct parts, which only join together by a narrow passage.[2] The first house . . . is the house belonging to the lord, and the adjoining one is called the harem, that is, the ladies' apartment . . . it has also a gallery running around it towards the garden, to which all the windows are turned, and the same number of chambers as the other, but more gay and splendid, both in painting and furniture. The second row of windows is very low, with grates like those of convents; the rooms are all spread with Persian carpets, and raised at one end (my chamber is raised at both ends) about two feet. This is the sofa, and is laid with a richer sort of carpet, and all around it a sort of couch, raised half a foot, covered with rich silk according to the fancy or magnificence of the owner. Mine is of scarlet cloth, with a gold fringe; round this are placed, standing against the wall, two rows of cushions, the first very large, and the next little ones; and here the Turks display their greatest magnificence. They are generally brocade, or embroidery of gold wire upon white satin;—nothing can look more gay and splendid. These seats are so convenient and easy, I shall never endure chairs as long as I live. The rooms are low, which I think is no fault, and the ceiling is nearly always of wood,[3] generally inlaid or painted and gilded. They use no hangings, the rooms being all wainscoted with cedar set off with silver nails or painted with flowers, which open in many places with folding-doors, and serve for cabinets, I think, more conveniently than ours. Between the windows are little arches to set pots of perfume, or baskets of flowers. But what pleases me best is the fashion of having marble fountains in the lower part of the room, which throw up several spouts of water, giving at the same time an agreeable coolness, and a pleasant dashing sound, falling from one basin to another. Some of these fountains are very magnificent. Each house has a bagnio, which is generally two or three little rooms, leaded at the top, paved with marble, with basins, cocks of water, and all conveniences for either hot or cold baths.[4]

Lady Montagu indicates that harem and *selâmlık* occupied equal amounts of space, and Lucy Garnett agrees with her, but this was not always the case. In the nineteenth-century *konak* of the Köprülü family on Divan Yolu, the harem took up about one-third of the building.[5] Sometimes the harem and *selâmlık* were entirely separate buildings, as is the case with the still extant nineteenth-century *yalı* of Refia Sultan at İstinye on the Bosphorus, where the harem is down at the water's edge, and the *selâmlık* some distance from it up a hill.[6]

The Ottoman family being patriarchal, one roof often sheltered the households of several members. Such was the Beylerbeyi *yalı* of Kâmil Pasha,[7] the man who was four times grand vizier in the late nineteenth and early twentieth centuries. His was a building of 50 rooms divided into three sections—one for Kâmil Pasha and his wife and family, one for his eldest daughter and her family, and one for his brother, Şakir Pasha, and Şakir's two wives and children.

An idea of the smaller objects of the upper-class Ottoman household can be gained from the list of items of the household of Selim III, turned in to the Treasury in 1790 to contribute toward the cost of the war with Russia. The sultan himself, the *valide*, the women *sultan*s, the princes, the *kadın efendi*s, the *kalfa*s, and even the smallest *cariye*s gave objects that included a wash basin, a ewer, a mug, a flower vase, a soap-holder, an incense-holder, a ladle, a candlestick, a *hamam* cup, a water vessel with a long handle, a coffee tray, an ink-stand and coffer, a brazier, a decanter, a vessel for cooling water with snow, and lanterns, all made of silver; and various articles made of gold, such as a plate and cup for sweets, a water cup, a bowl, a ceremonial basket woven with gold, an ice cream (*dondurma*) set, a candlestick set with mother-of-pearl inlay, a tray, and a pipe.[8] Many of these articles were undoubtedly richly embossed or otherwise decorated, as are their counterparts on display in the Topkapı Museum today.

To these we can add, as generally found in the upper-class Ottoman household, one or two *kavukluks*, turban stands hung on a wall, many of them painted or inset with mother-of-pearl; a set of pot and bowl for serving coffee; fancy spoons for eating *hoşaf*, the fruit in syrup that was a favorite Ottoman dish offered to guests; colorful embroidered napkins that slaves or servants held over their arms when passing the *ibrik* and *leğen* (pitcher and basin) for washing hands after a meal; metal- or porcelain-covered dishes for food; and, of course, the metal trays on which the food was served. There were also *zarfs*, pierced metal filigree coffee-cup holders, and porcelain coffee cups. In the palace these articles were sometimes made of gold, in the richer private houses of silver, elsewhere of copper. In the harem one would find silver-backed mirrors, an embroidery frame, a needle holder, and also an elaborate cradle and a *doğum iskemlesi* (birthing chair).

The rooms in which the Ottoman woman spent her time were sparsely furnished, empty, in fact, except for sofas, cushions, brazier, and rugs, but this simplicity of furnishing was compensated for by the elaborate architectural ornamentation. The ceiling was decorated, often in rich colors and gold. The walls were painted in floral decorations or tiled, and at intervals lined with graceful niches, each of which held a *gülâbdan* for rose water or a vase.

Slowly, beginning with the period of Mahmut II, Western items began to appear in the households of the great. Malek Hanım, who visited the palace of Esma Sultan in the early years of the Tanzimat, has left the following account of Esma's guest rooms:[9]

I drove to the palace, and on arriving at the garden entrance was received by more than a hundred slaves drawn up on each side of my carriage, and lining the way to a magnificent marble staircase leading to the harem. Several of them, taking me under the arms, assisted me to ascend. The *hasnadar housta*, or grand mistress, here met me, and conducted me to my apartments. These consisted of three rooms— drawing-room, bedroom and dining-room. Roses, white and red, adorned the walls; the curtains were of beautiful striped cashmere; costly carpets covered the floors; splendid mirrors were arranged at intervals; golden cups enriched with precious stones, and filled with sweetmeats, were placed here and there ... Besides comfortable divans, there were arm-chairs of European manufacture, and lamps were disposed together with large massive silver candlesticks in the Oriental style, resembling those used for tapers in the churches of France. All the rooms were furnished pretty much in the same fashion.[10]

We see that certain Western items have come into use: draperies, armchairs, and lamps. Yet there is no mention of a stove. At this period people

kept themselves warm with an apparatus called the *tandır*. Melek Hanım
describes it thus:

To make this original stove a large iron foot warmer is placed under a kind of flat,
circular wooden chest, lined with sheet-iron, and about a foot and a half high. It
is pierced at intervals with holes sufficiently large to allow persons sitting on it to
pass their legs underneath. The whole is covered with stuffs more or less rich,
according to the resources of the owner. In the centre is placed a circular table-
cloth, or covering, of silk or cashmere. Before each of the persons who take their
seats on this novel divan is a drawer, in which fruit and other things can be placed.

Their heads alone are visible, for their bodies, up to their shoulders, are under
cover. When the circle is composed of young girls, they . . . tease each other, throw
fruit and nuts, and excite themselves by playful interchanges of kicks and blows.
This kind of entertainment is sometimes attended with serious results, as the foot-
warmer occasionally gets overturned, and sets fire to the house.[11]

Lady Montagu describes the *tandır* somewhat differently. There is, she
writes,

a certain machine called a *tendour*, the height of two feet, in the form of a table,
covered with a fine carpet or embroidery. This is made only of wood, and they put
into it a small quantity of hot ashes, and sit with their legs under the carpet. At
this table they work, read, and very often sleep; and, if they chance to dream, kick
down the *tendour*, and the hot ashes commonly set the house on fire. There were
five hundred houses burnt in this manner about a fortnight ago.[12]

Melek Hanım's visit to Esma Sultan took place during the early years
of the Tanzimat, around 1848. European chairs were just coming into use,
but later on would crowd out the old divan.[13] During the Tanzimat the
mangal (brazier) on high legs also came into fashion. As the people moved
from sitting on low divans or on cushions on the floor to sitting on chairs,
the *mangal* moved up from very short legs to taller ones.[14]

In the late nineteenth century Western objects increased. Writing about
1875, Théophile Gautier passed on an account of a visit to a Turkish harem
by a European woman of his acquaintance. The lady of the house was a
pasha's wife, a *saraylı*, and thus able to afford whatever was most fashionable. Her drawing room was furnished with the usual divan and fine
carpet, and its ceiling was elaborately decorated with colored and gilded
arabesques. There was also a ewer of emerald-colored Bohemian glass,
and a mahogany chest of drawers with a marble top surmounted by an
ormulu clock, covered by a glass shade, standing between two vases of
artificial flowers, also under glass. The Victorian style had reached Istanbul.[15]

Some time in the 1860s Emmeline Lott, governess of little İbrahim Pasha
of Egypt, found herself in an old palace along the Bosphorus at some
distance from Bebek. The palace was being used for the summer by some

of the members of the khedival family. By this time it had lost much of its former splendor, yet it still had a nobility about it, as can be seen from Lott's description:

Landing on the pier, we entered an immense door, or gateway . . . then we passed into a magnificent marble-paved hall, lined on both sides with rooms. . . .

The only furniture it contained was a divan and a large table. The floor, like that of the other rooms, was matted, and the windows (which commanded a full view of the pier, and its prison-looking gates) were, together with the doors, hung with dark-brown curtains. . . .

Facing the grand entrance was a noble flight of marble stairs, covered with new matting, and the walls had been freshly whitewashed. Ascending the stairs, we approached a large door. . . . On its being opened, it led us unto the grand entrance of the noble marble hall of the Harem, along which ran a corridor, the entire length of which faced the Bosphorus.

It was lighted by five spacious windows, all of which commanded views of the sapphire-looking river. . . . In the centre stood a large marble fountain; at each end rooms branched off both right and left.[16]

There had been no attempt made to dress up the palace in an elegant fashion, and Lott deplored the lack of carpets and the worn-out condition of some of the fabrics. The furnishings were, except for the reception rooms, simplicity itself. For example, the bedroom of her charge's mother

was furnished with a plain iron bedstead, with crimson mosquito-curtains, a large mirror, and a divan cover of dark-brown chintz. The hangings of the door and windows were of the same material, with the addition of white muslin curtains; no other furniture of any kind. . . .

At the extremity of the hall was a large apartment used as Her Highness's wardrobe-room, in which the "*Kaftandji Ousta*", "Mistress of the Wardrobe" slept. Across it hung several lines on which were placed the Princess's jackets, dresses, etc.[17]

In another section of the palace she found a second "noble-looking" reception hall furnished with console tables on which were branched candelabra.

In the centre stood the grand staircase, which was well lighted by a handsome stained-glass cupola; and in the corridor, round which stood several marble fountains, the windows were decorated with dark-brown hangings.[18]

From this it appears that the public rooms were handsome, the private rooms simple. The servants' quarters were not even comfortable. This was a little-used palace and hence undoubtedly more simply furnished than most, yet it shows that the overfurnishing which had become fashionable in the West had not yet reached all the great houses in the Istanbul area.

In *Turkey of the Ottomans*, Garnett describes a provincial *konak* of the Young Turk period. There was always a lag in the adoption of new ways between Istanbul and the provinces, so the provincial *konak* of 1911 probably resembled a *konak* of Istanbul and its suburbs during the latter part of the nineteenth century:

A Turkish mansion, whether in town or country, is generally a tile-roofed, rambling, irregularly built edifice of two stories, surrounded by walled gardens and courtyards and divided internally into two parts, the *haremlik* and the *selamlik*. Many of the older houses are built entirely of wood, and, with their overhanging upper stories, their projections and recesses, bright colouring and verdant setting, are most picturesque in appearance. The partiality for light and air characteristic of the Ottomans leads them, however, to construct their dwellings with what appears to Europeans a superfluity of windows. In the upper story of a *konak* or *yahli* they are often set only a few inches apart, and the frames, being generally both ill-constructed and unpainted, become warped by the sun and rain, and let in the draughts in all directions.[19]

These drafts were a reason for the wadded and fur-lined jackets which were worn in the winter time, and for the custom of clustering around the *tandır*. Lacy Garnett goes on to say:

The lower parts of the *haremlik* windows are invariably screened by latticed blinds of unpainted wood, and by these a Moslem dwelling can always be identified.[20]

Her account of the harem portion of the house is the most detailed we have encountered:

The larger division of the house constitutes the *haremlik*, which has its separate entrance, courtyard and garden, and contains all the private apartments of the family. As in the generality of Eastern houses, the front door opens into a large hall, which gives access to rooms on each side of it, and has several windows at the opposite end. One of these rooms is the *kahve-ojak*, or "coffee-hearth", where an old woman may always be found presiding over a charcoal brazier ready to boil coffee at a moment's notice; the others are storerooms and sleeping apartments of the inferior slaves. The kitchen, which is very spacious, is generally an out-building. One side of it is occupied by the great arched cooking-stove with its numerous little grates, on which the contents of brightly burnished copper pans simmer over charcoal fires, fanned with a turkey's wing by the negress cook. A wide staircase leads from the entrance floor to the upper hall, the centre of which is generally occupied by a spacious ante-room, on which other apartments open. In some of the older houses the *divan-khane*, or principal reception room, contains a large alcove, the floor of which is raised about a foot above the level of the rest of the apartment. A low divan furnishes its three sides, and its most comfortable corner is the *hanum*'s habitual seat. If the *divan-khane* has not such a recess, one end and half the two adjoining wings of the room are usually occupied by a continuous sofa, and the fourth is furnished with a marble-topped console table surmounted by a mirror and candelabra, and flanked on either side by shelves in niches, containing rose-water sprinklers, sherbet goblets, and other ornamental objects. A few European chairs stand stiffly against the wall in every space left vacant, and one or two walnut tray-stools, inlaid with mother-of-pearl, are placed near the divan to hold cigarettes, ash-trays, matches, coffee-cups and other trifles. A few framed *yafta*s, or texts from the Koran, may be seen on the walls, but pictures are, generally, conspicuous by their absence....

Bedsteads are not used by old-fashioned Turks. Each room contains a large cupboard, built into the wall, in which the bedding is piled during the day, and at night the slaves come in, when summoned, to make up the beds on the floor. Other bedroom furniture in the shape of washstands, dressing-tables, and wardrobes is dispensed with as superfluous. For everyday ablutions there is a small washing-room with a hole in the floor for the water to escape through, and when it is proposed to wash the hands and face only, a slave brings in the *leyen* [*leğen*] and *ibrik* and pours the water; while, for special ablutions, the private *hammam*s or the public baths will be resorted to. The *hanum* "does her hair", or has it done for her, seated cross-legged in her corner of the divan; and the quaintly carved and painted walnut-wood chests and coffers in her treasure-room suffice to hold her gauzes and brocades, her silks and embroideries....

Such a mansion as described above may be found in every provincial town... though there may now be found, especially in the capital and its suburbs, a considerable number of new houses, handsomely and solidly built, and in outward appearance not to be distinguished—except by the wooden lattices at the windows— from the dwellings of Europeans. The disposal of the rooms is naturally that best suited to Osmanli customs, but the furniture will be rather European than Oriental.[21]

By the turn of the century, the Ottomans had been accustomed to Western furniture long enough for certain pieces to have become heirlooms. Emine Foat Tugay tells that when in 1897 her mother and father moved into the Mermer Konak in Moda, which was to be their home for most of their lives, her mother took with her "two high mirrors in elaborate carved gilt frames, with matching marble-topped tables, and an upholstered drawing-room set of massive carved mahogany, which had stood in her great grandfather İbrahim Pasha's study." Mermer Konak had been built by a Greek grocer who had been unable to afford to live anywhere in it except the basement. It was a large marble building, and when bought and furnished by Mrs. Tugay's parents became a stately home. It was lighted by gas until 1907 or 1908, when Muhtar Pasha, Mrs. Tugay's father, installed an engine and a dynamo in the stables to provide electric light for the house and grounds. Even at this late date, in a house completely furnished with European furniture, Turkish hospitality sometimes made the family revert to the old style, and bedding for the many guests would be brought out of cupboards and spread on the floor.[22]

Westernized decor reached its peak of extravagance in the palaces of Dolmabahçe and Beylerbeyi. There the mass of inlay, ormulu, gilt, crystal, and silver and gold pieces—elegant in themselves—is so overpowering that the effect of any single piece is lost in the competition. Gone was the beautiful simplicity of a building like the Amuca Hüseyin Pasha Yalısı, where the elaborate decoration was enhanced by spaciousness. Westernization may have made the home of the Ottoman woman more comfortable for modern living, but it did little to make it more beautiful.

These large houses needed a plenitude of help. As the nineteenth century turned into the twentieth and slaves were replaced by servants, the great houses contained a multitude of the latter. Seniha Moralı's family home, at Kanlıca on the Asiatic shore of the Bosphorus, was an example. She recalled

four or five maids in the harem, both Turkish and Greek, and at times one of them had a small child who lived in the house. An Armenian washer-woman called *dudu* (an old Turkish title later restricted to Armenian women) came once a month, and Farida, a Lebanese Christian, did the ironing and starching. In the *selâmlık* were an attendant, a dark Negro who had been a boatman but was too old to row any longer, and an *usta*, a jack-of-all-trades who did all the plumbing and carpentering and used the workshop in which my father [Sami Bey] spent a great deal of his time. Then there were cooks and kitchen boys from Bolu,[23] a dishwasher, and seven Albanian gardeners. My father had wonderful conservatories full of orchids and other exotic plants. There were also five boatmen, two coachmen, and stable boys. Driving was well nigh impossible through the narrow cobbled streets of the Asiatic shore, so the carriages and horses were kept at the town house or on the European shore. This would now seem a large household, but it was normal for a great house in those days.[24]

NOTES

1. There is to my knowledge no study of Ottoman furnishings, though it is a rich and interesting topic.

2. The passageway between the men's and women's divisions of the house, that is, between *selâmlık* and harem, was the *mabeyn*. In addition to this, the two were connected by a revolving cupboard called *dolap*.

3. An interesting and elegantly simple painted wooden ceiling has been uncovered in the Kıbrıslı Yalısı in Kandilli. Personal observation and interview with Nesterin Dirvana, August 1966.

4. Lady Mary Wortley Montagu, *Letters from the Right Honourable...1709-1762*, pp. 126-128.

5. Interview with Orhan Köprülü, August 1966.

6. Personal observation and interview with the then owner, summer, 1957; also information from Süphiye Gürün.

7. Personal interview with Perihan Arıburun, Kâmil Pasha's granddaughter, November 1967.

8. İsmail Baykal, "Selim III devrinde 'imdad-ı sefer' için para basılmak üzere saraydan verilen altın ve gümüş evanî hakkında," *Tarih vesikaları*, 3 (*Ağustos* 1944), pp. 26-50.

9. For pictures of some of these objects, *see* Musahipzade Celâl, *Eski İstanbul yaşayışı*, passim. For a detailed account and photographs of certain objects, *see* Katherine McClinton, "Influences in Turkish Silver Design," *The Connoisseur* (March, 1973), pp. 201-207.

10. Melek Hanım, *Thirty Years in the Harem*, p. 120. This is the handsome palace that Melling redesigned (*see* Chapter 13), and he has told us that in one of the rooms over the water a section of the floor could be removed so that Esma Sultan and her suite might indulge in fishing without being seen by the public (Antoine-Ignace Melling, *Voyage pittoresque de Constantinople et des rives du Bosphore d'auprès les dessins de M. Melling*). Sometime in the 1860s Emmeline Lott, governess to little İbrahim Pasha of Egypt, found herself in what may well have been that room. She and her charge were housed in a *yalı* at some distance from Bebek, which may have been in Beşiktaş. According to her description of the watery room, "some of the marble slabs with which it was paved were removable at pleasure." A spring was pressed, bolts slid back, "and then one of the marble slabs sank down. All the persons standing on that sunken slab found themselves suddenly let down into an immense room of marble, like a swimming-bath, filled with the water of the Bosphorus, which flowed into it from the five upright iron gratings outside" (Emmeline Lott, *Harem Life in Egypt and Constantinople*, pp. 297-298).

11. Melek Hanım, *Thirty Years*, pp. 11-12.

12. Montagu, *Letters*, p. 151. The difference between Melek Hanım's and Lady Montagu's descriptions of the *tandır* may be due to the fact that Melek Hanım was describing the object in the household of her Levantine family, who may have had one constructed a little differently from the Turkish *tandır*. An illustration of a *tandır*, in a copy of Mehmet Tevfik's *Tandırbaşı* which is in the author's possession, shows people covered by the *tandır* cloth only from the waist down. This is an 1881 publication. Charles White (*Three Years in Constantinople; or Domestic Manners of the Turks in 1844*, III, p. 139), in his description of the *tandır*, claims that among Greeks, where separation of the sexes was not observed, it gave opportunity for scandalous goings-on. Lucy M. J. Garnett (*Turkey of the Ottomans*, p. 205) says this about the *tandır*: "The warming apparatus commonly used by all the races of Turkey is a brass or copper pan containing charcoal buried in wood ashes. This is placed either on an elegantly shaped receptacle of wrought metal, or on a square heavy stand of polished wood from two to three feet square and about eight inches high which occupies the center of the room, or forms part of the *tandour*, a species of table round which the ladies sit with its heavy quilted covering drawn over their knees. The use of American stoves is, however, increasing every year." (She must have been writing shortly before 1911, when the book was published.)

13. Samuel S. Cox, *Diversions of a Diplomat in Turkey*, p. 515.

14. Personal interview with Fazile Keçeci, August 1966.

15. Théophile Gautier, *Constantinople*, p. 196.

16. Lott, *Harem Life*, pp. 293-295.

17. Ibid., pp. 295-296.

18. Ibid., p. 297.

19. Garnett, *Turkey of the Ottomans*, pp. 202-203.

20. Ibid., p. 203.

21. Ibid., pp. 203-205.

22. Emine Foat Tugay, *Three Centuries, Family Chronicle of Turkey and Egypt*, pp. 55, 215-216, 249-250; also personal interview, August 1966.

23. Bolu, in Western Anatolia, was known for its cooks.

24. Personal communication from Seniha Moralı.

13

Architecture and the Arts

ARCHITECTURE

The gift of a building to the community was a tradition among the Turks. Already during the reign of the Selçuks of Anatolia we find several structures that were built at the instigation of, or in memory of, women of the ruling class. One of the best known of these is the Döner Kumbet (turning conical tomb) of Şah Cihan (Ruler of the Universe) Hatun, a Selçuk princess, in Kayseri. In the same city there is a complex of buildings which was built under the auspices of Mahperi (Moon Fairy) Hatun, a Selçuk queen. The complex includes a mosque, a *medrese* (theological school), and a tomb. Mahperi was a wife of Alaeddin Keykubad I (ruled 1219-1236), one of the most famous Selçuk sultans of Anatolia.[1]

The handful of buildings connected with Selçuk women were but a foretaste of those to come under the Ottomans. The city of Istanbul and its environs are the more beautiful for the interest Ottoman women have taken in architecture. Their edifices were put up as *hayrat*, pious deeds, and frequently bore inscriptions asking the passerby to say a *fatiha* (first chapter of the Koran) for the soul of the donor. Although mosques and their dependencies, *mescit*s (chapels), and fountains were the most popular forms of *hayrat*, there were others: *medrese*s and other schools, *saray*s, *yalı*s, aqueducts, a new *mimber* (pulpit) for an old mosque, and, in the period covered by this work, even a *namazgâh* (place of prayer).

Hammer, translating from Hafiz Hüseyin el-Hac İsmail of Ayvansaray's *Hadikat-ül-cami* (Garden of Mosques) of the eighteenth century, lists 67 then extant mosques which had been built at the behest of or, in a few instances, in memory of women. Although in many cases Hammer does

not give dates, Tahsin Öz, in his study of Istanbul mosques, does. Therefore, we know that from about the beginning of the eighteenth century to
the end of the Empire women were responsible for the building or res-
toration of 33 mosques or *mescit*s.[2] As for the fountains, of the 491 extant
in Istanbul and its environs when İbrahim Hilmi Tanışık made his study
of them in the 1930s, 128, or 28 percent, were commissioned by women.
Of these women, about six percent were imperial women, and 29 percent
were *valides*.[3]

We shall begin with a discussion of mosques (*camiler*) and fountains
(*çeşmeler*).[4] The first donor of our period is the mother of Mustafa II and
Ahmet III, Râbia Gülnûş, or Gülnûş Ummetullah, who had been a *kadın*
of Mehmet IV. She was responsible for the no-longer-standing wooden
Valide Camii in Galata and the *medrese* connected with it. She had them
built in 1697 when Mustafa II was on the throne. In 1708, when the sultan
was Ahmet III, she commissioned the Yeni (New) Valide Camii, which
today can be found behind a low wall on the main street of Üsküdar. It is
an elegant building with a center dome supported by four half-domes, one
of the last of the classic mosques. Its *mihrap* (niche indicating the direction
of Mecca) and *mimber* (pulpit) are of marble. When it was built, it had
numerous annexes, including an *imaret* (kitchen to feed the poor) and a
mosque school. Later Saliha Valide Sultan added a fountain to one side.
Because there was a stone-worker shortage in Istanbul at the time the
mosque was built, a decree went out in 1708 to the *bostancıbaşı* (head of
the palace guard) of Edirne ordering him to send to the *valide*'s *kethüda*
in Üsküdar 40 stone-workers from the vicinity of Edirne to quarry marble
from the Island of Marmara for the mosque.[5] Râbia Gülnûş is buried in
her *türbe* (tomb) at this mosque.

It is widely believed that Râbia Gülnûş sponsored the building of the
long-gone *mescit* at the Slave Market in Istanbul in order to fulfill a vow
she had made while a slave there. Though romantic, the story is untrue.
Tahsin Öz has discovered from a *vakıf* register that this chapel was commissioned by a man.[6]

The next *valide*, Saliha, mother of Mahmut I, donated the fountain and
primary school connected with the Sokollu Camii in Azapkapı.[7] She restored another mosque and presented a *mimber* to a third.

Mihrişah, *kadın* of Mustafa III and mother of Selim III, was a great
patron of architecture. We know she was responsible for the mosque of
the *humbaracıyan* (bombardiers), built in their barracks in Hacıoğlu, on
the Asiatic shore of Istanbul. According to the *Hadikat-ül-cami*, one side
of the mosque was for the bombardiers, the other for the sappers (*lağım-
cıyan*), and it had a sultan's pew (*hünkâr mahfili*). Thus Mihrişah supported
her son's interest in improving the Empire's military forces. She also put
up the Küçüksu Mescidi (Chapel of the Little Water) which used to stand
near her lovely free-standing fountain in Anadolu Hisarı on the Asiatic

shore of the Bosphorus. A medical school, another school, two fountains in Stambul, seven in Beyoğlu (Pera), and two in Üsküdar are also credited to her. Like so many *valide sultan*s she commissioned her own tomb; this was in Eyüp.[8]

Besm-i Âlem, a *kadın* of Mahmut II who became the mother of Abdülmecit, is remembered for the Dolmabahçe Mosque that stands along the Bosphorus shore beside the palace of that name. It was begun in 1853, but she died before the year was out, and it was completed the next year by request of her son.[9] The architect was Serkiz Balyan, who was from an Armenian family that did much work for the sultans. The mosque shows the influence of his Western training.[10] Instead of the large dome of the classic Ottoman mosque supported by numerous half-domes to form a billowing roof covering a unified building, we find a dome set firmly on a low drum atop a square structure with turreted corners, the square structure attached to a separate rectangular section that carries the main portal and the two minarets. For a time during the Republic the building was used as the Naval Museum. It has a large clock tower which has been moved somewhat farther from the mosque than it originally stood.

Dolmabahçe means "filled garden," and the platform on which the palace and mosque rest is indeed man-made. Here, history tells us, during his conquest of Istanbul, Mehmet II's fleet began its overland journey on wheeled platforms to the Golden Horn, thus bypassing the chain boom which the Byzantines had strung across the mouth of the Horn to prevent the Turkish ships from entering it. Under later sultans this area was a small bay bordered by gardens. Ahmet I (1603-1617) and Osman II (1618-1622), wanting to extend their gardens, had the site filled in with stone.[11]

Added to Besm-i Âlem's list of architectural contributions are the Guraba Hospital, which is still in use,[12] and its mosque in Stambul, and even a hospital in Mecca. Her fountains add up to eight, four in Stambul and four in Beyoğlu.

Pertevniyal, Abdülaziz's mother and another *kadın* of Mahmut II, is remembered for the Gothic Valide Camii in Aksaray. Except for its slender Turkish minaret, it is devoid of traditional Ottoman architectural features. It too is a single-domed mosque, its dome set on a square structure like Dolmabahçe Camii, but the building as a whole has a somewhat more pleasing effect. Its arched Gothic windows point upward, as do its two minarets, so that the entire mosque gives a feeling of uplift until the eye meets the dome squatting on the top. However, the windows in the drum lighten the squatting effect somewhat, and the building has an architectural unity which Dolmabahçe Camii lacks. The mosque was designed by an Italian architect, Pietro Montani, and built about 1871.

Prior to the building of this mosque, Pertevniyal's *kethüda*, Hüseyin Ağa, expropriated the site, tore down a dilapidated mosque, and bought in behalf of the *valide* a number of coffee, *çörek*,[13] baking, tobacco, grocery, and shoemaker's shops to clear the area. To make room for the mosque he also took over some *konak*s and other home sites. While construction was in progress, he sent the *valide* a memorandum emphasizing the mosque's spaciousness: "I have made and presented to His Majesty a picture of the noble mosque. It is as big as the noble Ortaköy Mosque, but its courtyard will be wider, and when His Majesty the Benefactor of the World comes, the imperial soldiers and the officers of the *selâmlık* will stand there; streets have been opened and widened in accordance with the new style. My Lady, since you are not devoid of wisdom, you have given the order for the fountain and also a place for a great congregation there."[14]

Despite Hüseyin Ağa's pains, the Aksaray Valide Camii remains a pleasant, medium-sized mosque that cannot compete in spaciousness and grandeur with the classic Ottoman mosques.

On the day the foundation was laid in 1868, Pertevniyal traveled in disguise by carriage to the nearby house of a secretary and watched. At 4:15, the hour the chief astrologer (*müneccimbaşı*) had appointed, which coincided with the hour of afternoon prayer, the sacrifices were made and the prayers chanted by *hoca*s and *şeyh*s who had been invited, while pickaxes struck deep into the earth. In behalf of the *valide*, Hüseyin Ağa presented each of them with a watch worth from 3,000 to 4,000 liras.[15]

Finally, we come to Perestû, a *kadın* of Abdülmecit who became Abdülhamit II's foster mother and official *valide*. We know little of her work except that she added a *sebil* (public fountain) and a *muvakkithane*[16] to the fifteenth-century Bala Camii at Silivrikapı, in Istanbul.

*İkbal*s and *kadın*s did their share of building. Perhaps the most noteworthy of their works was the Simkeşhane Mescidi built at the old Simkeşhane[17] at Beyazıt[18] in 1707 by Emetullah, *baş kadın* of Ahmet III. Shortly afterwards, the Simkeşhane burned and was rebuilt by means of a commission from the same woman within the confines of Topkapı Palace. She added to it a school for the weavers of silver thread. The *mescit*, however, remained standing until it was torn down in 1956 to make way for the enlargement of Beyazıt Meydanı (Beyazıt Square).[19]

Âdilşah, a *kadın* of Mustafa III, commissioned the Hatice Sultan Camii at Tekfur Sarayı.[20] She was the mother of Hatice Sultan, of whom we shall hear later. In 1752 Hatice Usta, a slave of the chief black eunuch, the younger Beşir Ağa, donated a mosque near Beyazıt known as the Yahnikapanı Sokağı Camii, the Mosque of the Street of the Smart Boy.[21]

Women *sultan*s also contributed their share to the building of mosques and other religious edifices. Fatma, daughter of Ahmet III and wife of the grand vizier Nevşehirli İbrahim Pasha, in 1727 had a mosque built that stood across from the Istanbul Vilayet Konağı (the government house of the province of Istanbul). It lasted until 1957 when it fell victim to a public works project.[22] Her sister, Zeynep Sultan, put up the mosque across from Gülhane Park in the neighborhood of Topkapı Palace in 1765. This was only a few years before her death, and she had it built in accordance with the desire of a deceased sister. The mosque was originally accompanied by a school and a tomb, in the latter of which Zeynep was buried. Mahmut II held a reception in the mosque on June 16, 1826, after he had accomplished the destruction of the Janissaries. School and tomb eventually fell into ruins, and the princess's body was transferred to the cellar of her mosque.[23]

A very important *hayrat* was the building of an aqueduct. Two *valides*, Saliha and Mihrişah, were responsible for aqueducts. In 1732 Saliha Valide Sultan initiated the building of an aqueduct in Bahçeköy on the European side of the Bosphorus. The sultan, the *şeyhülislâm*, the grand vizier, and other viziers were all on hand for the stone-laying ceremony.[24] Mihrişah financed the building of an aqueduct to serve Tophane, Galata, and Beşiktaş;[25] it opened with a celebration prepared by her *kethüda*, Yusuf Ağa, on July 23, 1798.

Women were also responsible for the building of certain *medreses*. There was the one Fatma, Ahmet III's daughter, commissioned in Eyüp, the two *medreses* Valide Râbia Gülnûş constructed for her mosques in Galata and Üsküdar, the one founded by a woman named Ayşe in 1712,[26] and the one erected in the mid-nineteenth century under the auspices of Hüşyar, a *kadın* of Mahmut II, in memory of her two daughters, Mihrimah and Zeynep. Hüşyar created a *vakıf* to support her buildings.[27]

In the nineteenth century, when Western education got under way, some women commissioned the building of schools of the European type. A few of them still exist, like the Pertevniyal School for boys in Aksaray and the aforementioned Besm-i Âlem Rüştiyesi in the Çemberlitaş area.[28]

With the exception of mosques, the most elegant and impressive buildings were the palaces built by or for the women *sultans*. Unfortunately none of the eighteenth-century ones remains today. Since they were made of wood, they either burned or succumbed to the wear and tear of years. However, we do have information about some of them. The earliest in our period was never lived in by the *sultan* for whom it was intended. It was the palace Ali Pasha[29] prepared for Fatma Sultan when he became engaged to the five-year-old girl. It seems originally to have belonged to a former grand vizier and to have been restored by Ali Pasha.[30] It was torn down a few years later to make room for one of the pleasure palaces, Neşatabad,[31] of Ahmet III, Fatma Sultan's father. But it was seen by Lady Montagu, who has left us a description of it. Her words are particularly useful because the palace was built and restored before French influence entered Ottoman architecture.

It is situated on one of the most delightful parts of the canal [the Bosphorus], with a fine wood on the side of the hill behind it. The extent of it is prodigious. The guardian assured me there are eight hundred rooms in it; I will not answer for that number, since I did not count them; but 'tis certain the number is very large, and the whole adorned with a profusion of marble, gilding, and the most exquisite painting of fruit and flowers. The windows are all sashed with the finest crystalline glass brought from England; and all the expensive magnificence that you can suppose in a palace founded by a vain young luxurious man, with the wealth of a vast empire at his command. But no part of it pleased me better than the apartments designed for the bagnios. There are two built in exactly the same manner, answering to one another; the baths, the fountains, and pavements, all of white marble, the roofs gilt, and the walls covered with Japan china; but adjoining to them, two rooms, the upper part of which is divided into a sofa; in the four corners falls of water from the very roof, from shell to shell, of white marble, to the lower end of the room, where it falls into a large basin, surrounded with pipes, that throw up the water as high as the room. The walls are in the nature of lattices; and, on the outside of them, vines and woodbines planted, and form a sort of green tapestry, and give an agreeable obscurity to these delightful chambers.

'Tis yet harder to describe a Turkish palace than any other, being entirely irregular. There is nothing that can properly be called front or wings. . . . I shall only add that the chamber destined for the Sultan, when he visits his daughter, is wainscoated with mother-of-pearl fastened with emeralds like nails. There are others of mother-of-pearl and olive wood inlaid, and several of Japan china. The galleries, which are numerous and very large, are adorned with jars of flowers, and porcelain dishes of fruits of all sorts, so well done in plaster, and coloured in so lively a manner, that it has an enchanting effect. The garden is suitable to the house, where arbours, fountains, and walks, are thrown together in an agreeable confusion.[32]

As we know, Ali Pasha died at Peterwaradin before his marriage to Fatma Sultan could be consummated, and the next year, 1717, when she was 13, Fatma was married to Nevşehirli İbrahim Pasha, who was then in his 50s. During her marriage she lived in a palace opposite Topkapı on the street today called Cağaloğlu. It was Nevşehirli's headquarters when he was grand vizier and was, therefore, called Paşakapısı (the Pasha's Gate),[33] but was usually referred to as the Yeni Paşakapısı (the New Pasha's Gate) to distinguish it from the palace of the former grand viziers.[34] Fatma's palace ceased being the Paşakapısı upon the death of Nevşehirli, but regained that designation in 1739 and continued to be the seat of the grand vizier until it was destroyed by fire. The prevalence of fires in Istanbul led to the changing of the grand vizier's locale from time to time. The *konaks* of the highly placed being invariably large and impressive, two of them were chosen as Paşakapısı: Esma Sultan's in Kadırga after the 1754 fire and Zeynep Hanım's after the 1838 fire.[35]

Nevşehirli İbrahim Pasha became grand vizier in 1718 and straightaway began a building program to compensate for the neglect Ottoman architecture had suffered during a protracted period of war. In the spring of 1719, he began alterations on Fatma Sultan's palace. In the same year he repaired the *valide*'s palace in Eyüp on the Golden Horn because the sultan frequently visited there. By the following spring, he had completed a shore palace (*sahil sarayı*) for himself and his wife at Beşiktaş, [36] the palace where the celebrated illuminated entertainments took place. That year also saw the beginning of the improvements of the old promenade spot of Kağıthane. In 1721 Yirmisekiz Mehmet Çelebi came home from France with pictures and plans of Versailles, Fontainebleau, and other palaces. The pace of building quickened. The purpose changed from one of making amends for past neglect to one of building pleasure palaces for the sake of enjoyment. They were no longer laid out in the state of "agreeable confusion" which Lady Montagu spoke of, but in formal gardens adorned with pools in the best French fashion. [37] These were not built for women, but for Ahmet III and his cronies. Yet it is certain that ladies of the court and other highly placed women were from time to time allowed to enjoy them.

Meanwhile, feelings against this type of ostentation arose among the conservative elements of the population. The animosity centered largely on Nevşehirli İbrahim. In 1722, when the palace garden of Sadabad was being built at Kağıthane, an individual named Sem'danizade Süleyman Efendi wrote concerning Nevşehirli: "This vizier is a spendthrift and invents pleasure and enjoyment night and day. . . . High officials and women mingle, and when the poor women climb in and out of the hammocks, handsome youths take them in their arms, put them in the hammocks, and take them out again . . . they have illicit relations and sing songs with pleasing voices. . . . Women go on excursions without permission, saying they have the permission of their husbands . . . and otherwise demand divorce. . . . There are not five women in any quarter who can be called chaste wives. . . . He removes the mates and food and garments that belong to the people." [38] And again he wrote, regarding the building of Sadabad, "The vagabonds occupied with the transporting of wood and stones many times attached themselves to Jewish women in order to look on at the execrable acts." [39]

But still the building went on. In 1725 Ahmet III confiscated the debt-ridden shore palace of Osman Bey, located between Tophane and Salıpazarı, added to it a *yalı* similarly confiscated from one Gümrükcü Hüseyin Pasha, and had the sea filled in along the shore. On the resultant site he erected a large and handsome shore palace. The place was called Eminabad, "the abode of security." [40]

After the execution of Nevşehirli and the deposition of Ahmet III, the construction of new buildings stopped, but only for a short period of time. About 1735, we find Mahmut I's *valide* putting up kiosks, one near Çengelköy and another on the water in the village of Aliköy. [41]

Another spurt of building took place during the reign of Selim III. The main catalyst was Selim himself, but among the most devoted patrons of architecture were the sultan's mother, Mihrişah, and his sister, Hatice. As we have stated above, Hatice was allowed to visit the Bosphorus villa and gardens of the Danish ambassador, Baron de Hübsch, where she was undoubtedly received by Mme. de Hübsch, a noted hostess. Impressed with the Baron's building and grounds, she asked him to recommend a European architect to her, and he suggested Antoine-Ignace Melling.

Hatice had been given Neşatabad, the palace Ahmet III had put up on the site of Şehit Ali Pasha's palace. She asked Melling for ideas for rebuilding it, and he made her a set of models that were Western in concept. Hatice liked them and commissioned him to go ahead with his plans. The work was beset with intrigues and jealousies, but nevertheless Melling produced a beautiful two-story building stretching along the shore at Defterdar Burnu, in Beşiktaş. On the land side he bordered it with elaborate gardens with labyrinthine paths where Selim, reportedly to his delight, once found his sister's girl slaves playing hide and seek.[42] The central section of the palace contained a suite for Selim.[43]

Melling has left us some views of this palace, two of the exterior on the water side, and one of the reception hall, which shows a large, high-ceilinged room with windows on two sides, panels of flowers in vases set high on the wall of the third side, and the fourth side open to a corridor. A figure that is presumably the lady *sultan* herself sits in a corner of the divan which runs around three sides. Before her and roundabout stand various women. Some of them are her slaves, standing in an attitude of respect. Others are her visiting sister and retinue.[44] This is the palace that was equipped with a trapdoor over the water which enabled the *sultan* to fish without being seen.[45] It was probably the inspiration for the stories of the lady *sultan* who lured in *gâvur* (non-Muslim) men and once, when about to be caught by the Janissaries, let them out through a trapdoor into the Bosphorus.

Beyhan Sultan, Selim's full sister, was given the old Çırağan Palace, one of the sites of the Lâle Devri (Tulip Period) entertainments.[46] Beyhan Sultan restored it, which could perhaps be a reason she needed money so badly.[47]

Some of the later palaces that were built for the women *sultan*s are still standing today. One of these is now the Kandilli Kız Lisesi; another, with large high-ceilinged rooms, is in İstinye.

The mansions of the great families imitated the elegance of the imperial palaces to the extent that their owners were able to afford such extravagance. Suphi Pasha's *konak* in Fatih, still standing, is a fine example of those of the later period. Its ceilings are high and elaborately decorated with gilt and colored moldings. Its floors are tiled. Its stairway is spacious and opens from an enclosed entranceway into which carriages used to drive to deposit their occupants. When the *konak* was originally built in 1854 it had a separate harem. That building burned, and the upper floor of the main house was then turned into the harem and a separate *selâmlık* erected.[48] Certain *konak*s were larger than this and numbered from 60 to 100 rooms.[49]

Selim III built, on Sarayburnu (Palace Point), a beautiful kiosk that was known variously as Valide Yeri (Place of the Valide), Serdab Köşkü (Underground Kiosk) or Şevkiye Köşkü (Beloved Kiosk).[50] According to Barnette Miller:

[It] is said to have been lined with mirrored panels alternating with niches, wherein were set the ubiquitous pots and vases of fruits and flowers of the Louis Quinze and Louis Seize periods. So lovely was this kiushk that the mere recollection of it moved to tears the old custodian who related to Abdurrahman Efendi the story of its demolition at the time of the building of the railway which encircles Seraglio Point.[51]

Hospitals were also founded by women. We have said that Valide Besm-i Âlem, a person of many good works, established the Yenibahçe Valide or Guraba Hastahanesi (Hospital) located between Aksaray and the Gate of Topkapı.[52] Its *vakıf* deed arranged for hunters to provide meat for the hospital during such times in the winter as meat was scarce.[53] Zeynep Hanım founded, with her husband, the Zeynep Kâmil Hospital in Üsküdar.[54] We have seen that her *konak* at Beyazıt was used as a hospital.[55]

Among the good works of Besm-i Âlem was the Galata Bridge at Eminönü which replaced the original one of Mahmut II.[56]

CALLIGRAPHY

The decorative arts in which the Turks were so proficient were not to our knowledge practiced by women, except for calligraphy and embroidery. Among practitioners of the former was Ani Hatun of the late seventeenth and early eighteenth centuries, from the family of the *şeyhülislâm* Hoca Sadeddin Efendi. Famous in her time as a *hac-ı zenan* (a woman who had been on a pilgrimage), she was both a poet and calligrapher.[57]

Among other women calligraphers was Esma İbret, who wrote a *hilye-i şerif* (book of sacred recitations), which was shown to Selim III and his mother who arranged that she be sent 500 *kuruş* and 40 *akçes* daily from Customs.[58]

Esma was taught by her husband, Mahmut. One day he discovered this book, and thought it so good and so unwomanly that he did not believe it was actually by her hand. However, investigation proved that Esma had written it, so Mahmut arranged to have it presented at court. In case other skeptics might doubt that so fine a piece of calligraphy could have been done by a woman, Mahmut made a deposition explaining matters and attached it to the work. He concluded it with: "If the time comes when it is not believed that İsma is the İbret, who is the writer of the *hilye*, in order to repel suspicion, explanation is given." The book is now in the

Topkapı Palace Museum. Some of it is in *sülüs* script, some in *nesih*. Esma was entitled to sign her work *ketebe*, indicating she had received a diploma for calligraphy; she added *ibret* (strange) to show that her work was worth notice.[59]

Another woman calligrapher was Feride Hanım, the daughter of a poet who was a member of the *ulema* from Kastamonu. He was her teacher. She had memorized the Koran by the time she was seven, developed a passion for poetry, and began to imitate her father's verse. Eventually she was awarded a diploma for calligraphy. She married in 1852 and went to Istanbul with her husband, who died when she was only 21. The grieving widow wrote elegies for him and from then on occupied herself with literary and religious activity, which included copying the Koran and other religious books.[60]

Also in the mid-nineteenth century lived Zahide Selma Hanım, the daughter of one Ali Pasha. She had a talent for calligraphy which was cultivated by the study of *talik* script with Kazasker Mustafa İzzet Efendi, who was a neighbor of her family at Bebek. Her work was recognized, and it adorned the pulpit of the former Meccan Camii and the window of Şeyh Vefa's tomb.[61]

In the late nineteenth century came Emine Servet Hanım, the daughter of Şeyhülislâm Hasan Hayrullah Efendi, who was imprisoned in Tâif with Mithat and who died there. She studied *sülüs*, *nesih*, and *celî*, and in 1872 received her diploma.[62]

Emine Servet married unhappily and, because she could not stand the strains of a polygamous household, returned to her family. Her maternal grandfather was the *imam* of Arpacılar Camii, and she spent much time with him. She wrote nine *hilye-i şerif*s, one of which is in that mosque. She used to say, "Although I have no children of my own, I have nine children through God's mercy."[63]

Other women calligraphers were Trabzonlu Fıtnat Hanım,[64] Şerife Ayşe (who was the daughter of a *hırka-ı şerife şeyh*[65] and who wrote in *talik* in the late nineteenth century) and Cilve Naz Hanım (who wrote a *hilye-i şerif*[66] but whose identity is not known, although it is suspected that she was a *cariye* in the palace or in a great household).

Women calligraphers continued to exercise their talent well into the twentieth century. Among these later ones is Müşerref Hanım, the daughter and wife of a merchant. She memorized the Koran when she was very young, but she did not turn to calligraphy until her later years, when she took lessons in *sülüs*. She worked at it seriously, became an excellent calligrapher, and had her daughter taught the art.[67]

It should be noted that these girls all came from intellectual families where they were generally exposed to fine calligraphy, and that they were taught by someone very close to them.

EMBROIDERY

Virtually every Turkish girl learned the art of embroidery. As Maurice Moyal has pointed out in his article on Turkish embroidery, "You notice many signs bearing witness to a love of beauty nurtured by the Turks . . . streets lined with daintily carved wooden houses, the shoeshine man's mother-of-pearl inlaid box, the carts with gaily painted panels. . . . This instinctive quest for beauty has found its highest expression in embroidery, a truly popular art."[68]

Moyal discusses embroidery as it was practiced by the village girl, but the art was by no means limited to her. During the Empire all Turkish women knew how to embroider. It was part of every girl's education, the high and the low alike. Although perhaps the *büyük hanım* of a great house no longer practiced the art, she had acquired the necessary skill and had it taught to her daughters and slaves, and when they became *ev hanımıs* (housewives) they in turn had it taught to the girls under their guardianship.

It is an art that goes far back in Turkic history. As Moyal points out, it was a nomad art, "for patterns can easily be rolled and carried away as the herdsmen move from pasture to pasture." It was also practiced by the Selçuks. One day, when a man questioned the daughter of the Selçuk sultan Alp Arslan about a piece of work in her hand, she answered, "Yes, Iranians are amazed at seeing me occupied with handwork. However, in my family all the women, like me, are occupied with handwork. It is not suitable for our race to waste time."[69]

The girls worked both with and without patterns. Sometimes a girl drew a pattern on her material. Sometimes she had no pattern at all, and formed her design by counting the stitches. This is called *hesap işi* (reckoning work).[70]

Great patience was necessary and, as Moyal points out, so was an attitude that took no heed of time. Sometimes the changes in color are so gradual that one shade seems to fade into another. Yet each time a color changed the thread had to be changed. No knots or joints might show, and the wrong side had to be as finished as the right. The best work was very fine, three or four stitches to a millimeter.[71]

In the collections of Nuri H. Arlasez of Istanbul and Kenan Kent of New York are many very beautiful examples of Turkish embroidery. Only a few can be mentioned here. In the Arlasez collection there is a towel of many colors, each shade melting into the next, but in one little section a black thread is worked in (this was to show that the embroiderer did not aspire to the same degree of perfection as God). Another towel, of very fine material, is worked in pale colors but in a very bold design. A third, the finest in the collection, an Istanbul piece of the early eighteenth century, is worked with five stitches to the millimeter, in a floral design of many colors. The towels in the Arlasez collection have all been washed, yet the colors have neither run nor faded.

Many objects besides towels were embroidered: quilt facings; head scarfs; handkerchiefs; belts and sashes; the ubiquitous *bohças*, whose corners were usually embroidered and whose edges were decorated with the tatting-like lace in flower designs called *oya*; the *örtüs* that covered pillows, cradles, turbans, and the food dishes on their trays; caftans; wedding dresses; prayer rugs (*seccades*); and carpets (*nihales*).[72] In imperial circles, especially in the nineteenth century, some of these, such as the pillow covers and cradle covers, were so heavily encrusted with gold thread and precious stones as to have lost their flexibility. Coral and pearl work was especially popular in that century. Although impressive, in sheer beauty this elaborate work cannot compare with the more delicate embroidery.[73]

The colors used in a single work were few in earlier times. The most beautiful work comes from the sixteenth century, the high point of Turkish art. By the nineteenth century the embroiderer was working in several colors in one piece, such as in a towel in the author's possession. Each end is embroidered in eight colors: two shades of green; pink; two shades of blue; grey; gold; and black for outlining. The design is composed of leaves and flowers in an open circle. It is executed mostly in the Turkish stitch, in which one stitch covers three threads. The stitches are placed diagonally and close together so that they fill the allotted space. The wrong side is as perfect as the right. Each end of the towel has a border of simple counted stitches. It has great beauty.

Yet Macide Gönül shows another towel of the nineteenth century, which does not have the appeal of the simpler work. The ends are embroidered with a multitude of motifs, including cypresses, leaves, sprays of flowers, and even a building, forming a complex design that is crowded and devoid of unity. Its stitch is *muşabak*.[74]

The motifs in Turkish embroidery are taken largely from nature. We see tulips, hyacinths, carnations, roses, violets, cypresses, oaks, plane trees, vines, grapes, pomegranates, pears. In the embroideries of the eighteenth and nineteenth centuries the moon, the sun, clouds, kiosks, palaces, tents, ships, arcs, and broken lines are also represented.

Wedding dresses were heavily embroidered. The author has examined a deep red velvet nineteenth-century one embroidered in gold in a rose and spray pattern. The work was probably done by specialists in the bride's native city. It is embroidered in the *dival* stitch, a very old stitch that was used on quivers, books, and Koran covers. In the case of this wedding dress the *dival* work is supplemented by a simple stitch in gold in a pattern of open squares, and by gold sequins sewn on here and there with red thread. It is a heavy, stiff garment, but magnificent.

Another example of interesting Turkish embroidery is shown by Malek Celâl in her book, *Türk işlemeleri*.[75] It is a late eighteenth-century napkin (*yağlık*) which combines Chinese and baroque influences. Earlier examples in her book have clear colors and are embroidered in the formalized floral designs that may have had their origin in the animal art of Central Asia. In the nineteenth century the style began to show French influence and grew heavier. Yet the floral sprays never lost their popularity.

So important was the art of embroidery as a feminine accomplishment that the *görücü* who came to visit a house to shop for a bride often looked over the girl's embroidery to see how well executed it was. This, it was said, gave her an idea of the girl's character.[76]

LITERATURE[77]

Women have always been active in the realm of Turkish literature, in both folk poetry and in *divan* (classical) poetry. As Nihat Sami Banarlı has said: "As a natural result of the rich and historical poetic tradition and the popular cultures among the Turkic people we have had many women poets who have sung all sorts of quatrains on the life of pleasure. They have sung songs for those they loved, lullabies for their infants, tales for their children, epics for their soldiers, and laments for their martyrs."[78] These women composed verses with genuine sentiments, about things they knew first hand.

But there was another type of female writer, namely, the woman *divan*[79] poet. She used the form and meter of the male *divan* poet, and even adopted his vocabulary and subject matter. In a sense her work was synthetic, for though she lived a secluded harem life, she wrote about wine and wine shops, youths and love, and even the male homosexual love celebrated by the male poets.[80] Hers was a vocation or avocation removed from life and, as such, required more artistry than art.

In our period the first of these woman *divan* poets was Fıtnat Hanım. Fıtnat was a pen name; her own was Zübeyde. She came from a learned family, being sister, niece, and granddaughter of *şeyhülislâm*s. Her father was Esat Efendi, a poet, the compiler of an Arabic-Persian-Turkish dictionary, and also a historian of music. In a household dominated by such a man, it is not surprising that a bright girl should have turned to poetry. She must have wanted to be a part of the life she admired, and poetry was the one way open to her. At this time no one had ever heard of an Ottoman woman prose writer, but in poetry others had paved the way. She showed her first efforts to her father and her teachers, and the praise they gave encouraged her to continue.[81]

Since her father held high *ulema* posts, she grew up in a palace atmosphere. However, her greatest fame came in the days of the vizierate of Koca Ragıp Pasha (1756-1763), who became grand vizier in the last days of Mahmut I and continued to serve in that capacity for six years under Mustafa III. She wrote a sonnet (*kaside*) to Ragıp Pasha, wrote parallels (*nazireler*) to some of his poems, and engaged in witty poetic contests with him.[82]

Fıtnat was married to a man named Derviş Efendi, whose accomplishments were far inferior to hers although he held fairly high *ulema* positions, and it is generally thought that she was not happy. It is said that she was a woman of considerable wit, quick in repartee. She published a *divan* of classic poetry on time-honored themes. Perhaps her most famous poem is a *müseddes* (poem with six-line stanzas) on spring, each stanza ending with the line: "The tulips and roses are opened, once again the season of spring has come."[83] She is also credited with having knowledge of jurisprudence and is said to have helped her father in his work.[84] Undoubtedly a woman of great character, she had a mosque and dependencies built in memory of her father in Shumen, Bulgaria, the town from which her family came.[85] She became famous in her own lifetime, and many think that she was the finest of the women *divan* poets. She died in 1780.[86]

There was another Fıtnat Hanım, also a *divan* poet, although a lesser one. She was born in Trabzon where her father, Haznedar Ahmet Pasha, was governor. Trabzonlu Fıtnat was born in 1842 and died in either 1909 or 1911. She married early a man who was very jealous. He forbade her to wear beautiful clothing, to write poems, and even to read. It is not surprising that she separated from him and took up her studies again. She married a second time. Besides having a gift for poetry, this Fıtnat, as we have seen, produced beautiful calligraphy.[87]

With *divan* poetry so popular an art form, there were naturally several women who tried their hand at it. One of them was Şeref Hanım (1809-1858). She seems to have been an unoriginal but skillful versifier. She was the daughter of a Nebil Bey, who wrote some poetry and was a teacher of Persian. Like several other woman poets, she was related to a *şeyhülislâm*. Being a member of the Kadirî and Mevlevî orders, she wrote some mystic poetry, but her work is very varied.[88]

Sırrı Hanım, from Diyarbakır, was also of the *divan* school. She wrote a *kaside* and a letter of presentation to Mithat Pasha when he was governor of Baghdad. She was a prolific poet and wrote a famous elegy (*mersiye*). Her dates are 1814-1877.[89]

Other noteworthy Ottoman women poets who wrote in a traditional vein were Nakiye, Seniye, Mahşah and Leylâ. Nakiye (1848-1898) was the daughter of a court astrologer (*müneccimbaşı*) and the niece of Şeref Hanım. She learned to read the Koran when very young and finished her education at the *Darülmuallimat*, where she later taught. She wrote poetry in the old style and with a slight mystic bent.[90] Seniye of Trabzon (1836-1905) was taught to read and write by her father. She took part in poetic contests with men, and wrote in stress (*hece*) as well as in measured (*aruz*) meter.[91] Mahşah (1864-1902) was born in Trabzon but lived in various places, including Istanbul. She entered several religious orders, and wrote poetry of a mystical character.[92] Leylâ, whose birthdate is unknown, came from an *ulema* family, being the daughter of Moralızade Hamit Efendi, a *kazasker*. She learned the art of poetics from her uncle, Keçecizade İzzet Molla, the father of Keçecizade Fuat, the Tanzimat statesman. She too was unhappily married, and she separated from her husband right after the marriage ceremony. Those who have made a study of Leylâ's poetry have found it sensitive, intelligent, lyrical, and written in a simple style. Because of her musical verse, she was called Bülbül (Nightingale). She too was famous in her lifetime and had a *divan* published in three volumes. She became a member of the Mevlevî order, perhaps through the influence of İzzet Molla, who was a Mevlevî. Leylâ Hanım died in 1824. Fatma Aliye, in a work entitled *Famous Women of Islam* (*Namdaran-ı zenan-ı İslâmiye*), says that on Leylâ's wedding night, when she was still in wedding dress and veil, her husband showed her a cut on his arm kept open by a chick-pea and told her to dress it. Horrified, she ran out of the room and never returned.[93]

Some women *sultan*s also tried their hand at writing traditional poetry. We have the most information about Âdile Sultan (1826-1899), daughter of Mahmut II and Zernigâr Kadın. She followed the *divan* tradition, writing *nazire*s to Fuzulî, Muhibbî, and Şeyh Galip, but she is not outstanding in either feeling or technique. Her life lasted long enough for her to have become a modern poet, but she was faithful to the classic tradition which was still strong, particularly in the palace. Moreover, she was a member of the Nakşibendî order.[94]

The first Ottoman woman poet to write of emotions she herself had experienced was Nigâr Hanım (1856-1918). Fuat Köprülü has called her the first sincere woman poet and the greatest up to his time. Whereas the others were concerned with the old rules of prosody and the nuances of the Ottoman language, Nigâr went beyond this to sing of emotional reality.[95]

She was the daughter of a Hungarian convert to Islam, Osman Nihalî, who had been aide-de-camp to Serdar-ı Ekrem Ömer Pasha in the Crimean War, and of Emine Hanım, the daughter of the *mühürdar* of Keçecizade Fuat Pasha. Her father, popularly known as Macarlı (Hungarian) Osman Pasha, taught German at Harbiye, the officers' training school, and was a musician and a lover of music; her mother had a passion for poetry. These influences melded in Nigâr Hanım.[96]

Her schooling was more extensive than that of most upper-class girls of her time. She was taught both at home and at the French school in Kadıköy. She learned several languages, including Persian, Arabic, French, and German. She studied Turkish with a member of the Educational Council. She read voluminously both the French and the Ottoman writers, and her favorites are said to have been de Musset among the French and Fuzulî among the Ottomans. Perhaps under the influence of de Musset as well as of her own emotions, she first wrote an elegy, "Efsus" ("Alas!"), which was dedicated to her dead brother. It was published when she was 14. Other influences on her work were the poets of the Tanzimat, especially Abdülhak Hamit and Recaizade. "Efsus" was followed by two collections of prose and poetry, some of it translations from the French, called *Niran* (*Shining Things*) and *Aks-ı seda* (*Echo*). She also published a book of love letters, *Sefahat-ı kalb* (*Phases of the Heart*), on the basis of which Köprülü called her a very good prose writer, and she contributed various articles to *Hanımlara mahsus gazete*.[97] The first issue of this magazine for women contains a poem written by her congratulating Abdülhamit II on the anniversary of his accession to the throne, apparently one of her few non-personal poems.[98]

Nigâr Hanım too was not happy in her marriage, which is perhaps why she poured so much emotion into poetry. Except in the matter of clothes where she stayed with *ferace* and *yaşmak*, she was very modern and participated in the *Servet-i Fünun*. Even before the Young Turk Revolution she entertained foreign literary and artistic personalities in her *konak* and was one of the popular figures in the *mehtap*s that took place on summer evenings on the Bosphorus. Her house on the Bosphorus and her *konak* in Nişantaşı[99] were places of rendezvous of the literary and the great. Her favorite haunt was Göksu, where she frequently heard her poems recited.[100] The last poem she wrote was dedicated to Rauf Bey, a literary figure who died at a young age.[101]

Nigâr signed her works Nigâr bint-i (daughter of) Osman or Nigâr bint-i Osman Paşa, which at first was thought to be the pseudonym of a man.[102]

Less famous than Nigâr, but still well known, was Makbule Leman, who was born in 1865 and died in 1898. She was the daughter of the *kahvebaşı*[103] (principal coffee server) of Murat V and the wife of a member of the Council of State, who was also a poet. She studied first in a *rüştiye* and then followed the upper-class pattern of having private teachers. For the last 14 years of her life she was an invalid; the melancholy turn of her poetry is usually ascribed to her precarious state of health. Her verse has rhythm, her thought sensitivity. She published two volumes of verse, *Solgun şükûfem* (*My Wilted Flowers*) and *Ah sıhhat* (*Ah, Health*), and several articles in *Hanımlara mahsus gazete*. For her writing she received the Order of Şefkat (Compassion), an honor given to women at the time. Her life was short; she was only 33 when she died. Tevfik Fikret wrote an elegy to her.[104]

A third prominent woman poet of the last years of the Ottoman Empire was İhsan Raif, who was born in Beirut in 1897 and moved to Istanbul ten years later. Her father was Raif Pasha, one of the last Ottoman viziers. In 1912 she published a book of verse in *hece* (stress) that was harshly criticized, perhaps because the *hece* meter was thought inelegant at the time. At any rate, her later work was more appreciated. Some of her poems are patriotic, some pastoral. Her best known work is called *Göz yaşları* (*Tearful Eyes*). She died in 1926 in Paris.[105]

One ought also to mention Yaşar Nazihe, who lived from 1880 to 1934 or 1935. She came from an uneducated family and, because of her father's ignorance, had very little schooling. Nevertheless she taught herself and eventually published close to 50 poems in *Kadınlar dünyası* (*Women's World*).[106]

Certain other literary women, principally writers of prose, were of outstanding importance. Two such were Fatma Aliye (1864-1924)[107] and Emine Semiye (1868-1944), daughters of the statesman and historian, Ahmet Cevdet Pasha. They were educated by private teachers and by their father in the family *konak*, much of the time in Aleppo, where he was governor. As the historian of literature Nihat Sami Banarlı has pointed out, these two played a historic role in giving women the courage to formulate their ideas and to write about them. Both were versatile and wrote in many fields, largely in prose.

Fatma Aliye, when she was ten years old, decided she wanted to learn French. At first her father thought her too young, but he was soon persuaded to engage a French teacher for her. Her drive to write started almost as early. Her first effort was a translation from the French of Georges Ohnet's novel *Volonté*, which she called *Meram* (*Desire*). She signed it only "A Lady." Thereafter, she frequently signed herself "Translator of *Meram*." Many thought it the work of a man until Ahmet Mithat, who was one of her teachers, wrote a monograph on her and let it be known that the author was Fatma Aliye. Eventually she took her respected place in Ottoman letters and signed her own name. Many articles by her appeared in *Hanımlara mahsus gazete*. Among these are pieces on educational subjects and a serialization of a later book of hers, *Women of Islam* (*Nisvan-ı İslâm*).[108]

She wrote the first novel by a Turkish woman, *Muhadderat* (*Devout and Virtuous Woman*), about a love that killed a first love. This was the first work she signed with her own name.[109] This and a later novel, *Udî* (*The Lute-Player*), were widely read by the women of the old families and reduced many of their readers to tears.

Among other works Fatma Aliye wrote a summary of Ottoman history and a monograph on her father. She was the first woman Turkish writer to arouse interest outside her own country. Her work was shown in the Chicago exhibition of 1893 and discussed in the Chicago newspapers of the time.[110] She was also active in women's affairs and became the first president of the Cemiyet-i İmdadiye, the Society of Help (for the refugees of the Balkan Wars).[111]

The writing of her sister, Emine Semiye, leaned more toward the didactic, although Emine Semiye also wrote novels and short stories. Z.

Duckett Ferriman, an Englishman who was in Turkey in the early twentieth century, says her work reflects the charms and strength of her personality and did a great deal for the moral and intellectual progress of her countrymen. Her older sister had paved the way for her somewhat. She was able to take the then extraordinary step of studying in Paris and followed this up with work in psychology and sociology in Sweden. *Hanımlara mahsus gazete* published letters she wrote from abroad, as well as many other pieces by her. She wrote on a variety of subjects, including spiritual beauty (*Cemal-ı manevî*), health (*Sıhhat*), and dress (*Moda ve korse*). Nevertheless the central endeavor of her life was teaching, and she taught in Istanbul and Edirne until close to her death in 1944. Among her works were novels and stories for children. She married, but not happily.[112]

Of lesser importance in the world of letters but not to be overlooked is Abdülhak Mihrünnisa (1864-1943), the sister of Abdülhak Hamit. She was a child of the Tanzimat, much under the influence of both her brother and Namık Kemal, and wrote in the more modern language of their time. She was privately educated and, like so many of her literary sisters, married unhappily and separated from her husband when still young. Only scattered examples of her work remain with us today.[113]

These women, beginning with Nigâr Hanım, might be called the first crop of the seeds of Westernization among women. Another group came to the fore in the *Meşrutiyet* (Constitution) period. A little earlier, and serving as a link between the old and the new, was Leylâ Saz, who was born in 1850 and died in 1936. She was the daughter of Hekimbaşı İsmail Pasha, who was originally a Greek from Chios and who was imperial surgeon to Mahmut II and head doctor of Abdülmecit and Abdülaziz. Because of her father's position, she had access to the palace as a child and learned music there. All her life she remained interested in music, both à la turka and à la franga. She played the piano and wrote many musical compositions, largely songs and marches. Her interest in music led her to take *saz* (the name of a musical instrument) as her family name. Her father became governor of Crete, and there she learned French and Greek. She married Giritli Sırrı Pasha, who served as governor of various provinces.[114]

Leylâ Saz wrote poetry in both the *divan* and the Tanzimat style, and also her memoirs, which the scholar Fahir İz calls her most valuable contribution. They describe daily life in the imperial harem. A portion of these memoirs appeared in the Istanbul newspapers *Vakıt* (*Time*) and *İleri* (*Progress*). The part of the memoirs having to do with the palace was translated into French by her son.[115] She lived to a ripe old age, dying at 86. Like that of Nigâr Hanim, her life was much connected with the Bosphorus, and she participated in the *mehtap*s there.[116]

By far the most important woman writer of the twentieth century and perhaps the most important in Turkey to date was Halide Edip (Adıvar).

Although she did most of her work under the Republic, she began her career during the Empire and thus comes within our period. Her background and education have already been discussed. Otto von Spiess, the German student of Turkish literature, has said about her, "She is a real artist. She has a style of her own, which has been influenced by an American and English education. She writes charmingly and vividly."[117] Most of the work of which Spiess is speaking came later in her career; yet during the late years of the Empire her writing career was already in full bloom, especially in the realm of politics. Köprülü has called her the greatest prose figure of Nationalist literature.[118] She wrote to help promote a national consciousness and to advertise the need for a new and more liberal outlook.

Halide Edip's first writing venture was a translation of an obscure American book, *Mother in the Home*, by a pedagogue of the 1860s, Jacob Abbott. This so delighted her father that he had a thousand copies printed and distributed to the wives of soldiers. He even showed it to Abdülhamit II who consequently gave Halide a decoration.[119]

The first published work which was truly her own was a patriotic poem offered in the garb of an address by Osman Gazi, the first Ottoman sultan. It exhorted the Fourth Army Corps to uphold the Young Turk Revolution of 1908.[120]

The Young Turk Revolution brought to life a number of newspapers of opinion, thus providing a forum for writers interested in socio-political subjects; Halide Edip took advantage of this opportunity. She was a frequent contributor to *Tanin* (*Reverberation*) and her articles provoked heated debates. Once she even received a letter threatening her if she didn't stop publishing.[121] She had prepared well for writing by devouring the excellent library (which included French books) of her first husband Salih Zeki Bey. She was acquainted with the political and literary movements of the time, and with her quick mind, interest in political affairs, and talent she communicated her ideas well.

Because of her political activities she was forced to flee during the 1909 Counter-Revolution and made her way first to Üsküdar and then to Egypt. From Egypt she was invited to England and while there wrote *Yeni Turan*. The novel was an immediate success, exemplifying as it did the nascent nationalist yearnings of the Turks. From then on Halide Edip was constantly busy as a writer of articles and novels, and in demand as a public speaker. A series of articles which she wrote on education brought her a request to teach from the Ministry of Education, which added one more facet to a busy life. Even at her lowest ebb, when sick in heart and body in 1911 after her divorce from her first husband, Halide Edip continued writing.

Meanwhile her public grew. During the Italo-Turkish War a letter came to her from six Turkish officers in Tripoli who had been moved by *Yeni Turan*, an incident she later used in another story. In the period before

World War I she wrote and helped produce for Türk Ocağı (Turkish Hearth) a children's play, "The Shepherds of Canaan," about Joseph and his brothers. This work was never published in its original form, but later became the libretto for an opera written by the Syrian musician, Vedi Sabra.

Halide Edip not only wrote, but in 1908 or 1909 she helped found a women's organization, the aforementioned Teali-i Nisvan Cemiyeti, the Society for the Elevation of Women. By the time Turkey's War of Independence broke out, Halide Edip was a well-known political, literary, and educational figure.[122]

There are other *Meşrutiyet* women writers worthy of mention: Şükûfe Nihal Başar (b. 1896), who was a graduate of the Edebiyat (Literature) Fakültesi of the University of Istanbul and a teacher (she wrote on educational and economic matters);[123] Halide Nusret Zorlatuna (b. 1901), a teacher of English who wrote poetry, novels, and newspaper articles;[124] Müfide Ferit, whose *Pervaneler* (*Moths*), a novel about young girls in foreign schools, attracted a great deal of attention;[125] Güzide Sabri Aygün (b. 1883), a popular novelist;[126] Sabiha Zekeriye Sertel (b. 1897), who wrote for both adults and children, and with her husband wrote for the newspaper *Tan* well into the era of the Republic. She was educated in New York at Columbia University.[127]

One cannot fail to note that almost all of these women came from the educated class, many from *ulema* families. It was in these families, with their tradition of private teaching, that the literate women were produced.

In the last years of the nineteenth century, publications aimed directly at women readers were launched (which is in itself an indication of the increased literacy of women). The first of which we have found a record is a weekly women's supplement to the publication that bore the title *Terakki* (*Progress*), which was founded in 1868.[128] Among others was *Resimli kitap* (*The Illustrated Book*), a monthly (occasionally bimonthly) journal that existed from September, 1908, until May, 1923. Its contributors included Fatma Aliye, Emine Semiye, Nigâr Hanım, and Halide Edip, who wrote for it romantic essays which were signed Halide Salih.[129] There were also *Mehasin* (*Good Qualities*) and *Süs* (*Elegance*). By 1911 there were seven women's magazines, owned by men but with women contributors. Also in 1911 the first magazine to be published by women, *Kadınlar dünyası* (*Women's World*), appeared. Its editors were Turkish women who made it the official organ of the Müdafaa-ı Hukukî Nisvan Cemiyeti (Society for the Defense of Women's Rights) which we have previously mentioned.[130]

One of the editors and writers of this publication was the first woman in the Ottoman Empire to go up in an airplane. She was Belkis Şevket, who flew in the *Osmanlı* in 1913, throwing out over Istanbul cards enjoining Turkish women to contribute money to purchase a new plane for the Turkish army, a plane to be called *Kadınlar Dünyası*. The *Osmanlı* was piloted by the Balkan War hero Fethi Bey.[131]

The best known of the women's publications was *Hanımlara mahsus gazete*, published by Mehmet Tahir. The first issue was dated August 19, 1311 (1893). It opened with an editorial congratulating Abdülhamit II on the anniversary of his accession to the throne and, as we have said, contained a poem on that subject by Nigâr bint-i Osman. The formalities having been disposed of, the magazine went on to discuss the issues of the day that were of particular interest to women. Its contributors were both men and women. We have mentioned articles by Fatma Aliye, Emine Semiye, and Nigâr Hanım. These and other authors wrote on the advisability of women wearing the veil, on the bringing up and educating of children, on dress, on European women. There were poems as well as works of fiction translated from the French; news of dressmaking and handwork; recipes; pictures of foreign places; and advertisements ranging from Singer sewing machines to pianos and music teachers. In general, it tended to educate the Ottoman woman in the Western way of life.[132]

The magazine continued to be published for several years and as time went on became more and more Westernized. Beginning with the October 15, 1901 issue it carried a French logotype beneath the Ottoman one, which read: *Journal des dames, illustration hebdomadaire littéraire et scientifique paraissant les jeudis.*[133]

There were a number of other magazines that catered both to a woman's intellectual life and to her personal life.[134]

In this period several women's organizations came into being. We have mentioned the Cemiyet-i İmdadiye and the Teali-i Nisvan Cemiyeti (founded in 1912). To encourage women to work outside the home there was also the Kadınlar Çalıştırma Cemiyeti (The Society for Women's Work), run by upper-class women for the benefit of poor women. It was connected with the Red Crescent Society (Hilâl-i Ahmer, today's Kızılay).

This was a time when the yeast of the women's movement in Turkey was rising, and nowhere was it more productive than in literature. The gains were noted even abroad. In the last years of the Ottoman Empire, women writers were no longer measured by their ability to imitate men. They had given up the traditional world of letters for one of ideas and emotions that touched them and the women who read them. In so doing they had metamorphosed from imitators to artists and thinkers in their own right.

NOTES

1. Ülkü Ü. Bates, "Women as Patrons of Architecture in Turkey," *Women in the Muslim World*, pp. 245-260; Tamara Talbot Rice, *The Seljuks* (New York, 1961), plate 34 and text, p. 263, and plates 35, 36, and text, pp. 261, 263 for Selçuk buildings built by or for women.

2. Tahsin Öz, *İstanbul camileri*, I and II, passim.

3. İbrahim Hilmi Tanışık, *İstanbul çeşmeleri*, I and II, passim.

4. The information concerning mosques, *mescit*s, and *medrese*s is from Joseph de Hammer-Purgstall, *Histoire de l'Empire ottoman depuis son origine jusqu'à nos jours*, XVIII, pp. 1-138 and Öz, *İstanbul camileri*, I and II, passim. The descriptions are from personal observation.

5. Ahmet Refik [Altınay], *Hicri on ikinci asırda İstanbul hayatı (1100-1200)*, No. 63, p. 42.

6. Öz, *İstanbul camileri*, I, p. 52, no. 109.

7. A district of Istanbul.

8. The places named are all in or near Istanbul.

9. Öz, *İstanbul camileri*, II, p. 20.

10. Reşat Ekrem Koçu, "Bezmiâlem Valide Sultan," *İstanbul ansiklopedisi*, V, p. 2733.

11. Hilary Sumner-Boyd and John Freely, *Strolling Through Istanbul* (Istanbul, 1972), pp. 471-472.

12. Tezer Taşkıran, *Women in Turkey*, p. 25.

13. *Çörek* is a kind of shortbread in the shape of a ring.

14. Halûk Y. Şehsüvaroğlu, *Asırlar boyunca İstanbul*, p. 155.

15. Ibid. Every time a new building was put up in Turkey it was consecrated by means of an animal sacrifice (Sir William M. Ramsay, *The Revolution in Constantinople and Turkey*, p. 298.

16. Öz, *Camiler*, I, p. 31. A *muvakkithane* was a room that held both timepieces and instruments for observing the stars. The officials who set, regulated, and repaired clocks were called *muvakkitler* (Mehmet Zeki Pakalın, *Osmanlı tarih deyimleri ve terimleri sözlüğü*, II, p. 587).

17. The Simkeşhane was the place where gold and silver thread was made.

18. Beyazıt is the district in Istanbul now known as Hürriyet Meydanı (Freedom Square) where the University of Istanbul is located.

19. Information from Yılmaz Güngör, formerly with the Eski Eserler (Old Works) section of the Istanbul Belediye (Municipality). Also Öz, *İstanbul camileri*, I, p. 122, no. 289, and Barnette Miller, *Beyond the Sublime Porte*, p. 161.

20. Öz, *İstanbul camileri*, I, pp. 68 and 69, n. 137. Tekfur Sarayı was a Byzantine palace, the remains of which still stand near the eastern end of the Theodosian Wall.

21. Öz, *İstanbul camileri*, I, p. 151, n. 341.

22. Ibid., I, p. 59, n. 113.

23. Ibid., I, p. 158; Şehsüvaroğlu, *Asırlar*, p. 224.

24. P. G. İnciciyan, *XVIII. asırda İstanbul*, pp. 84, 97.

25. All districts in the newer part of the city.

26. Öz, "Selim III. ün sırkâtibi tarafından tutulan ruzname," *Tarih vesikaları* (*Mayıs* 1949), p. 197; İnciciyan, *İstanbul*, pp. 94, 156. It has not been possible to locate this *medrese*.

27. M. Çağatay Uluçay, *Haremden mektuplar*, pp. 176-177.

28. Information on the location of the Besm-i Âlem Rüştiyesi from Yılmaz Güngör.

29. Later known as Şehit Ali Pasha, *şehit* meaning "one who died in battle."

30. Hammer (*HEO*, XIII, p. 195) writes that Ali Pasha restored for Fatma Sultan the palace of the grand vizier Bıyıklı (the Mustached) Mustafa.

31. Neşatabad means the Abode of Gaiety.

32. Lady Mary Wortley Montagu, *Letters from the Right Honourable . . . 1709-1762*, pp. 173-174. The description of this building, with its floral decorations and mother-of-pearl inlay, indicates a resemblance to the Amucazade Hüseyin Pasha *yalısı* at Anadolu Hisarı. They would have been built about the same period, although the Amucazade *yalısı* is a bit earlier. The plaster flowers and fruits suggest the Ahmet III kiosk of Topkapı Palace (*see* Fanny Davis, *The Palace of Topkapı in Istanbul*, pp. 243-244). Şehit Ali Pasha's palace passed to the government upon his death. One day Ahmet III chanced to admire the site, on a promontory of the Bosphorus at Beşiktaş, which was all that was needed for an imperial palace to be erected there. The new palace was Neşatabad (M. Münir Aktepe, *Patrona isyanı (1730)*, pp. 45-46).

33. *Kapı* (gate) was used in the Ottoman Empire to denote the residence of the grand vizier or the central office of the government (Pakalın, *Deyimler ve terimler*, II, p. 166).

34. Paşakapısı was the name of the grand vizier's residence before the period of Abdülhamit I, when it came to be called Bab-ı Âli (Mithat Sertoğlu, *Resimli osmanlı tarihi ansiklopedisi*, p. 263).

35. This Esma Sultan was probably the daughter of Ahmet III. Zeynep Hanım was the youngest daughter of Mehmet Ali of Egypt. Her *konak* became a military hospital in World War I (*see* Halit Ziya Uşaklıgil, *Saray ve ötesi son hatıralar*, III, p. 101). It stood on the site of the present Fen Fakültesi of the University of Istanbul.

36. Altınay (*İstanbul hayatı 1100-1200*, No. 89, pp. 64-69) gives the text of an order for marble for a pond to be built at the Beşiktaş *yalı* of Nevşehirli İbrahim. It is dated 1718/19.

37. Aktepe, *Patrona isyanı*, pp. 50-51.

38. Ibid., p. 44.

39. Ibid., p. 24.

40. Ibid., pp. 51, 55.

41. Hammer, *HEO*, XIV, p. 307. Çengelköy is on the Bosphorus, Aliköy on the Sea of Marmara.

42. Antoine-Ignace Melling, *Voyage pittoresque de Constantinople et des rives du Bosphore d'auprès les dessins de M. Melling*, II, plates.

43. On March 24, 1794, a *ferman* was issued for the decoration of a modern *kışlak* (winter quarters) for the imperial arrival at Neşatabad (Öz, "Ruzname," No. 69, pp. 195-196).

44. Melling, *Voyage pittoresque*, II, plates. There is a model of this room in the Belediye Müzesi in Istanbul.

45. Ibid., I.

46. This Çırağan is not the palace whose ruins still stand up the Bosphorus from Yıldız; the latter was built by Abdülaziz and burned in 1910.

47. Öz, "Ruzname," No. 69, p. 196 and p. 196, n. 2.

48. Interview with Demir Tanrıöver, grandson of Suphi Pasha, August 1966.

49. Interview with Nesterin Dirvana, whose family *konak* at the end of the Empire numbered 60 rooms.

50. İnciciyan, *İstanbul*, p. 22.

51. Miller, *Beyond the Sublime Porte*, p. 129.

52. This Topkapı is a gate in the land walls of Istanbul.

53. Information from Yılmaz Güngör.

54. Emine Foat Tugay, *Three Centuries, Family Chronicle of Turkey and Egypt*, p. 122.

55. According to Tugay (*Three Centuries*, p. 127) after Zeynep Hanım's death her *konak* became part of Istanbul University and later burned. Mrs. Tugay further relates that a fifth of the land of this woman's estates was given over to charitable purposes.

56. J. H. Mordtmann, "Constantinople," *Encyclopaedia of Islam*, first edition pp. 867-876. For further discussion of women's influence on architecture, *see* also Bates, "Women as Patrons of Architecture in Turkey," pp. 245-260.

57. Reşat Ekrem Koçu, "Ani Hatun," *İstanbul ansiklopedisi*, I, pp. 522-523.

58. Mahmut Kemal İnal, *Son hattatlar*, pp. 85-87.

59. Ibid.

60. Ibid., pp. 775-776; also İbrahim Alâettin Gövsa, *Türk meşhurları ansiklopedisi*, p. 135. Gövsa says that she was married at 15 and widowed three years later.

61. İnal, *Son hattatlar*, pp. 616-617.

62. Ibid., p. 825.

63. Ibid.

64. Gövsa, *Türk meşhurları*, p. 143.

65. Sheikh charged with guarding the Holy Mantle of Muhammad.

66. İnal, *Son hattatlar*, p. 621.

67. Ibid., p. 95.

68. Maurice Moyal, "The Art of Turkish Embroidery," *The Islamic Quarterly*, 4 (January 1958), pp. 162-167.

69. Faruk Sümer, "Eski Türk kadınları," *Türk yurdu*, 3 (*Eylül*, 1954), pp. 191-194.

70. Interviews with Nuri Arlasez, July 1967, Beraet Bulayır, August 1967, and Kenan Kent, April 1971.

71. For a general discussion of Turkish embroidery *see Sanat ansiklopedisi*, II, pp. 849-851, illus. pp. 846, 848, 850, and plate CXXXV.

72. Collections in the Topkapı Sarayı Müzesi and the Belediye Müzesi, Istanbul; Tahsin Öz, *Güzel sanatlar*, passim; also interview with Fazile Keçeci, Istanbul, 1966.

73. *See* Topkapı Sarayı Müzesi.

74. Macide Gönül, "Some Turkish Embroideries in the Collection of the Topkapı Sarayı Museum in Istanbul," *Kunst des Orients*, 6 (1969), pp. 43–76; information on embroidery also from interviews with Beraet Bulayır and Fazile Keçeci, Istanbul, 1966.

75. Melek Celâl, *Türk işlemeleri*, plates.

76. Personal interview with Nuri Arlasez, Istanbul, 1966.

77. For much of the information here and for a general understanding of the subject, the author is indebted to Fevziye Abdullah Tansel.

78. Nihat Sami Banarlı, *Resimli Türk edebiyat tarihi*, p. 289.

79. A *divan* is a collection of poems by one poet.

80. Banarlı, *Türk edebiyat*, p. 289.

81. İsmail Hikmet, *Koca Ragıp Paşa ve Fıtnat*, pp. 26-27; Gövsa, *Türk me-*

şhurları, pp. 142-143; E. J. W. Gibb, *Ottoman Poems*, p. 217 and *History of Ottoman Poetry*, IV, pp. 150-159; İsmail Hakkı Uzunçarşılı, *Osmanlı tarihi*, IV, pp. 395, 478-479. Fahir İz ("Fıtnat," *Encyclopaedia of Islam*, second edition II, p. 931) says she was the daughter of a *şeyhülislâm* and that she was inspired by both the poets Nabi and Nadim.

82. Hikmet, *Koca Ragıp*, pp. 26-27; Gövsa, *Türk meşhurları*, pp. 142-143; Uzunçarşılı, *Osmanlı tarihi*, IV, pp. 395, 478-479; Murat Uraz, "Fıtnat," *Resimli kadın şair ve muharririmiz*, pp. 32ff.

83. Hikmet, *Koca Ragıp*, p. 31.

84. Charles White, *Three Years in Constantinople*, II, p. 174.

85. Herbert W. Duda, *Balkantürkische Studien*, pp. 74-75.

86. Gövsa, *Türk meşhurları*, pp. 142-143; Banarlı, *Türk edebiyat*, pp. 214-215.

87. Gövsa, *Türk meşhurları*, p. 143; Uraz, "Fıtnat," pp. 84ff.

88. Banarlı, *Türk edebiyat*, p. 236; E. J. W. Gibb, *Ottoman Poetry*, IV, pp. 349-350; Gövsa, *Türk meşhurları*, pp. 368-369; Uraz, "Şeref," *Muharririmiz*, pp. 48ff.

89. Uraz, "Sırrı," *Muharririmiz*, p. 55.

90. Uraz, "Nakiye," *Muharririmiz*, pp. 69ff. *See* also Mehmet Zeki Pakalın, *Son sadrazamlar ve başvekiller*, I, p. 301, and K. L. Basmadjian, *Essai sur l'histoire de la littérature ottomane*, p. 217.

91. Uraz, "Seniye," *Muharririmiz*, pp. 82f.

92. Uraz, "Mahşah," *Muharririmiz*, pp. 95ff.

93. Uraz, "Leylâ," *Muharririmiz*, p. 41. *See* also Banarlı, *Türk edebiyat*, p. 236; Gibb, *Ottoman Poetry*, IV, pp. 342-349; İz, *Encyclopaedia of Islam* 2, V, p. 710. Gibb (*Poems*) found her sentimental and addicted to a pattern. *See* also Gövsa, *Türk meşhurları*, p. 229.

94. Uraz, "Âdile," *Muharririmiz*, p. 68; Koçu, *İstanbul ansiklopedisi*, I, pp. 142-143. Lucy M. J. Garnett (*Home Life in Turkey*, p. 175) mentions Hebetullah Sultan, sister of Mahmut II, as a poet.

95. Fuat Köprülü, "Nigâr Hanım," *Bugünkü edebiyat*, pp. 297-313.

96. Banarlı, *Türk edebiyat*, pp. 289-290; Gövsa, *Türk meşhurları*, p. 285; Uraz, "Nigâr," *Muharririmiz*, pp. 98ff.

97. İsmail Habip, *Yeni "edebî yeniliğimiz" Tanzimattan beri*, II, pp. 343-344.

98. *See Hanımlara mahsus gazete*, issue of August 19, 1893, for the poem to Abdülhamit, and issues of 1311 and 1312 (1893-1895) for Nigâr Hanım in general.

99. A section of Istanbul in the newer city north of the Golden Horn.

100. Uraz, "Nigâr," pp. 98ff.

101. Interview with the late Nesrin Moralı, Rauf Bey's daughter, July 1966.

102. Köprülü, "Nigâr Hanım," pp. 297-313.

103. In the Ottoman Empire to serve the sultan personally was considered an honor.

104. Uraz, "Makbule Leman," *Muharririmiz*, pp. 108ff; Gövsa, *Turk meşhurları*, p. 238.

105. Banarlı, *Türk edebiyat*, pp. 403-404; Gövsa, *Türk meşhurları*, p. 187; Uraz, "İhsan Raif," *Muharririmiz*, pp. 126ff.

106. Uraz, "Yaşar Nezihe," *Muharririmiz*, pp. 142ff.

107. Banarlı, *Türk edebiyat*, pp. 131-132; Habip, *Tanzimattan beri*, I, p. 356; M. Şakir Ülkütaşır, *Cevdet Paşa—hayatı—şahsiyeti—eserleri (1822-1898)*, p. 60; Uraz, "Fatma Aliye," *Muharririmiz*, pp. 209ff.

108. Gövsa, *Türk meşhurları*, pp. 131-132.
109. Uraz, "Fatma Aliye," *Muharririmiz*, pp. 209ff.
110. Habip, *Tanzimattan beri*, I, p. 356.
111. Uraz, "Fatma Aliye," *Muharririmiz*, pp. 209ff.
112. Banarlı, *Türk edebiyat*, p. 290; Gövsa, *Türk meşhurları*, p. 114; Z. Duckett Ferriman, *Turkey and the Turks*, p. 322.
113. Banarlı, *Türk edebiyat*, p. 290; Gövsa, *Türk meşhurları*, p. 9; Uraz, "Abdülhak Mihrünnisa," *Muharririmiz*, pp. 136ff.
114. Gövsa, *Türk meşhurları*, p. 229; İz, *Encyclopaedia of Islam 2*, V, pp. 710-711. Tugay, *Three Centuries*, pp. 309-310; Uraz, "Leylâ," *Muharririmiz*, pp. 92ff; also interviews with Emine Foat Tugay and the late Belkis Erad, August 1966.
115. Unfortunately the author has been unable to obtain a copy of this book, which is a very rare one. However, portions of it having to do with the woman slave have been quoted by Emine Foat Tugay in *Three Centuries*, pp. 309-310 and by Pakalın in "Esir tuccarı," *Deyimler ve terimler*, I, pp. 554-555.
116. Gövsa, *Türk meşhurları*, p. 229; Uraz, "Leylâ," pp. 92ff; İz, "Laylā Khānum," *EI²*, V, pp. 710-711.
117. Otto von Spiess, *Die türkische Prosliteratur der gegenwart*, p. 40.
118. Köprülü, "Ottoman Turkish Literature," *EI¹*, IV, p. 956.
119. Gertrude Emerson, "Halideh Hanoum," *Asia* (January 1920), pp. 80-89.
120. Ibid.
121. Information on Halide Edip comes from her *Memoirs*, pp. 261-264, 270, 270-284, 292, 295, 297, 310-311, 331, 338-339, 369; Banarlı, *Türk edebiyat*, pp. 404-406; Gövsa, *Türk meşhurları*, pp. 15-16; Fahir İz, "Khālide Edīb," *EI²*, IV, pp. 933-936; Uraz, "Halide Edip," *Muharririmiz*, pp. 241ff.
122. Communication from Tezer Taşkıran, via Seniha Moralı, 1978.
123. Banarlı, *Türk edebiyat*, p. 403; Gövsa, *Türk meşhurları*, p. 63.
124. Banarlı, *Türk edebiyat*; Gövsa, *Türk meşhurları*, p. 415.
125. Banarlı, *Türk edebiyat*, p. 404; personal interview with Fahir İz, 1966.
126. Banarlı, *Türk edebiyat*, p. 402.
127. Gövsa, *Türk meşhurları*, p. 350. Uraz, "Sabiha Zekeriya Sertel," *Muharririmiz*, pp. 482ff.
128. A. Ziyaeddin Fahri Fındıkoğlu, *Zia Gökalp, sa vie et sa sociologie*, photostat opposite p. 164. Also Vedad Günyol and Andrew Mango, "Djarīda," *Encyclopaedia of Islam 2*, II, p. 474. The only other mention we have found of the women's supplement to *Terakki* is in the *Quarterly Review* of the International Council of Women in a piece by İffet Halim Oruz entitled "The Turkish Press and Women," in the issue for the first quarter of 1960, p. 12. In this it is called *The Ladies' Journal*.
129. Personal communication from Seniha Moralı, 1978. Salih was the name of Halide Edip's first husband; her second was Dr. Adnan Adıvar.
130. Information from Fevziye Abdullah Tansel.
131. Halide Edip, *Conflict of East and West*, p. 262; Koçu, "Belkis Şevket Hanım," *İstanbul ansiklopedisi*, V, pp. 2483-2484.
132. *Hanımlara mahsus gazete*, issues for 1311-1312 and 1319-1320, in the author's possession.
133. Ibid.
134. A. Afetinan, in *Tarih boyunca Türk kadınlarının hak ve görevleri*, has given a list of the Ottoman women's magazines and newspapers, including the year of

the first appearance of each: *Kadın* (*Woman*), 1908; *Kadın bahçesi* (*Woman's Garden*), 1912; *Kadınlar dünyası* (*Women's World*), 1912; *Kadın hayatı* (*Woman's Life*), 1912; *Kadın duygusu* (*Woman's Feelings*), 1913; *Kadınlar âlemî* (*Women's Universe*), 1913; *Kadın kalbı* (*Woman's Heart*), 1919.

14

Religion

We have seen in previous chapters how rigorously the upper-class Ottoman woman's life was circumscribed by the rules of Islam. Although she could not be a member of the *ulema*, the religious institution, nor retire to a convent if her life did not suit her, she could be accepted as a teacher of Islam. Certain religious women gained great influence in this way, as did the one who persuaded Süleyman I to give up the pleasures of music.[1]

It would be difficult to exaggerate the importance of religion to the Ottoman woman. It was her mainstay. Though the world outside the harem was largely beyond bounds for her, though she not only often had to share her husband but also was usually denied participation in a large part of his life, though her social intercourse was restricted to women, there remained this field into which she might pour herself unrestrainedly. No wonder she followed Islam with passionate piety.

Religion was the one subject on which she was sure to have been instructed. We have already mentioned the *hoca hanım*s who came to the harems to teach the girls the tenets and practices of Islam.[2] A girl began by learning to read the Koran in Arabic and by learning her prayers. If she belonged to certain families with high standards of education, she also learned the Arabic language, so that in time she understood what she was reading.[3]

A girl was about eight when she was first taught her prayers.[4] Being a woman, she did not go to the mosque, but prayed at home (except during Ramazan). First she made her ablutions according to the ritual prescribed by the Koran: "When ye rise up for prayer, wash your faces, and your hands up to the elbows, and lightly rub your heads and (wash) your feet up to the ankles."[5] According to Julia Pardoe she then veiled herself in white, which probably means that she threw a white scarf over her head.[6] Her ritual prayers, called *salat* or *namaz*, were the same which the men performed. She put down her prayer rug, very likely in an upper-class harem a handsome Gördes or some other finely made *seccade*, and went through the required number of *rekat*s (prayer positions) for each prayer.[7]

Julia Pardoe gives us a glimpse of the Ottoman woman at prayer:

The Turkish women are intuitively pious; the exercises of religion are admirably suited to their style of existence. In the seclusion of the harem the hour of prayer is an epoch of unvarying interest to the whole of its inhabitants; and there is something touching and beautiful in the humility with which, when they have spread their prayer-carpets, they veil themselves with a scarf of white muslin, ere they intrude into the immediate presence of their Maker.[8]

The piety of the Ottoman woman often included a belief in visions. Emine Foat Tugay has told us that her mother experienced a religious vision when the latter was a little under 12 years of age.[9]

The Ottoman woman was taught, by either the *hoca hanım* or an elderly Turkish man, something of the history of Islam, its beliefs and duties. She knew that Muhammad had come into the world to reveal the word of God to the *Müminin* (the Believers) and that, in the line of Prophets or revealers of the word of God that began with Adam, Muhammad was the last, the seal. She learned the six doctrines of her faith: belief in God, in His angels, in His Book, in His Prophets, in the Last Day, and in Predestination. She knew her fate had long been engraved on tablets in heaven. It was therefore easier to be resigned to it. She had been taught the five duties of her faith: belief that there is but one God and that Muhammad is His Prophet; prayer five times a day; almsgiving; fasting during the holy month of Ramazan; and, if financially possible, the *hac* or pilgrimage to the holy cities of Mecca and Madina.[10]

The first of these duties, attestation to the belief in God, she performed each time she said her ritual prayer. She prayed at home because it was considered indecent for a woman to pray in a public mosque unless she was old, and even then she was obliged to confine herself to a place set aside for that purpose. She could not be in the same line as men.[11] In the ritual prayer she was allowed to raise her hands only as high as her shoulders, whereas a man raised his to his ears. When a group of women prayed together, it was better for the leader to be a man, but if it had to be a woman, she was advised to stand not at the head of the group, as a male *imam* would have done, but modestly in the center.[12] A woman was forbidden to pray at all during her menstrual period, which was set at not less than three or more than ten days, nor when she was ill or pregnant, although the latter two prohibitions were in a less stringent category.[13]

The injunction to pray at home came into being gradually, as did the other restrictions on women in Islam. Among the first Muslims there appears to have been no law or regulation which prevented women from praying in mosques. But some time after Muhammad's death the question came up, and the Arabs attempted to settle it, as they did so many other matters, by means of traditions. Since there were two opposing opinions, there came into being two contradictory sets of traditions.[14] One, related by al-Bukhārī, states that Muhammad said, "When a woman of any of you asks permission to go to a *masjid*, do not deny her"; whereas another tradition advises, "It is better for women to say their prayers within their houses than in the courtyards of them; but their closets are still more excellent for them."[15]

Omar is credited with placing the first restrictions on women. It is related that he said, "Keep women captive ... because when they have liberty to go out of their houses a great deal, they do not lack seeing what pleases them, even though their husbands may be more handsome and pleasing and those who please them may be less noble."[16]

We read little of women appearing in mosques outside of the month of Ramazan from this time on, except in Central Asia, where as late as A.H. 1222 (1807-1808) women in Samarkand were going to the mosque in answer to the call to prayer.[17]

Since in the Ottoman empire the higher a woman's social status the more closely she was guarded, most observers found them in mosques rarely.[18] De Tott thought this a good idea, since it kept order and silence.[19] However, in imperial mosques there was a room with a grilled screen, from behind which imperial women could participate in the service without being seen.[20] This shows again how privileged in some ways the imperial women were.

In spite of the fact that women were not excluded from worshipping in mosques during Muhammad's time, Islam was, from the beginning, a male-oriented religion. "Men are in charge of women," says the Koran, "because Allah hath made the one to excel the other."[21] One of Muhammad's criticisms of the pagan Arabs was that the idols they worshipped were women.[22] There was, in fact, considerable controversy over whether or not a woman had a soul. Though it is clear enough in the Koran that Muhammad believed she does have a soul that outlasts the body and enters Paradise,[23] opinion was sometimes to the contrary. Sir Edwin Pears reported instances of women admitting they had no souls and a group of them in Anatolia reciting, as directed by an *imam*, "We are asses. We are beasts." On the other hand Pears claims that many Ottoman Turks thought that women did have souls.[24]

In any case, upper-class women of Istanbul were, it seems, generally conceded a soul. There is plenty of evidence for this in the inscriptions on tombstones, on public fountains, and on other monuments erected by women, in which the passerby is asked to say a *fatiha* for the soul of the deceased.[25] Pears himself quotes the inscription on the gravestone of a woman in Hasköy: "Grant my soul the blessing of prayer."[26] The very fact that women built public works as pious deeds is evidence that they believed they had souls about whose welfare they were concerned.

Charity was an obligation upon all Muslims, but perhaps particularly upon women because, says a *hadith*, "Ye are mostly of hell on the day of resurrection." For that reason the same *hadith* urges them to "Give alms, though it be of your gold and silver ornaments."[27] It was advice faithfully heeded. For example, the admonition to befriend the needy and the wayfarer[28] beautified Istanbul with many public fountains.[29] We have already pointed out that mosques were built and renovated with funds provided by women, especially the imperial women.

The institution of the *vakıf* (pious foundation) was closely connected with the duty of almsgiving. The Turks were undoubtedly already familiar with its Islamic form when they entered Anatolia.[30] Köprülü has pointed out that in the thirteenth century the Anatolian Selçuks used the institution extensively, their sovereigns, great men and women, and merchants all establishing foundations for hospitals, *imaret*s, *medrese*s, schools, and *tekke*s.[31]

In Ottoman times, numerous foundations were set up by women. Although many were established for the purpose of protecting heirs against the confiscation of wealth by the state, some were also established for a wide range of charitable purposes. The latter included dispensaries, general and mental hospitals, medical schools, mosque schools, kitchens for the poor, shelters, and money for poor girls' trousseaus and for books and excursions for poor children.[32]

For the period of this study, Kunter has recorded a *vakıf* of 1707-08 by Ummehani Hatun for help to the Istanbul poor in paying their taxes, and another of 1856-57 by Züleyha Hanım for clothes and provisions for poor children, widows, and old people.[33] Ahmet III's daughter, Fatma Sultan, and her husband, Nevşehirli İbrahim Pasha, set up a *vakıf* for a library and school for traditions near Şehzade Camii and provided for its maintenance by means of vineyards to be worked by two Greek *zimmi*s.[34] In the early twentieth century Fatma Hanım, a daughter of the Khedive İsmail, turned her palace at Bulak-Takrur in Gizeh into a *vakıf* for the benefit of the University of Cairo and provided for its maintenance with 400 feddans of fertile land. In her will she bequeathed 30,000 pounds to Istanbul University, but the government of Egypt prevented the University from receiving it.[35]

A most important religious observance was the *ramazan* fast, which was a duty faithfully performed in the Ottoman household. The stringency of the days was made up for by the nights. Especially lavish was the *iftar*, the meal taken at sundown. Julia Pardoe, who was invited to participate in such a feast, describes it thus:

We fasted until about half past six o'clock, when the cry of the muezzin from the minarets proclaimed that one of the out-watchers . . . had caught a glimpse of the moon. Instantly all were in motion; their preliminary arrangements had been so zealously and carefully made that not another second was lost; and, as a slave announced dinner, we followed her to a smaller apartment where the table, if I may call it such, was already laid.

The room was a perfect square, totally unfurnished, save that in the centre of the floor was spread a carpet, on which stood a wooden frame, about two feet in height, supporting an immense round plated tray, with the edge slightly raised. In the centre of the tray was placed a capacious white basin, filled with a kind of cold bread soup; and around it were ranged a circle of small porcelain saucers, filled with sliced cheese, anchovies, caviare, and sweetmeats of every description: among these were scattered spoons of box-wood, and goblets of pink and white sherbet, whose rose-scented contents perfumed the apartment. The outer range of the tray was covered with fragments of unleavened bread, torn asunder; and portions of the Ramazan cake, a dry, close, sickly kind of paste, glazed with the white of eggs, and strewed over with aniseeds.[36]

There were many in the house: the old family nurse, an orphaned grand-son, several neighbors and friends, among them a newly widowed woman seeking advice on her affairs, along with the immediate family which con-sisted of a middle-aged couple, their son and daughter-in-law, their daugh-ter and son-in-law, and an adopted son. After all had eaten their fill, they returned to the first room where a *masalcı* entertained them with tales. Coffee was prepared and the *büyük hanım* settled down with her pipe. At this point a slave announced the imminent arrival of the gentlemen, where-upon the visitors fled from the room, the *masalcı* veiled herself, and

the Juno-like daughter . . . flung a handkerchief over her head, and fastened it beneath her chin: while the son's wife caught up a *feridjhe*, or cloak, and withdrew, muffled in its folds, to her own apartment. The older lady was the only one of the party undisturbed by the intelligence: she never raised her eyes from the carpet, but continued inhaling the aroma of the "scented weed", gravely grasping her long pipe, her lips pressed against its amber mouthpiece, and her brilliant rings and diamond-studded bracelet flashing in the light.[37]

The head of the house and his sons came in, bringing little gifts of choice foods. The middle-aged wife filled and lighted the bowl of her husband's pipe; a slave held it for him while one of his sons held a brass dish in which to rest it. At the call to prayer the old man laid the pipe in the dish, spread out his prayer-rug, and performed his *namaz*, during which time the rest of them chatted and smoked.[38]

Pardoe reported that she then went to bed, but the rest of the party had another meal between two and three in the morning and sat up sipping coffee, listening to stories, and passing on the news until dawn. Just before the day's fast began they all took opium pills wrapped in one, two, or three coatings of goldleaf which were supposed to free the pills at time-intervals and thus reduce the pangs of hunger throughout the day-long fast.[39]

The word *ramazan* comes from the Arabic root *ramaza*, which means "to be burning."[40] It is the month when sins are burned away by the pain of fasting. There are three duties which must be performed each day of this month: fasting, saying the *teravih*, the special Ramazan prayer, and *zekat*, giving alms or help to others.[41]

We notice that all three were observed at the house of Julia Pardoe's host. Family and guests fasted. The old man performed the *teravih*, apparently on behalf of the entire family. When it came to the time of *iftar*, not only did the household invite neighbors as guests but also a widowed woman. Many great houses were open to all comers. Even when households became more Westernized in table accoutrements, the traditions of Ramazan remained largely unchanged.[42]

During the hours of the fast not only were food and drink disallowed, but all sexual relations and even caresses were taboo. Dispensations from fasting were allowed only to the sick, travelers, pregnant women, wet nurses, women with menses or who had gone through childbirth less than 40 days previously, the starving, the insane, minors, and the aged.[43]

The seclusion of women was relaxed slightly during Ramazan, and in the nineteenth century one finds that after sunset they drove about the city of Istanbul in their *araba*s. Lady Blunt reported seeing them on the esplanade of Süleymaniye.[44] Apparently they also drove up and down the hill of Divan Yolu, for White says the sultan watched from an apartment there, probably the Alay Köşkü (Procession Kiosk), and now and then sent an officer to warn of his displeasure should they be too lightly veiled or insufficiently covered.[45]

Adolphus Slade, with ever an eye for the mischievous, reports that during Ramazan "the harems were enlivened by dancing girls, wandering singers, fortune tellers." He believed a certain amount of illicit lovemaking went on then, the couples meeting in the apartments of old Jewesses. Undoubtedly tales of such goings on circulated, although it is difficult to know how much credibility to give them.[46]

Three nights before the end of Ramazan came *kadir gecesi*, the Night of Power. This is the night, it is believed, when the first *sura* (chapter) of the Koran was revealed to Muhammad. Worship at that time is worth a thousand months of worship on other nights and insures to the worshipper the remission of his smaller sins.[47]

During the time of the Empire, according to Emine Foat Tugay, on *kadir gecesi* the whole family went to the mosque. Hers went to Ayasofya, where "large, round chandeliers, lit by oil-wicks, shed a soft light over hundreds of worshippers who listened to the chanting of the Qur'an." Some worshippers, she says, stayed at prayer till dawn in the hope of seeing the special light thought to descend on this night as a sign of Divine Grace.[48]

The *ramazan bayramı*, also called the Breaking of the Fast,[49] and the Alms Bayram (now *şeker bayramı*, the Festival of Sweets) arrived the first three days of *Şevval*, the month succeeding Ramazan. "On the first day of Bairam," writes Lucy Garnett, "every well-to-do person makes a present to his children, his slaves, and his subordinates, besides giving liberally to the poor. In the morning the streets are thronged with people in holiday costume, who go from house to house paying complimentary visits."[50]

The very devout woman also observed other religious days, among them *mevlut kandili*, the feast on the eve of the Prophet's birthday;[51] *berat gecesi*, the celebration of the revelation to Muhammad of his mission;[52] and *kurban bayramı*, the festival that celebrates Abraham's offering of his son in sacrifice and God's acceptance of a sheep in his place.[53]

On *kurban bayramı* every Muslim who can afford it sacrifices a sheep, which is divided into three parts—one for the poor, one for relations, and one for the household. Again people wear new clothes, give gifts, particularly toys to children, and women call on one another.[54]

The fifth duty of Islam, the *hac* or pilgrimage to the holy cities, is incumbent on women as well as on men, although fewer women perform it. The chief reason for this in Ottoman times was, and in many Islamic lands still is, the restrictions that hedge a woman. She must be accompanied either by her husband or by a male relative who has reached the age of majority, is of sound mind and of trustworthy character. She must have the wherewithal for the journey and be ritually clean. Widows are not eligible, with the result that in the past many widows took nominal husbands for the journey.[55] In return for his protection the woman provided the man with his keep en route. Another method by which a widow could qualify was to marry an Arab in Mecca. This custom of temporary marriage led to some embarrassing situations, for the husband thus acquired was not always easily dismissed. Şehsüvaroğlu ran across an elderly Turkish woman whose Arab husband wanted to return to Istanbul with her and who was understandably worried as to how her children and grandchildren would receive their new relative. On a trip back to Istanbul Şehsüvaroğlu met on shipboard, politely ignoring one another, a young female *hacı* (pilgrim) and an old jurist who had married each other on the trip out and were now divorced.[56]

Since the *hac* is one of the pillars of Islam, a woman is allowed to make it without the permission of her husband, a proviso of which, in the Ottoman era, obviously only a woman rich in her own right could take advantage.[57] A repudiated wife might not go during her period of *iddet* (the three-month interval after divorce which enables a possible pregnancy to show itself). Although the free woman needed no permission to go on the pilgrimage, a slave woman might go only with the permission of the master and a minor girl only in the company of her parents; but neither of these was considered a true *hacı*.[58]

The *hac* traditionally starts 14 days before *kurban bayramı*. The Ottomans began it in Istanbul with the pilgrims gathering in a square of the old city and forming a procession. Lucy Garnett has written a vivid description of it in the days of Abdülhamit II:

This comprises a number of camels with gorgeously ornamented saddles bearing the coffers containing the Sultan's gifts to the holy shrines, together with the alms and presents of his well-to-do subjects for the religious trustees of their respective families in the cities of Mecca and Medina. Other camels carry a kind of palanquin covered with costly silken stuffs in which lady pilgrims will perform part of the journey. A company of picturesquely garbed Arabs who accompany the caravan exhibit at every halting-place, to the accompaniment of kettle drums, feats of swordsmanship to the crowds of spectators which surround and follow the procession and its military escort through the streets and across the long bridge spanning the Golden Horn on its way to Yildiz Kiosk, where the pilgrims salute the Sultan before embarking. The best view of this quaint procession is obtained as it mounts the steep road leading to the palace of Yildiz, now lined with the troops of the Imperial guard. The rising ground on either side has the appearance of a flower garden, covered as it is with the variously hued cloaks and white headgear of thousands of Turkish women of the lower orders. The Sultan, himself unseen, is believed to be at one of the windows of Yildiz Kiosk to receive the salutation of the departing pilgrims, who, after offering up in union a prayer for the success of their undertaking, retrace their steps to the quay, whence they embark for the Asiatic shore. Before the construction of the existing railway the pilgrim caravan, after crossing the Bosphorus, made the long journey to Arabia by land; at Damascus it was joined by thousands of pilgrims from Africa, Asia Minor, and Syria, and thence, under the command of a special officer styled the "Steward of the Offerings",[59] and escorted by troops, it began its long journey across the desert to the Holy Cities.[60]

Before starting out on the pilgrimage the Ottoman woman made certain preparations: She repented her sins, paid her debts, gave alms, and sought a spiritual frame of mind by reading and reciting the Koran.[61]

There are two kinds of pilgrimage a person may make: *umre*[62] or the shorter pilgrimage, and *hac* or the greater pilgrimage. The former consists of a visitation to Mecca with appropriate ceremonies; the latter adds to this visits to nearby holy places with attendant ceremonies.[63] Since a woman, unlike a man, was unlikely to repeat the journey, the Ottoman woman probably tended to make the greater pilgrimage. In the eighteenth century she joined the caravan that proceeded from Üsküdar to Mecca; in the nineteenth she had the choice of a steamship to Jidda.

Outside the sacred territory of Mecca, she put on the *ihram*, two white sheets sewed together that covered her body. According to the rules, a woman's face is supposed to be uncovered during the actual pilgrimage, but women got around this by wearing a mask so fixed that it did not actually touch the skin of the face.[64] Otherwise only the palms of her hands might show. This act put her in the state of *mühim* (importance) and meant that she must not engage in sex nor come near nor kiss her sex partner, nor even make any remarks that might have a sexual meaning. She must not cut her nails nor her hair nor use perfume nor wear fabricated clothing or inner household shoes. (There are other provisions that do not apply to women, such as that against hunting.)[65]

Once in the sacred area (*Harem-i Şerif*) it was her duty to repeat over and over again the *telbiye*, [66] a rite in which she said that she came with pleasure and alacrity.[67] Carefully moving to the left and keeping the Black Stone on her right, she performed the *tavaf* or circumambulation of the Kaaba seven times. (The Arabic root *haja* originally meant "to go around, to go in a circle.") She prayed two *rekat*s facing the Makam-ı (place of) İbrahim and the Kaaba, and ran seven *savt* or courses[68] between the towns of Safa and Merve. She could then, if she chose, enjoy normal life for a while by ritually cutting a piece of her hair and discarding the *ihram*. The sex act, however, might not be performed until after the *tavaf* of the *ihaze* (*see* below). This deconsecrated condition is called *temettü*, "enjoyment, pleasure,"[69] and in return for it she had to offer a special sacrifice sometime during the *hac*.[70]

This was and is the extent of the *umre*. It can be performed at other times, but the preferable time is during Ramazan. If the Ottoman woman wanted to be in Mecca during that holy month, and wanted to perform the greater *hac*, she had also to be on hand three months later to take up the duties that begin on the eighth of *zilhicce*. That day is the *yevm-üt-terviye*, [71] the day of providing water, which some believe to be a vestige of an ancient rain rite. In any case, on that day the Ottoman lady's attendants saw to it that she was supplied with water for the next few days on the desert. That night she left Mecca afoot or on camelback for the wide valley of Arafat, 15 miles[72] to the east, where her *akkam*[73] pitched her tent. There the next day she performed the *vukuf*, [74] "a standing" in front of the Hill of Mercy (*Cebel-ür-Rahmet*), which lies in the valley. Beginning at noon she and the thousands of pilgrims around her said the prayers of *zuhur*, "midday," and *asır*, "mid-afternoon," in which she emphasized the Oneness of God in words such as: "There is no god but the One God, Who has no associates; to Him belongs the power, to Him belongs the glory. He holds all in His hands and has power over everything." Protected by her tent from the hot desert sun, she heard the murmur of a sermon being preached in memory of the one preached by Muhammad, and though she was too far off to make out the words, she was elated in just being a part of that throng of worshippers.[75]

That evening after sunset she began the *ifaze*, which is a running or hurrying back toward Mecca. At Müzdelife, a holy place between Arafat and Mecca, she again said prayers, the *mağrip*, the sunset prayer, and the *işa*, the prayer of nightfall. Then, with the rest of the women, she went on to Mina, leaving the men to spend the night at Müzdelife.[76]

The next three days were spent largely at Mina, although she probably slept in her tent at Arafat. On the tenth, called the *yevmünnahr*, "the day of sacrifice" (this is the Turkish *kurban bayramı*),[77] she began the day with the *salât-i fecir*[78] (dawn prayer) and then proceeded with the ritual of stoning the devil. This involved throwing 77 small stones at the *cemre-i akabe*.[79] After this came the animal sacrifice. If she had not previously done so, she now offered a separate sacrifice for her *temettü*.[80] If that was already done, she ritually cut her hair. Then she returned to Mecca and made a *tavaf* around the Kaaba now resplendent in the new hangings that had been sent out from Islamic countries. This circumambulation is the *tavaf* of the *ifaza* (running).[81] She now took off her *ihram* and was released from her state of sanctity; from here on she wore her ordinary clothes.

The three days of the 11th, 12th, and 13th are social days, the *eyyam-üt-teşrik*,[82] during which the slain animal's flesh is exposed to the sun to dry. These are feast days, during which the Ottoman lady and her entire entourage consumed a part of the animal sacrificed and gave the rest to the poor. Following the *sunna* (custom) of the Prophet, each day she went to Mina between midday and sunset to throw seven stones at each *cemre*,[83] in this order: first *el-cemret-ül-ula*, then *el-cemret-ül-vusta*, both on the main street of Mina, and then up the hill to the third and final *cemre-i akabe*. Each *cemre* is surrounded by a wall and columns which, while she stoned them, she called *şeytan* (satan).[84] These sites have been sacred since pre-Islamic times.[85] Tradition has it that Satan was stoned there, according to one tradition by Adam, according to another by Abraham, Hagar, and Ishmael.[86]

Finally she made a last *tavaf* around the Kaaba, this one the *sadır* or "going out." Perhaps she also visited other holy places in the area and went to Madina to worship at the tomb of the Prophet, although these were not requirements.[87]

In 1849 the British traveler, Albert Richard Smith, found himself on a ship transporting pilgrims from Istanbul and noted six or seven women among them. Half the afterdeck was railed off for the pilgrims, and they cooked, ate, slept, and prayed there. When it rained, their only cover was a canvas. Among the party was the head eunuch of the palace, a resplendent individual in yellow and scarlet silk *entari* and blue trousers, worn with European boots.[88]

Since the *hac* could be performed by proxy, it sometimes happened that a rich woman willed that a pilgrimage be made in her behalf after her death, its cost to be defrayed by her estate. Such a request was made by a woman named Hamko, the mother of Ali Pasha of Janina. However, it was a requirement of the *hac* that the funds for the purpose be legally acquired, and when it was discovered that the lady had obtained her wealth by defrauding Christian owners of their land, the pilgrimage in her behalf was disallowed.[89]

With great numbers of people crowded together in Mecca and its environs, infections spread rapidly during the *hac*. B. N. Şehsüvaroğlu reports that dysentary and trachoma were still widespread in the Hejaz as late as the twentieth century and that tuberculosis was still spreading. In the days when the Hejaz was part of the Empire, the Porte tried to improve the health situation. Pertevniyal, the mother of Abdülaziz, built hospitals in the Harem-i Şerif, and young Turkish doctors went out from Istanbul to man them. Yet the patient load remained far greater than the facilities, with the result that it took hours every day just to remove the dead and dying from the pilgrims' dormitories.[90]

Up until sometime in the nineteenth century a great health hazard was the lack of pure water, and typhoid fever was the result. To combat this the Porte put cisterns in Jidda, installed pipes and set up water-storage facilities in both Jidda, the port for Mecca, and Yenbu, the port for Madina.[91]

There was also always the danger of bandits on the land route. To ward against this the Porte paid protection to certain Bedouin tribes residing in the regions which were traversed by the pilgrims.[92] Still, women as well as men considered the grace to be gained greater than the danger to be run and made the *hac*.

If the woman survived the dangers and returned home, she was permitted to prefix the title *hacı* (pilgrim) to her name and thus became a *hacı kadın*. As evidence of her pilgrimage she bore a small tattoo mark on one arm and another between the thumb and forefinger of one of her hands. From then on she was a person of some consequence in her quarter.[93] Through the *hac*, a woman could gain a social footing almost equal to that of a man.

For Ottoman women the *hac* was the one time they could move about among men freely, unveiled. Otherwise in classical Islam, which the upper-class women of the Ottoman Empire followed, the only men who might see a woman's face were those to whom she was *mahrem* or so closely related that they were forbidden to marry her.[94]

Among the Turks it would seem that popular Islam was sometimes at odds with classical Islam on the position of women. While classical Islam kept men and women apart and relegated women to an inferior position, popular Islam had its women saints and, above all, Fatma, the daughter of Muhammad, whom it placed high in the Muslim spiritual hierarchy. At the same time that the one emphasized the indivisibility of God, the other induced women to pray to Fatma much as Christian women prayed to the Virgin Mary.[95]

Fatma became part of the apparatus of piety. But when piety is overdone, fanaticism results, and Istanbul had its share of women fanatics. Smith reported that a group of veiled women rushed at him with clumps of earth and stone at a sacred spot called the Giant's Grave on the Asiatic side of the Bosphorus.[96] When Robert College first opened at Rumeli Hisarı, the wife of the local *imam* led the community in attacking the infidel institution. However, she later changed her mind and apologized thus: "We thought you were bad people and would corrupt our village and were determined to drive you out, but we found that you are much better than we are and we are sorry for what we did."[97]

Much of the antipathy to the *gâvur* (infidel, *i.e.*, non-Muslim) came from fear—especially of the Russians. One Western observer after another reported evidence of it. In 1828 MacFarlane noted that "Mussulman fathers, and mothers, and wives trembled at an amplified idea of the prowess and ferocity of the Moscovites." He heard a pipeseller in the Istanbul bazaar declare that he would stab his wife and children if need be to keep the *gâvur*s from touching them.[98] In the vicinity of the Egyptian bazaar in Istanbul, Slade heard a woman say to her child, "Run, my child, the evil eye of the infidel is on thee!" At Edirne he met a Turkish woman who had been disowned by her coreligionists for being too friendly with the conquering Russians, but she nevertheless "received us haughtily, and motioned us, with the air of a sultana, to be seated on the sofa at some distance from her . . . her Mohammedan pride making her feel that, though downgraded in the eyes of her own caste, she was yet superior to Christians."[99]

Ayesha, the daughter of Melek Hanım and Kıbrıslı Mehmet Pasha, hesitated to go to a Christian country even when pursued by the wrath of the husband and father she was escaping, so great was her horror of *gâvur*s. Only the imminent danger of prison convinced her to flee with her mother to France.[100] Morgenthau, during the Gallipoli campaign of World War I, found the "Turkish populace aflame with fear that the English and the French, when they reached the city, would celebrate the event by a wholesale attack on Turkish women."[101] The belief that the *gâvur* was dangerously uncivilized was strong. In those instances where a Turkish woman accepted a Christian woman as friend, the greatest compliment she could pay was to say, "So nice a woman should be a follower of the true religion of God."[102]

Fear of the *gâvur* came partly from the belief that he possessed the evil eye. Superstition played a great part in the religion of the women of the Middle East. The country was full of old women like the one reported to Pears, who sold rejuvenating pills from a room "full of skulls, snakes, scorpions, pots and pans for concoctions, fantastic figures, and a black cat." Men and women astrologers and other types of fortune-tellers foretold the future. Even as late as the time of Abdülhamit II there was an official court astrologer, the *müneccimbaşı*, although he was there because of tradition rather than the sultan's belief in his powers.[103]

Children and animals wore blue beads as protection against the evil eye.

It was thought that a redhead had a special power to cast the evil eye and that blue and grey eyes were dangerous. Houses were inhabited by *ev sahibi*s, good jinns who brought prosperity. One could hear them walk by the tinkle of the little bells on their clothes. Rivaling them were the bad jinns that made strange noises at night. If a woman found a dress wrinkled, she knew the bad jinns had been using it for their nocturnal revels and straightaway had it blessed by some *imam, baba*,[104] or *şeyh*. These holy men had the power to remove evil by the laying on of a hand, blowing, breathing, or reciting the name of God.[105] Though these notions were of heterodox provenance, they were nevertheless held by many women of the upper class.

We have already noted that classical Islam relegated woman to an inferior position. It can be argued that to the extent the Turks followed their nomadic Turkic traditions and stood aloof from classical Islam, their women had physical freedom. Thus the village woman was not secluded while the urban woman was. On the surface the upper class of urban society was thoroughly Islamized and Persianized. Yet even in the cities there remained an area of freedom behind the closed doors of the Bektaşi *tekke*s (dervish lodges), where men and women jointly participated in religious ceremonies.

According to John Kingsley Birge, there is historical evidence that "a man named Haji Bektash came to Asia Minor in the thirteenth century, settled in the neighborhood of Kir Shehir [Kirşehir] in the village later bearing his name; was part of the general movement of Turkmen *baba*s who under orthodox guise carried the social and religious practices of earlier Turkic life and the mysticism of the Central Asian Sufi, Ahmet Yesevî. He won recognition among the tribes as a saint, and gained followers; taught a simple ritual including the candle, the ceremonial meal, and the dance. He and his followers wore characteristic headpieces and sent out apostles in different directions.[106]

Hacı Bektaş is closely associated with women. According to the popular tradition, "he approached a woman named Kadincik . . . washing at a fountain. He pleaded hunger . . . and she brought bread and oil from her own house. The next day her jar of oil was refilled. Later she bore two children as a result of having drunk the water with which Haci Bektaş had performed his ablutions, mixed with the blood of his nose."[107] It was believed that he had included women in his ritual and had taught the rites and beliefs to a certain Ana Hatun, who passed them on.[108]

The way women are interwoven into the fabric of tradition and their participation in the ceremonies may well be, as Köprülü thought, a survival of the Central Asian tradition in which there was not complete separation of the sexes and, in fact, the shamaness was often an important figure. According to him, "The Turkic nomads considered as shamans the sufis of their race who converted them to Islam. This is why men and women could very well assist at the ritual seance, listening to, in place of the incantations of the shamans, the hymns of the mystics composed in their national language."[109]

Hacı Bektaş was supposed to have had the power to make a woman conceive by simply handing her a piece of grain, and to have passed this power on to his disciples. Birge reported meeting a well-educated Albanian who said his mother had borne several girl babies by such ministrations.[110]

Even after orthodox Islam gained the upper hand in the Ottoman Empire, the Bektaşis continued to admit women to their ceremonies on equal terms with men, but held their rites in secret behind closed doors.[111] The other dervish orders, although they admitted women, segregated them in a gallery behind lattices.[112] Bektaşi practices inevitably gave rise to gossip, "some of which may have been based on fact."[113]

Lady Blunt thought that Bektaşi wives generally had more freedom than other women and did not have to wear the veil in front of male family friends. She had observed them when her husband was stationed in Albania, where the Bektaşis were strong, and concluded that a Bektaşi man lived polygamously only when his wife "had some defect or infirmity."[114]

Although the Bektaşis suffered periodic persecution after the abolition of the Janissaries, whose patrons they were, they still retained their influence, sometimes in high places. Besm-i Âlem, the mother of Abdülmecit, is supposed to have been a Bektaşi and to have been responsible for the publication of two Bektaşi books, the *Vilayetname* (*Book of Friendship*) in 1871 and the *Aşkname* (*Book of Love*) in 1876.[115] When the Turkish Republic finally abolished all dervish orders, a Bektaşi named Ziya Bey wrote that the Bektaşis were willing to accept the new situation because the purpose of their order had been accomplished. Women had been freed from the veil and from social restraint.[116]

NOTES

1. Ogier Ghiselin de Busbecq, *Imperial Ambassador at Constantinople, 1554-1562, The Turkish Letters of*, p. 180.

2. One elderly Turkish woman interviewed by this writer said that when she was a small girl of seven or eight she was brought all the way from Büyükdere on the upper Bosphorus to Istanbul for Koran lessons with a special *hoca*. This was thought necessary because her mother was a Westerner. The lessons continued until she entered a French school at the age of ten (personal interview with Leylâ Cebesoy, August 1966).

3. The daughters of Sami Bey who gave the large *mehter* concerts on the Bosphorus in the late nineteenth century were taught Arabic, as was Emine Foat Tugay (personal interviews with Seniha Moralı, Sami Bey's daughter, August-September, 1966; Emine Foat Tugay, *Three Centuries, Family Chronicle of Turkey and Egypt*, p. 240).

4. Personal interviews with Seniha Moralı, August-September, 1966.

5. Mohammed Marmaduke Pickthall, *The Meaning of the Glorious Koran*, V:6, p. 97.

6. Julia Pardoe, *The City of the Sultans and Domestic Manners of the Turks in 1836*, I, p. 387.

7. According to Sir Hamilton A. R. Gibb (*Mohammedanism, an Historic Survey*, pp. 54-55), "Each ritual prayer consists of a fixed number of 'bowings' (called *rak'ah*), the 'bowing' itself consisting of seven movements with their appropriate recitations: (1) the recitation of the phrase, *Allahu akbar*, 'God is most Great', with the hands open on each side of the face (for women the hands are lower); (2) the recitation of the *Fatihah* or opening sura of the Koran, followed by another passage or passages, while standing upright; (3) bowing from the hips; (4) straightening up; (5) gliding to the knees and a first prostration with face to the ground; (6) sitting back on the haunches; (7) a second prostration. The second and later 'bowings' begin with the second of these movements, and at the end of each pair of 'bowings' and the conclusion of the whole prayer the worshipper recites the *shahada* and the ritual salutations. The set times are at daybreak (2 *rak'ah*s), noon (4 *rak'ah*s), mid-afternoon (4 *rak'ah*s), after sunset (3 *rak'ah*s), and in the early part of the night (4 *rak'ah*s)." (It will be noticed that the Turks have palatalized *rak'ah* into *rekat*. Likewise *akbar* has become *ekber*.) The Turkish terms for the five ritual prayers are: *sabah, öğle, ikindi, akşam*, and *yatsı namazı* (Ahmet Hamdi Akseki, *İslâm fıtrî, tabiî ve umumî bir dindir*, p. 295).

8. Pardoe, *The City*, I, pp. 286-287.

9. Tugay, *Three Centuries*, pp. 198-199.

10. Arthur Jeffery, *Islam, Muhammad and His Religion*, pp. 85-147, 155-211.

11. Ignatius Mouradgea d'Ohsson, *Tableau général de l'Empire othoman*, II, pp. 121-122.

12. Ibid.

13. A. Hamdi Akseki, *İslâm dini, itikat, ibadet, ve ahlâk*, pp. 176-187. Akseki says a woman is considered *hayız*, capable of menstruating, between the ages of nine and 55.

14. V. R. and L. Bevan Jones, *Women in Islam*, pp. 259-260.

15. Ibid.

16. Mansour Fahmy, *La Condition de la femme dans la tradition et l'évolution de l'Islamisme*, pp. 78, 108.

17. Vasilii Vladimirovich Bart'old, *Turkestan Down to the Mongol Invasion*, p. 451. We read sometimes of women praying in the mosques in the Ottoman empire, but have no knowledge as to what class they belonged. Lajos İrta Fekete (*Budapest a törökkorban*, p. 273) says that in the seventeenth century in Hungary, women went to the small and large mosques where they participated with men in prayers, but only in the background or on a balcony. However, some old women formed unofficial pious gatherings elsewhere for spiritual communion. They would go to the grave of some saint to pray, usually on a Thursday night. They went in procession, carrying candles which they lit at the grave of the holy man, where they said the *fatiha*. This act was to prepare them for the next life. The group leaders often made a profession of reciting such prayers and were paid for their services. In 1628 a pension for having been such a reciter was awarded to a woman in Buda and a fee for the same services was given to her daughter. The woman's

husband was a *şeyh*, her son a Mevlevî. We may be sure this practice was not limited to Buda, for the Turks there followed Ottoman customs.

18. Lady Fanny Blunt, *The People of Turkey*, II, p. 280; Aaron Hill, *A Full and Just Account of the Present State of the Ottoman Empire*, pp. 41-42; James E. P. Boulden, *An American Among the Orientals*, p. 128.

19. Baron de Tott, *Mémoires sur les Turcs et les Tartares*, I, p. 266.

20. Barnette Miller, *Beyond the Sublime Porte*, p. 97.

21. Koran, LV:34. Cf. Paul's *Epistle to the Ephesians*, v:23: "For the husband is the head of the wife, even as Christ is the head of the Church" (King James version of the Bible).

22. Koran, iv:117.

23. Ibid., xii:23.

24. Sir Edwin Pears, *Turkey and Its People*, p. 329. According to Lucy M. J. Garnett (*Home Life in Turkey*, pp. 126-127), Montesquieu took the position that Islam denies women souls. She cites Koranic texts to refute him, but her references are wrong.

25. İbrahim Hilmi Tanışık, *İstanbul çeşmeleri*, passim. Many public fountains in Istanbul bear inscriptions pointing out that the erection of the fountains were intended as *hayrat*s, or pious deeds.

26. Pears, *Turkey and Its People*, p. 329.

27. Stanley Lane-Poole, *The Speeches and Table-Talk of the Prophet Mohammed*, p. 163.

28. Koran, ii:315.

29. Tanışık, *İstanbul çeşmeleri*, passim.

30. Köprülü thinks that the Islamic *vakıf* is perhaps of Byzantine origin, influenced somewhat by similar institutions in the Central Asian countries which the Caliphate conquered. *See* Fuat Köprülü, "L'Institution du Vakouf, sa nature juridique et son évolution historique," *Vakıflar dergisi*, 2 (1942), pp. 3-44.

31. Köprülü, *Les Origines de l'Empire ottoman*, p. 74.

32. Other *vakıf*s established for charitable purposes provided funds necessary for the setting up of a place for prayer, *namazâh*, or a school for Koran readers, *dârülkurra*, or money to have the Koran read for the benefit of the soul of a deceased person, often the donor. Sir Hamilton A. R. Gibb and Harold Bowen (*Islamic Society and the West*, I, 2, p. 168) mention Zeynep Hatun, who set up the last-named type of *vakıf* in Istanbul in the sixteenth century. Halim Baki Kunter ("Türk vakıfları ve vakfiyeleri," *Vakıflar dergisi*, 1, 1938, pp. 118-120) gives the text of this *vakıf*-deed. He also gives the text of a nineteenth-century *vakfiye* of a woman named Rikne for olive oil for the Mevlevîhane at Yenikapı (ibid., pp. 121-122).

33. Kunter, "Türk vakıflar," p. 123.

34. Ahmet Refik [Altınay], *Hicrî on ikinci asırda İstanbul hayatı (1100-1200)*, pp. 72-73.

35. Tugay, *Three Centuries*, p. 168; İbrahim Alâettin Gövsa, *Türk meşhurları ansiklopedisi*, p. 132.

36. Pardoe, *The City*, I, pp. 21-23.

37. Ibid.

38. Ibid.

39. Ibid.

40. J. G. Hava, *Arabic-English Dictionary* (Beirut, 1951), p. 270. However, Kâmil Miras (*Ramazan musahabeleri*, p. 9) says "*Güneş sıcağında yalınayak yürüyüp yanmağa denir*" ("It means to be walking alone in the heat of the sun").

41. Miras, *Ramazan musahabeleri*, p. 9.

42. Tugay, *Three Centuries*, pp. 252-253.

43. D'Ohsson, *Tableau général*, III, pp. 15-19.

44. Blunt, *The People of Turkey*, II, p. 283.

45. Charles White, *Three Years in Constantinople; or Domestic Manners of the Turks in 1844*, III, pp. 118-119.

46. Adolphus Slade, *Records of Travels in Turkey, Greece, etc.*, II, p. 202.

47. Miras, *Ramazan musahabeleri*, pp. 54-55.

48. Tugay, *Three Centuries*, p. 263.

49. *İd-i fitir*, "The festival of the breaking of the fast" (H. C. Hony, with the advice of Fahir İz, *A Turkish-English Dictionary*, Oxford, 1957, p. 154). On that day people greet their friends, saying, "İdiniz sait olsun!" (May your festival be happy!).

50. Garnett, *Home Life In Turkey*, pp. 146-147.

51. Miras, *Ramazan musahabeleri*, passim.

52. Hony, *TED*, p. 240.

53. Ibid., p. 38.

54. Garnett, *Home Life in Turkey*, pp. 147-148; Edward William Lane, *The Manners and Customs of the Modern Egyptians*, p. 493.

55. Apparently it was not always nominal, according to Şehsüvaroğlu, who says that in what he calls a religious marriage "one can taste the small worldly pleasures along with the great religious ones" (Bedi N. Şehsüvaroğlu, *Hac yolu*, pp. 42-43).

56. Ibid.

57. Fatma Hanım, the daughter of the Khedive İsmail, made the *hac* in her old age (Tugay, *Three Centuries*, p. 168).

58. D'Ohsson, *Tableau général*, III, pp. 59-60. To be considered a true *hacı* a woman slave had to make the pilgrimage ten times and a freeborn minor girl had to repeat it again when she became of age (ibid.).

59. *Emir-ül-hac*.

60. Garnett, *Home Life in Turkey*, pp. 152-155.

61. Arthur T. Jeffery, lecture notes.

62. *Umre*: A minor pilgrimage to Mekka (at any time of the year) (Sir James W. Redhouse, *A Turkish and English Lexicon*, Constantinople, 1921, pp. 1, 321).

63. "The hadjdj is in fact an *umre*, that is a rite of visiting the Ka'ba, which is completed by the rites of visiting the Holy Places in the neighborhood of Mecca" (A. J. Wensinck and J. Jomier, "The Islamic Hadjdj", *EI²*, III, pp. 33-37).

64. G. E. von Grunebaum, *Muhammedan Festivals*, p. 27.

65. Ibid., İsa Ruhi Bolay, *Hac rehberi*, p. 17; B. N. Şehsüvaroğlu, *Hac yolu*, pp. 14-15.

66. *See* Redhouse, *TED*, p. 578.

67. Ibid., p. 1625. Von Grunebaum (*Muhammedan Festivals*, p. 28) translates this as "at Thy service."

68. Bolay, *Hac rehberi*, p. 17; F. Steingass, *A Comprehensive Persian-English Dictionary* (London, 1957), p. 766.

69. Steingass, *PED*, p. 323.

70. Wensinck and Jomier, "The Islamic Hadjdj."

71. Redhouse, *TEL*, p. 539.

72. Thirteen miles, according to A. J. Wensinck and H. A. R. Gibb, " 'Arafa," *EI²*, I, p. 604.

73. *Akkam* (A. Vahid Moran, *Türkçe-Ingilizce sözlük, A Turkish-English Dictionary*, Istanbul, 1945, p. 26): "(obs.) an attendant on pilgrims (in Arabia); a tent-pitcher." For a description of the *akkam, see* Musahipzade Celâl, *Eski İstanbul yaşayışı*, p. 104.

74. Redhouse, *TEL*, p. 2146: " 'the halt' on the plain of Arafat." According to von Grunebaum (*Muhammedan Festivals*, p. 32) the *vukuf* at Arafat is the "essential ceremony and he who misses it has missed the *hajj*."

75. Wensinck and Jomier, "The Islamic Hadjdj."

76. Ibid.

77. Redhouse, *TEL*, p. 2073.

78. Ibid., p. 1366.

79. Wensinck and Jomier, "The Islamic Hadjdj"; R. Buhl and J. Jomier, "al-Djamra", *EI²*, II, p. 438. Wensinck and Jomier say seven stones; Buhl and Jomier say 77. *Cemre*: one of the heaps of small pebbles at Mina, near Mecca (Redhouse, *TEL*, p. 675); *aqabe*: a steep mountain road, a pass (ibid., p. 1310).

80. Wensinck and Jomier, "The Islamic Hadjdj."

81. Ibid.

82. Redhouse, *TEL*, p. 550. These days, plus the tenth, form the Greater Bayram (ibid.).

83. Wensinck and Jomier, "The Islamic Hadjdj."

84. Buhl and Jomier, "al-Djamra."

85. A. J. Wensinck, "The pre-Islamic Hadjdj," *EI²*, III, pp. 31-33.

86. Buhl and Jomier, "al-Djamra."

87. Wensinck and Jomier, "The Islamic Hadjdj"; Bolay, *Hac rehberi*, p. 17.

88. Albert Richard Smith, *A Month in Constantinople*, p. 157.

89. Garnett, *Home Life in Turkey*, p. 158.

90. B. N. Şehsüvaroğlu, *Hac yolu*, pp. 18-19; today great health precautions are taken regarding the pilgrims (Wensinck and Jomier, "The Islamic Hadjdj").

91. B. N. Şehsüvaroğlu, *Hac yolu*, p. 170.

92. Stanford J. Shaw, *The Budget of Ottoman Egypt 1005-1006/1596-1597*, pp. 158 and n. 134, p. 160 and n. 140; pp. 164, 166.

93. Blunt, *The People of Turkey*, II, p. 285.

94. Reuben Levy, *The Social Structure of Islam*, p. 104; Koran, iv:23.

95. This semideification of Fatma can perhaps be explained by the influence of the Astarte mother-goddess cult which the Turks found being practiced in Asia Minor in the form of worship of the Virgin Mary. Or it may be something as simple as the human need for a woman as a confidante, in this case someone close to the source of grace and power. But for the Turks, in particular, veneration of Fatma may have been inspired, at least in part, by their former worship of the Central Asian goddess Umay to whom, in the Orkhon inscriptions, Bilge Han likened his mother (Vilhelm Thomsen, "Inscriptions de l'Orkhon déchiffrées," *Mémoires de la Société Finno-Ougrienne*, V, Helsinfors, 1896, p. 108). Further, prayer to Fatma was frequently for the purpose of warding off evil spirits, even as the shamaness was used to ward them off in Central Asia.

96. Smith, *A Month in Constantinople*, pp. 107-108.

97. George Washburn, *Fifty Years in Constantinople and Recollections of Robert College*, p. 72.

98. Charles MacFarlane, *Constantinople in 1829*, II, pp. 27, 36.

99. Slade, *Records of Travels*, I, p. 371; II, pp. 152-153.

100. Melek Hanım [Melek Hanum], *Thirty Years in the Harem*, pp. 290, 317-320.

101. Henry Morgenthau, *Ambassador Morgenthau's Story*, p. 194.

102. Halil Halit [Khalil Khalid], *The Diary of a Turk*, p. 47. The remark was made by Halil Halit's mother about the wife of a British consul.

103. Pears, *Turkey and Its People*, pp. 81, 113.

104. *Lit.*, "father"; here, a religious figure.

105. Garnett, *Home Life in Turkey*, pp. 131-137.

106. John Kingsley Birge, *The Bektashi Order of Dervishes*, p. 50.

107. Ibid., p. 38.

108. Ibid., p. 46.

109. Fuat Köprülü, *Influence du chamanisme turco-mongol sur les ordres mystiques musulmans*, p. 8. In the Golden Horde the women shamans took part in burial ceremonies, muttering incantations and sprinkling water (Lajos Ligeti, *Bilinmeyen İç-Asya*, p. 105).

110. Birge, *The Bektashi Order of Dervishes*, p. 39.

111. Raphaela Lewis, *Everyday Life in Ottoman Turkey*, p. 49.

112. For the various dervish orders, *see* Gibb and Bowen, *Islamic Society and the West*, I, 2, pp. 179-206. For the Mevlevî, *see* Théophile Gautier, *Constantinople*, pp. 127-137; for the Howling Dervishes, *see* Edward David Clarke, *Travels in the Various Countries of Europe, Asia and Africa*, III, p. 54f.

113. Ernest Edmondson Ramsaur, Jr., *The Young Turks, Prelude to the Revolution of 1908*, p. 111.

114. Blunt, *The People of Turkey*, II, pp. 275-279.

115. Birge, *The Bektashi Order of Dervishes*, pp. 80-81.

116. Ibid., p. 20, quoting Ziya Bey from "Bektaşilik," in *Yeni Gün*, January 26-March 8, 1931. Elias John Wilkinson Gibb, (*History of Ottoman Poetry*, I, p. 358, n. 1) gives a proverb having to do with the Bektaşi practice of allowing both sexes at their ceremonies: "When the candle goes out the girl (daughter) cannot be distinguished from the woman (wife)." Incest was sometimes imputed to them.

15

Illness, Old Age, and Death

Like the rest of the world, in matters of health the Turks of earlier times relied to a large extent on superstition. Yet interest in and respect for medicine were ever present, even among women, who were on the whole more superstitious than men. In Asia Minor in pre-Ottoman times several hospitals were founded by Turkic women.[1]

In Istanbul there were always doctors, both native and foreign. In the period of Ahmet III (ruled 1703-1730) medicine was especially valued by the grand vizier, Nevşehirli İbrahim Pasha, because both his wife, Fatma Sultan, and the ruler were subject to illnesses.[2] Yet the Englishman, Aaron Hill, writing in the early years of the eighteenth century, thought that native doctors were not competent and that the Turks, apparently sharing his conviction, were likely to trust any Christian quack.[3] Lady Craven found that Turks would ask any European for a cure in the belief that all of them possessed an intuitive knowledge of "physic."[4] Nevertheless the Turkish physician, the *hekim*, always had status. He was allowed into the harem even as early as Süleyman's time, though he was not allowed to give his patients a physical examination.[5] Madden, a British doctor of the early nineteenth century, has told how he was called in to treat a sick woman who, although old and ugly, would let him talk to her only via a door held ajar, and how another, younger woman would let him touch her wrist only through a piece of gauze.[6] Madden was usually asked for medicines that would put on weight, a little fatness being considered an attribute of beauty, and for potions to induce fertility.[7]

There were occasionally women who had the title of doctor. This has been attested to as far back as the time of Süleyman I. A sixteenth century *fetva* even allowed them, if old, to treat men.[8]

There was always, it appears, a belief in the efficacy of medicines. Forty-nine different remedies were kept on hand in the pharmacy of the Maltepe Asker Hastahanesi in 1835.[9] Some *konak*s had their own pharmacies, and some people were inveterate medicine-users. It is said that the *şeyhülislâm* at the end of the eighteenth century personally used 38 kinds of medicine that included acids, oils, ointments, powders, pills, and plant concoctions. Topkapı Palace had its own pharmacy, the Hekimbaşı Odası whence, every year at Nevruz, a gift of aphrodisiac paste was sent to the sultan.[10] Nor were doctors the only people to dispense drugs. Feleksu, a slave of Behice Sultan, daughter of Abdülmecit,[11] lived apart from the palace because she was suffering from malaria. She was being treated by a doctor, yet she looked forward to the ministrations of one Pertev Kalfa who "knows many medicines."[12] In the palace there were woman nurses called *hanım anne* (lady mother), caring even for the young men in the palace. These women were undoubtedly elderly.[13]

Although the Ottoman Empire stood behind Europe in health and sanitary matters generally, there was one phase of medicine in which it was well ahead, and that was as regards innoculation against smallpox. Vaccination seems to have been developed in the Caucasus. De la Motraye, who traveled in Circassia in the early eighteenth century, described in detail the process as he saw it followed in a Circassian village.[14] At about the same period Lady Mary Wortley Montagu found vaccination being practiced in Istanbul. September was the favored month for the innoculation, when the summer heat was over. It was done by scratching a vein with a large needle. Lady Montagu had her son vaccinated in this fashion.[15]

Beyond this, the average Turkish woman, even in the nineteenth century, had to rely on a doctor who had had only *medrese* training in a medicine that was still taught according to the ancient principles of Galen and Avicenna. The modern medical school, founded in 1827 and transferred to Galatasaray in 1838, trained only military doctors. Yet after the opening of the medical school, students were sent abroad to study from time to time.[16] Abdülhamit II sent his palace physician, İsmail Pasha, to Rome.[17]

At the end of the nineteenth century the medical school was improved and enlarged and the whole medical picture began to change in Turkey. With modern medicine becoming more widely practiced in the early twentieth century, some of the harem restrictions began to be removed.[18] In the closing years of the Empire the Constantinople Women's College opened a medical department and an American Hospital in Istanbul, with the result that medical courses were given in the college and nurses were trained in the hospital.[19] Meanwhile, one enterprising young graduate of the college had gone to Germany to study medicine. She was Safiye Ali of the class of 1916, and she became the first Turkish woman physician.[20] We have already discussed the training of the *ebe* or midwife.[21]

But in spite of this, superstition continued to play an important role in the treatment of illness well into the twentieth century. Mehmet Halit Bayrı, who has made a study of Istanbul folklore, lists 12 types of folk cures, all of them purely superstitious. He gives them in this order: to pour lead, to extinguish fire, to pour sherbet, to cut spleen, to cut jaundice, to expunge fear, to singe, to fumigate, to tie a fever, to perform *kırklama* or to go through some folk rite 40 times, to nail, and to read. In addition, letting and leeching blood were also customary remedies.

Many of these cures had to be administered by someone who was *ocaklı* and *izinli*, that is, someone who belonged to a family that had been performing this type of cure for generations and who had been formally instructed in applying the method by the family. Usually, at the time of the cure, some prayers were read or the *besmele* said. Some cures required a *hoca*, some were performed by old women, and a few could be performed by any person, including even the sick person himself.

The list of illnesses believed to be cured by these folk methods is long. For example, rheumatism, head, eye and ear aches, erysipelas, sleeplessness, loss of appetite, shortness of breath, and diarrhea could all supposedly be cured by the patient's being read over by a *hoca*. "Such *hoca*s," writes Bayrı, "went about in the costume of a religious man or a dervish and acted in such a way as to show themselves knowledgeable, esteemed, and the possessor of influence." Some of them could barely read and write, but that did not prevent them from attempting to cure illnesses by reading. (The ability to read seemed to be a magic property). They wrote out charms to tell a girl's fate, to bring back someone who had been sent into exile, to reconcile couples, to protect someone from the evil eye or to save a person from a spell. They interpreted dreams and even prepared medicines. No one seems to know the origin of these *hoca*s, although they were supposed to be *ocaklı* and *izinli*, nor exactly what they read, how they prepared their medicines, or of what the charms they wrote consisted. These *hoca*s were especially influential with women, and it is suspected that they often attempted to keep women under their influence in order to obtain money from them.[22]

One of the most widely used of these folk cures was the pouring of lead. Bayrı says that it was indicated for illnesses of the brain, the nerves, and the "soul." The philosophy behind it was that the illness was caused by some offense to the jinns and the peris, and therefore they had to be propitiated. The *kurşuncu kadın* (the woman who poured the lead) had to be both *ocaklı* and *izinli*. With anyone else the cure was not supposed to work. The woman put 250 to 300 grams of lead into a metal ladle and melted it over a fire. Then the head and body of the sick person were covered with a bath towel and water was put into a metal container. The *kurşuncu kadın* held the container with her left hand over the head of the patient, and with her right ladled the melted lead into the water. While doing so she said, "This is not my hand but the hand of our mother, Ayşe

Fatma," a favorite saying for a pouring cure. This process was repeated over the patient's navel and feet, and once again over the threshold of the room or house. Then the sick person swallowed a few mouthfuls of the water, and some of it was rubbed on his forehead, wrists, palms, and feet. Bread was broken up in the water and thrown to the street dogs, and finally the *kurşuncu kadın* sprinkled some water in a corner for the jinns and peris. If the melted lead in the ladle was very dirty, it meant that the evil spell was strongly entrenched; but if there was a gleaming piece in the lead, that indicated that the sick person's heart was clean and that he would soon recover. The *kurşuncu kadın* was paid for her services, and might be called to treat a person more than once.[23]

The belief in spells, both good and bad, was widespread. According to Lady Blunt, "A Turkish lady, however high her position, invariably attributes to the influence of magic the neglect she experiences from her husband, or the bestowal of his favour on other wives. Every Hanoum I have known would go down to the laundry regularly and rinse with her own hands her husband's clothes after the wash, fearing that if any of her slaves performed this duty she would have the power of casting spells to supplant her in her husband's good graces." These spells were usually cast by means of a *büyü bohçası* (a packet of charms) which, Lady Blunt explained, "is composed of a number of incongruous objects, such as human bones, hair, charcoal, earth, besides a portion of the intended victim's garment, etc., tied up in a rag." After the death of Abdülmecit, 50 of these were found stuffed into his sofa, hidden there by favorites of the moment who hoped thereby to continue their sway over him. The palace women believed that the eccentricities of Abdülaziz could be attributed to magic spells that intriguers had cast on him. *Büyü bohçası*s were found under the mats of his floor.[24]

Probably nothing was more feared by the women of the Ottoman Empire than the evil eye. Lady Blunt, whose interest in superstition led her to acquire a good deal of information, had this to say about it:

The evil eye is supposed to be cast by some envious or malicious person, and sickness, death, and loss of beauty, affection, and wealth are ascribed to it. Often when paying visits of condolence to Turkish harems, I have heard them attribute the loss they have sustained to the *Nazar* [look]. I knew a beautiful girl, who was entirely blinded and disfigured by small-pox, attribute her misfortune to one of her rivals, who, envying in her the charms she did not herself possess, used to look at her with the peculiar *fena guz* (bad expression) so much dreaded by Turkish women. . . . I knew a lady in Broussa whose eye was so dreaded as to induce her friends to fumigate their houses after she paid them a visit.[25]

The means used to nullify the effects of the evil eye were numerous and ran the gamut of fumigations, incantations and charms. A great variety of objects were considered efficacious, among them garlic, wild thyme, boars' tusks, hares' heads, alum, blue grass, turquoise and other stones, eggs, and written amulets.[26]

An example of the tying of knots as a cure, mentioned by Bayrı, has also been given by Lucy Garnett. She saw a dervish tie knots in a cord for a young woman to guard her from female ills. One knot was tied "for each relative in the first degree of herself and her husband."[27] Bayrı, on the other hand, found that the cords were usually multiple and were used principally to cure fever. It was not, he thinks, essentially an Istanbul custom, but one that persons settling in Istanbul had brought from the provinces.[28]

As time went on, among the upper classes it came to be principally the old women who continued to believe in folk medicine. Halide Edip tells the story of her grandmother's belief in one Arziye Hanım, a woman skilled in magic. It was thought that the peris had taken possession of her spirit "and she became a clairvoyant and went to all the fashionable houses, as well as the poor ones, in sickness, childbirth, or other calamity, such as when people were under the influence of witchcraft, sorcery, or the evil of those they called Themselves." Edip Bey, who patronized foreign doctors, undoubtedly did not know that Halide's grandmother took her to this woman and had her prayed over and breathed on.[29]

Superstition was not the only resource of old age. As the Ottoman woman grew older, it was thought fitting for her to devote herself to prayer and pious deeds in preparation for Ezrail, the Angel of Death, who would announce the *ecel*, or moment of death which was predetermined for everyone. Death itself was a word to be avoided and was replaced by a number of euphemisms such as the "Return" and "Cupbearer of the Sphere."[30]

In spite of an increased concern with approaching death, many elderly Ottoman ladies continued to lead rich and varied lives. Halide Edip has given us an excellent portrait of an elderly upper-class Turkish woman in her novel, *Sinekli bakkal*. The woman is Sabiha Hanım, the wife of a pasha. Sabiha Hanım was more interested in life than in death, and in her old age gave of her time and affection to a poor young girl with a beautiful voice, Râbia, the granddaughter of the neighborhood *imam* and the heroine of the novel. Halide Edip describes the old lady thus:

She was of mature years; her husband and everyone else close to her was intimating that the time had come to devote herself to prayer and to give more time to the hereafter. However, she further wrinkled up her already wrinkled face as if she were not at all pleased by thoughts of the hereafter. Wormy and scorpion-infested ground, damp and dark and cold. . . . Would her soul perhaps go up from there to heaven? That, however, was not a very merry place. Undoubtedly musicians and singers would be forbidden there.[31]

Sabiha Hanım, who loved music, happened to hear Râbia sing and said to her husband, "Today I heard the granddaughter of the *imam* at the

Valide Mosque. I haven't heard anything comparable in thirty years. Send word to the *imam* asking him to let the girl come evenings and read for me." The pasha did so, and Râbia was summoned to the *konak*.

With hesitant and bashful eyes she looked at the old woman stretched out on the cushion . . . . There was nothing fearful or haughty about her.

On her several chins and around her wrinkled eyes rouge and face powder had collected in every fold of the flabby flesh. The child found this kind of toilette a little strange. But, wonderfully, the face had a smile that gave confidence, and her eyes were friendly. She stretched out a white, emerald-ringed hand for Râbia to kiss.[32]

The old lady quickly set Râbia at her ease and talked to her about her father, an *orta oyunu* actor whose name was forbidden utterance in her grandfather's household. From Sabiha Hanım, the child drew the courage to admit her love for her father. Then:

When the housekeeper entered, Sabiha Hanım quickly forgot the *imam*'s granddaughter with whom she had been so occupied. She administered her *konak* by relying on the information brought her every evening by her housekeeper, like a commander waiting for the report from the general staff. A chronic rheumatism chained her to her room. Despotic and inquisitive, if she did not learn what everyone under her command had done and what they were thinking, she was restless. The housekeeper's answers were a riddle to Râbia.

"What is the bearded one doing this evening?"

"He is carving wood again. I heard the sound of the saw in the hall."

The bearded one was Selim Pasha. His position as Minister of Police was both difficult and delicate. So in his spare time he made cigarette stools, corner pieces, and back scratchers. He had no hobby outside of this. People who detested the official Selim Pasha couldn't find a thing to say about his personal life.

He was a good family man and especially attracted to his wife. There had been just one bitter event in their shared lives of thirty years of love, an event his wife would not forget. Yet it had had a very reasonable cause.

The pasha had wanted a male child who would be like him, to whom all his own greatness would descend.[33]

Sabiha Hanım's only child turned out to be a frail boy, and so the pasha took another wife and settled her in a house far from the *konak*.

In this one chapter Halide Edip spans the life of the elderly Ottoman woman of station, showing how she spent her time, what her worries and joys were. She depicts a matriarchal figure who ruled her household and her family with a firm hand.

When the Sabiha Hanıms of the Empire reached the final days of their lives, they were comforted by the last rites of the Muslim religion. Very likely even those who had recited "We are asses, we are beasts" now hoped that a merciful Allah would show them the way across the Bridge of Sırat, which was finer than a hair and sharper than a sword.[34] And they would think back on whatever sacrifices they had made in life, knowing that if there had been enough of them, a sheep would carry them safely over.[35]

When Halide Edip sent for a doctor to care for her dying grandmother, she also sent for a *hoca* "who would chant the Koran softly and breathe its healing effects over her, which soothed her and made her feel safe on her road to heaven."

On her deathbed the old lady was still mindful of the proprieties. When her doctor, Dr. Adnan (later Adıvar) came into the room, Halide Edip "saw a look of horror on her face instead of the pleasure I had expected . . . . But he walked to her bed, took her white veil, which had been taken off to put ice on her head, and covered her head, which immediately brought back the usual look to her eyes."[36]

To receive the visit of Ezrail, the Angel of Death, a patient was turned with her face toward Mecca.[37] She and her family forgave one another whatever transgressions they might have committed against one another.[38] The dying person often made some last bequest, a favorite being to free slaves.[39] The *imam* read the 36th sura of the Koran, called *Ya' Sin*, the sura of mourning.[40] And if the dying *hanım efendi* did not understand the Arabic words, she was nonetheless comforted by her belief in their sanctity. The *hoca* or *imam* followed this up with the *şahadet*, the profession of the faith in which, if she were able, the woman joined. If possible, her last words proclaimed: "There is no god but God." At the same time, a member of her family perfumed the room with aromatic substances.

Once she had ceased to breathe, the women around her set up mournful cries, while her closest relative gently closed her eyes, straightened her limbs, bandaged her forehead and chin, and stretched her out on her *rahat yatağı*, her bed of rest. The *imam* sent the particulars of her death to the police to be recorded and called in the old neighborhood woman whose profession it was to prepare the dead for burial.

The old woman then took over, placing the body on a special low table, a *teneşir*, brought from the mosque for the purpose.[41] She washed the body in pure water and rubbed powered camphor on those eight parts of it that touched the ground during prayer—the knees, hands, feet, nose and forehead. She covered the body with a shirt and a one-piece white shroud called the *kefen*, and arranged the dead woman's hair in two strands on her breast. She placed the dead woman on a perfumed bier (*tabut*), the face toward Mecca. If the dead woman had been rich, the bier was built especially for her, perhaps in advance on her own orders. Poor women used a bier supplied by the local mosque.

For a woman of an important family the muezzin announced her death

from a minaret of the local mosque,[42] and close friends and relatives con-
gregated there. The *imam* or a close relative recited a short prayer, the
muhit namazı (neighborhood prayer).[43] Then the *imam* asked the congregation for their opinion of the dead woman, a ceremony known as *tezkiye*.
On getting their answer, which was always favorable, he asked them to
perform the *helâl*, the giving up of the dead woman to God.

The body was next put into a coffin—temporary for all but the rich—
and shawls and rich fabrics thrown over it. A *çember* (neckerchief) was
placed at its head. (A fez or a turban was placed at the head of a man's
coffin.) The body lay on its couch of rest for a time to make sure that
death had taken place and then the procession to the cemetery took place.
Burial was relatively soon. Whatever the distance, the body was carried
on foot by four pallbearers. These often changed, for it was an act of merit
to help carry a body, and therefore many wanted a chance.[44]

At the cemetery the body was reverently lowered into the grave, the
face toward Mecca. A woman's face was covered, a man's left uncovered.[45]
Burial was always underground, even if a large tomb was erected over the
grave. The usual marker was a slender vertical slab, with perhaps a sun-
flower or lotus leaf carved at its head (a fez or turban for a man) and a
verse asking God's blessing.[46]

At the grave the *imam* read the moving prayer for the dead called *telkin*,
and followed it with the *fatiha*.[47] Alms were distributed to the pack of poor
that followed the body to the cemetery. Then the mourners left, but the
imam stayed behind to help the deceased give the right answers to the two
questioning angels, *Münker* and *Nekir*,[48] who would soon question the
dead woman on her faith. A good Muslim would know the answers, an
indifferent Muslim would have forgotten them. The right answers enabled
the *hanım efendi*'s soul to take its first step on the path to Paradise. A
wealthy family might also hire theological students to read the Koran over
the grave throughout the night.

On the third day after death *lokma*, a kind of doughnut, was baked and
sent to friends in return for their prayers for the dead. Some families had
the *Mevlûd*, Süleyman Çelebi's poem on the birth of the Prophet, read on
the 40th day after death and, if they were so minded, once a year afterwards. A funeral could be an expensive affair, as Hüseyin Rahmi Gürpınar
shows in his story of the funeral of a pasha's wife in his work, *Pages From
Life*.[49] When word of the *hanım efendi*'s death reached the street in her
quarter:

Everyone ran to put on beggars' clothing in order to be properly dressed to accompany the corpse. The married women covered themselves in green. They carried
needles and water jugs. Beggar men gathered.

Hacer, pushing the crowd to one side of the street, awakened the sleeping old
beggar, Abdullah, with a couple of blows. She embraced the decrepit old man.

She hung a Koran case around his neck as if he were a child. She put a stick in his hand and gave him directions for the route, with the warning, "Don't go astray when you read the *Âşir*[50] at the grave or by God I'll leave you hungry tonight."

The woman's child carried the clothes for the corpse on her back, clothes sewn from entirely new material. In fact each of the arms was made from a different piece, so that more people would be entitled to take the money when a hand scattered it at the grave. . . .

Pitcher, tin plate, metal pot, cudgel, and stick in hand, men, women, the old, the young with families poured in crowds into the street. The water-carrier, in costume and with saliva dripping from his mouth into the engraved copper cup in his hand, cried out the *arak*[51] in a rasping voice: "Three-year-olds, seven-year-olds, four-year-olds, those at puberty, those who are pure, the *ulema*, the expounders of the law of Islam. . . . " The fat-thighed beggar who sat sniffing the air like a disabled cat in a corner of an Eyüp *kebabcı*'s . . . the slovenly, deceitful child of adultery who pulls fishlines from the tails of drivers' horses . . . Ağır Aksak Ruhi who passes three entire hours on the Unkapanı bridge in invocation . . . Molla Uryani, the preacher without a congregation who, at the place for shoes in the mosque on the Night of Power, looks around and starts out with: "When His Excellency Yunus Aleyhisslani takes up his home in the belly of the fish. . . . " Hoş-Neva Zakir Rıza, who thrusts his turban into the wine-shop of Silâhtar Ağa in the spring and attracts a group of revelers with his song: "May the Ceyhun see my weeping eyes that search."

This troop drew near the cemetery. Though the corpse had not yet arrived, there was a small group at the grave that was being prepared. The stone was at one side, the soil was heaped on the other side, and some people were working in and around the pit. There was a dispute between the civil *efendi* who swung a thick gold chain on his fat stomach and a turbaned, fearsome man who was the head keeper.

The turbaned man: "I am in charge here; I will not bury the corpse unless I receive twenty-five liras."

The civil servant: "I am the representative of the pasha. I will bury the corpse here without giving anyone even one *para*."

The turbaned man: "Don't do it! This is not the world's work; it would be a sin. This is an honored place because it is near the tomb there. If you want me to, I will bury it on the land over on the other side for five lira."

While they carried on their dispute like this, the prayer-reciter and his flock filled the graveyard like a flood. A train of the blind was coming from among the cypresses with the guidance of a single eye out in front, moving as a ship rolls. Elbowing and pushing one another about in order to get close to the front row, they surrounded the pit on all sides as if it were a feast. This feast had first, second and third positions. The guild official wanted everybody in his following to go over to where they ought to be. They were supposed to perform without fee, and they were all struggling hard to rise above the matter of fee. . . . Elevated to the sky along with the *zikirs*[52] of the old men and the scent of the aloeswood of which the smoke poured from the incense-holders, the coffin changed shoulders as heads turned right and left. Once every minute it was raised above the red of the fezes and the green of the turbans and, carried on respectful shoulders, it moved ponderously. The group rushed into the tomb. The open mouth of the grave, from which the black earth had been scattered on all sides, was waiting to swallow a life. They lowered the coffin. The old men gave out a long "Hu!" The *zikir* stopped. The husband of the deceased, a pasha, seemed sad and plunged in thought. Among those who had gotten out of the carriage was a thin, pale child of fifteen or sixteen who didn't know where to stand. . . . He loved his mother very much, but he suddenly moved back as if not to be pulled into this pit with her. . . .

The chanting was ended; they had prayed, and all the rites were completed. Now money was being scattered to the poor. The officials in this matter were three men, the *kâhya efendi*, the *imam*, and the *bekçi* [watchman]. The guild official, Ömer Ağa, tried to keep the business in order with the stick in his hand. The money to be given was emptied from a large purse into handkerchiefs by the handful, clanking and uncounted. Suddenly all the beggars' arms were stretched out as if money were to rain from the air.

Swiftly fifteen or twenty rushed up to those who were distributing the money, and with the skill of a knave the hand of each was quickly filled. Empty hands stretched out again, and however much alms was dispersed, it was impossible to lessen the number of beggars. . . .

Finally the purse was empty. . . .

Hacer, in her green headgear, arrived with her stick in her hand. . . . "May you dwell in light! Are you going to bury the eminent *hanım efendi* with only two *kuruş* worth of water? When she was in health and came to the *hamam*, was not water truly given?"

Uşak: "She didn't go to the *hamam* in the market. There was a *hamam* in the *konak*. . . . Have the women read the *Âşir*?"

Hacer: "They will read the glorious verses, but they have not finished. . . ."

Uşak: "All right, how much money do you want to read the *Âşir*?"

"My two eyes are illiterate. I do not read, my husband reads. . . . The world of the reader is like light. If you give money into my hand, he will read it; if you don't, he won't. My husband will make the grave as it should be. He will make it glow to the zenith."

Hacer kept up her pleading for money and her talk about how poor but pious she and her husband were. Finally, realizing that she could get nothing more out of the pasha, she turned her cries on the dead woman's son.

"Ah, my chick, live to be a thousand. You are generous, exactly like your mother. Oh, how I weep for that *hanım efendi*. . . . Have you seen the son of great lineage, have you seen the son of good family, have you seen this educated one? May the hand that gives see no trouble! Give, give, son of my benefactress; give, my darling; give, give, my young bull; give!"

All the beggars, seeing Hacer's easy success, made a rush. All had read the *Âşir*, all had carried water, each had been energetic and left some difficult situation because of the obligation to go to the corpse, for which he had been paid only a trifling amount. . . . The beggars did not all leave until the carriage had reached the Eyüp dock.

Some Western observers have commented on the simplicity and lack of lugubriousness in Turkish funerals, and have noted the atmosphere of quiet dignity which prevails on those occasions. But such observations tend to be subjective and based upon cultural clichés. People accustomed to the "hysteric and often mechanical yells . . . of the most frantic nature"[53] with which the Greeks mourn their dead no doubt find the Turks' demeanor a model of self-control. Yet Melek Hanım recounted that Kıbrıslı Mehmet Pasha beat his head against the wall at the death of his first son.[54] And in addition to the human need to give expression to grief, a formality-loving people like the Turks cannot let death pass without some sort of social ritual. Innumerable visits of condolence from relatives and friends are an integral part of the ceremony of death.[55]

Hüseyin Rahmi Gürpınar has satirized this custom in a short story entitled "Condolences."[56] He tells how a mother's grief at the death of a small son is exacerbated by an endless stream of female visitors. One woman tells her that it would do her good to cry. Another says that an *imam* has declared that it is a sin to weep. At first only the neighbor women call in, then friends and relatives from other quarters of the city, and eventually those from even farther off. The wailing and weeping goes on week after week. The woman's mother exacts a promise from the visitors not to talk about the dead child, but they manage to do so nonetheless. In desperation she orders the servant not to open the door to visitors, but the servant forgets. Finally, worn down by her grief, the young mother dies only a month after her son.

Then a fresh spate of calls begin, this time to console Şefkure, the grandmother. Having had all she can take, Şefkure arms herself with a stick to keep the visitors out. At this the neighbors, thinking her mad, have her confined in an asylum. This does not end the stream of condolences but only redirects it. Now the people call at the asylum. To escape their endless chatter, poor Şefkure finally does go mad.

The Westerners' opinion that the Turks did not show their feelings at a death in the family perhaps derived partly from the fact that Muslims do not wear mourning clothes or observe a period of seclusion, as was customary among Christians, and partly from the notion that the Muslim belief in a preordained date of death may sometimes lessen grief when that date arrives. Lady Blunt fell into this error when she wrote: "At the approach of death, his [the Turk's] friends [are] reconciled to the thought of his approaching end. No *imam* or servant of God is called in to soothe the

departing spirit. . . . The friends and relatives weep in silence."[57] As we
have seen, Lady Blunt could scarcely have been more wrong.

In the period under discussion we find no ferment for change in the
death and funerary customs of the Ottoman woman. The feminists were
concerned not with the Ottoman woman's death but with her life. Their
emphasis was on education and on changes in marriage and divorce laws.
Their attitudes would soon alter life for all the urban women as it had
already altered it for the few.[58]

Writing at the beginning of the nineteenth century, Fazıl Bey had thought
that a woman's most important attribute was her chastity.[59] By the end of
the century women were a topic of wider interest and Tevfik Fikret was
writing of them: "In the moral evolution of mankind, the great question
of their share and their rights is acknowledged. We now admit that they
are the foundation of our life."[60]

NOTES

1. There was the one put up by Gevher Nesibe, probably the daughter of the
Selçuk ruler, Kılıç Arslan I, in Kayseri, in 1205. Together with the medical school
founded by her brother, Giyasüddin Keyhüsrev I, it was the oldest Turkic medical
institution in Anatolia. There was also a hospital in Divrik, the Turan Melik Şi-
faiyesi, given in 1228 by the wife of Ahmet Shah of the Al Mengücek *beylik*. In
Amasya a hospital was provided at the instigation of Ildus (Yıldız) Hatun, wife of
the Ilhanid ruler, Ölceytü Sultan, although it was actually built by her slave, Anber
bin Abdullah. In addition, there was a treatment center, the Yoncalı İlica, built
in Kütahya by Gülsüm, daughter of Ramazan, in 1233. In other Turkic-dominated
lands, hospitals built by or for women were also going up. Kutluk Turkân Hatun
of the Kara Kitai state built a hospital in the environs of Isfahan in 1271-1281.
Erbil Atabeg in Mosul opened a building for the care of widows and orphans and
a home for children gathered from the streets. He even provided wet nurses for
children who needed them. *See* A. Afetinan, *Herkesin bir dünyası var*, pp. 129-
137 and A. Süheyl Ünver, "Büyük Selçuklu İmparatorluğu zamanında" Vakıf
hastahanelerinin bir kısmına dair," *Vakıflar dergisi*, I (1938), pp. 17-24.

2. Ahmet Refik [Altınay], *Lâle devri*, p. 96.

3. Aaron Hill, *A Full and Just Account of the Present State of the Ottoman
Empire*, p. 74.

4. Lady Elizabeth Craven, *A Journey Through the Crimea to Constantinople
(1786)*, pp. 230-231.

5. Albert Howe Lybyer, *The Government of the Ottoman Empire in the Time
of Suleiman the Magnificent*, pp. 121-122. See also Baron de Tott, *Mémoires sur
les Turcs et les Tartares*, I, p. 80.

6. R. Robert Madden, *Travels in Turkey, Egypt, Nubia and Palestine in 1824,
1825, 1826 and 1827*, I, p. 45.

7. Ibid., pp. 32-33.

8. *See* Tezer Taşkıran, *Women in Turkey*, p. 22.

9. A. Süheyl Ünver, *Osmanlı Türklerinde hekimlik ve eczacılık tarihi hakkında*, pp. 17-18.

10. Ibid., p. 12.

11. A. D. Alderson, *The Structure of the Ottoman Dynasty*, Table XLVII.

12. M. Çağatay Uluçay, *Haremden mektuplar*, p. 204.

13. Taşkıran, *Women in Turkey*, p. 22.

14. A girl of between four and five, who had first been purged with a concoction boiled from dried fruit, leaves, and roots, was brought to a boy of nine whose pox had begun to suppurate. An old woman then took three needles fastened together, pricked the pit of the girl's stomach, a point over her heart, her navel, her right wrist and the ankle of her left leg until blood came and then applied to these points matter from the boy's pox. She then bound the places with angelica leaves and young lamb skins, whereupon the mother wrapped the daughter up in a skin and carried her home. There the girl was kept warm and fed on a light diet for four or five days until the smallpox came out, presumably a very light case. According to De la Motraye no one knew how ancient this custom was, but he found it prevalent. Parents with a handsome girl would ride a day's journey to find a child with pox so their daughter could be innoculated (*see* Aubrey de la Motraye, *Travels Through Europe, Asia, and into Parts of Africa*, II, p. 75).

15. Lady Mary Wortley Montagu, *Letters from the Right Honourable . . . 1709-1762*, p. 124. Samuel Cox, who was American ambassador to Turkey in the latter half of the nineteenth century, has told a fantastic story of 150 palace women being vaccinated by an Italian surgeon through a hole in a screen and the surgeon's head being covered with a shawl as soon as the proceeding was over. Cox does not vouch for the story, which was probably gossip; the palace women would have been vaccinated in childhood.

16. Bernard Lewis, *The Emergence of Modern Turkey*, pp. 82-83.

17. Interview with Kadri Cenani, August 1966.

18. Sir Edwin Pears, *Forty Years in Constantinople*, pp. 320-321 and *Turkey and Its People*, pp. 62-63.

19. The University of Istanbul trained women in nursing during World War I in classes attended by upper-class women. Among them was Makbule Eldeniz, the daughter of Kâmil Pasha. She nursed the wounded during the Dardanelles campaign.

20. Mary Mills Patrick, *Under Five Sultans*, pp. 331-333.

21. Trained, officially appointed midwives practice today in the rural areas of Turkey (personal observation).

22. Mehmet Halit Bayrı, *İstanbul folkloru*, pp. 91-99.

23. Ibid.

24. Lady Fanny Blunt, *The People of Turkey*, II, pp. 237-239.

25. Ibid., pp. 241-242.

26. Ibid., p. 244.

27. Lucy M. J. Garnett, *Home Life in Turkey*, p. 138.

28. Bayrı, *İstanbul folkloru*, p. 96.

29. Halide Edip [Adıvar], *Memoirs of Halide Edip*, pp. 42-44.

30. Blunt, *The People of Turkey*, II, pp. 134-135; Garnett, *Home Life in Turkey*, p. 249; Koran xxxii:11.

31. Halide Edip, *Sinekli bakkal*, pp. 17-23.

32. Ibid.

33. Ibid.

34. A. Vahid Moran, *Türkçe-Ingilizce sözlük, A Turkish-English Dictionary*, Istanbul, 1945, p. 1115.

35. Information on popular beliefs from the late A. Ahmet Gürün.

36. Edip, *Memoirs*, pp. 355-356. This event took place before Halide Edip married Dr. Adnan Adıvar.

37. This account of the preparation of the body and of the funeral is taken largely from Ignatius Mouradgea d'Ohsson, *Tableau général de l'Empire othoman*, II, pp. 299-306 and Charles White, *Three Years in Constantinople; or Domestic Manners of the Turks in 1844*, III, pp. 328-336. Other sources differ in some details, but these accounts appear to be the most meticulously researched. Where other sources are used, they will be noted.

38. Z. Duckett Ferriman,*Turkey and the Turks*, pp. 231-237.

39. Garnett, *Home Life in Turkey*, p. 251.

40. Arthur Jeffery, *A Reader on Islam*, pp. 49-53. The following verses are from Prof. Jeffery's translation from the Arabic:

> 12. It is We who bring to life the dead, and write down what they have sent ahead and the traces they have left behind. Everything have We reckoned up with a Codex (Imam) that makes clear.
>
> . . . .
>
> 77. Does not man see that We have created him from a drop? Yet, behold, he is a manifest disputer.
>
> 78. And has set forth for Us a parable, and forgotten his creation, saying: "Who will bring these bones to life when they have decayed?"
>
> 79. Say: "He will bring them to life Who produced them from the first time, since He knows about every created thing."
>
> 80. He who gave you fire from the green tree, behold, ye kindle flame from it.
>
> 81. Is not He Who created the heavens and the earth powerful enough to create their like? Yea, indeed, He is the Creator, the Knower.
>
> 82. His only command when He wishes anything is to say to it: "Be!", and it is.
>
> 83. So glory be to Him in Whose hand is the dominion over everything, seeing that to Him ye will be brought back.

41. In later years the washing and preparation of the body sometimes took place at the mosque (information supplied by Şehbal Teilmann).

42. Blunt, *The People of Turkey,* II, p. 136.

43. Ibid.

44. White says all funeral processions took place afoot, but later writers speak of carriages (*Three Years in Constantinople*, III, p. 336).

45. White, *Three Years in Constantinople*, III, p. 335.

46. Garnett, *Home Life in Turkey*, p. 255 and Adolphus Slade, *Records of Travels in Turkey, Greece, etc.*, II, p. 274.

47. D'Ohsson gives the prayer for the dead in French (*Tableau général*, II, pp. 296-299). The following is a translation of his text:

O my God, have mercy on the living and on the dead, on those present and on those absent, on the insignificant and on the great, on the men and on the women among us. O my God, let live in Islam those among us to whom You have given life, and let die in the faith those to whom You have given death. Honor the dead with the grace of repose and tranquillity, with the grace of Your mercy and Your divine satisfaction. O my God, add to his excellence if he be among the excellent, and pardon his wickedness if he be among the wicked. Accord him peace and salvation, let him enter and dwell near Your eternal throne; save him from the torments of the tomb and from the eternal fires; allow him to remain in Paradise in the company of the blessed souls. O my God, transform his tomb into a place of delights equal to those of Paradise, and not a pit of sufferings like those of Hell. Have mercy on him, O Most Merciful of Beings.

48. Ferriman, *Turkey and the Turks*, pp. 231-237.
49. Hüseyin Rahmi Gürpınar, *Hayatın sahifeleri*, from an unpublished anthology by Fevziye Abdullah Tansel.
50. *Âşir*: a portion of ten verses in the Koran (Moran, *Sözlük*, p. 74).
51. *Arak*: a tune of à la turka music (Mehmet Ali Ağakay, *Türkçe sözlük*, Ankara, 1966, p. 44).
52. *Zikir*: recitation of the attributes of God (H. C. Hony, with the advice of Fahir İz, *A Turkish-English Dictionary*, Oxford, 1957, p. 414).
53. White, *Three Years in Constantinople*, III, p. 332.
54. Melek Hanım [Melek Hanum], *Thirty Years in the Harem*, p. 51.
55. According to Blunt (*The People of Turkey*, II, p. 142) the conventional expression of sympathy was: *Siz sağ olun evlatlarımız sağ olsun* (May you be sound in body, and may your children be sound in body).
56. Hüseyin Rahmi Gürpınar, "Ecir ve Sabır," from Yaşar Nabi's *Türk edebiyatının en güzel hikâyeleri antolojisi*, pp. 10-21.
57. Blunt, *The People of Turkey*, II, p. 140.
58. There is an entertaining short story by Memduh Şevket Esendel entitled "Feminist" (from Yaşar Nabi's *Türk edebiyatının en güzel hikâyeleri*, pp. 52-57) about a man who tried to find out what a feminist was. Nobody could tell him, but he asked the question so often that he was nicknamed "Feminist" and invited to address gatherings as an authority on the subject.
59. Fazıl Bey [Fazıl Hüseyin Enderunlı], *Le Livre des femmes (Zenan-name)*, p. 20: "La femme est fausse et méchante—malgré ses graces elle ne peut échapper à cela—mais je la veux vierge, intacte et que, chez elle, le lien de la virginité subsiste dans toute sa force. Si elle n'est vierge, je la dédaigne: il ne m'importe alors de distinguer si toute une caravane y a passé ou si elle n'a été qu'à peine déflorée."
60. Kenan Akyüz, *Tevfik Fikret*, p. 285. Akyüz quotes this passage from "Nevha-ı bi-süt," in *Servet-i fünun* (Istanbul, 1314/1891), p. 400.

Glossary

abla	An elder sister
acemi	A novice
ağa	In this case, a black eunuch or a palace page
Ağa Yeri	The playing field of the palace pages on the grounds of Topkapı Palace
ağırlık	The portion of the dowry paid before marriage
ahsan	Better
akarsu	*Lit.*, flowing water, *i.e.*, a diamond necklace
akit	A contract
akkam	An attendant on the pilgrimage to Mecca
al-Azhar	A Muslim university in Cairo
altın	Gold, a gold coin
Altın Yol	The Golden Way, a corridor in the harem of Topkapı Palace
ana okulu	A nursery school
anne	Mother
ansiklopedi	An encyclopedia
araba	A carriage, a wagon (today, also an automobile)
araştırmak	To search
arslan	A lion
asır	The same as *ikindi namazı*; also a century
askı	A bride's throne or chair

askıcı	A bridal attendant
ayan	A notable of the European lands of the Ottoman Empire
ayet	A verse of the Koran
azatlık	A pension for a palace eunuch
baba	Father; here, a male religious leader
Bab-ı Ali	The Sublime Porte, later name of the palace of the grand vizier
Bab-ı Hümayun	The Imperial Gate of Topkapı Palace
bacı	A child's nurse
baltacı	A halberdier
baskın	A raid
baş ağa	A head black eunuch in the service of the imperial family
baş ikbal	*See ikbal, baş*
baş kadın	*See kadın, baş*
baş kalfa	A woman in charge of a palace service
baş usta	*See usta, baş*
başlanmak	The ceremony when a child first went to school
başmaklık, paşmaklık	Money for the personal use of a palace woman, called slipper money
bayram	A holiday or festival
bekçi	A watchman
Bektaşi	A member of the religious order of that name
belge	A document
bendegân	*Lit.*, servants; here, palace courtiers
berat gecesi	The night when Muhammad received his mission
besmele	*See bismillah*
beşik	A cradle
beşik kertiği	Betrothing children in the cradle
beşik kertme nişanlı	A person betrothed in the cradle
bey	A title indicating a gentleman
beylik	A district governed by a *bey*, in this case a pre-Ottoman principality of Asia Minor
bid'at	An innovation
bismillah	A prayer meaning "in the name of God"

bohça	A square of cloth used for wrapping
bohçacı	A tradeswoman who carried her wares in a *bohça*
bostancı	*Lit.*, a gardener, also a palace guard
bostancıbaşı	Head *bostancı*
boş kağıdı	A paper of divorce
boyunca	Along
boza	A fermented drink made of millet
börek	A pastry
buhurdanlık	An incense burner
bürümcük	Gauze
büyü	A spell
büyü bohçası	A package of charms
büyük	Big, great
camekân	The dressing room of a bath
cami	A mosque
can	The soul, life
canım bey efendi	Dear soul (*lit.*, my soul) gentleman lord
cariye	A woman slave
cedit	New
celi	A type of calligraphy
cemiyet	A reception
cemre-i akaba	A rite denoting the stoning of the devil during the pilgrimage
çalgı	A musical instrument
çarşaf	A veil
çatmak	To encounter
çekmece	A box or chest
çember	A neckerchief
çengi	A girl dancer
çengi kolubaşı	The head of a troupe of dancing girls
çeşm-i bülbül	*Lit.*, nightingale's eye; colored glass with spiral stripes
çeşme	A fountain
çifte hamamı	A double bath, one side for men, one side for women
çırak	An apprentice

çocuk	A child
çöğür	The lute
çubuk	A pipe
dadı	A child's nurse
dalkavuk	A turban-nodder, *i.e.*, a sycophant
damat	A son-in-law; here, an imperial son-in-law
darphane emini	The superintendent of the mint
dârülkurra	A school for Koran readers
dârülmuallimat	A school to train women teachers
dârüssaadet ağası	The *ağa* of the House of Felicity, the same as the *kızlar ağası*
deli sultan	The mad princess
dellâliye	A broker's fee
dergi	A magazine
devlet	The state
dil	Language
Divan	The imperial council
divan poetry	Classic Ottoman poetry
Divan Yolu	The Council Road that led from the Old Palace to the New or Topkapı Palace
divanhane kakması	A setting for a jeweled ring
dışarı	Outside; here, living with the groom's parents
doğum iskemlesi	A birthing chair
dolap	A revolving cupboard
dolma	A food in which something is stuffed
Dolmabahçe Sarayı	The nineteenth-century imperial palace on the Bosphorus
donanma	A decking out
dondurma	Ice cream
dua	A prayer
düğün	A feast, usually wedding or circumcision activities
düğün saşısı	A wedding gift
dünya	The world
ebe	A midwife
ebe kadın	The same as *ebe*
ebelik	The profession of midwifery

Edirne Sarayı	The imperial palace at Edirne (now destroyed)
efendi	Master, lord, a term of respect
emirname	A letter of command
en aşağı	*Lit.*, the lowest; the lowest rank of palace eunuch
enderun	*Lit.*, interior; here, the women's apartments of the palace
enderun hoca	A palace teacher
esir	A slave
esirci	A slave dealer
esirci esnafı	The slave-dealer guild
esir tuccarı	A slave merchant
Eski Saray	The Old Palace, now the site of the University of Istanbul
evkaf	The Arabic plural of *vakıf*
evlatlık	An adopted child
ev hanımı	A housewife
ev sahibi	*Lit.*, master of the house; here, good jinns
eyalet	A province
eyalet valisi	A governor of a province
Eyüp (Eyoup)	A suburb of Istanbul up the Golden Horn; a companion of the Prophet is supposedly buried there
eyyam-üt-teşrik	The days of sharing during the pilgrimage
ezan	The call to prayer
fatiha	The first verse of the Koran, often recited
Fatimids	A Turkic dynasty of medieval Egypt
ferman	A decree of the sultan
fetva	An opinion on Islamic law given by a *müftü*, a Muslim jurist
fincan	A small coffee cup
fiskiye	A water jet
gâvur	An unbeliever, *i.e.*, a non-Muslim
gayret kuşağı	*Lit.*, a girdle of effort; a band put around the body of a new baby
gazete	A newspaper
gecelik	A nightgown

gedikli	*Lit.*, a chosen one; a servitor
gelin	A bride
gelinlik yatağı	A couch for a woman who has just given birth
gelin yüzü	Swaddling for a baby
giyim	Wearing apparel
giyinmek	To dress up
göbek adı	*Lit.*, navel name; the name given to a child when the navel cord is cut, not usually the name by which the person is thereafter known
görev	Duty
görücü	Viewer; a woman who goes about viewing girls on behalf of a prospective bridegroom
gözde	*Lit.*, in the eye; *i.e.*, a favorite
gül	Rose, flower
gümrük emini	The chief of customs
gündelikçi	A woman who sews by the day
gyz tanysu	A Central Asian song of a bride's farewell to her childhood home
hac	The pilgrimage to Mecca
hacı	A pilgrim
hacı kadın	A woman who has made the pilgrimage
hacı zenan	The same as *hacı kadın*
hacle	The bridal chamber
hadith	A tradition supposedly stemming from the Prophet Muhammad
hafız	One who has memorized the Koran
hak	The right
halvet	Privacy
hamam	A bath
hamamcı	A bath attendant
hamam takımı	Bath paraphernalia
hamam tası	A bathing bowl
han	An inn
hanım	A title meaning lady, wife
hanım, büyük	*Lit.*, great lady; the first wife in a polygamous household
hanım efendi	A term of respect for a lady
hanım iğnesi	*Lit.*, lady's needle; a slender variety of caique

hanım sultan	A daughter of a woman *sultan*
harem	The women's quarters in a household; the sacred territory of Mecca and Madina
harem ağaları	The black eunuchs who guarded the imperial harem
harem-i hümayun	The imperial harem
harem-i şerif	The sacred area of Mecca and Madina
haremeyn-i şerifeyn	The holy cities of Mecca and Madina
has	Belonging to the person of the sovereign, *i.e.*, crown land
haseki	The favorite official concubine of the sultan
haseki kadın	The same as *haseki*
hasen	Good
has odalık	A favorite concubine of the sultan
hat	A decree of the sultan
hat-ı hümayun	An imperial decree
hat-ı şerif	The same as *hat-ı hümayun*
hatun	An old form of *kadın*
havlu	A towel
havuz	A pool
hayal-i zil	The same as Karagöz
hayat	Life
hayrat	Pious deeds
hazine-i hassa defteri	The register of the imperial treasury
hazine-i hümayun kâhyası	The steward in charge of the imperial treasury
haznedar	Treasurer
haznedar gedikli	A woman in the service of the treasury of the imperial harem
haznedar kalfa	The same as *haznedar gedikli*
haznedar usta	The woman in charge of the treasury of the imperial harem
hekim	A physician
hekimbaşı	The head doctor of the palace
helâl	*Lit.*, lawful; the part of the Muslim funeral service in which the dead is given up to God
helva	A sweet
heşap işi	An embroidery stitch
hicrî	Indicating a date of the Muslim calendar

hil'at	A robe of honor
hilye-i şerif	A book of sacred recitations
hıdrellez günü	A spring holiday, popularly considered as the beginning of summer
hırka-i şerif	The Blessed Mantle, Muhammad's cloak
hırka-i şerif şeyh	The sheikh of the Blessed Mantle
hoca	A teacher
hoca hanım	A lady teacher
hoşaf	Stewed fruit
humbaracıhane	The headquarters of the bombardiers
humbarcıyan	The bombardiers
hutbe	The Friday sermon in a mosque
hüküm	A written command
hümayun	Imperial
Hümayunname	A book written about a sultan
hünkâr	The ruler
hünkârı çatmak	To encounter the ruler
hünkâr mahfili	The sultan's pew in a mosque
ibret	An example
ibrik	A pitcher
içeri	Inside; here, indicates living with the bride's parents
idadiye	A secondary school, corresponding to senior high school
iddet	The three-month period of chastity for a woman after a divorce
ifaze	A pilgrimage rite
iftar	The meal that breaks the daily fast during *ramazan*
ihram	A cloth covering; also a ritual garment for the pilgrimage
ihtisap ağası	A tax official
ikbal	A girl favorite of the sultan, higher in rank than an *odalık* and not so high as a *kadın*
ikbal, baş	Head *ikbal*, next in rank to the fourth *kadın*
iliklik	The tepid room of a bath
ilm-i hal	Catechism
ilm-ül-musiki	Knowledge of music
imam	A prayer leader

imaret	A kitchen of food for the poor
ince yemek	*Lit.*, fine food, *i.e.*, delicacies
irade	A decree
irmik helvası	A sweet made of semolina
istifa	A type of embroidery
istihare	Divination by dreams
işa	The same as *yatsı namazı*
izinname	A marriage license
Kaaba	The building in which the black stone of Mecca is embedded
kadı	A judge
kadın	*Lit.*, a woman; in palace parlance one of the four official concubines of the sultan
kadın, baş	Head *kadın*
kadın cubuğu	A woman's pipe
kadın efendi	A title of the sultan's official concubines
Kadınlar Sultanatı	The Women's Sultanate
kadınlık	The four women who were the sultan's official concubines
kadir gecesi	The Night of Power, when the Koran was first revealed to Muhammad
kahve	Coffee
kahveci	One who serves coffee
kâhya	A steward
kâhya kadın	*Lit.*, a woman steward; the woman in charge of the imperial harem
kalfa	The same as *gedikli*
kalfa, nöbetci	A rank of the guard of the black enunchs of the palace
kalın	The part of the dowry paid before marriage
kalym	An old Turkic word for the dowry payment
kandil gecesi	A night of Muslim celebration when the mosques are illuminated
kanun	A dulcimer; a law
kaplan	A tiger
kaptan paşa	The head of the Navy
Karagöz	The shadow theater
karagözcü	The man who operates the shadow theater

kaside	A poem of praise of not more than 15 lines
kâtibe	A woman scribe or clerk
kavaltı	Breakfast
kavuk	A wadded turban
kavukluk	A turban stand
kayık	A caique
kaymak	Cream
kaymakam	The assistant to the grand vizier who took his place when the grand vizier was out of Istanbul
kaynana	Mother-in-law
kazasker	A high official in the Ottoman judiciary
kebapçı	A seller of *kebap* or roasted lamb
kefen	A shroud
keman	A violin
kese	A purse
ketebe	A diploma for excellence in calligraphy
kethüda	The same as *kâhya*
kibit	A *yurt*, a habitation
kıra	A tradeswoman who went from house to house
kılavuz	A guide; here, the same as *görücü*
kına	Henna
kına gecesi	The evening of the bride's henna ceremony
kırk hamamı	The bath given a woman 40 days after childbirth
kırklama	A bathing ceremony for a child performed 40 days after birth; a folk healing rite
kırlangiç	*Lit.*, swallow; a variety of caique
kışlak	Winter quarters
kıyafet	Costume
kız	A girl, daughter
kız ağası	*Lit.*, *ağa* of the girls; the chief black eunuch in charge of the imperial harem
kız kaçırma	Abduction of a girl, elopement
Kız Kulesi	An island tower at the point where the Bosphorus and the Sea of Marmara meet, also called Leander's Tower
kız rüştiyesi	A girls' primary school
kız sanayi mektebi	A girls' craft school
koçu	A coach
kolağası	A rank in the Ottoman army

koltuk	A ceremony in which the bridegroom gave his arm to the bride
konak	A mansion
koz bekciyan	A group in the outer service of Topkapı Palace
kule	A tower
kurban bayramı	The sacrifice holiday
kurna	The basin of a fountain
kurşuncu kadın	A woman who pours lead, a folk healer
kuruş	A coin, a unit of currency
kuşbaz	The official who looked after the sultan's hunting birds
küçük	Small, little, young
lağımcıyan	Sappers
lâlâ	A servant in charge of a boy; in the palace a black eunuch in charge of a prince
lâledan	A tulip vase
Lâle Devri	The Tulip Period
lebbeyk	*Lit.*, I answer twice to thy summons; to come with pleasure and alacrity
leğen	A basin
lise	A lycée
loğusa	A woman who has just given birth
loğusa yatağı	A couch for a woman who has just given birth
lokma	A kind of doughnut
lokum	The candy called Turkish Delight
maarif	Education
mabeyn	The area between the harem and the *selâmlık*
mağrip	West, sunset
mahalle	Neighborhood, quarter
mahrem	Closely related and therefore forbidden in marriage
makat	A divan or cushion cover
makataa	A tax farm
makrama	A handkerchief
mangal	A brazier
mani	A four-line folk poem

mani torbası	A bag in which four-line poems were put during a folk rite
masalcı	A female story-teller
masjid	The same as *mescit*
maşallah	*Lit.*, What wonders God hath wrought!—an exclamation of wonder or admiration
meddah	A male story-teller
meddahlık	The profession of story-telling
medrese	A theological school
mehâsin	Good qualities
mehd-i ülya	*Lit.*, cradle of the great, *i.e.,* the mother of the sultan
mehr	A marriage settlement
mehtap	Moonlight, a moonlight concert on the Bosphorus
mehter	Band of musicians which played in palaces
mehterbaşı	The head of a band of musicians
mehterhane	The military band of the grand vizier
mektep	A school
mektup	A letter
mescit	A small mosque
mesihat	The office of the *şeyhülislâm*
meşhur	Famous
meşrutiyet	The period of Ottoman constitutional government under the Young Turks
methiye	A hymn of praise
Mevlevî	A member of the Whirling Dervishes
mevlûd	A poem on the birth of Muhammad by Süleyman Çelebi; a ceremony during which this poem is chanted
Mevlûd Kandili	The celebration of the eve of Muhammad's birthday
meydan	A city square
mezeler	Appetizers
mihr-i muaccel	The prompt payment of the dowry
mihr-i müeccel	The deferred payment of the dowry
millet	In Ottoman times a religious community, as the Greek Orthodox
mimber	A pulpit
Mısır	Egypt

molla	A doctor of Muslim law
muhrim	A state of holiness
muvakkıthane	A place where timepieces are kept
müftü	A Muslim jurist
mühürdar	A keeper of the seal
müjdeci	A bearer of good news
müminin	Believers, *i.e.*, Muslims
müneccimbaşı	The head astrologer of the palace
mürebbiye	A governess
müsahip ağası	The black eunuch who attended the sultan in the harem
müseddes	A poem with six-line stanzas
müsendereci	The black eunuch disciplinary officer in the palace
myrsa	A Circassian noble
nafaka	Maintenance allowance of a divorced wife
nahil	A branch of date palms
nakkaş	An artist
namaz	A ritual prayer
namaz bezi	The white scarf women wear over their heads while praying
namazgâh	An open-air prayer place
namazı, akşam	The evening prayer
namazı, ikindi	The afternoon prayer
namazı, mühit	The neighborhood prayer of a funeral
namazı, öğle	The midday prayer
namazı, sabah	The morning prayer
namazı, yatsı	The bedtime prayer
namazı, zuhur	The same as *öğle namazı*
nargile	A water pipe
nazar	The evil eye
nazar takımı	A bundle of charms to ward off the evil eye
nazire	A poem parallel to another one
nesih	A type of calligraphy
nev	New
nevruz	The New Year
ney	A flute

nikâh	The legal marriage ceremony
ninni	A lullaby
nişan	*Lit.*, a sign; an engagement to marry
nişan bohçası	The package of engagement presents from the bride to the bridegroom
nişanlı	Engaged to be married
nişan makraması	The handkerchief sent to signify an engagement
nişan takımı	The set of engagement presents sent from the groom to the bride
nişan yüzüğü	An engagement ring
nizam	Order
nizam-ı cedit	The new order
nizamname	A regulation
nöbet gecesi	*Lit.*, night turn; a concubine's turn to be made love to by the sultan
nur	Light
ocak	Hearth; here, guild home
oda	A room
Oda, Ocaklı	The Room with the Hearth in the harem of Topkapı Palace
odalık	An odalisque
oda takımı	A set of furniture
ortak	A co-wife
Orta Kapı	The Middle Gate of Topkapı Palace
ortancı	The middle rank of black eunuchs of the palace
orta oyunu	A folk play in the round
Osmanlı	Ottoman
ot	A depilatory paste
oturak âlemi	A male drinking party at which a girl dances
oya	A kind of lace that resembles tatting
örtü	A cover for the hair, a pillow or other object
paça günü	The feast of sheep trotters on the last day of wedding festivities
padishah (*padişah*)	The sultan
para	A coin, money
paşa	A pasha

Paşakapısı	The Pasha's Gate, the residence of the grand vizier
paşalık	A district governed by a pasha
peçiç	A game
pencik	A tax on the sale of slaves
pencik emini	The superintendent of the *pencik*
peştemal	A large towel
peynir şekeri	A soft candy
piçhane	A house for illegitimate children
pilav	Boiled rice
puşide	A bed coverlet
rahat yatağı	*Lit.*, bed of rest; the couch on which a dead person is laid out
rak'ah	The same as *rekat*
rakı	An alcoholic drink
ramazan	The ninth month of the Muslim year, during which Muslims fast from dawn to dusk
reis efendi	The same as *reis-ül-küttap*
reis-ül-küttap	The state secretary, later the foreign minister
rekat	Worship, going through a set of prayer positions
resim	A picture
rical	Men of importance
rikab-ı hümayun	*Lit.*, imperial stirrup; a member of the sultan's suite
rüştiye	A high school
sadır	The chief minister, *i.e.,* the grand vizier; the rite of "going out" during the pilgrimage
sadrazam	The grand vizier
sahil sarayı	A shore palace
sahur	The meal before the daily *ramazan* fast
sakusum	The bride's last dance before her marriage
salât	The same as *namaz*
salât-ı fecir	The same as *sabah namazı*
sancak	A subdivision of a province
sancakbeyi	The governor of a *sancak*
sandal	A rowboat

saray	A palace
Saray-ı Atik	The Old Palace (Eski Saray)
saraylı	A woman trained in the palace
saray ocağı	*Lit.*, palace hearth; here, palace guild
saray terbiyesi	Palace training
savt	A course, a rite of the pilgrimage
sazende	A lute player, a musician
sazendebaşı	A head musician
sebil	A public fountain
seccade	A prayer rug
sedir	A divan or sofa
sedye	A sedan chair
sekbanbaşı	The head of a certain regiment of Janissaries
selâmlık	Here, the men's apartments of an Ottoman household
sene	A year
ser hanende	A head singer
silâhtar	The sword-bearer
sipahi	A cavalryman
sitil	A bowl on chains in which a coffee pot is set
sıbyan mektebi	A mosque primary school
sıcaklık	The warm or steam room of a bath
sıracı	A group of four girl musicians
sır kâtibi	Confidential secretary to the sultan
sırma	Gold or silver embroidery
sırmalı	Embroidered with gold or silver thread
sofra	A set dining table
soğukluk	The cooling room of a bath
soyuncu kadın	A woman who greeted wedding guests and cared for their outer clothing
söz	Word
sözlük	A dictionary
sultan	When referring to a woman, a daughter of the sultan
suna	Muslim rules and practices derived from the habits of the Prophet
sübek	A urinal for a baby
sülüs	A type of calligraphy
sünnet düğünü	Circumcision festivities

sürme	Kohl
sürre	The procession of gifts sent to Mecca each year by the sultan
süs	Elegance
süslemek	To adorn
sütana	*Lit.*, a milk mother; i.e., a wet nurse
synsu	A central Asiatic Turkic wedding dance
şagird	An apprentice
şahadet	The profession of faith
şarkı	A song
şehriyar	The sultan
şehzade	A prince
şeker bayramı	The candy holiday at the end of *ramazan*
şeriat	The Muslim holy law
şevval	The tenth month of the Muslim year
şeyh	Here, the head of a religious order
şeyhülislâm	The head of the Ottoman religious establishment
şeytan	Satan
şıbr	A unit of measurement
tabut	A bier
takrir	An official memo
talâk	Divorce
talâk-ı tevkil	Divorce by repudiation
talebe	A student
talik	A type of calligraphy
talika	A closed coach
tambur	A guitar
tandır	A warming arrangement consisting of a brazier under a table which has a cloth cover that goes over the knees of the people sitting around the table
Tanzimat	The period of reform between 1839 and 1876
tarak	A comb
tarih	History
taşlık	A paved courtyard
tavaf	Circumambulation of the Kaaba

tekbir	The formula, God is Great
tekke	The convent of a religious order
tel	Strands of tinsel
telbiye	A rite during the pilgrimage
temenna	The Ottoman salute, which included a low bow
temettü	A rite of the pilgrimage
teneşir	A bench on which a corpse is laid
teravi	The evening *ramazan* prayer
teşrifatçı	The official in charge of imperial ceremonies
tevcit	The art of reading or reciting the Koran in the proper rhythm
tezkiye	Praise of the deceased during a Muslim funeral
Topkapı Sarayı	The palace at Saray Burnu or Palace Point in Istanbul, formerly called the New Palace; its present name means Palace of the Cannon Gate
tuccar	A merchant
tuğ	A horsetail, Ottoman emblem of rank
tuyuğ	An early Turkic quatrain
türbe	A tomb
ulema	The religious hierarchy
umm-ül-veled	Mother of a child, a legal status
umre	The short pilgrimage
usta	Here, a woman who oversaw women slaves
usta, baş	Head *usta*
usta, berber	The woman in charge of the imperial harem hairdressing service
usta, çamaşır	The woman in charge of the imperial harem laundry service
usta, çaşnigir	The woman in charge of the sultan's tasting service in the harem
usta, hastalı	The woman in charge of the sick in the imperial harem
usta, ibriktar	The woman in charge of the imperial harem pitcher service
usta, ikinci	The second woman in charge of an imperial harem service
usta, kahve	The woman in charge of the imperial harem coffee service

usta, kilerci	The woman in charge of the imperial harem pantry service
usta, külhane	The woman in charge of heating water for the harem baths
ut	A lute
vakfiye	A *vakıf* deed
vakıf	A pious foundation
vali	The governor of a *vilayet*
valide	Mother; here, mother of the sultan
valide alayı	The procession of the sultan's mother from the Old Palace to the New, that is, to Topkapı Palace, on the accession of her son to the throne
valide paşa	The mother of the khedive of Egypt
valide sultan	The mother of the sultan
valide taşlığı	The paved court of the mother of the sultan in Topkapı Palace
valilik	The position of governor of a *vilayet*
vekil	A representative
vesika	A document
vilayet	A province
vukuf	*Lit.*, a standing; a rite of the pilgrimage
yağlık	A napkin
yalı	A house on the shore built partly over the water
yalı köşkü	A shore pavilion
yaşayış	A manner of living
yaşmak	Veil worn by Ottoman women
yatağan	A long curved knife
yatak	A bed
yatalık	A bedstead
yavrum	*Lit.*, my little chick, a term of endearment
yazı	Writing
yazma	A printed fabric
yazma yemini	A printed kerchief
yelpaze	A fan
yemek	Food, the evening meal
yenge	An aunt, the elderly woman who attends a bride

yenge kadın	The same as *yenge*
Yeni Saray	The New Palace, now Topkapı Palace
yevm-ül-nehar	The same as *kurban bayramı*
yevm-üt-terviye	The day of providing water on the pilgrimage
Yıldız Sarayı	The imperial palace on the hill in Beşiktaş, Istanbul; its name means Star Palace
yurt	A habitation
yüz görümlüğü	A present from the bridegroom to the bride when he first saw her face
yüz yazısı	The ornamenting of the bride's face
zarf	*Lit.,* envelope; a coffee-cup holder
zekat	Alms
zifaf	The entry of the bridegroom into the bridal chamber
zikir	Recitation of the attributes of God
zilhicce	The twelfth month of the Muslim year
zimmî	A non-Muslim subject of the Ottoman Empire

Note: For terms indicating clothing, see Chapter 11.

Bibliography

ABBREVIATIONS

EI¹   *Encyclopaedia of Islam*, first edition

EI²   *Encyclopaedia of Islam*, second edition

HEO   Joseph de Hammer-Purgstall's *Histoire de l'Empire ottoman*

İA   *İslâm ansiklopedisi*

SA   Celâl Esat Arseven's *Sanat ansiklopedisi*

SOURCES IN ENGLISH

Afetinan, A., *The Emancipation of the Turkish Woman*. The Hague, 1962.

Alderson, A. D. *The Structure of the Ottoman Dynasty*. Oxford, 1956.

Amicis, Edmondo de. *Constantinople*. Translated from the Italian by Caroline Tilton. New York, 1896.

"The Awakening of the Turkish Woman," *The American Review of Reviews*. 49 (June 1914), pp. 743–745.

Bart'old, Vasilii Vladimirovich. *Turkestan Down to the Mongol Invasion*. Translated by H. A. R. Gibb. London, 1928.

Bates, Ülkü Ü. "Women as Patrons of Architecture in Turkey," *Women in the Muslim World*. Lois Beck and Nikki Keddie, eds. Cambridge, Mass., 1978.

Belgiojoso, Princess (Christina Trivolzio de). *Oriental Harems and Scenery*. Translated from the French. New York, 1862.

Bevan Jones, V. R. and Bevan Jones, L. *Women in Islam*. Lucknow, 1941.

Birge, John Kingsley. *The Bektashi Order of Dervishes*. Hartford and London, 1937.

Blunt, Lady Fanny. *My Reminiscences*. London, 1918.

———. *The People of Turkey. By a Consul's Daughter and Wife*. Two volumes. Edited by Stanley Lane-Poole. London, 1878.

Boulden, James E. P. *An American Among the Orientals*. Philadelphia, 1855.

Bowen, Harold. *See* Gibb, Sir Hamilton, A. R.

Braudel, Fernand. *The Structure of Everyday Life, Civilization, and Capitalism, 15th–18th Century*. New York, 1981.

Brockelmann, Carl. *History of the Islamic People*. New York, 1960.

Brown, D. V. *Haremlık*. New York, 1909.

———. *The Unveiled Ladies of Stamboul*. New York, 1923.

Brunschvig, R. " 'Abd," *EI²*, I, pp. 24–40.

Buhl, R. and Jomier, J. "al-Djamra," *EI²*, II, p. 438.

Busbecq, Ogier Ghiselin de. *The Turkish Letters of the Imperial Ambassador at Constantinople, 1554–1562*. Oxford, 1927, 1963 (reprint). Translated by Edward Seymour Forster.

Cahen, Claude. *Pre-Ottoman Turkey*. New York, 1968.

Castellan, Antoine Laurent. *Turkey, Being a Description of the Manners, Customs, Dresses and Other Peculiarities Characteristic of the Inhabitants of the Turkish Empire*. Translated from the French by Frederic Shoberl. Philadelphia, 1829.

Clarke, Edward David. *Travels in the Various Countries of Europe, Asia and Africa*. Three volumes. London, 1816–1824.

Clement, Clara Erskine. *Constantinople, the City of the Sultans*. Boston, 1895.

Covel, Dr. John. "Extracts from the Diaries of Dr. John Covel, 1670–1679," *Early Voyages and Travels in the Levant*. Hakluyt Society, New York (reprint), n.d. Pp. 101–286.

Cox, Samuel S. *Diversions of a Diplomat in Turkey*. New York, 1887.

Craven, Lady Elizabeth. *A Journey Through the Crimea to Constantinople (1786)*. London, 1789.

Creasy, Edward S. *History of the Ottoman Turks*. Beirut, 1961.

"Curbs Dress Reform of Turkish Woman," *The New York Times*. (January 21, 1913), p. 5.

Czaplicka, M. A. *Aboriginal Siberia*. Oxford, 1914.

———. *The Turks of Central Asia, in History and at the Present Day*. Oxford, 1918.

Davey, Richard. *The Sultan and His Subjects*. London, 1907.

Davis, Fanny. *The Palace of Topkapi in Istanbul*. New York, 1970.

Davison, Roderic H. *Reform in the Ottoman Empire, 1856–1876*. Princeton, 1963.

Dengler, Ian C. "Turkish Women in the Ottoman Empire: The Classical Age," *Women in the Muslim World*. Lois Beck and Nikki Keddie, eds. Cambridge, Mass., 1978.

Deny, J. "Wālida Sulṭān," *EI¹*, IV, pp. 1113–1118.

D'Ohsson, Mouradgea. *See* Ohsson, Mouradgea d'.

Edip, Halide [Adıvar]. *Conflict of East and West in Turkey*. Lahore, 1935. Second edition.

———. *Memoirs of Halide Edip*. New York, 1926.

———. *The Turkish Ordeal*. New York, 1928.

Ekrem, Selma. "Flutist of old Istanbul," *The Christian Science Monitor*. (November 26, 1966), Boston, Mass.

Ellis, Ellen Deborah and Palmer, Florence. "The Feminist Movement in Turkey," *The Contemporary Review*. 105 (January–June, 1914), pp. 857–864.

Ellison, Grace and Melek Hanum. *Abdul Hamid's Daughter*. London, 1913.

Emerson, Gertrude. "Halideh Hanoum," *Asia*. (January, 1920), pp. 80–89.

Encyclopaedia of Islam. First edition. Leyden, 1913–1934. Four volumes.

Encyclopaedia of Islam. Leyden, 1960–. Second edition.

Esin, Emel. *Turkish Miniature Painting*. Tokyo and Rutland, 1960.

Essad-Bey. *Twelve Secrets of the Caucasus*. New York, 1931. Translated from the German by C. Chychele Waterston.

Evrenol, Hilmi Malik. *Revolutionary Turkey*. Ankara and Istanbul, 1936.

Farmer, H. G. "Musiki," *EI¹*, III, pp. 749–755.

Ferriman, Z. Duckett. *Turkey and the Turks*. London, 1911.

Freely, John. *See* Sumner-Boyd, Hilary.

Freygang, Wilhelm von. *Letters from the Caucasus and Georgia*. London, 1823. Translated from the French.

Fyzee, Asaf A. A. *Outlines of Muhammadan Law*. Oxford, 1955.

Garnett, Lucy M. J. *Home Life in Turkey*. New York, 1909.

———. *Turkey of the Ottomans*. London, 1911.

———. *Turkish Life in Town and Country*. New York, 1904.

Gautier, Théophile. *Constantinople*. New York, 1875. Translated by Robert Howe Gould.

Gibb, Elias John Wilkinson. *History of Ottoman Poetry*. London, 1900. Five volumes. Leyden (reprint), 1958.

———. *Ottoman Poems*. London, 1882. Translated into English in the original forms.

Gibb, Sir Hamilton A. R. *Mohammedanism, an Historic Survey*. New York, 1955.

———. *The Travels of Ibn Baṭṭūṭa, A.D. 1325–1354*. London, 1958–1959. Two volumes. Translated and edited by C. Defrémery and B. R. Sanguinetti.

———, and Bowen, Harold. *Islamic Society and the West*. New York, 1957. Vol. I, Parts 1 and 2.

Gökalp, Ziya. *Turkish Nationalities and Western Civilization*. New York, 1959. Translated by Niyazi Berkes.

Gönül, Macide. "Some Turkish Embroideries in the Collection of the Topkapı Sarayı Museum in Istanbul," *Kunst des Orients*. 6 (1969), pp. 43–76.

Grigsby, W. E., trans. *The Medjelle or Ottoman Civil Law*. London, 1895.

"Growth of the Mohammedan Feminist Movement in Turkey," *Current Opinion*. 57 (August, 1914), pp. 118–119.

Grunebaum, G. E. von. *Muhammedan Festivals*. New York, 1951.

Günyol, Vedad and Mango, Andrew. "Djarīda", *EI²*, II, pp. 473–476.

Habesci, Elias. *The Present State of the Ottoman Empire*. London, 1784. Translated from the French.

Halit, Halil. *See* Khalid, Khalil.

Haslip, Joan. *The Sultan: The Life of Abdul Hamid*. London, 1958.

Hill, Aaron. *A Full and Just Account of the Present State of the Ottoman Empire*. London, 1709.

Hisar, Abdülhak Şinasi. "Moonlight on the Bosphorus." An unpublished condensation and translation by Nesrin Moralı, n.d.

Huart, Clément. "'Adile Khātūn," *EI²*, I, p. 199.

Ibn Baṭṭūṭa, *The Travels of. See* Gibb, Sir Hamilton A. R.

İsmail Kemal. *The Memoirs of Ismail Kemal Bey*. London, [1920 ?]. Edited by
    Sommerville Storey.
İz, Fahir. "Fıtnat", *EI²*, II, p. 931.
————. "Khālide Edib," *EI²*, IV, pp. 933–936.
————. "Laylā Khānim," EI², p. 710.
————. "Laylā Khānim (Leylâ Saz)," *EI²*, V, pp. 710–711.
Jeffery, Arthur. *Islam, Muhammad and His Religion*. New York, 1958.
————. *A Reader on Islam*. The Hague, 1962.
Jenkins, H. "A Word About Turkish Women," *Open Court*. 25 (May, 1911), pp.
    264–270.
Jomier, J. and Buhl, R. *See* Buhl, R.
Kai Kā'ūs ibn Iskandar, Prince of Gurgan. *A Mirror for Princes, the Qābūs Nāma*.
    New York, 1951. Translated from the Persian by Reuben Levy.
Khalid, Khalil. *The Diary of a Turk*. London, 1903.
Kohn, Hans. *A History of Nationalism in the Near East*. London, 1929.
Köprülü, Fuat. "Ottoman Turkish Literature," *EI¹*, IV, p. 938ff.
Kramers, J. H. "Sulṭān," *EI¹*, IV, pp. 543–545.
Lane, Edward William. *The Manners and Customs of the Modern Egyptians*. New
    York, 1923.
Lane-Poole, Stanley. *The Speeches and Table-Talk of the Prophet Mohammed*.
    London, 1882.
————. *Turkey*. New York, 1899.
Lane-Poole, Stanley, editor. *See* Blunt, Lady Fanny.
Layard, Sir Austin Henry. *Autobiography and Letters*. Two volumes. London,
    1903. Edited by the Hon. William N. Bruce.
Levy, Reuben. *The Social Structure of Islam*. Cambridge, 1957.
Lewis, Bernard. *The Emergence of Modern Turkey*. New York, 1961.
————. *Istanbul and the Civilization of the Ottoman Empire*. Norman, 1963.
Lewis, Raphaela. *Everyday Life in Ottoman Turkey*. New York, 1971.
Longrigg, Stephen Hemsley. *Four Centuries of Modern Iraq*. Oxford, 1925.
Lott, Emmeline. *Harem Life in Egypt and Constantinople*. London, 1867.
Lybyer, Albert Howe. *The Government of the Ottoman Empire in the Time of
    Suleiman the Magnificent*. New York, 1966 (reprint).
MacFarlane, Charles. *Constantinople in 1829*. London, 1829. Two volumes.
Madden, R. Robert. *Travels in Turkey, Egypt, Nubia and Palestine in 1824, 1825,
    1826 and 1827*. London, 1833. Two volumes.
Mamboury, Ernest. *The Tourist's Istanbul*. Istanbul, 1953. Translated by Malcolm
    Burr.
Marghīnānī, 'Alī ibn Abū Bakr, Burham al-Din. *The Hedaya, or Guide; a Com-
    mentary on the Mussulman Laws*. London, 1870. Translated by Charles
    Hamilton.
Massé, Henri. *Persian Beliefs and Customs*. New Haven, 1954. Translated by
    Charles A. Messner.
Melek Hanum and Ellison, Grace. *Abdul Hamid's Daughter*. London, [1913].
Melek Hanım [Melek-Hanum]. *Thirty Years in the Harem; or the Autobiography
    of*. New York, 1872.
Midhat [Mithat], Ali Haydar. *The Life of Midhat Pasha*. London, 1903.
Miller, Barnette. *Beyond the Sublime Porte*. New Haven, 1931.

————. *The Palace School of Muhammad the Conqueror.* Cambridge, Mass., 1941.

Montagu, Lady Mary Wortley. *Letters from the Right Honourable . . . 1709–1762.* New York, 1906.

Mordtmann, J. H. "Constantinople," *EI*[1], I, pp. 867–876.

————. "Dāmād," *EI*[2], III, p. 103.

Morgenthau, Henry. *Ambassador Morgenthau's Story.* Garden City, 1918.

Motraye, Aubrey de la. *Travels Through Europe, Asia, and into Parts of Africa.* London, 1723. Two volumes.

Moyal, Maurice. "The Art of Turkish Embroidery," *The Islamic Quarterly.* 4, Nos. 3 and 4 (London, January 1958), pp. 162–167.

Muftizade K. Zia Bey. *Speaking of the Turks.* New York, 1922.

Neave, Lady Dorina. *Romance of the Bosphorus.* London, n.d.

Nerval, Gerard de. *The Women of Cairo (1842–1843).* New York, 1930. Two volumes.

Orga, İrfan. *Portrait of a Turkish Family.* New York, 1957.

Oruz, İffet Halim. "The Turkish Press and Women," *Quarterly Review* of the International Council of Women. (First quarter, 1960.)

Pardoe, Julia. *The City of the Sultans and Domestic Manners of the Turks in 1836.* London, 1837. Two volumes.

Patrick, Mary Mills. *Under Five Sultans.* New York, 1929.

"The Patriotic Awakening of the Turkish Woman," *The Literary Digest.* 46 (January 1913–June 1913), pp. 563–564. New York.

Pears, Sir Edwin. *Forty Years in Constantinople.* London and New York, 1916.

————. *Turkey and Its People.* New York, [1911].

Penzer, N. M. *The Harem, an Account of the Institution as it Existed in the Palace of the Turkish Sultans with a History of the Grand Seraglio from its Foundation to the Present Time.* Philadelphia, 1936.

Pickthall, Mohammed Marmaduke. *The Meaning of the Glorious Koran.* New York, 1953.

————. *With the Turk in Wartime.* London and Toronto, 1914.

Poynter, Mary A. *When Turkey Was Turkey, In and Around Constantinople.* New York and London, 1921.

Ramsaur, Ernest Edmondson, Jr. *The Young Turks, Prelude to the Revolution of 1908.* Princeton, 1957.

Ramsay, Sir William M. *The Revolution in Constantinople and Turkey.* London, 1909.

Robson, James M. A. *Tracts on Listening to Music.* London, 1938. Edited and translated by James M. A. Robson.

Rycaut, Sir Paul. *The History of the Present State of the Ottoman Empire.* London, 1670. Three volumes.

Sanderson, John. "Sundrie the Personall Voyages Performed by John Sanderson of London, Merchant, Begun in October 1584. Ended in October 1602. With an Historical Description of Constantinople," *Hakluytus Posthumus or Purchas His Pilgrims.* New York, 1905 (reprint).

Schiltberger, Johann. *The Bondage and Travels of* ————, *a Native of Bavaria, in Europe, Asia, and Africa, 1396–1427.* London, 1879. Translated from the Heidelberg MS. edited in 1859 by Professor Karl Friedrich Neumann, by Commodore J. Buchan Telfer, R.N., F.S.A., F.R.G.S. With Notes by Professor P. Brunn, of the Imperial Academy of South Russia, at Odessa, and a Preface, Introduction and Notes by the translator and editor.

Senior, Nassau W. *A Journal Kept in Turkey and Greece in the Autumn of 1857 and the Beginning of 1858.* London, 1859.

Shaw, Stanford J. *Between Old and New, the Ottoman Empire Under Sultan Selim III, 1789–1807.* Cambridge, Mass., 1971.

———. *The Budget of Ottoman Egypt 1005–1006/1596–1597.* The Hague and Paris, 1968.

———, and Shaw, Ezel Kural. *History of the Ottoman Empire and Modern Turkey.* Cambridge, Mass., 1977. Vol. II.

Shay, Mary Lucille. *The Ottoman Empire from 1720 to 1734 as Revealed in Dispatches of the Venetian Baili.* Urbana, 1944.

Siyavuşgil, Sabri Esat. *Karagöz, its History, its Characters, its Mystic and Satiric Spirit.* Ankara, 1955.

Slade, Adolphus. *Records of Travels in Turkey, Greece, etc., and of a Cruise in the Black Sea, with the Captain Pasha, in the Years 1829, 1830, and 1831.* London, 1832. Two volumes.

Smith, Albert Richard. *A Month in Constantinople.* London, 1851.

Sourdel-Thomine, J. "Hamam," *EI²*, IV, pp. 139–144.

Sönmez, Emel. *Turkish Women in Turkish Literature of the 19th Century.* Leiden, 1969.

Spencer, Edmund. *Travels in Circassia, Krim Tartary, etc., Including a Steam Voyage Down the Danube, from Vienna to Constantinople and Round the Black Sea, in 1836.* London, 1838. Two volumes.

Stevens, E. S. "The Awakening of the Turkish Woman," *The Outlook.* 98 (August 5, 1911), pp. 757–758.

———. "The Womankind of Young Turkey," *The Living Age.* 270 (July, 1911), pp. 137–146.

Sumner-Boyd, Hilary. *Strolling Through Istanbul.* Istanbul, 1973.

Szyliowicz, Joseph S. *Political Change in Rural Turkey: Erdemli.* The Hague, 1966.

Taşkıran, Tezer. *Women in Turkey.* Istanbul, 1976.

Tekin, Talat. *A Grammar of Orkhon Turkic.* Bloomington, 1968.

Tokarev, S. A. "The Caucasus." Multigraphed translation from the Russian by Aert Kuipers. Columbia University, n.d.

Toledano, Ehud R. *The Ottoman Slave Trade and Its Supervision: 1840–1890.* Princeton, 1982.

Tugay, Emine Foat. *Three Centuries, Family Chronicle of Turkey and Egypt.* London, 1963.

Turkish Music. Turkish Information Office. New York, n.d.

Ubicini, M. Abdolonyme. *Letters on Turkey.* London, 1856. Translated from the French by Lady Easthope. Two volumes.

Uluçay, M. Çağatay. "The Harem in the XVIIIth Century," *Akten des Vierundzwanzigsten Internationalen Orientalisten-Kongresses, München, 28 August Bis 4. September, 1957.* Wiesbaden, 1959.

Vaglieri, L. Veccia. "Ḥafṣa," *EI²*, III, pp. 63–64.

Walsh, Rev. R. *A Residence in Constantinople.* London, 1936. Two volumes.

Washburn, George. *Fifty Years in Constantinople and Recollections of Robert College.* Boston and New York, 1911.

Wensinck, A. J. "The pre-Islamic Hadjdj," *EI²*, III, pp. 31–33.

———, and Gibb, H. A. R. " 'Arafa," *EI²*, I, p. 604.

———, and Jomier, J. "The Islamic Hadjdj," *EI²*, III, pp. 33–37.

White, Charles. *Three Years in Constantinople; or Domestic Manners of the Turks in 1844*. London, 1845. Three volumes.

Winner, Thomas G. *The Oral Art and Literature of the Kazakhs of Russian Central Asia*. Durham, 1958.

Withers, Robert. *The Grand Signor's Seraglio—c. 1620*. An unacknowledged translation of Ottavio Bon, *Il Seraglio del Gransignore—1608*. Published in *Purchas His Pilgrims*, IX, pp. 322–400, Hakluytus Posthumas. New York, 1905.

Woods, John E. *The Aqquyunlu, Clan, Confederation, Empire*. Minneapolis and Chicago, 1976.

SOURCES IN TURKISH

Abdülhamit II. *Abdülhamit'in hatıra defteri*. Istanbul, 1960.

Afetinan. *See* İnan, A. Afet.

Ahmet Midhat. "Bir kına gecesi," *Jön Türk* (Istanbul, 1908) in *Metinlerle edebiyat*, pp. 136–138. Edited by Vasfi Mahir Kocatürk. Istanbul, 1955.

Ahmet Refik. *See* [Altınay].

Akseki, Ahmet Hamdi. *İslâm dini, itikat, ibadet, ve ahlâk*. Ankara, 1950.

———. *İslâm fıtrî, tabiî ve umumî bir dindir*. Istanbul, 1966.

Aktepe, M. Münir. *Patrona isyanı (1730)*. Istanbul, 1958.

Akyüz, Kenan. *Tevfik Fikret*. Ankara, 1957.

"Alemdar'ın evlât ve torunları," *Tarih dünyası*, No. 3 (Istanbul, 1950), p. 39.

[Altınay], Ahmet Refik. *Hicrî on ikinci asırda İstanbul hayatı (1100–1200)*. Istanbul, 1930.

———. *Lâle devri*. Istanbul, 1928.

Arpınar, Seval. "İlk kadın gazetesi (Kadınlar mahsus gazete)," *Belgelerle Türk tarihi dergisi*, 16 (*Aralık*, 1969), pp. 29–33.

Arseven, Celâl Esat. "Lâle," *Sanat ansiklopedisi*, III, pp. 1217–1218. Istanbul, 1950.

———. *Sanat ansiklopedisi*. Istanbul, 1943. Four volumes.

Ayapbek, Mecit M. "Kazak Kirgiz folklorunda dair bir kaç söz," *Türk yurdu*, (*Ağustos* 1954), pp. 139–142.

Banarlı, Nihat Sami. *Resimli Türk edebiyat tarihi*. Istanbul, n.d.

Baykal, İsmail. "Selim III devrinde 'imdad-ı sefer' için para basılmak üzere saraydan verilen altın ve gümüş, evanî hakkında," *Tarih vesikaları*, 3, No. 13 (*Ağustos* 1944), pp. 26–50.

———. "Silâhdar-ı Şehriyari ve Dârüssaade ağası tâyinleri hakkında hattı hümayunlar," *Tarih vesikaları*, 2, No. 11 (*Şubat* 1943), pp. 338–341.

Bayrı, Mehmet Halit. *İstanbul folkloru*. Istanbul, 1947.

Bolay, İsa Ruhi. *Hac rehberi*. Konya, 1948.

Bulut, Rukiye. "İstanbul kadınlarının kıyafetleri ve II. Abdülhamid'in çarşafı yasaklaması," *Belgelerle Türk tarihi dergisi*, 8 (*Mayıs* 1968), pp. 34–36.

———. "Lâle devrinde araba saltanatı," *Belgelerle Türk tarihi dergisi*, 16 (*Aralık* 1969), pp. 34–38.

Celâl, Melek. *Türk işlemeleri*. Istanbul, 1939.

Celâl, Musahipzade. *See* Musahipzade Celâl.

Celâl Nuri. *See* [İleri].

Cenkman, Emin. *Osmanlı sarayı ve kıyafetleri.* Istanbul, 1948.

Edip, Halide. *Sinekli bakkal.* Istanbul, 1949.

Emin, Mehmet. "Mürebbiye," *Hayat,* 4, 89 (*Ağustos* 6, 1928), pp. 1–2.

Emine Semiye. "Moda ve korse," *Hanımlara mahsus gazete,* 59 (*Nisan* 11, 1312 A.H.), pp. 1–2.

Ergin, Osman. *Türkiye maarif tarihi.* Istanbul, 1940. Three volumes.

Erim, Necmeddin. "Yusuf İzzeddin'e dair yeni vesikalar," *Tarih dünyası,* 1, No. 15 (*Haziran* 15, 1950), pp. 211–213.

Esendal, Memduh Şevket. "Feminist," *Türk edebiyatının en güzel hikâyeleri,* pp. 52–57. Edited by Yaşar Nabi. Istanbul, 1947.

Eyice, Semavi. "İstanbul (tarih eserler)," *İA,* V, Part 2, pp. 1214/44–1214/144. Istanbul, 1967.

Fatma Aliye. "İzdivaç dair," *Hanımlara mahsus gazete,* (*Nisan,* 24, 1319 A.H.), pp. 175–176.

Gökbilgin, M. Tayyip. "Başmaklık (Paşmaklık)," *İA,* II, pp. 333–334.

Gövsa, İbrahim Alâettin. *Türk meşhurları ansiklopedisi.* Istanbul, 1946.

Günaydin, Nimet. "İlk kadın memurları," *Hayat tarih mecmuası,* (*Mayıs*), pp. 66–67.

Günyol, Vedat. "Mektep," *İA,* VII, p. 659.

[Gürpınar], Hüseyin Rahmi. "Ecir ve sabır," *Türk edebiyatının en güzel hikâyeleri antolojisi.* Istanbul, 1947. Edited by Yaşar Nabi.

———. *Hayatın sahifeleri.* From an unpublished anthology by Fevziye Abdullah Tansel, n.d.

———. *Mürebbiye.* Istanbul, 1927.

Habip, İsmail. *Yeni "edebî yeniliğimiz" Tanzimattan beri.* Istanbul, 1940, 1943. Two volumes.

Hanımlara mahsus gazete. See İbn el-Hak Mehmet Tahir.

Hurşit Paşa. "Cariyeler hakkında, saray hatırları," *Hayat tarih mecmuası,* 5 (*Haziran* 1965), pp. 60–64.

İbn el-Hak Mehmet Tahir. *Meşrutiyet hanımları.* Istanbul, 1910.

———, editor. *Hanımlara mahsus gazete.* Istanbul, 1311/1312-? A.H.

[İleri], Celâl Nuri. *Kadınlarımız.* Istanbul, 1331 A.H.

İnal, Mahmut Kemal. *Son hattatlar.* Istanbul, 1955.

İnan, Abdülkerim. "Türk düğünlerinde exogamie izleri," *Türk dili ve tarihi hakkında araştırmalar,* 1 (Ankara, 1934), pp. 105–113.

İnan, A. Afet. *Herkesin bir dünyası var.* Ankara, 1958.

———. *Tarih boyunca Türk kadınlarının hak ve görevleri.* Istanbul, 1968.

İnciciyan, P. G. *XVIII. asırda İstanbul.* Istanbul, 1956. Translated and annotated by Hrand D. Andreasyan.

İslâm ansiklopedisi. Istanbul, 1950-.

İsmail Baykal. *See* Baykal, İsmail.

İsmail Hikmet. *Koca Ragıp Paşa ve Fıtnat.* Istanbul, 1933.

İsmail Mevlevî. *Mecmua-ı esam-ı cariye.* Ms., Belediye kütüphanesi, M. Cevdet collection, K63. Istanbul, n.d.

İstanbul ansiklopedisi. See Koçu, Reşat Ekrem.

Karal, Enver Ziya. *See* Uzunçarsılı, İsmail Hakkı.

Karaosmanoğlu, Yakup Kadri. "Baskın," *Bir serencam*. Istanbul, 1943.
————. "Bir kadın meselesi," *Bir serencam*. Istanbul, 1943.
————. *Hep o şarkı*. Istanbul, 1956.
Kemal, Namık. *See* Namık Kemal.
Kocatürk, Vasfi Mahir. *Metinlerle edebiyat II*. Istanbul, 1955.
Koçu, Reşat Ekrem. "Ani Hatun," *İstanbul ansiklopedisi*, I, pp. 522–523.
————. "Belkis Şevket Hanım," *İstanbul ansiklopedisi*, V, pp. 2483–2484.
————. "Benli Ayşe Hanım," *Türk düşüncesi*, 2, No. 10 (*Eylül* 1, 1954), pp. 254–256.
————. "Bezmiâlem Valide Sultan," *İstanbul ansiklopedisi*, V, p. 2733.
————. "Çubuktar Mehmet Paşa," *Türk düşüncesi*, 2, No. 11 (*Ekim* 1, 1954), pp. 326–328.
————. *İstanbul ansiklopedisi*. Istanbul, 1946-.
————. "Meddah Yusuf ve Ayşe Reis hikâyesi," *Türk düşüncesi*, 2, No. 9 (*Ağustos* 1954), pp. 170–173.
————. *Tarihimizde garip vakalar*. Istanbul, 1952.
————. *Türk giyim kuşam ve süslenme sözlüğü*. Ankara, 1969.
Konyalı, İbrahim Hakkı. "Cariyeler ve esir pazarı," *Türk dünyası*, (*Mart* 15, 1960), pp. 72–74.
Koşay, Hâmit Zübeyr. *Türkiye Türk düğünleri üzerine mukayeseli malzeme*. Ankara, 1944.
Köprülü, Fuat. "Nigâr Hanım," *Bugünkü edebiyat*. Istanbul, 1924.
Kunter, Halim Baki. "Türk vakıfları ve vakfiyeleri," *Vakıflar dergisi*, 1 (1938), pp. 103–129.
Ligeti, Lajos. *Bilinmeyen İç-Asya*. Ankara, 1946. Translated by S. Karatay.
Mehmet Emin. *See* Emin, Mehmet.
Mehmet Tevfik. *See* Tevfik, Mehmet.
Midhat, Ahmet. *See* Ahmet Midhat.
Miras, Kâmil. *Ramazan musahabeleri*. Istanbul, 1949.
Mithat, Ali Haydar. *Hatıralarım 1872–1946*. Istanbul, 1946.
Moralı, Seniha Sami. "Arkeoloji Müzesi, Suriye ve Lübnan ile Kanlıca Körfezine dair," *Hayat tarih ve edebiyat mecmuası*, (*Nisan* 4, 1978), pp. 56–61.
————. "Çarşaf modası bize Suriye'den geldi," *Hayat*, (*Eylül* 30, 1960), pp. 4–5.
————. "Çocuk esirgeme kurumu'nun kurucularından Hamiyet Hanım," *Hayat tarih mecmuası*, 1 (*Şubat* 1969), pp. 69–71.
Musahipzade Celâl. *Eski İstanbul yaşayışı*. Istanbul, 1946.
Namık Kemal. "Aile," *İbret gazetesi*, pp. 199–211. Istanbul, 1938.
————. "Maarif," *İbret gazetesi*, pp. 86–90. Istanbul, 1938.
Osman, Rifat. *Edirne sarayı*. Published by S. Ünver. Ankara, 1957.
Osmanoğlu, Ayşe. *Babam Abdülhamit*. Istanbul, 1960.
Öz, Tahsin. *Güzel sanatlar*. Istanbul, 1929.
————. *İstanbul camileri*. Ankara, 1962, 1965. Two volumes.
————. "Selim III, Mustafa IV ve Mahmut II zamanlarında ait bir kaç vesika," *Tarih vesikaları*, 1 (*Haziran* 1941), pp. 20–29.
————. "Selim III. ün sırkâtibi tarafından tutulan ruzname," *Tarih vesikaları*, (*Ağustos* 1944), pp. 26–43; (*Ekim* 1944), pp. 102–116; (*Mayıs* 1949), pp. 183–199.
Özön, Mustafa Nihat. *Namık Kemal ve İbret gazetesi*. Istanbul, 1938.
————. *Son asır Türk edebiyatı tarihi*. Istanbul, 1945.

Öztuna, Yılmaz. "Büyük bestekâr Hacı Ârif Bey," *Hayat tarih mecmuası*, 2 (*Temmuz* 1966), pp. 20–26.

Pakalın, Mehmet Zeki. *Osmanlı tarih deyimleri ve terimleri sözlüğü*. Istanbul, 1946–1954. Three volumes.

————. *Son sadrazamlar ve başvekiller*. Istanbul, 1940. Five volumes.

Pedersen, Johannes. "Mescid: Talebeler," *İA*, VIII, p. 69.

Raşit Efendi, Mehmet. *Tarih-i Raşit*. Istanbul[?], 1282 A.H. Six volumes.

Refik, Ahmet. *See* [Altınay], Refik Ahmet.

Ruska, J. "Kına," *İA*, VI, pp. 708–709.

Safa, Peyami. *Türk inkılâbına bakışlar*. Istanbul, n.d.

Sezai, Samipaşazade. *Sergüzeşt*. From an unpublished anthology by Fevziye Abdullah Tansel. Ankara, 1960.

Siyavuşgil, Sabri Esat. *Karagöz*. Ankara, 1955.

Seniha Sami. *See* Moralı, Seniha Sami.

Sertoğlu, Mithat. *Resimli osmanlı tarihi ansiklopedisi*. Istanbul, 1958.

Sümer, Faruk. "Eski Türk kadınları," *Türk yurdu*, 3, (*Eylül* 1954), pp. 191–194.

Sümer, Tülin. "Türkiye'de ilk defa kurulan kadınları çalıştırma derneği," *Belgelerle Türk tarih dergisi*, 10 (*Temmuz*, 1968), pp. 59–63.

Şakir, Ziya. "Enver Paşa ile Emine Naciye nasıl evlendiler?" *Resimli tarih*, 10 (*Ekim*, 1950), pp. 376–378.

Şapolyo, Enver Behnan. *Mustafa Reşit Paşa ve Tanzimat devri tarihi*. Istanbul, 1945.

Şehsüvaroğlu, Bedi N. *Hac yolu*. Istanbul, 1948.

Şehsüvaroğlu, Halûk Y. *Asırlar boyunca İstanbul*. Istanbul, n.d.

————. *Sultan Aziz, hususi, siyasi, hayatı, devri ve ölümü*. Istanbul, 1949.

Tahir, İbn el-Hak Mehmet. *See* İbn el-Hak Mehmet Tahir.

Tanışık, İbrahim Hilmi. *İstanbul çeşmeleri*. Istanbul, 1945. Two volumes.

Tansel, Fevziye Abdullah. *Ziya Gökalp külliyatı, II*. Ankara, 1965.

Tarama sözlüğü. Istanbul, 1945. Five volumes.

Taşkıran, Tezar. "Şemseddin Sami ve kadınlar," *Türk yurdu* (*Haziran* 1955), pp. 946–950.

Tevfik, Mehmet. *İstanbul'da bir sene*. Istanbul, 1299 A.H. German translation and notes by Theodore Menzel (Berlin, 1905).

Tuğlacı, Pars. *Osmanlı döneminde İstanbul kadınları*. Istanbul, 1984.

Tunalı, Tahsin. "Türk bestekârlarının asıl meslekleri," *Hayat tarih mecmuası*, 1 (1 *Haziran*, 1965), pp. 27–33.

Türk Dil Kurumu. *Söz derleme dergisi—folklor sözleri*, VI, Ankara, 1952.

Türkay, Cevdet. "Esircilerle ilgili bir belge," *Belgelerle Türk tarihi dergisi*, 2 (*Ağustos* 1968), p. 60.

Türkgeldi, Ali Fuat. *Görüp işittiklerim*. Ankara, 1951.

Uluçay, M. Çağatay. *Haremden mektuplar*. Istanbul, 1956.

————. *Padişahların kadınları ve kızları*. Ankara, 1980.

Uraz, Murat. Articles in *Resimli kadın şair ve muharririmiz*. Istanbul, 1940.

Uşaklıgil, Halit Ziya. *Aşk-ı memnu*. Istanbul, 1963.

————. *Saray ve ötesi, son hatıralar*. Istanbul, 1940–1942. Three volumes.

Uzunçarşılı, İsmail Hakkı. *Midhat Paşa ve Tâif mahkûmları*. Ankara, 1950.

————. "Nizam-ı Cedit ricalından Valide Sultan Kethüdası meşhur Yusuf Ağa ve Kethüdazade Arif Efendi," *Belleten*, 20, fasc. 79 (*Temmuz* 1965).

———. *Osmanlı devletinin saray teşkilâtı.* Ankara, 1945.

———, and Karal, Enver Ziya. *Osmanlı tarihi.* Ankara, 1951–1964. (Uzunçarşılı wrote vols. I-IV; Karal wrote vols. V-VII). Seven volumes.

Üçok, Bahriye. *İslâm devletlerinde kadın hükümdarlar.* Ankara, 1965.

Ülgen, Ali Saim. "Hamam," *İA*, V, pp. 174–178.

Ülkütaşır, M. Şakir. *Cevdet Paşa—hayatı—şahsiyeti—eserleri (1822–1898).* Ankara, 1945.

Ünver, A. Süheyl. "Büyük Selçuklu İmparatorluğu zamanında. Vakıf hastahane-lerinin bir kısmına dair," *Vakıflar dergisi*, 1 (Ankara, 1938), pp. 17-24.

———. *Geçmiş yüzyıllarda kıyafet resimlerimiz.* Ankara, 1958.

———. *Levnî.* Istanbul, 1951.

———. *Osmanlı Türklerinde hekimlik ve eczacılık tarihi hakkında.* Istanbul, 1952.

Wickerhauser, Moriz. *Eine Deutsch-Türkische Chrestomathie.* Vienna, 1853. In Ottoman Turkish with German translation.

Yalçin, Hüseyin Cahit. "Görücü," from *Hayat-ı muhayyel* (Istanbul, 1899), quoted in Mustafa Nihat Özön, *Son asır Türk edebiyatı tarihi*, pp. 249–253. Istanbul, 1945.

Yatman, Nurettin. *Türk kumaşları.* Ankara, 1945.

Yener, Enise. "Eski Ankara kadın kıyafetleri ve giyiniş tarzları," *Ankara Üniversitesi dil ve tarih-coğrafya fakültesi dergisi*, 13, No. 3 (*Eylül* 1955), pp. 21–37.

Zorlatuna, Halide Nüsret. "Meslek hatırları, Musul'dan sonra Kerkuk," *Türk yurdu*, (*Ocak* 1960).

SOURCES IN OTHER LANGUAGES

Aristarchi Bey, Grégoire. *Législation ottomane.* Constantinople, 1874. Seven parts.

Arseven, Celâl Esat. *L'Art turc depuis son origine jusqu'à nos jours.* Istanbul, 1939.

———, (Djelal Essad). *Constantinople de Byzance à Stamboul.* Paris, 1909.

Basmadjian, K. L. *Essai sur l'histoire de la littérature ottomane.* Paris and Constantinople, 1910.

Bratianu, G. I. *Recherches sur le commerce génois dans la Mer Noire au XIIIè siècle.* Paris, 1929.

Christensen, Arthur. *Iran sous les Sassanides.* Copenhagen, 1944.

Depping, Georges Bernard. *Histoire du commerce entre le Levant et l'Europe depuis les Croisades jusqu'à la fondation des colonies d'Amerique.* Paris, 1930. Two volumes.

Duda, Herbert W. *Balkantürkische Studien.* Vienna, 1949.

"L'Envolée de Belkis Hanoum," *The Levant Herald*, (December 2, 1913), p. 2.

Ethem, Halil. *See* Halil Ethem.

Fahmy, Mansour. *La Condition de la femme dans la tradition et l'évolution de l'Islamisme.* Paris, 1918.

Fazil Bey [Fazıl Hüseyin Enderunlı]. *Le Livre des femmes (Zenan-name).* Paris, 1879. Translated from the Turkish by J. A. Decourdemanche (Osman Bey).

Fekete, Lajos. *Budapest története III: Budapest a törökkorban.* Budapest, 1944.

Feldmann, Wilhelm. "Die Türkischen Frauengesellschaften," *Die Welt des Islam*, (December 15, 1914), pp. 20–21.

Fındıkoğlu, A. Ziyaeddin Fahri. *Essai sur la transformation du code familial en Turquie*. Paris, 1936.

———. *Ziya Gökalp, sa vie et sa sociologie*. Nancy, Paris, Strasbourg, 1935.

Flachat, Jean-Claude. *Observations sur le commerce et sur les arts*. Lyon, 1766.

Fonton, Félix de [Feliks Petrovich]. *La Russie dans l'Asie Mineure, ou Compagnes du Maréchal Paskevitch en 1828 et 1829*. Paris, 1840.

Goldziher, Ignácz. *Muhammedanische Studien*. Hildesheim, 1961. Two volumes.

Grelot, Guillaume-Joseph. *Relation nouvelle d'une voyage de Constantinople*. Paris, 1680.

Halil Ethem. *Nos mosquées à Stamboul*. Istanbul, 1934. Translated from the Turkish by E. Mamboury.

Hammer-Purgstall, Joseph de. *Histoire de l'Empire ottoman depuis son origine jusqu'à nos jours*. Paris, 1835–1843. Translated from the German by J. J. Hellert. Eighteen volumes.

Hartmann, M. "Die Türkische Frau," *Die Welt des Islam*, (December 15, 1914), pp. 15–20.

Heyd, Wilhelm. *Histoire du commerce du Levant au Moyen-Âge*. Amsterdam, 1959. Translated from the German and augmented by the author. Two volumes.

Huart, Clément. *Histoire de Baghdad dans les temps modernes*. Paris, 1901.

———. "Midhat Pacha," *Revue du monde musulman*, 8 (1909), pp. 419–430.

Koch, Karl. *Der Kaukasus*. Berlin, 1882.

Köprülü, Fuat. *Influence du chamanisme turco-mongol sur les ordres mystiques musulmans*. Istanbul, 1929.

———. "L'Institution du Vakouf, sa nature juridique et son évolution historique," *Vakıflar dergisi*, 2 (1942), pp. 3–44.

———. *Les Origines de l'Empire ottoman*. Paris, 1935; Philadelphia, 1978. Edited by E. de Boccard.

Loti, Pierre. *See* Viaud, Julien.

Mantran, Robert. *Istanbul dans la seconde moitié du XVIIè siècle*. Paris, 1962.

Maury, Lucien. "P. S. à 'Faut-il tuer l'éditeur?' " *Revue bleue*, 5, No. 64 (March 6, 1926), pp. 153–154.

Melling, Antoine-Ignace. *Voyage pittoresque de Constantinople et des rives du Bosphore d'auprès les dessins de M. Melling*. Paris, 1819. Two volumes.

Midhat Bey, Ali Haydar. *Midhat-Pacha, sa vie—son oeuvre, par son fils*. Paris, 1908.

Millingen, Frederick (Osman Bey, Major Vladimir Andrejevich). *Les femmes de Turquie*. Paris, 1883.

———. *Les Anglais en Orient, 1830–1878, vrai version du livre "Trente Ans au Harem."* Paris, 1877.

Mordtmann, J. H. "Die jüdischen Kira im Serai der Sultans," *Mitteilungen des Seminars für orientalische, Sprachen auf der K. Friedrich-Wilhelms Universität zu Berlin: West asiatiche Abteilung* (January 1955), pp. 1–38.

Ohsson, Ignatius Mouradgea d'. *Tableau général de l'Empire othoman*. Paris, Vols. I–IV, 1791; Vols. V–VII, 1824.

Osman Bey. *See* Millingen, Frederick.

Rodinson, Maxime. "Sur l'Araba," *Journal asiatique*, 216 (1957), pp. 273–280.

Saussey, Edmond. "Le Théâtre populaire," *Études orientales*, 4 (Paris, 1936), pp. 73–98.

Spiess, Otto von. *Die türkische Prosliteratur der gegenwart.* Leipsig, 1943.

Thomsen, Vilhelm. "Inscriptions de l'Orkhon déchiffrées," *Mémoires de la Société Finno-Ougrienne*, V (Helsinfors, 1896), pp. 1–224.

[Timur], Mehmet Hıfzı. *Le Lien de mariage à travers l'histoire juridique turque.* Paris, 1936.

Toderini, Gian-Battista. *De la Littérature des Turcs.* Paris, 1789. Translated by l'Abbé de Cournand. Two volumes.

Tott, Baron de. *Mémoires sur les Turcs et les Tartares.* Amsterdam, 1784.

Ubicini, Abdolonyme. *La Turquie actuelle.* Paris, 1855.

Viaud, Julien (Loti, Pierre). *Aziyadé.* Paris, 1895.

———. *Les Désenchantées.* Paris, 1906.

Young, Sir George. *Corps de droit ottoman.* Oxford, 1905–1906. Seven volumes.

Index